THE UNIVERSITY OF
WINCHESTER

The Invention of Suspicion

The Invention of Suspicion

Law and Mimesis in Shakespeare and Renaissance Drama

Lorna Hutson

OXFORD

UNIVERSITY PRESS

Great Clarendon Street, Oxford OX2 6DP

Oxford University Press is a department of the University of Oxford.
It furthers the University's objective of excellence in research, scholarship,
and education by publishing worldwide in

Oxford New York

Auckland Cape Town Dar es Salaam Hong Kong Karachi
Kuala Lumpur Madrid Melbourne Mexico City Nairobi
New Delhi Shanghai Taipei Toronto

With offices in

Argentina Austria Brazil Chile Czech Republic France Greece
Guatemala Hungary Italy Japan Poland Portugal Singapore
South Korea Switzerland Thailand Turkey Ukraine Vietnam

Oxford is a registered trade mark of Oxford University Press
in the UK and in certain other countries

Published in the United States
by Oxford University Press Inc., New York

© Lorna Hutson 2007

The moral rights of the author have been asserted
Database right Oxford University Press (maker)

First published 2007

British Library Cataloguing in Publication Data
Data available

Library of Congress Cataloging in Publication Data
Data available

Typeset by Laserwords Private Limited, Chennai, India
Printed in Great Britain
on acid-free paper by
the MPG Books Group

ISBN 978–0–19–921243–9

10 9 8 7 6 5 4 3 2

For Cathy Sprent and Ellie Yong An Hutson

Acknowledgements

I am pleased to be able to acknowledge the generous support of the John Simon Guggenheim Memorial Foundation, which enabled me to spend the year 2004–5 working on this book. I am also grateful to the University of St Andrews for granting me sabbatical leave in the spring of 2006, and to the Arts and Humanities Research Council of Great Britain for funding leave for the autumn of 2006 in which to write up my research. I am grateful to the Masters of the Bench of the Inner Temple for permission to reproduce the illumination of the Court of the King's Bench, c.1450 (Fig. 3), and to the Honourable Society of the Middle Temple for permission to reproduce their painting of the Judgment of Solomon (c.1570, Fig. 4). The Reverend Jim Hill of Charlton Mackrell church, Somerset, kindly allowed me to visit the church to photograph a carved bench end depicting a writing devil (Fig. 1), the reproduction of which here I gratefully acknowledge. Thanks to the British Library for permission to reproduce a woodcut from *Der Ritter vom Turn* (Fig. 2) and William Lambarde's 1592 table of 'what things be materiall to induce Suspicion' (Fig. 5). Portions of this book have appeared, in slightly different versions, in the journal *Representations*. Chapter 2 appeared in a slightly different form as 'Rethinking the "Spectacle of the Scaffold": Juridical Epistemologies and English Revenge Tragedy', *Representations*, 89 (Winter 2005), 30–58, and parts of Chapter 3 appeared in *Representations*, 94 (Spring 2006), 80–109, as 'Forensic Aspects of Renaissance Mimesis'. I am grateful to the editorial board of *Representations* for permission to reproduce this material in altered form here.

This book's genesis owes a great deal to colleagues at the University of California at Berkeley. I owe most of all to Victoria Kahn, who believed in the argument of this study when it hardly existed at all, and without whose interest, enthusiasm, and generous support it would certainly never have become a book. I am also grateful, for discussion and friendship at early stages in the work's genesis, to Berkeley colleagues Janet Adelman, Joel

Altman, Albert Ascoli, David Bates, Carol Clover, Cathy Gallagher, Jeffrey Knapp, and Steve Justice, and to the editorial board of *Representations* whose discussion of a version of Chapter 2 helped shaped the book in my mind at a formative time. I would like to acknowledge here also the friendship of the late Nick Howe, whose advice about writing and reviewing was invaluable, and delivered with a warmth, sharpness, and energy now sadly missed. My intellectual debts to one other Berkeley colleague—Barbara Shapiro—are apparent throughout the book. I thank Daniel Javitch for his most generous support, Bernadette Meyler for sharing her unpublished work with me, and Peter Goodrich for inviting me to speak at the Law, Culture and Humanities Conference in New York, 2003, and for kindness in correspondence on many issues. Hilary Schor, Nomi Stolzenberg, and Rebecca Lemon invited me to present work from the book at the University of Southern California Center for Law, Culture and Humanities, for which I am grateful.

Since I returned to Britain, I have accumulated more debts of gratitude: I would like to thank David Norbrook for support on many occasions, and for inviting me to present some of this work at Oxford in 2005. Thanks to Ros Ballaster, as ever, for friendship and for asking a really smart question which got me thinking. I would like to thank Andrew Hadfield as a generous reader, and for inviting me to Sussex. Thanks to the organizers of the conference on the Inns of Court in September 2006—Jayne Archer, Elizabeth Goldring, and Sarah Knight—for a unique opportunity to learn from many experts on so many aspects of early modern legal culture. My colleagues in the School of History at St Andrews, Paul Hammer, John Hudson, and Andrew Pettegree, have listened to some of these ideas and offered very helpful suggestions, and my colleagues in the School of English are the most supportive, sane, and friendly community of scholars imaginable. Especial thanks to Neil Rhodes, who read the Introduction. Julian Luxford in the School of Art History has patiently responded to some very ignorant questions about medieval iconography. With wonderful scholarly generosity, Peter Holland, William Sherman, and Mark Jenner shared their knowledge in response to my queries about plague bills and Jonson's *Alchemist*.

I am grateful to the Central Executive Committee of the Folger Institute for offering me the opportunity to teach a late spring seminar in June 2006, at which I was able to try out some of the ideas presented here on unsuspecting seminar participants. I thank the participants for stimulating and enthusiastic discussions, and am especially grateful to those with whom I am still occasionally in correspondence about these legal and literary matters: Edward Gieskes, Lisa Klotz, Virginia Strain, and Owen Williams. During my time at the Folger I enjoyed many discussions with Heather James, for which I thank her. Holger Schott-Syme has been a most energetic and engaged correspondent on many legal and literary topics of shared interest, and I have learned a great deal from our electronic discussions. I have likewise learned from discussions with Bradin Cormack and Subha Mukherji, both of whose work on this topic I have been lucky enough to encounter in unpublished form. Bradin Cormack also kindly read and made characteristically subtle and stimulating comments on a version of Chapter 4.

I am grateful to Margaret Grundy of the Interlibrary Loans section of St Andrews' University Library for going to great lengths to acquire numerous items for me, and I would like to acknowledge, too, the especial helpfulness of librarians at Duke Humphrey's Library at the Bodleian. Andrew McNeillie has been the most delightful and reassuring commissioning editor, and Jacqueline Baker has been patient and sympathetic about my difficulties with making a deadline imposed by the Research Assessment Exercise. I am very grateful, too, for the legal knowledge and critical astuteness of an anonymous reader of my manuscript for Oxford University Press: few authors, I think, can have had such helpfully pertinent criticisms.

My greatest debts, as usual, are to my family: Cathy Sprent, with a generosity no mention on an acknowledgements page can repay, allowed me to spend weeks thinking about almost nothing but the book, neglecting all sorts of other chores and commitments, and Ellie has put up patiently with a parent utterly distracted for months and months by a pile of books and a computer, for no apparent reason.

Contents

List of Figures

Introduction

This book argues that important changes took place in the rhetoric of dramatic narrative—or the way of telling a story on-stage—in late sixteenth-century England that corresponded closely to developments in popular legal culture. My title, *The Invention of Suspicion*, fuses the terminology of law and of rhetoric in a way that encapsulates this argument. In sixteenth-century England, the word 'invention' did not have, as its primary meaning, the currently dominant sense of originating a new technology, or a new method of doing something ('inventing television', for example). Rather, it was a rhetorical term referring to the processing of 'finding' (the word comes from the Latin *invenire*, 'to find') the most appropriate arguments, figures of speech, and topics to use in a particular kind of oration, or persuasive discourse. Cicero's *De inventione* ('On Invention') accordingly explained this part of rhetoric: how to find arguments. As such, it was (as most histories of Renaissance rhetoric inform us) one of the most important texts in the basic rhetorical curriculum of the schools and academies in the first age of print. What those histories tend not to explain, though, is that *De inventione*, like another enormously important Latin treatise on rhetoric, Quintilian's *Institutio oratoria* ('Institutes of the Orator') was concerned with judicial, or forensic, oratory: that is to say, these books were designed to teach lawyers how to find arguments to prove the likely innocence or guilt of a defendant in a particular case. In learning even elementary lessons in grammar and composition, then, sixteenth-century writers inevitably absorbed ways of thinking about proof and evidence, for, as Richard Hooker said when setting out to use forensic rhetoric to investigate the question of church government, 'that judiciall method ... serveth best for the invention of truth'.[1]

---

[1] Richard Hooker, *On the Lawes of Ecclesiastical Politie* (London, 1593), 99.

many edited collections published and forthcoming which are helping to define it.[5]

Specific to this book, however, is a historical argument about the relation of cultural change to formal developments in English drama. In suggesting that aspects of formal development in literary practice and theory can be explained in relation to cultural-historical changes, I align my work on English Renaissance drama with work of the kind being done by Andrea Frisch on French sixteenth- and seventeenth-century tragic drama. Frisch argues that the well-known commitment to aesthetic distance between audience and the tragic stage, which was a central tenet of the dramatic theory and practice of Corneille and Racine, 'arose in the wake of a political discourse that emphasized the gains to be had from forgetting one of the most painful periods of French history', the French wars of religion.[6] As Frisch argues that formal qualities specific to the development of norms and expectations of representation on the French stage can be attributed to particular historical and discursive conditions, so I will argue that qualities later thought to distinguish English from French drama—such as Dryden's examples of 'variety and greatness of characters' and 'copiousness and well-knitting of intrigue' in English plays—are partly explicable in relation to the development of a particular kind of popular evidential awareness in late sixteenth- and seventeenth-century popular legal culture.[7]

After the English Reformation, the relationship of English common law to the jurisdiction of the church changed. This is not to say that the church courts declined, as an older historical narrative once declared, but that the vigorous revival of church court business in the latter half of the sixteenth century should be seen as part of the intensification of popular litigiousness and of local moral governance, rather than as a precise continuation of the pre-Reformation jurisdiction over the internal forum, the soul, by means of mandatory annual confession. At the same time, statutory changes in the criminal law and in local judicial administration, as well as the growth of popular litigiousness and general law-mindedness,

---

[5] Cormack's work is forthcoming as *A Power to Do Justice* (Chicago: University of Chicago Press, 2008). Collections include *Rhetoric and Law in Early Modern Europe*, ed. Victoria Kahn and Lorna Hutson (New Haven: Yale University Press, 2001); *Literature, Politics and Law in Renaissance England*, ed. Erica Sheen and Lorna Hutson (Basingstoke: Palgrave Macmillan, 2005); *The Law in Shakespeare*, ed. Constance Jordan and Karen Cunningham (Basingstoke: Palgrave Macmillan, 2007).

[6] Andrea Frisch, 'French Tragedy and the Civil Wars', *Modern Language Quarterly*, 67, no. 3 (2006), 287–313.

[7] John Dryden, 'Of Dramatic Poesy' (1668), in *Selected Criticism*, ed. James Kinsley and George Parfitt (Oxford: Oxford University Press, 1970), 55.

meant that the roles played by voluntary officers responsible for keeping the peace (Justices of the Peace and constables) as well as those played by ordinary people (as litigants, victims of crime, participants in the hue and cry, members of juries, etc.) increasingly involved the exercise of discretion, judgment, and a sense of how to weigh evidence. This gradually increasing awareness of the importance of evidential concepts, while neither formalized nor at all sophisticated by the standards of the law and related epistemologies in later periods, was significant because it was socially pervasive, and because it resulted in the investigative procedures of the common law acquiring a new cultural centrality and moral exemplarity. Spiritual allegories could be written in which the conscience was likened to an investigating Justice of the Peace, and God could figure as the providential processes of detection and of evidence evaluation in the new printed literature of the discovery and punishment of murder.

The relationship of these shifts in cultural sensibility to the strategies of representation favoured in various kinds of theatre, popular, erudite, and courtly, is not straightforward, but the connection is argued throughout this book. The primarily sacramental drama of the fifteenth century was profoundly concerned with the procedures of secular justice. However, as I show in Chapter 1, one of the ways in which secular judicial procedure figured in sacramental drama was as the diabolic, merely procedural and exteriorized double of the truly just and merciful jurisdiction of God's representative, the priest, over the internal forum of the soul. As one of the four daughters of God, Justice can never win the debate against Mercy in the drama for the capture of the soul of humankind. Consequently, the presence of evidence in the drama of the soul's salvation is always a threatening one: evidence means a record of the soul's sinfulness. Since sacramental drama presents confession and penance as the solution to the devil's gathering evidence of sin, it can never represent dramatis personae as engaged in testing or trying to prove the validity of the knowledge they have; sacramental drama is not *evidential*.

Chapter 2, however, 'Rethinking Foucault: The Juridical Epistemology of Renaissance Drama', does not, as one might expect, go on to trace some kind of slow evolution of evidential awareness through the drama of the sixteenth century. Rather, it confronts the difficulty of arguing that English participatory justice offers an epistemological model relevant to English Renaissance drama. Foucault's genealogy of disciplinary power, which traces its origins in the state's appropriation of the church's techniques of spiritual examination, has been extremely influential in providing a model for a culturally and historically aware criticism of English Renaissance drama. However, as Chapter 2 argues, the Foucauldian genealogy depends on a history of prosecution techniques and a system of proof in early modern criminal law that is specifically French. Where Foucault portrays an *ancien régime* epistemology of judgment based on a 'system of "legal proofs" . . . known only to specialists' and speaks of 'the singularity of this judicial truth', the sixteenth-century English epistemology of judgment could rather be said to be based on the participation of lay persons (justices, victims, neighbours, jurors) in deciding what was to count as knowledge.[8] The English criminal justice system, as Barbara Shapiro writes, put 'great faith both in witness observers and in jurors as "judges of fact" ', that is, as evaluators of contradictory witness testimony.[9] Sixteenth-century developments in the participatory justice system involving the taking of written examinations by Justices, and the need for jurors to evaluate evidence at the bar, were directly engaging the very same questions of probability and likelihood with which dramatists were beginning to be concerned. The question of the extent to which jurors were, in this period, able to evaluate testimony meaningfully is one which has exercised both social and legal historians, and this chapter engages with that debate, using printed accounts of trials, manuscripts of Justices' examinations, and transcripts of Justices' notebooks. Finally, Chapter 2 concludes with an exemplary reading of Shakespeare's *Titus Andronicus* as a play in which the sequence of events, or plot, makes sense if it is regarded as the displacement of the open, participatory trial of the evidence which had been suppressed early in the play by a tyrannical regime.

Chapter 3, 'Judicial Narrative and Dramatic Mimesis', moves away from legal history to try and find a way of speaking about what it is that might make one kind of dramatic fiction seem more 'lifelike' than another. This chapter engages, in other words, with the difficulty of discussing what makes us respond to drama as if its personae had inner lives and histories. In the most prestigious kind of cultural criticism currently practised, mimetic reading continues to be—though in a somewhat veiled fashion—the norm. Yet cultural criticism itself is little help when it comes to investigating our tendency to interpret certain dramatic texts mimetically (that is, by ascribing consciousness to the people represented) while feeling less inclined to do so in interpreting others. If, as Peter

---

[8] Michel Foucault, *Discipline and Punish*, trans. Alan Sheridan (Harmondsworth: Penguin, 1977), 37.

[9] Barbara J. Shapiro, *A Culture of Fact* (Ithaca, NY: Cornell University Press, 2000), 13.

Womack writes, our conviction of 'the characters having minds at all is an optical illusion generated by the text', then we need to investigate why some textual strategies are better at producing the 'optical illusion' of characters' minds than others.[10] Chapter 3 argues that Renaissance schoolboys were given lessons in making a sequence of events appear both naturally ordered and, at the same time, more intensely motivated and vividly intelligible than a sequence would be in real life. It demonstrates, moreover, that these lessons derived from the judicial or forensic rhetorics of Cicero and Quintilian, in which advocates were taught how to open a case with an irrefutable *narratio*, or 'narrative of the facts'. Both the mid-nineteenth-century discovery of 'double time' in Shakespeare, and late nineteenth-century character criticism can thus be read as properly forensic responses to clues that have really been planted in the texts by dramatists who have absorbed the evidential lessons of circumstantial narrative. In addition, the chapter suggests that this judicial pedagogy of narrative fostered an awareness of the 'facts' as having been generated by the order and coherence of their telling. In other words, it fostered a tendency to represent dramatis personae as, on the one hand, forensically engaged in persuading one another of the truth of highly disputable 'facts', and, on the other, as suspiciously testing and trying out the grounds for belief in one another. In this way, the diffusion of judicial rhetoric through the education system facilitated the kind of writing which produces the illusion that behind speech headings and speeches are the consciousnesses of 'characters'.

Chapter 4, 'From Intrigue to Detection: Transformations of Classical Comedy, 1566–1594', moves into a more detailed historical and formal analysis of the relationship of legal culture to the writing of intrigue comedy at the early Elizabethan Inns of Court. The chapter first explains, drawing on Adele Scafuro's work on Greek and Latin New Comedy, that sixteenth-century readers would have understood that action in Roman comedy depends on the opportunistic use of forensic strategies of argument. As the first generation of dramatists to engage in the translation and adaptation of Latin drama in Elizabeth's reign were closely connected with London's legal schools, the Inns of Court, one might expect them to have enjoyed translating and imitating these comedies, as they translated and imitated Seneca. However, these men were also closely involved with Parliamentary debates on the reformation of local government through the ecclesiastical courts, quarter sessions, and assizes. Their

---

[10] Peter Womack, *Rereading Literature* (Oxford: Basil Blackwell, 1986), 6.

response to Latin comedy, and its Continental imitations, was complicated in these decades by recognition that the very strategies by which
criminal deceptions and fraudulent arguments were rendered vividly convincing or 'probable' were exactly the same as the evidential techniques
or techniques of proof on which they were increasingly asking Justices
of the Peace and officers of the law to rely in order to administer justice.
(Remember that Hooker thought the 'judiciall method ... serveth best
for the invention of truth'.) The result was a profound ambivalence in
this tight-knit community of Inns of Court men, Members of Parliament,
and writers of dramatic poetry towards the perceived subversions of civic
order inherent in the imitation of Italian models of Roman New Comedy. This ambivalence, however, produced a new, hybrid subgenre of
English neoclassical plot making, exemplified in the work of Philip Sidney, George Gascoigne, and George Whetstone, in which the fraudulent
or merely strategic uses of forensic rhetoric typical of the Latin playwrights
became the morally righteous methods of detection and evidence evaluation employed by magistrate-heroes. This subgenre, I argue, was wittily
transformed by Shakespeare in his own first Inns of Court comedy, *The
Comedy of Errors*.

The last three chapters of the book all deal, to some extent, with the
legacy of the 1560s and 1570s for the popular stage in the 1590s. The
chapters take their starting premises from the work of Scott McMillin
and Sally Beth Maclean on the dramaturgy of the Queen's Men, which
dominated the London stage in the 1580s.[11] McMillin and Maclean
argue that the Queen's Men favoured a form of dramatic writing that
depended on what they characterize as brilliant stagecraft and surplus
narrative explanation. Shakespeare seems to have rewritten no fewer
than four of the Queen's Men's plays, and his rewriting, I argue in
Chapter 5, crucially introduces the mimetic and characterological effects
that an awareness of forensic rhetoric—of understanding speeches as
attempts to prove a set of dubious 'facts', or to test one's suspicions about
the motives of others—can produce. These chapters also argue that the
1570s 'reformation' of Latin intrigue comedy as a genre of civic detective
work affects the plotting of Shakespeare's plays and their thematic concern with civic justice. Chapter 6 returns to the question, introduced in
Chapter 2's reading of *Titus Andronicus*, of how revenge tragedy as a genre
relates to legal thought and practice. The chapter argues that Protestant

[11] Scott McMillin and Sally-Beth Maclean, *The Queen's Men and their Plays* (Cambridge:
Cambridge University Press, 1998).

8

providential theology does not merely figure evidence as divinely disclosed by God, but represents the deferral of discovery—the protracted processes of detection, pre-trial examination, trial, and evidence evaluation—as God's satisfying of our consciences that justice has truly been done. A reading of Thomas Kyd's *Spanish Tragedy* reveals how the play's scenic form mingles the older 'theatrical literalism' of the Queen's Men's dramaturgy with a new dramaturgy of drawing inferences and acting on suspicion. Turning from revenge tragedy to romantic comedy, Chapter 6 goes on to explore the ambivalence discernible in writers like Lyly and Shakespeare towards the suggestion of sexual scandal that inheres in the classical model of a comic 'recognition'—that is, the discovery of a character's legitimate paternity—brought about by merely probable signs. The plays *Mother Bombie* and *Love's Labour's Lost* are read as responses to this scandal.

Chapter 7 concludes the book with a comparative reading of Shakespeare's and Jonson's plots revolving around the use and abuse of forensic rhetoric and the invention of suspicion in the 1590s and early 1600s. While Jonson's variation on Shakespeare's 'invention of suspicion' may seem to be more intently focused on questions of contemporary manners, the chapter attempts to refute the common view that Jonson's art is therefore slavishly striving to imitate, as exactly as possible, the world outside the plays. Rather, I suggest, whereas Shakespeare presents the forensic strategist as a villain who abuses proofs and persuades people that they have witnessed what they could not have, Jonson openly celebrates his heroes, and the theatre itself, for being capable of such *deceptio visus*, and thus, in a sense, endorses the theatre's and the poet's capacity to transform the boundaries of morality and law.

The image of the Judgement of Solomon on the cover and in Chapter 4 aptly captures the essence of this book's intervention in debates over theatre, politics, and law in the late sixteenth and early seventeenth centuries. The painting, commissioned (possibly by the eminent lawyer Edward Plowden) to adorn the newly rebuilt hall of the Middle Temple around 1570, carries a legend revealing contemporary interest in its depiction of justice as a work of inference on the basis of evidential signs. Solomon, says the legend, was able, in his act of judgement, to disclose the secrets of the heart; the false mother is shamed by the discovery of her fiction.[12] Yet, as James I was later to point out in a

---

[12] For the legend in full, and for the probable circumstances of the painting's commission, see p. 198 below.

1

From Penitence to Evidence: Drama and the Legal Reformation

Evidential Awareness in English Renaissance Drama: Two Examples

In the 1590s for the very first time, English dramatists began to make use, for mimetic purposes, of the practice of raising and then *not answering* questions about how to interpret evidence. That is to say, dramatists were newly concerned with casting doubt on the reliability and probability of the signs and indications on which people base judgements about one another. This new awareness of the mimetic uses of evidential uncertainty has been overlooked in histories of English Renaissance drama largely because its effects were so successful as to seem, to later generations, like dramatic naturalism. Dramatists of the 1590s began to focus their attention on the ways in which agents in a story actually gain their knowledge about the events supposed to have taken place in that story and infer, from various speeches and signs, what each other thinks about these events. Such a focus is constitutive both of complex social interaction and of apparent psychological depth. It allows for verisimilitude in the dramatic representation of questions of politics and justice as well as in what we think of as the more private questions of intimacy and love. In its generic versatility, then, this innovative focus on evidential uncertainty cuts across the strict tragic and comic divisions which characterize the neoclassical drama of France and Italy; but in spite of this, it cannot be traced to any native English tradition of dramatic storytelling. It did in fact, as we shall see, derive from the same Latin dramatic sources as gave rise to Continental neoclassicism, but it adapted these sources to representational conditions peculiarly constituted by developments in thinking about evidence in English common law. Rather than generalizing further at this point, however, it would seem better to offer a couple of examples of the uses of evidential uncertainty from early plays by Shakespeare: one, a tragic moment in a chronicle history, and the other, the opening of a courtship in a romantic comedy.

My first example comes from Act 3 of the play now known as *2 Henry VI*, which was published in 1594 as *The First Part of the Contention betwixt the two Famous Houses of York and Lancaster*. The sequence of actions in question—the discovery of the murder of Duke Humphrey—is conceived similarly in both the 1623 Folio (F) and the 1594 Quarto (Q), so the conception undoubtedly belongs to the 1590s. In F, Act 3, Scene 2, opens with the stage direction: *Enter two or three running over the stage, from the murder of Duke Humphrey.*[1] In the Q, a fuller stage direction tells us that we see first two men smothering Humphrey in his bed, and then the Duke of Suffolk coming toward them.[2] We learn from the next exchange between the murderers and the Duke of Suffolk that Duke Humphrey is to appear to have died peacefully in his bed: 'Have you laid fair the bed?', asks Suffolk (3. 2. 11) in F, and in Q he asks them to smooth down the bedclothes.[3] The King and peers enter: this is the appointed time of Humphrey's trial for trumped-up charges of treason, on which we saw him arrested and taken into custody in the previous scene. As the pathos of the King's ineffectuality expresses itself in his hope that trial proceedings against Duke Humphrey will be conducted in accordance with 'true evidence', Suffolk makes the fatal announcement: Humphrey has been found 'Dead in his bed'. Confusion ensues. Then the Earls of Warwick and Salisbury enter, with the commons audible off-stage, and Warwick reports to the King that the commons are ready to commit violence, believing, in defiance of Suffolk's testimony, that the Duke has been murdered. Someone must 'view' Humphrey's body. Again, stage directions differ slightly, but both texts indicate that the bed is now visible on-stage. Warwick then

---

[1] Folio readings refer to line numbers in *The Norton Facsimile of the First Folio of Shakespeare*, prepared by Charles Hinman, with a new intro. by Peter Blayney (New York: W. W. Norton, 1996). Act, scene, and line references to Shakespeare's plays refer, unless otherwise specified, to *The Riverside Shakespeare*, ed. G. Blakemore Evans (Boston: Houghton Mifflin Company, 1997); American spellings have been silently altered. The question of the relation between Quarto (Q) and Folio (F) texts of *2 Henry VI* has been the subject of much debate, and will be discussed more fully in Ch. 5.

[2] *The First Part of the Contention* (1594), ed. William Montgomery, Malone Society Reprints (Oxford: Oxford University Press, 1985), 35.　　　　　　　　　　　　　　[3] Ibid. 35.

vows solemnly that he, too, now believes Duke Humphrey to have been murdered, and when asked for 'instance', replies with this speech (as it is in Q):

> Oft have I seene a timely parted ghost,
> Of ashie semblance, pale and bloodlesse,
> But loe the blood is setled in his face,
> More better coloured than when he liv'd,
> His well proportioned beard made rough and sterne,
> And fingers spred abrode as one that graspt for life,
> Yet was by strength surprisde, the least of these are probable,
> It cannot chuse but he was murthered.[4]

This speech, though admittedly less eloquent than its counterpart in F, deserves no less than the latter to be called a 'rare and early example of forensic reasoning'. [5] The signs adduced by Warwick are inconclusive: the corpse's livid colouring, grasping hands, and tousled beard could indicate strangulation *or* suffocation. The fact that the murder has already been staged in Q has led one critic to argue for Q's inauthenticity, as if authentic Shakespeare could only be proved by the tallying of the signs of strangulation adduced in the speech with what 'really' happened. 'Shakespeare', as this critic rather absurdly writes, 'on the evidence of the Folio . . . opted for a simple strangulation, offstage.'[6] There is, of course, no need to speculate about what an authentic Shakespeare might imagine as authentically taking place off-stage. The play in both versions distinguishes what the audience knows from what Warwick and the King suspect, and the speech performs a process of reasoning probably from uncertain signs as an explicitly forensic (and hence morally righteous) activity, with Warwick in the position of the coroner at an inquest. The word 'view', spoken twice (in F, 3. 2. 132 and 3. 2. 149) indicates this: in English law, the coroner was required to inquire into unexplained deaths *super visum corporis*, on the viewing of the corpse.[7] '[H]ee shall see the dead bodie when hee doth make the inquirie, or otherwise the inquirie is not good', as Ferdinando

---

[4] *The First Part of the Contention*, 37.

[5] David Thatcher, 'Cover-up', *The Shakespeare Newsletter* (2000–1), 105–18, at 114.

[6] See Claire Saunders, ' "Dead in his Bed" Shakespeare's Staging of the Death of the Duke of Gloucester in *2 Henry VI*', *Review of English Studies*, n.s. 35 (1984), 19–34, at 23. Saunders decides on the evidence of the Folio version of Warwick's speech that 'strangulation, rather than smothering' is 'the obvious verdict'—a strangely literal response to the play's positioning of the audience as at an inquest.

[7] Andrew S. Cairncross glosses 'view' as 'the usual term in the direction to a coroner's jury'; see *The Second Part of King Henry VI*, ed. Cairncross (London: Methuen, 1957), 85. See also R. F. Hunniset, *The Medieval Coroner* (Cambridge: Cambridge University Press, 1961), 19.

Pulton wrote in *De Pace Regis*.[8] In formulating this evidential speech as a response to sounds of the commons off-stage, threatening violence until the report of Duke Humphrey's murder be investigated, Shakespeare does a remarkable thing. At the mid-point of the play in which he is most cynical about legal process (the first half being full of arbitrary and corrupt judgments, the second taking the form of a brutal series of mock trials enacted by the commons in vengeance), the playwright for a moment shapes public anger into the demand for a judicial inquiry, implying the possibility that the 'rude multitude' are capable of evaluating evidence, and that participatory judicial process can be a way of calling a corrupt government to account.[9]

My second example comes from an early comedy, *Love's Labour's Lost* (printed in 1598). No critic has, to my knowledge, commented on the curious fact that the romantic courtship of this comedy follows from the deferral of a process of litigation over a debt. The Princess of France arrives at the court of the King of Navarre on an embassy to reclaim her father's title in Aquitaine, a country bound over to Navarre as part surety for a loan, half of which (the Princess maintains) her father has already repaid. Navarre's response is to dispute this repayment (once again, to stress that this conception belongs to the 1590s, I quote from the Quarto text of 1598):

> Madame, your father heere doth intimate,
> The payment of a hundred thousand Crownes,
> Being but the one halfe of, of an intire summe,
> Disbursed by my father in his warres.
> But say that he, or we, as neither have
> Receiv[e]d that summe, yet there remaines unpaide
> A hundred thousand more, in suretie of the which,
> One part of *Aquitaine* is bound to us,
> Although not valued to the monies worth.
> If then the King your father will restore,
> But that one halfe which is unsatisfied,
> We will give up our right in *Aquitaine*,
> And hold faire friendship with his Majestie.
> But that it seemes he little purposeth:
> For here he doth demaund to have repaide,
> A hundred thousand Crownes, and not demaunds,

---

[8] Ferdinando Pulton, *De Pace Regis et Regni* (London, 1609), fol. 250ᵛ.

[9] For a reading of the scenes of the Cade rebellion as a carnivalesque inversion of faulty and corrupt judicial processes shown in the first half of the play, see Craig Bernthal, 'Jack Cade's Legal Carnival', *Studies in English Literature, 1500–1800*, 42, no. 2 (2002), 259–74.

> On paiment of a hundred thousand Crownes,
> To have his title live in *Aquitaine*:
> Which we much rather had depart withall,
> And have the money by our father lent,
> Than *Aquitaine*, so guelded as it is.[10]

The Princess objects that Navarre is wrong to claim that the first hundred thousand had not been paid:

> You do the King my father too much wrong ...
> In so unseeming to confesse receit
> Of that which hath so faithfully been paide.[11]

Navarre, in response, challenges the Princess directly to 'prove it': if she can produce proof, he says, he will pay the sum back, or yield up his title. She then commands Boyet, her attendant lord, to produce 'acquittances'—a technical term for legally admissible written evidence of repayment—which her father received from Navarre's father. Boyet, however, explains to the Princess that he can't produce the evidence right away: 'So please your Grace, the packet is not come, | Where that and other specialties are bound', and he concludes, mischievously, 'Tomorrow you shall have a sight of them.'[12]

This deferral of the 'sight' of specialties and acquittances—the written instruments and evidences without which, according to the English common law action of debt, there could be no proof conclusive as to the existence of a debt or its discharge—can only be an ostentatious joke in a play so self-conscious about time and dramatic decorum that it ends with Berowne's declaration that a year and a day of penance is 'Too long for a play'.[13] Here the withholding of the sight that would be proof functions, paradoxically, like Warwick's invitation to 'see' the blood in Humphrey's face, to introduce a notion of probability, of hermeneutic uncertainty. For the debtor who could not produce an acquittance from his or her creditor as proof of the debt's discharge was the stock example in early modern legal literature of the litigant who might have a case 'in reason and conscience', but whom the common law, with

---

[10] Shakespeare, *A Pleasant Conceited Comedie called Loves Labors Lost*, sig. C1ʳ.
[11] Ibid.   [12] Ibid.
[13] Ibid., sig. K1ᵛ. For the necessity, in common law, of the plaintiff producing a 'specialty' to avoid the defendant waging his law (swearing with compurgators that he owed nothing), and for the importance of the debtor producing an 'acquittance' as common law proof of the debt's discharge, see W. T. Barbour, *The History of Contract in Early English Equity* (Oxford: Clarendon Press, 1914), 34, 38, 84–5, 99, and *passim*. See also A. W. Simpson, *A History of the Common Law of Contract* (Oxford: Oxford University Press, 1975); S. C. F. Milsom, *Historical Foundations of the Common Law*, 2nd edn. (Toronto: Butterworths, 1981), 250.

its rigid adherence to proof in writing or under seal, could not help.[14] The language of the spiritual courts and the equity courts (or courts of conscience) appears in the Princess's indignation at Navarre's refusal to acknowledge 'receipt' of a sum 'faithfully' repaid, inclining us to think that she has a case in conscience. But our suspicion hovers over her motives—or those of her father—as well. What thinking lies behind her personal appearance at Navarre's court to enter a 'plea' for Aquitaine? Aquitaine, as Boyet points out, might serve as 'Dowrie for a Queene', and his complimentary description of her father's creditor as 'Matchles *Navar*' slyly notes Navarre's opportune bachelorhood, implying that love might be an alternative to litigation.[15] The equivocal set-up, with its hints of disingenuousness on both sides, bears resemblance to innumerable legal cases brought by subpoena, in the fifteenth and sixteenth centuries, to the Lord Chancellor, who could directly examine the consciences of the litigating parties according to Roman canon law rules of evidence, and could, by evaluating the circumstances and applying canon law presumptions of likely motivation, discover a more detailed, inward narrative of the intentions behind each litigant's actions.[16] The deferral of the sight of written proof locates the Prince's courtship of the Princess in what Navarre explicitly calls a '[m]eantime' of evidential uncertainty, an interim, in which questions of reason and conscience—the motives behind courtship, justifications for making and breaking oaths, equivocations about just how 'faithfully' or how opportunistically the labour of love might be undertaken—are comically under scrutiny, under suspicion.

Sacred Theatre after the Reformation: Recent Critical Accounts

Evidential uncertainty was not a feature of the native English interlude, or morality play. In Thomas Preston's *Cambises* (*c*.1575), a scene of popular protest against judicial corruption involves three actors performing the parts of 'Commons Complaint', 'Proof', and 'Trial'. Each declares who he is, and the declaration itself enacts the appropriate legal procedure. 'Commons Complaint' dares to speak; this prompts 'Proof' to 'appeal' (formally accuse) the corrupt judge, reiterating the complaint, and 'Trial'

---

[14] Barbour, *History of Contract*, 91; J. H. Baker (ed.), *The Reports of Sir John Spelman* (London: Selden Society, 1978), ii. 38.

[15] Shakespeare, *Pleasant Conceited Comedie*, sig. B3ʳ.

[16] See Barbour, *History of Contract*, 84–90, 147–8, and the appendix of cases, 169–234.

Eucharist. He proposes that a heightened Protestant reflexivity and wariness about what externals conceal is combined, in Shakespeare's theatre, with an involuntary physical response to the language and presence of the actor.[22]

My own argument locates a crucial difference between the morality play—which Robert Potter persuasively defined as a kind of penitential theatre—and the drama of the English Renaissance in the ways each type of theatre relates to existing judicial institutions and represents or enacts social relations as, in some sense, relations involving justice.[23] For my account it matters, then, that both Purgatory and eucharistic transubstantiation—institutions and doctrines whose fiercely contested afterlives have been invoked to explain the psychological intensity of Renaissance drama—had, prior to the Reformation, a juridical and social dimension as part of the sacrament of penance. Many of the recent cultural-historical accounts of Renaissance theatre's fascination with pre-Reformation beliefs and practices have been influenced by revisionist historians' accounts of the survival of these in Elizabethan England. However, the historian Ethan Shagan has assaulted revisionist accounts of the survival of this kind of notional convergence of traditional belief and practice after the Reformation precisely because of religion's social and juridical dimension: belief and practice can never be understood solely as a private exercise reflecting the conscience of a parishioner, unmediated by the relation of the Church's jurisdiction to that of the State.[24]

In pre-Reformation theology, the annual reception of the Eucharist went with a legal obligation to be 'shriven' (confessed) so as to be made worthy to receive the host. But shriving, or confession, was not just a private affair: it involved relationships with God, with the priest, and with the community at large. Part of its aim was the achievement of reconciliation among parishioners, and mending broken ties of 'charity' or love by the restitution of any goods wrongfully withheld.[25] If, as Beckwith persuasively argues, the sacramental theatre of Corpus Christi expressed an understanding of the Eucharist as the bonds of community, broken by

---

[22] Anthony Dawson, 'Performance and Participation', in *The Culture of Playgoing in Shakespeare's England*, ed. Dawson and Paul Yachnin (Cambridge: Cambridge University Press, 2001).

[23] Robert Potter, *The English Morality Play* (London: Routledge & Kegan Paul, 1975), 16.

[24] Ethan H. Shagan, *Popular Politics and the English Reformation* (Cambridge: Cambridge University Press, 2003), 9.

[25] See John Bossy, 'The Social History of Confession in the Age of the Reformation', *Transactions of the Royal Historical Society*, 5th ser., 25 (1975), 21–38; Peter Biller and A. J. Minnis (eds.), *Handling Sin* (York: York Medieval Press, 1998); Susan Brigden, *London and the Reformation* (Oxford: Clarendon Press, 1989), 19–21, and Beckwith, *Signifying God*, 92.

sin and restored by love, then this way of experiencing and thinking about theatre could not survive the severance of the Eucharist from penitential theology and the juridical imperative to be 'shriven', or make confession, once a year. We cannot, that is, separate pre-Reformation beliefs in eucharistic transubstantiation and in Purgatory from the economic and juridical organization of social and intersubjective relations through the sacrament of penance of which each was a part.

The Church's penitential jurisdiction was exercised through confession, made mandatory once a year by the Fourth Lateran Council in 1215. By the end of the thirteenth century, writes Elizabeth Fowler, 'confession was considered to be a formal legal jurisdiction complementary to that of the external forum of the ecclesiastical courts'.[26] Penitential manuals, the literature of confession, developed an enormously complex legalistic casuistry to enable the just calculation of penances according to degrees of intentional guilt, the material circumstances of the sin, and the possibility or otherwise of performing direct restitution. So authoritative and sophisticated was this legal discourse of intentionality that, in England, presenting juries in late thirteenth-century cases of homicide were using phrases drawn from *summa confessorum*—manuals written for confessors—in order to distinguish unintentional from intentional slaying.[27] The European Reformation is associated with the rejection of this penitential literature of the confessional: Luther's burning of the 'diabolical' *Summa Angelica* is the exemplary instance.[28] But in England, where action to bring about the Reformation was precipitated initially less by doctrinal opposition to the Catholic Church than by lay and lawyerly discontent with the Church's jurisdiction, something rather different happened. A lawyer called Christopher St German united the genre of the *summa confessorum* (specifically drawing on Angelo Carletti's *Summa Angelica*) with the pedagogical genre of the hypothetical legal case arising from a reading on a statute.[29] He literally put these two genres into dialogue, personifying them as the interlocutors known as 'Doctor' and 'Student'—a university doctor of divinity, or canon law, and an Inns of Court 'Student in the

---

[26] Elizabeth Fowler, *Literary Character* (Ithaca, NY: Cornell University Press, 2003), 49.

[27] See Naomi D. Hurnard, *The King's Pardon for Homicide before A.D. 1307* (Oxford: Clarendon Press, 1969), 69–77; Anthony Musson, *Medieval Law in Context* (Manchester: Manchester University Press, 2001), 113–14.

[28] See Thomas N. Tentler, 'The Summa for Confessors as an Instrument of Social Control', in *The Pursuit of Holiness in Late Medieval and Renaissance Religion*, ed. Charles Trinkhaus and Heiko A. Oberman (Leiden: E. J. Brill, 1974), 123–4.

[29] On readings at the Inns of Court, see *Readings and Moots at the Inns of Court in the Fifteenth Century*, ii: *Moots and Readers' Cases*, ed. Samuel E. Thorne and J. H. Baker (London: Selden Society, 1990), pp. xv–lxxvi.

Lawes of Englande'.[30] This dialogue effectively prepared for a translation of the Church's penitential jurisdiction over conscience into a common law jurisdiction over the evidential reconstruction of intention. This chapter will explore the imaginative underpinnings of the relation of canon and common law just prior to the Reformation, in order to establish a historical context for understanding the differences between fifteenth-century penitential drama and what I shall call 'evidential drama'—the drama of the Renaissance. We need to start, then, with a question: what representations of 'evidence gathering' can we find in the dramatic, liturgical, and visual culture of the late Middle Ages, when the jurisdiction of confession was at its height?

Medieval Evidence Gathering: Tutivillus, the Writing Demon

At a bench end in the church of the Blessed Virgin Mary in Charlton Mackrell, Somerset, is the carving of a demon who holds a pen in his claw, apparently engaged in writing down something on a long roll of parchment which curls around his figure (Fig. 1). Like the two demons represented in a woodcut in Geoffrey de La Tour Landry's *Der Ritter vom Turn* (1495) this particular devil has a burdensome task (Fig. 2).[31] It is his job to record, in writing, all the sins of inattention to God and lack of charity to neighbours—the malicious gossip, the mumbled prayers and psalms, the evidence of wandering thoughts and bodily distractions—that no gathering of living Christian souls, however devout, can fail to provide. For this busy scribbler is the 'recording demon', Tutivillus, the most popular and often-represented among devils, the only one, apparently, 'whose name and activities seem to have been generally familiar' in the late medieval period.[32]

Stories, dramatizations, and images of Tutivillus span a distinct legal era, ranging chronologically from the first decades after the convening of the Fourth Lateran Council in 1215, which forbade trial by ordeal and made annual confession obligatory, to 1530, the very moment of the Reformation which in England saw the end of the continuum between

---

[30] See Christopher St German, *St German's Doctor and Student*, ed. T. F. T. Plucknett and J. L. Barton (London: Selden Society, 1974), 7. On St German's use of Angelico Carletti, see Simpson, *History of the Common Law of Contract*, ch. 6.

[31] Geoffrey de la Tour Landry, *Der Ritter vom Turn von den Exempeln der gotsforcht un erberkeit* (Augsburg, 1495), sig. C5ʳ.

[32] M. D. Anderson, *Drama and Imagery in Medieval Churches* (Cambridge: Cambridge University Press, 1963), 173.

Figure 1. Carved bench end, *c*.1530, Charlton Mackrell church. Author's photograph.

Figure 2. Devil tearing parchment, from Geoffrey de la Tour Landry, *Der Ritter vom Turn* (1495), sig. C5^r. Reproduced with permission from British Library, I. B. 6827.

the confessional and the jurisdictions of ecclesiastical and royal courts over property and crime.[33] Literary appearances of the writing demon, then, coincide with the period in which all Christians were enjoined to confess their sins at least once a year to their own priest and to perform the penance that the same priest imposed. Indeed, Tutivillus himself is deployed as part of this penitential system, the threat of his record keeping serving to admonish sinners to make timely amendment in this life, as one fourteenth-century manual says, 'Wyth schryfte of mouth and penaunce clere'.[34]

[33] Margaret Jennings traces the earliest references to the *Sermones Vulgares* of Jacques de Vitry (*c*.1220s) and the *Dialogus Miraculorum* (*c*.1230) of Caesarius of Heisterbach in 'Tutivillus: The Literary Career of the Recording Demon', *Studies in Philology*, 74, no. 5 (1977), 1–95, at 11–13. Jennings refers to the demon as 'Tutivillus', though he is also referred to as 'Titivillus'. I refer to him as 'Tutivillus' except when quoting from *Mankind*, where he is designated 'Titivullus'.

[34] *Robert Mannyng of Brunne's 'Handlyng Synne', A.D. 1303*, ed. Frederick J. Furnivall, EETS, o.s., pt. 2, no. 123 (London: EETS, 1903), 292. The line about 'shryfte of mouth' is only in MS Bodl. 415.

Yet it is quite clear that the scribbler Tutivillus also derives some of his attributes from developments of secular as well as ecclesiastical judicial procedure in the period from the thirteenth to the fifteenth centuries. The fact that in one manifestation he not only witnesses secret sin, but records what he has witnessed in *writing* links his life in the popular imagination to the increasing use of writing as a form of legal evidence in English local and crown courts from the thirteenth century onward.[35] The Latin word *evidentia* is a rhetorical term meaning distinctness or clarity. Richard Firth Green, however, notes that a peculiarly English sense of the word 'evidence' as designating ' "information proving the truth of a statement or claim" seems first to have appeared in the Anglo-Norman terminology of thirteenth-century common lawyers, and … seems to have referred exclusively to written documents'.[36] In the Wakefield Judgement play the demon Tutivillus responds to the trump of doomsday by showing the other demons his bags of 'rolles', or parchments, full of writings recording the sins of unrepentant souls, and announcing proudly that he is a 'courte rollar', a clerk or scribe of a legal court.[37] This modelling of the imagined scene of the Last Judgement on technical developments in earthly legal procedure is not in itself surprising. 'In all religions in which the dead are judged', as Jacques Le Goff observed, there are close conceptual ties between 'earthly justice and the divine justice meted out in the hereafter'.[38] But Le Goff's observation itself raises fascinating questions about the conceptual and imaginative consequences of interrelated legal and theological change.

Le Goff himself proposed that the emergence of the complex penal system of the afterlife known as Purgatory was a consequence of a new theological and judicial emphasis, in the twelfth century, on the part played by intention in sin, which produced the division between *culpa* and *poena*, guilt and punishment. According to the influential new theology of this period, guilt (*culpa*) would normally lead to damnation, but could be effaced by contrition of heart, confession, and absolution by a priest, while the *poena* or punishment that remained due to God for the guilty deed in question was satisfied by penance imposed by the priest as a condition for absolution. However, because *poena* might remain unsatisfied even in

---

[35] See Michael T. Clanchy, *From Memory to Written Record* (London: Edward Arnold, 1979).

[36] Richard Firth Green, *A Crisis of Truth* (Philadelphia: University of Pennsylvania Press, 2002), 37.

[37] *The Towneley Plays*, ed. Alfred W. Pollard, EETS, extra series, no. 71 (Oxford, 1897), l. 211; Clanchy, *From Memory to Written Record*, 74–7, 187–9.

[38] Jacques Le Goff, *The Birth of Purgatory*, trans. Arthur Goldhammer (Aldershot: Scolar Press, 1990), 22.

Sins' change of heart, but confident that he has, safely written down in his book, the evidence that will damn them. When he opens the book, however, the record has been erased: 'Il n'y at cy ne mot ne le*tt*re!', he exclaims angrily to his clerk.[46] Judicial accusation in writing has been defeated by inward contrition and shrift of mouth, or confession before a priest.

The moment of erasure in the representation of the writing demon is, then, not conceptually distinct from, but complementary to, the 'economic' imagery of the sack-carrying demon. For in a sense, the erasure of writing is precisely what constitutes it as material: it is not refuted by probable argument, but materially vanishes or becomes ritually remedial. This, in turn, establishes the relationship between inward contrition and the exteriority of language as antithetical—unless ritually efficacious language is tied to the heart's intention in the moment of utterance, it is 'false', acquiring material weight in the scales that measure what is due to the satisfaction of eternal justice. The antithesis of interior and exterior, inward contrition and confession *versus* the legalistic exactions of *poena* no matter how small or unintentional the wrong, may be seen in two ways. In one sense, this antithesis implicit in stories of the devil as record-keeper seems to express the paradoxical supplementarity of *poena* to *culpa* as the residue of a formalistic concept of law that does not want to concede everything to intention: satisfaction must still be made, penance must be done, even though, inwardly, repentance is sincere. In another sense, we can see that the concept of *poena* is expressed by analogy with the formalism of human law, especially, perhaps, with the 'hellish bureaucracy' of the King's Law, with its centralized system of writs.[47] Thus, the aspect of divine justice that is imagined as oppressive—the exaction of satisfaction for venial sin—is expressed both diabolically and by analogy with the formalistic exteriority of English common law, as the latter is perceived as contrasting with the inwardness of sacramental theology.

However, sacramental theology's residual legal formalism—that aspect of the theology that requires the performance of penance, and the complex economic exchanges between the living on earth and the dead in Purgatory to 'purge off' the unsatisfied debts from the divine account—is also expressed in the devil's scribbling and sack-carrying habits. Among the now rather indeterminate objects at the writing demon's feet in the Charlton Mackrell carving, for example, may be an inkpot or, equally,

---

[46] *Moralité des Sept Péchés Mortels*, l. 2359.   [47] Clanchy, *Memory to Written Record*, 188.

the sacrament of penance. '[T]o see how penance works as and in sacramental theater is to see again how theology and theater work through each other', Beckwith writes; 'if early penitential theology was markedly contritionist and remarkably focused on the relation between priest and penitent... the liturgical and ritual aspects of Holy Week articulated absolution not so much as the sole prerogative of the priest, but as the reconciliation of the entire community.'[54] Yet, surprisingly, perhaps, the language of one such penitential play—*Mankind*—resonates no less with references to secular courts of judgment than it does with references to penance. If sacramental theatre, as Beckwith proposes, requires the audience's complicity in the theatrical medium as the penitent community participates annually in communal reconciliation, then it may be that, once again, the role of common law in such theatre is that of sacrament's diabolic double.

Before turning, however, to *Mankind*, and to a sequence of sermons sometimes thought to be a source for *Mankind*, known as *Jacob's Well*, I need to make a few, necessarily superficial, comments on developments in the criminal procedures of the common law in the period 1215–1530. For, from the late thirteenth century on, even as confession was being opposed to ordeal as a form of judicial investigation more able to reveal (and keep concealed for the sinner's own sake) degrees of intentional guilt, the common law was undergoing its own transformation. It is often said that the so-called irrational proofs of the ordeal, abolished in 1215, were 'replaced' by jury trial.[55] It would be seriously misleading, however, to think that the jury trial of the period 1275–1450 bore any resemblance to the fact-evaluating bodies of modern Anglo-American common law. Rather, juries originated as sworn inquests of members of the community whose 'verdict' or truth-saying was based on local knowledge and memory, and not on the oral presentation of evidential narratives of facts under dispute during a trial. To supplement the private prosecution system of appeal, whereby an injured party appealed (formally accused) another, and proof was by judicial combat, Henry II introduced, in 1166, the beginnings of a public prosecution system which made use of the folklaw inquest. Men of each hundred and vill were required to report suspects to royal officers: these were juries of 'presentment'.

---

[54] Beckwith, *Signifying God*, 91; see also Potter, *English Morality Play*, 16: 'If we are to understand the plays, we must clearly understand the action which they promulgate and ultimately represent. It is the acknowledgement, confession and forgiveness of sin, institutionalised in medieval Christianity as the sacrament of penance.'

[55] See, e.g., Barbara Shapiro, *'Beyond Reasonable Doubt' and 'Probable Cause'* (Berkeley: University of California Press, 1991), 3.

The suspects presented had to make proof by compurgation or ordeal. After 1215, the discrediting of ordeal led gradually, by about 1275, to trial by countryside, or by petty juries, which initially had some overlap in personnel with the presenting juries.[56] Indictment, leading to trial by country (that is, by a jury), was thus, unlike appeal, at the King's suit, though it seems that later in the period, 'contemporaries saw indictments as originating from individuals'.[57] Thus royal justice centralized and made state use of a local, folklaw system and attempted to reconcile locality and centre by means of itinerant royal justices or assize commissioners, who would, on their circuits through the counties, deliver the gaol and try accused prisoners with the help of local juries.[58]

Recently, Richard Firth Green has opened up unexpected implications in Michael Clanchy's influential account of how, in the period 1066–1307, the truth of memory came to be replaced, in law, by the truth of written evidence. Green explains how, through the late Middle Ages in England, increasing reliance on royal writs and written evidential records forced a traumatic confrontation between the old folklaw understanding of ethical truth—the truth of the juries' sworn verdict—and the intellectual, depersonalized truth of the written legal record. In both civil and criminal cases, medieval inquests or juries had traditionally sworn not on the basis of an investigation of the facts of the case presented orally in the trial, but on the basis of their own 'troth', their own support, as an ethical community bound by certain customary procedures, for the claim being made by the disputant.[59] The word 'evidence' first seems to appear, in a legal context, with reference to written documents shown to early juries in support of claims to seisin and title. In one such case from about 1200, the jury, as James Bradley Thayer comments, 'made short work of a charter', rejecting the written evidence on the grounds that 'they knew nothing of our chartularies or private agreements', deciding the

---

[56] Milsom, *Historical Foundations of the English Common Law*, 407–10; Roger D. Groot, 'The Early Thirteenth Century Criminal Jury', in *Twelve Good Men and True* (Princeton: Princeton University Press, 1988), 3–35; Naomi D. Hurnard, 'The Jury of Presentment and the Assize of Clarendon', *English Historical Review*, 56, no. 223 (1941), 374–410.

[57] J. G. Bellamy, *The Criminal Trial in Later Medieval England* (Stroud: Sutton Publishing, 1988), 24.

[58] See John Hudson, *The Formation of the English Common Law* (New York: Longman, 1996), 9–11; Marianne Constable, *The Law of the Other* (Chicago: University of Chicago Press, 1991); Green, *A Crisis of Truth*, 127. On writs, see J. H. Baker, *An Introduction to English Legal History* (London: Butterworths, 1979), 49–61, and on the innovative takeover of local by royal justice, see ibid. 1–15.

[59] Green, *A Crisis of Truth*, 100–6; see also Andrea Frisch, *The Invention of the Eyewitness*, (Chapel Hill, NC: University of North Carolina Press, 2004), 41–60.

case rather on the basis of their own memory of the descent of the title.[60]

Green gives a number of similar examples from the period 1269–1341 in which local inquests or juries swear verdicts in cases of dispute over land which are later found to be in direct contradiction to the rights of the case as set out by records discovered in manorial court rolls.[61] These cases, as Green argues, show how difficult it had become, by the mid-fourteenth century to maintain confidence in the illusion of community coherence founded on the jury's ethical truth. In criminal cases, as Green shows, too, writing 'froze legal procedure, even procedure that was no longer appropriate or just, into a set of inflexible rules justified by an appeal to tradition that quickly became tyrannical'.[62] The gradual replacement of the appeal procedure (brought by the victim of the wrong, and tried by battle) with the indictment procedure (brought nominally at the suit of the Crown, by means of the coroner's holding an inquest *super visum corporis*, or upon view of the wounded or slain body) introduced a new emphasis on the importance of the formal accuracy of the written indictment.[63] Up to the mid-sixteenth century, Justices of the King's Bench were, in J. H. Baker's words, 'very pernickety' about minute matters of form in indictments.[64] Moreover, along with this inequitable insistence on the written went an extremely ill-fitting match between formal judicial procedure, whereby the accused had to oppose the plaintiff's account point by point, while the inquests or juries impanelled to give life or death verdicts on these were less and less likely to be the neighbours and character witnesses than they had once been in the earliest years of sworn inquest trial.[65] By the early fifteenth century, according to Edward Powell, efforts made 'to ensure that juries in criminal

[60] James Bradley Thayer, *A Preliminary Treatise on Evidence at the Common Law* (Boston: Little, Brown and Company, 1898), 104–6.
[61] Green, *A Crisis of Truth*, 39–40.　　[62] Ibid. 127.
[63] Ibid.; Baker, *Introduction to English Legal History*, 413–15. Sir John Baker, *The Oxford History of the Laws of England*, VI: *1483–1558* (Oxford: Oxford University Press, 2003), 522.
[64] Sir John Baker, *Oxford History of the Laws of England*, vi. 522, 524 n.; Baker (ed.), *Reports of Sir John Spelman*, offers numerous reports of criminal cases, or pleas of the Crown, in which inaccuracy in the indictment was an issue. See i. 45, 55, 57. Gradually, questions of the accuracy of the indictment became less material; see below, Ch. 2, p. 84.
[65] See *Placita Corone, or La Corone Pledee devant Justices*, ed. J. M. Kaye, Selden Society, Supplementary Series, 4 (1966), 26–7, in which appellees are advised to take exception to every point made in the appeal against them, for 'if it is found in the coroners' rolls that he [the appellor] has varied, in making his counts, in any one of the points...his appeal will fail'. *Placita Corone* was written in the second half of the thirteenth century, but was still being copied in the early fifteenth century (p. xi). On the transition from juries of neighbours to juries of strangers, see J. M. Mitnick, 'From Neighbor-Witness to Judge of Proofs', *American Journal of Legal History*, 32 (1988), 201–35.

soul ready for the Easter houseling.[80] The entire festive and sacramental action of *Mankind* is framed by an injunction to remember the Last Judgement, and so haste to confess and purge one's soul; Mercy addresses the audience directly, reminding them that there will be a 'streyt examynacyon' at 'the last jugement', when 'The corn xall be sauyde, the chaffe xall be brente'—the audience must have 'premedytacyon' of this trial to come.[81] The play, of course, goes on to create its audience as a penitential community by irresistibly implicating it in a refusal to heed these opening words of Mercy's, deflected as it is by the carnivalesque pleasures of language and the body that constitute the subsequent dramatic action. Thus, immediately, Mercy's invocation of the universal Judgement Day is challenged by Myscheff, who reappropriates Mercy's spiritual metaphor of corn and chaff for the linguistic and physical pleasure of punning, thematized as the body's resistance to Mercy's terrifying spiritual distinctions (l. 57). Thereafter, the audience is pleasurably implicated though the spectacle of frenetic, levelling dance (the Vices try to make Mercy take off his long priest's robes and join in), raucous Christmas songs with infectiously repetitive and lewd refrains ('But he wyppe hys ars clen, but he wyppe hys ars clen', etc., l. 340), rampant linguistic and physical obscenity and hilariously subversive, anticlerical punning. Repeated address to the audience also implicates it, as an alehouse audience, in bodily pleasures and needs; for example, when Mankind excuses himself when he needs to urinate ('I wyll into thi[s] yerde, souerens, and cum ageyne sone', l. 561), and when the Vices appropriate the audience's food and drink, and borrow a football from the host (ll. 634, 732).

It is this profound, ritualistic, and non-mimetic implication of the audience in the play's densely physical and scatalogical festivity that enables the emotional power of the play's climactic moments, when a despairing, self-loathing Mankind meets a loving, solicitous Mercy, who reminds him of God's mercy, and begs him to desire it in words: 'yet for my lofe ope thy lyppys and sey, "Miserere mei, Deus!" '. The sense of efficacy in Mercy's final absolution of Mankind depends on this dramatization of Mankind's speaking voluntarily from a contrite heart. The play thus poses a question about the relation of words to the truth of inwardness. 'Idle' or

---

[80] See Walter K. Smart, 'Some Notes on *Mankind*', *Modern Philology*, 14 (1916), 45–8; Coogan, *An Interpretation*, 1–21; C. Davidson, *Visualising the Moral Life: Medieval Iconography and the Macro Plays* (New York: AMS Press, 1989), 17–18.

[81] *Mankind*, ll. 29–44. Hereafter references to line numbers of the play in the EETS edition will appear in the text.

insincere words are, as critics have noted, the play's type of venial sin.[82] After listening to the irreverent punning of the Vices, Mercy asks, 'How may yt be excusyde befor the Justyce of all | When for euery ydyll worde we must yelde a reson?' Mankind should not listen to the vices: 'Gyff them non audyence.' The ironies of giving audience or being an audience, however, emerge at the midpoint of the action, with the ritualistic arrival of the devil, Titivillus.[83] Titivillus momentarily arrests the action with the aplomb of a Hollywood star turning up in an episode of a television soap. The rest of the Vices cease, for a moment, to be their allegorical selves, and go about among the audience collecting money: 'Gys ws rede reyallys yf ye wyll se hys abhomynable presens', they demand. The 'presens' of Titivillus is clearly the highlight of the show, the carnivalesque inversion, or double, of the exactions of confession embodied in Mercy, who insists, in the name of the Judgement Day, that reasons be given for all idle words, including ones spoken at a play.

To speak of Titivillus as Mercy's 'double' in this way is to invoke Beckwith's argument about the doubleness of sacramental theatre, the space it shares with the sacred rituals of blessing and absolution. It is this theatre's proximity to sacrament that lends so much power to its Shrovetide inversions (Titivillus's left-handed blessing, obscene parodies of papal pardon, Myscheff's reversal of the Ten Commandments, and so forth).[84] But Titivillus furthers the action in another way, too, a way which, as we shall see in later chapters, faintly adumbrates the English adaptation of classical comic intrigue or legal trickery to Christian tragic forms. For Titivillus's iconographic peculiarity in this play is that he 'goes invisible' and carries neither a sack, nor a scroll, but a net. During Mankind's first shriving by Mercy, the priest warns him that Titivillus 'lesyth no wey, | that goth invysybull and wyll not be sen. | He wyll ronde in yowr ere and cast a nett befor yowr ey' (ll. 301–3). If the invisibility and the net are, as they seem to be, conveyed by gestures and props (for Titivillus announces to the audience, 'before his ey *thus* I wyll hange my nett'), the meaning of both relates to Mercy's insight that the devil 'lesyth no wey', that is, turns everything into a way, or a means. The net appears in the medieval iconography of Satan as fowler, capturing birds with

---

[82] Kathleen M. Ashley, 'Titivillus and the Battle of Words in *Mankind*', *Annuale Mediaeval*, 16 (1975), 128–50, at 130, 136.

[83] Robert Weimann, *Shakespeare and the Popular Tradition in the Theater* (Baltimore: Johns Hopkins University Press, 1978), 112–20; Smart, 'Some Notes on *Mankind*'.

[84] Anthony Gash, 'Carnival and the Poetics of Reversal', in *New Directions in Theatre*, ed. Julian Hilton (New York: St Martin's Press, 1993), 87–119, at 99.

snares of seductive words.[85] Thus the metaphor of invisibility and the net hung before the eye ('To blench hys syght', as Titivillus says, l. 531), anticipates the transformation of a ritual theatre into a theatre of disguise and deceit, but not in such a way as (again in Beckwith's words) 'destroys community'.[86] Titivillus's blenching of Mankind's sight can be paralleled in the later dramatic developments of the name-changing 'masquerading Vice' and the forensic rhetorical invention of the ingenious parasite.[87] This is to say that Titivillus's invisibility and his 'net' are implicitly identified—as was his scroll and pen, in a different manifestation—with trickster quality that is the formalism of any justice system, the capacity of its rules to be unethically manipulated.

The implication of Titivillus's 'game' in the procedural moves of judges and felons is evident from the bargain struck between the devil and the Vices to pay for Titivillus's services in bringing 'Mankynde to myscheff and to shame' (l. 606). Titivillus, having been, like a Justice of the Peace, 'informyde of all the matere' (l. 500) of Mankind's beating of the Vices, vows he will avenge their wounds, but they, in turn, must go about the country and steal what they can.[88] 'Ye that haue goode hors, to yow I sey caueatis!', Titivillus then roars to the East Anglian audience, some of whom may have felt like going home at this point to check the stables. The Vices pick on likely local targets from villages around Cambridge. 'I xall spare Master Woode of Fullbourn', says Nowadays, 'He ys a noli me tangere.' Nought plans to spare 'Master Alyngton of Botysam ... | For drede of in manus tuas qweke' (ll. 511–12, 514–16). Nowadays and Nought are canny burglars: William Allington of Bottisham was made a Justice of the Peace in 1457, and Alexander Woode of Fulburne in 1472. Nought's 'in manus tuas' evokes Christ's words on the cross (Luke 23: 46), '*In manus tuas commendo spiritum meum*'. The soul's commendation

[85] Ashley, 'Titivillus and the Battle of Words in *Mankind*', 139.

[86] Beckwith, *Signifying God*, 92.

[87] In Henry Medwall's *Nature* (1500), Pride introduces himself to Man by the name of 'Worship', 'For to blere hys eye', as another Vice later says. In John Foxe's *Titus et Gesippus* (1544), the parasite Phormio decides that 'Everyone's eyes must be blinded', while in George Gascoigne's *Glasse of Government* (1575), the parasite Eccho, encountering a stern Tudor schoolmaster, muses that he 'must find device to bleare his eye for a while'. Henry Medwall, *Nature*, l. 1203, in *The Plays of Henry Medwall*, ed. Alan H. Nelson (Woodbridge, Suffolk: D. S. Brewer, 1980), 121; John Foxe, *Titus et Gesippus*, i. 4. 20, in *Two Comedies by John Foxe the Martyrologist*, ed. John Hazel Smith (Ithaca, NY: Cornell University Press, 1978), 72–3; George Gascoigne, *The Glasse of Government*, 2. 4, in *The Complete Works of George Gascoigne*, ed. John W. Cunliffe, 2 vols. (Cambridge: Cambridge University Press, 1910), ii. 38.

[88] See Bellamy, *Criminal Trial*, 102.

to God, however, is interrupted by 'queke', a choking squeak as the noose tightens round the neck: what Nought dreads so evocatively is hanging.[89] But New Gyse suggests a further precaution against this eventuality: all they need to do is to 'con well', he says, what he calls, in the *OED*'s first recorded use of the term, their 'neke-verse'. The 'neck-verse', thus precisely codified as a legal dodge, is, of course, the tricksterish double of what Mercy invites Mankind to say truly, with a contrite heart: 'Yet for my lofe ope thy lyppys and sey, "Miserere mei, Deus!"'' (l. 830). Mercy's words, as Coogan points out, suggest the formula of absolution without 'duplicating' it, as happens in *Wisdom, Everyman, Castle of Perseverance*, and other penitential plays.[90] The doubleness/duplication of theatre, its proximity to sacred ritual, is thus precisely identified with the sacrament's mockery in the earthly approximations of justice that are, in fact, more like devilish games.

When the Vices next return to the stage having had a 'nere rune' with justice (New Gyse enters with the halter about his neck; Myscheff bears the marks of fetters, but was saved because he 'coude hys neke-verse', l. 619), Titivillus has already completed his 'game' with Mankind. These imagined actions—the Vices' off-stage thefts, homicides, and run-ins with the law, Mankind's being deluded by the invisible Titivillus with his net of lies—are clearly paralleled. Implicit here, as in the iconographical tradition that links Titivillus with the 'hellish bureaucracy' of legal writs and records, is a formalistic and ritualistic rather than rhetorical conception of legal language and procedure. Titivillus lulls Mankind to sleep and then whispers in his ear, perhaps in the form of a dream, that Mankind's priest, Mercy, is a marred man, and a cattle-thief, and has run off to France to escape the gallows. It is this belief that prompts Mankind to join the Vices in theft and lechery. The translation of the Vices' scatalogical, anticlerical punning into the efficacy of Titivillus's anticlerical rumour makes sense only according to a paradigm of the subject as split between the body's enmity towards its own inwardness (the soul), as words are split between their materiality (in puns, mumbled prayers, lies, and the procedural legal fictions of writs) and their spiritual efficacy (in the formulae of absolution, excommunication, and contrite prayer). At no time in the play are words considered evidential and probable, just as at no time are common law processes considered to be resources of justice rather than procedural hoops in the Vices' 'game'. When Mercy,

---

[89] See Eccles's excellent notes, *The Macro Plays*, 222; also Coogan, *An Interpretation*, 119.
[90] Coogan, *An Interpretation*, 16.

lamenting Mankind's fellowship with the Vices, seeks him with the cry, 'Mankynde, ubi es?', Nowadays mockingly suggests that he 'must speke to the schryve [sheriff] for a cape corpus', or else he must 'be fayn to return wyth non est inventus' (ll. 780–1). Nowadays's joke transforms Mercy's concern for Mankind's soul into the cumbrous writ procedure for ensuring the presence of a defendant who had not, in spite of previous writs of attachment, appeared in court. This involved a filazer, or officer of central courts, issuing a *capias* to the local sheriff to arrest the defendant. *'Non est inventus'*, 'he cannot be found', was a possible response that the sheriff could make to this writ, and it became, as Baker has written, a 'common fiction for use by sheriffs who could not be persuaded to take positive action', since the law could not take knowledge of whether or not the sheriff had actually looked.[91] The common law here appears as a grotesquely formal and ineffective parody of the essential path to Mercy, who, at the Last Judgement, 'schall rewle the mater wythowte contauersye' in favour of those who duly and contritely make confession (l. 842).

In a late sixteenth- or seventeenth-century play, a figure like Mankind, hearing in a dream, or by way of a rumour or a ghost, that a loved and trusted friend was in fact a criminal, would question the probability of the dream or rumour *as evidence*. Indeed, as Macolm Gaskill writes, seventeenth-century Protestant discourses of crime do not abandon the idea of ghosts, dreams, and apparitions, but fashion them increasingly in evidentially probable terms by linking them to other suspicious circumstances.[92] A printed pamphlet of 1690 describes how a vision of Mary Barwick, wife of William Barwick of Yorkshire, appeared one day to her brother-in-law. He, slightly puzzled, told his wife that he had seen an apparition of her sister. Together they recalled how William Barwick had told them of sending his wife to stay with his uncle, and 'laying Circumstances together', the couple 'inferr'd ... that her Sister was ... *Murder'd*', which, on subsequent investigation, turned out indeed to be the case.[93]

If we can imagine a late sixteenth- or seventeenth-century version of *Mankind*, then, it would surely be one in which much of the action subsequent to Titivillus's causing of the dream would be spent in the hero's seeking out further signs of guilt or innocence; uncertainty and suspicion would drive him on, prompt him to engage in further, testing dialogues

[91] Baker, *Introduction to English Legal History*, 52–3.
[92] Malcolm Gaskill, *Crimes and Mentalities in Early Modern England* (Cambridge: Cambridge University Press, 2000), 92, 219–20, 232–3, 271–2, 309.
[93] *A Full and True Relation of the Examination and Confession of W. Barwick and E. Mangall* (London, 1690), 2.

and strategic uses of play acting and pretence. *Mankind* would be like *Hamlet*. That the fifteenth-century Mankind does not, however, spend a moment questioning the likelihood of Mercy's sudden transformation into a gallows-bird testifies both to Titivillus's identification as the demonic irresistibility of legal accusation, and to the inconceivable nature of a rhetorical discourse of probability, or evidential uncertainty, in a sacramental theatre. Indeed, the paronomastic materialization of words that is the hallmark of the Vices finds its counterpart in a Purgatorial concept of justice not as the equitable hearing of words as evidential stories, but as the erasing of material marks from parchment and the ritual blessing of Mankind by Mercy, which Mankind extends outward to the audience, 'God send ws all plente of hys gret mercy!'.

'All lawes Cannon be not the lawes of god': The Legal Reformation

About 150 years after *Mankind* was being performed, and *Jacob's Well* was (if it ever was) being preached, an enthusiastic reading public (later to include John Bunyan) was buying up copies of a new kind of spiritual allegory of conscience examination, Richard Bernard's *The Isle of Man: Legall Proceeding in Man-shire against SIN* (1627).[94] In this same 150 years a seismic shift in the relative powers of the spiritual and temporal jurisdictions had taken place. In addition to the abolition of lay confession, sanctuary for felons had been almost completely done away with, and benefit of clergy had undergone 'a remarkable secularization'.[95] Certain kinds of spiritual action, such as defamation and *fidei laesio*, or the action for breach of sworn promise, now had common law equivalents. While ecclesiastical courts enjoyed something of a revival from 1570 to 1640, their work had to a great extent been harnessed, like that of constables, Justices of the Peace, and other non-professional local officers, by a central government concerned 'to try and control crime and disorder and regulate many aspects of social life' through the institutions of local and parish governance.[96] Ecclesiastical jurisdiction no longer represented a

---

[94] See *DNB* entry on Richard Bernard by Richard L. Greaves. Greaves says that *The Isle of Man* was first published in 1627 and went through six editions by 1683, but the title-page of the 1659 edition declares it to be the thirteenth. See Richard Bernard, *The Isle of Man* (London, 1659).

[95] Baker (ed.), *Reports of John Spelman*, ii. 327–34; on sanctuary, ii. 334–9.

[96] Martin Ingram, *Church Courts, Sex and Marriage in England, 1570–1640* (Cambridge: Cambridge University Press, 1987), 29.

sacramental alternative to the jurisdiction of the common law; rather, both had become instrumental in achieving administrative and judicial 'commonweal' at a local level. Richard Bernard, indeed, though himself a product of the educational reformation of the ministry between 1570 and 1620, had such respect for the evidential procedures of the common law that he grants them a certain kind of spiritual authority.[97]

For our purposes what is most striking about Bernard's allegory, by contrast with *Jacob's Well* or *Mankind*, is the way in which the obvious theological shift—from a penitential theology stressing shrift and works of mercy to a Protestant theology of dutiful self-examination and repentance—combines with a new moral confidence, expressed in the procedural detail of the common law allegory, in the investigative and evidential processes of the jury trial. Thus, whereas the priest who wrote *Jacob's Well* asked his parishioners to imagine themselves either as pleading clergy or as taking sanctuary in order to evade the process of indictment and trial 'by the country', or by sworn inquest, Richard Bernard devotes the entire two books of his allegory to an exhaustive rehearsal of the processes of hue and cry, arrest, pre-trial examination, challenging the jury, and evidence giving by witnesses both for and against at the oral trial, all of which have point-for-point analogies as aspects of the sinner's own self-examination, sincere repentance, and self-condemnation before God. Thus 'Godly Jealousie' first spies out the malefactor, Sin, and gets the Deputy Constable—who is 'commonly some neighbour, intreated to perform the Office', and who represents 'understanding darkened'—to attach the felon, and bring him before the Justice of the Peace, for pre-trial examination. The Justice, who represents *'well-informed Judgement'*, engages in a long examination of the fact, 'and the nature of it, with the occasions, causes, and degrees, with the associates, evident signes, the fruits and effects thereof; so this spiritual Justice is to examine sin'.[98] Having examined the felony, and found the suspect not bailable, the Justice binds over 'True Repentance...to give evidence against this *felon Sin*, which hee is very ready to do; for it cannot bee, (if a mans judgement be well informed upon a serious examination with a carefull and considerate remembrance of all his sins) but that he must needs perforce bee made to sorrow for them, and upon true repentance, pursue them to the death with a deadly

---

[97] On the reformation of the ministry, see Rosemary O'Day, *The English Clergy* (Leicester: Leicester University Press, 1979), 126–43.

[98] Bernard, *Isle of Man*, 76. Indeed, so detailed and exact is Bernard's allegory that one historian of the criminal law has referred extensively to it as a factual source for evidence of proceedings at the late medieval and sixteenth-century criminal trial. See Bellamy, *Criminal Trial in Later Medieval England*, 113, nn. 89–93.

hatred.' Finally, at the oral trial, which fills the whole of Bernard's second book, evidence is brought against various sins by witnesses who testify before the jury. For example, against Covetousness, evidence is brought by witnesses called 'Master Church, Master Commonweal, Master Houshold, Master Neighborhood, Master Good-Work', as well as by 'Master Proof' and 'Master Signs'.[99]

Bernard's allegory offers what can only be described as a lovingly detailed description of processes of pre-trial examination and jury trial as these had developed by the early years of the seventeenth century. As we can see, by this time criminal jury trial had acquired some of the features we still associate with it: though there was as yet no counsel for the prosecution and defence, witnesses are nevertheless brought on to give testimony before a jury who no longer swears for or against the character of the defendant, but who now listens to competing narratives of the facts and decides, on the strength of their probability, as to the defendant's guilt or innocence. In the years that intervened between the writing of the legal allegory of *Jacob's Well* and Bernard's influential *Isle of Man*, then, there had taken place not only a doctrinal but a legal Reformation. The elements of legal procedure in which the priestly author places so much trust—the trial by clergy for those able to plead clergy, and the recourse to sanctuary and abjuration of the realm by known felons and homicides—had been more or less abolished, and the statutory requirement that Justices of the Peace take pre-trial examinations of suspects before bailing them had breathed new life into the petty jury as a body whose task was to decide the facts based on hearing the evidence.[100] And thus, as Bernard's allegory amply demonstrates, the position of spiritual and moral authority once accorded to the sacrament of penance and canon law procedure has been decisively reversed. Spiritual and moral authority now rests at least as much with evidential processes of the participatory justice system—the collaboration of semi-official representatives of the common law—the Justice of the Peace, constables, tithing men, and so forth—and the ordinary people of the jury.

In a book that is primarily about the impact of evidential awareness on drama, it is arguable that we do not strictly need to know how this conceptual transformation came about. However, some account of the conditions

---

[99] Ibid. 212–26.

[100] On the importance of the legislation of 1555 and 1556 which obliged Justices of the Peace to make pre-trial examination of suspects, see Langbein, *Prosecuting Crime in the Renaissance*. This topic will be treated in more detail in Ch. 2.

that made it possible will help clarify representational questions—to do, for example, with English attitudes to the forensic rhetoric of classical comedy—that will become important in later chapters. So the last section of this chapter will take up some of the issues raised by the jurisdictional clash of the English Reformation, primarily as these arise in the passionate debate over canon and common law procedures argued out by Thomas More and Christopher St German.

First, a couple of caveats are in order. We need to be clear that the concepts that enabled the participatory system of common law jury trial to become more evidentially sophisticated originated in Roman canon law. The work of Barbara Shapiro and Michael Macnair has shown how these evidentiary concepts—concepts of suspicion, common fame, presumption, circumstantial evidence, satisfied conscience—migrated from the civil law and from the ecclesiastical courts into common law procedures of search and seizure, pre-trial examination, grand jury investigation, and trial by petty jury in the course of the sixteenth and seventeenth centuries.[101] The process, then, was one of popular diffusion: where once these evidentiary concepts had been deployed by the civil or ecclesiastical judge, common law procedures required them to be applied by lay officers and members of the public.

The second caveat involves the historiography of the ecclesiastical courts. Many studies since that of Martin Ingram in 1987 have shown that these courts were vigorously active in the Elizabethan and Jacobean period, and have thus superseded an older historiography of their decline, which relied heavily on contemporary Puritan and common law attacks.[102] A simple illustration from dramatic and pedagogical literature will suffice to show how the choice between recourse to common and recourse to ecclesiastical courts was thought of in practical terms. The same Richard Bernard who wrote *The Isle of Man* also translated the plays of Terence into English for schoolboys learning Latin. Bernard is even-handed and precise in his translations of variations on the frequently occurring Latin phrase involving legal actions in the plays. In a single play, he translated *'tibi scribam dicam'* ('I'll bring a case against you') as 'I...will enter an action against you', while later the phrase *'in ius ambula'* ('come with me to court') is translated as 'Come on and walke with me to the consistory'. In other words, Bernard suggests that the first court

---

[101] Shapiro, *'Beyond Reasonable Doubt' and 'Probable Cause'*; Michael R. T. Macnair, *The Law of Proof in Early Modern Equity* (Berlin: Duncker & Humblot, 1999).

[102] Ingram, *Church Courts*, 8; see also Laura Gowing, *Domestic Dangers* (Oxford: Oxford University Press, 1996).

referred to is a common law court, and the second is the bishops' or consistory court.[103] Bernard's late sixteenth-century translation of Terence allows readers to imagine these ancient litigious plots comfortably accommodating themselves to the native landscape of county and parish courts.

These caveats notwithstanding, it is clear that it was discontent with the Church's jurisdiction on the eve of the English Reformation that offered the opportunity for a radical rethinking of the place of conscience in the common law, which, in turn, permitted the increase in the common law's prestige and moral authority relative to that of the canon law, and made room for some of the evidential developments to be discussed in later chapters. Whether we understand this discontent as motivated by the self-interest of common lawyers or by the legitimate grievances of lay subjects, its effects are nevertheless undisputed.

Sarah Beckwith has distinguished the jurisdictional critique enacted in Corpus Christi theatre from Lollardy, and from programmes of Protestant reform. Corpus Christi plays, she says, 'are critical of *all* forms of jurisdiction, but such criticism is not done within an evangelical and utopian program of reform, but rather a sense of renewed polity through the dissemination of the body of Christ outside of any particular jurisdiction'.[104] It is hard to imagine, though, how other forms of drama could enact such renewal 'outside of any particular jurisdiction', for the Church's jurisdictional power over the sacramental community was inescapably felt in the repetitions of the articles of greater excommunication, or anathema. *Jacob's Well* begins with no fewer than nine chapters of articles of the greater excommunication curse, which, the author stipulates, must be read to parishioners four times a year, 'solemnly', with the cross upheld, bells ringing, and candles burning. We must show, he says, that the accursed soul is 'dampnyd & departyd fro god, and fro alle prayerys and suffragys of holy cherch, and fro alle the sacrymentys. And we schewe hem to be taken by the powere of sathan, the fend, to deth, & to damnacyoun of body and of soule, tyl thei come to amendement be verry penaunce, & ben assoyled.'[105]

The very first article concerns jurisdictional boundaries: 'We denounce acursed...thei...that pursewyn wryttes or letterys in ony lay court, to lettyn the proces of lawe of holy cherche in swyche causys that schulde

[103] Richard Bernard, *Terence in English* (London: John Legatt, 1629), 371–3, 421–3. On the terminology of going to court in Roman New Comedy, see Adele C. Scafuro, *The Forensic Stage* (Cambridge: Cambridge University Press, 1997), 86–7.
[104] Beckwith, *Signifying God*, 134.   [105] *Jacob's Well*, ed. Brandeis, 14.

be demyd be non other lawe.'[106] This seems to limit the curse to those who illegitimately hinder ecclesiastical due process, but it actually tries to pre-empt any debate over the question of which causes should be deemed or judged in which court. Yet in the late fifteenth and early sixteenth century, some litigants were choosing common law alternatives, and common lawyers were disputing the Church's right to adjudicate debts by the action *fidei laesio*. Attempts to use the common law writs of prohibition and *praemunire* to prevent the ecclesiastical courts from hearing property disputes became more and more frequent in the early years of the sixteenth century.[107] It was at this time, in 1505, that Bishop Nykke of Norwich wrote to Archbishop Warham that he wished to 'curse all . . . maintainers of the praemunire as heretics' for hindering the ecclesiastical jurisdiction.[108] The first salvo of the reformers, Simon Fish's famous *Supplication for the Beggars* of 1529, directly charged the Church with preventing all common law actions against the clergy by accusing the bringers of such actions of being heretics.[109] The charge became a frequent one during the Parliament of 1529. The Mercers' Company in London complained to the King that his subjects 'were vexed and trobled by citations with cursyng oon day and absoilyng the next day' in the church courts, while Edward Hall, the common lawyer, chronicled the House of Commons' discussion of six articles against the clergy, commenting that before this time no man would have dared voice such complaints for fear of being called a heretic and losing all his possessions.[110] Reformation historians argue about the motivations of bishops and common lawyers in these years of bitter jurisdictional dispute, but for our purposes, the central point to grasp here is that Henry VIII's divorce proceedings forced a confrontation of jurisdictions which centred, ultimately, on the question of either's capacity to decide whether a defendant was lying or telling the truth. That is to say, one jurisdiction (the common law), which had traditionally relegated such questions to the verdicts of a jury or to supplementary equitable proceedings in Chancery, was now in explicit and open conflict with another (the canon law), which,

---

[106] *Jacob's Well*, ed. Brandeis, 14.   [107] Baker (ed.), *Reports of John Spelman*, ii. 66.

[108] Ibid. 64–70; Ralph Houlbrooke, 'The Decline of Ecclesiastical Jurisdiction under the Tudors', in *Continuity and Change: Personnel and Administration of the Church of England 1500–1642*, ed. R. O. Day and F. Heal (Leicester: Leicester University Press, 1976), 239–42; Christopher Haigh, *English Reformations* (Oxford: Clarendon Press, 1993), 76; W. T. Waugh, 'The Great Statute of Praemunire', *English Historical Review*, 37 (1922), 173–205.

[109] Simon Fish, *A Supplication for the Beggars*, in *The Yale Edition of the Complete Works of St Thomas More*, vii, Appendix B, 409–22, 417.

[110] Stanford E. Lehmberg, *The Reformation Parliament 1529–1536* (Cambridge: the University Press, 1970), 81–3.

through the discretion permitted to ordinaries to examine circumstances and require oaths *ex officio*, as well as through the penitential jurisdiction of confession, claimed to be able to examine and adjudicate questions of truth telling directly.[111]

The high moral and material stakes of this jurisdictional conflict emerge, if not always clearly, from the repetitious yet passionate arguments over procedural technicalities that fill the pages of the famous debate between two men matched in lawyerly expertise and spiritual integrity, Christopher St German and St Thomas More.[112] Each of these disputants defends an idea of the primary accountability of the individual conscience (or what St German calls 'the entent inwarde in the herte') to God.[113] They divide sharply, however, over the question of the methods that law is permitted to use to examine conscience. More, having little faith in the jury system, prefers the civil and ecclesiastical legal models which permit the judge discretion to examine witnesses secretly and evaluate their testimony according to canon law presumptions and codified fractions of proof. St German would rather place conscience beyond secret investigation by any coercive system of law, while at the same time remedying the common law's defectiveness in failing to take account of other than written evidences by absorbing the equitable processes of Chancery as a necessary supplement. The legal and doctrinal questions over which More and St German come into collision can be divided into two broad categories: one concerns the distribution of goods, imagining justice as debts being paid and restitution made for wrongs, whether in this life or in Purgatory. The other involves comparison between ecclesiastical procedure in heresy trials and common law procedure in felony trials. What these areas have in common—as we might have imagined, bearing in mind the disputed debt repayment in *Love's Labour's Lost* and Warwick's suspicions of Suffolk's involvement in the death of Duke Humphrey in

---

[111] As Milsom points out, the Christian courts are 'the earliest in England that would have looked to us like courts of law. Documents survive from actual litigation very nearly as old as the earliest rolls of the king's courts; and what we see is a single judge trying to find out what had happened by considering and comparing the evidence of witnesses, and applying to the facts so found rules of law which could be looked up in books' (*Historical Foundations*, 25). The documents to which Milsom refers are to be found in *Select cases from the ecclesiastical courts of the Province of Canterbury, c.1200–1301*, ed. Norma Adams and Charles Donahue, Jr. (London: Selden Society, 1981).

[112] More's spiritual integrity is not in doubt; anyone who wants to know about St German's can read his writings and John Guy's account of how he dealt with beneficiaries whom he worried had not received their bequests from a friend's will. See John Guy, 'Christopher St German: His Legal and Political Career up to 1534', in *The Yale Edition of the Complete Works of St Thomas More*, x. (New Haven: Yale University Press, 1987), pp. xxx–xxxi.

[113] St German, *Doctor and Student*, 230.

1 Contention—is the problem of how law is to judge whether or not someone is *lying*.

The More–St German controversy began toward the end of 1532 or at the beginning of 1533, months after More had resigned as Lord Chancellor, following the Submission of the Clergy, and two years after the publication of an English text of St German's theoretical repositioning of conscience in relation to common law, the *Dialogue in English betwixt a Doctor of Divinity and a Student of the Laws of England* (1530).[114] This book, published first in Latin in 1528, was to become enormously influential, functioning as a standard legal textbook until the nineteenth century. Its innovative move, as John Guy has explained, was to bring English common law into theoretical harmony with the laws of God and Nature—'despite the fact that conscience might sometimes speak directly contrary to general rules of common law in specific instances'—by redefining conscience as a hermeneutic principle (equity) to be managed from within the common law itself.[115] Not only did this theory, as Guy says, enhance the prestige of the common law in relation to canon law; it effectively denied the canon law's claim, as the law of God, to have jurisdiction over 'inward things', redefining the internal forum of conscience as at once beyond sacerdotal jurisdiction and at the same time susceptible to equitable reconstruction within the common law.

St German's *Doctor and Student* announced a relocation of the casuistry of conscience from its expected place in the *summae* or handbooks of priestly confessors. The prologue to the Latin edition explicitly identified the book as a collection of 'cases of conscience' resolving potential conflicts between procedures in English property law and the imperatives of salvation. St German says that he has collected doubtful cases, 'the knowledge of which is not only necessary for the rendering of justice in the king's courts, but also for leading all those who heed them in the internal forum (*in foro anime*) to a good and healthy conscience'.[116] He goes on to invoke the canon law requirement that made confessors unable to grant absolution to contrite penitents until they had performed restitution. 'So when St Augustine tells us that the sin is not remitted until the thing is restored', his prologue concluded, 'English law tells us which

---

[114] Guy, 'The Political Context of the *Debellation*', in *The Yale Edition of the Complete Works of More*, ix, p. xviii.

[115] John Guy, *Christopher St German on Chancery and Statute* (London: Selden Society, 1985), 19–20; see also *idem*, 'Law, Equity and Conscience in Henrician Jurist Thought', in *Reassessing the Henrician Age*, ed. J. Guy and A. Fox (Oxford: Basil Blackwell, 1986), 178–98, and Zofia Rueger, 'Gerson's Concept of Equity and Christopher St German', *History of Political Thought*, 3 (1982), 1–30.   [116] St German, *Doctor and Student*, 2–3.

taking is just and which unjust; and so law is the best guide whether restitution is due or not.'[117] In this extraordinary claim, 'English law' stands exactly where one would expect the priestly confessor and his canon law *summa* to be. By citing St Augustine's famous predication of forgiveness of sin on the act of restitution, St German explicitly trespasses on the territory of the sacraments of the Church, specifically, the sacrament of penance.[118]

According to canon law, restitution of any property unjustly acquired was a prerequisite for absolution from sin, and the confessor was not to assign penance until restitution had been made.[119] Historians such as John Bossy who stress the work of social reconciliation performed through pre-Reformation confession, make restitution central to the sacrament: 'an annual settlement of social accounts', as Bossy puts it.[120] Though theologians might distinguish the 'satisfaction' due to God through *poena*, or penance, from the restitution due to neighbours for wrongs, most people, as Bossy notes St Bonaventura remarking, could not distinguish between satisfaction and restitution.[121] Sarah Beckwith's account of the sacrament of penance as a communal ritual of 'truth and reconciliation' likewise depends on invoking the condition of restitution. She quotes from the fifteenth-century *Speculum Sacerdotal*, which contains a treatise on penance derived from the influential pseudo-Augustinian *Liber de vera et falsa poenitentia*. The treatise advises the confessor thus: 'And if ther be eny siche that hath getyn through sotilte, thefte, or oker heritage [usury], felde, money, clothe, hows, houshold or what good so-euer it be, loke that thei be noght asoylid vn-to that which was wrongefully with-holde and withdrawen be restorid ageyn, *scilicet*, yif he haue wherof and his power mowe do it.'[122]

Why, then, should a treatise on common law concern itself with restitution? The reason can be found in the fact that, as Eamon Duffy explains, 'the whole notion of penance turned on the idea of a debt discharged by a pious activity' so that 'every bequest for a soul in Purgatory

---

[117] Ibid. 3–5.

[118] For a translation of the letter in which St Augustine stipulates restitution, see letter 153 in *Writings of St Augustine, Letters* (vol. 3), trans. Sister Wilfrid Parsons (New York: Fathers of the Church, 1953), 296–7.

[119] See Henry Charles Lea, *A History of Auricular Confession and Indulgences in the Latin Church*, 3 vols. (New York: Greenwood Press, 1968), ii. 43–63; Tentler, 'Summa for Confessors as an Instrument of Social Control'; Bossy, 'Social History of Confession in the Age of Reformation'.

[120] Bossy, 'Social History of Confession', 25.   [121] Ibid.

[122] *Speculum Sacerdotale*, ed. Edward H. Weatherly, EETS, o.s., no. 200 (London, 1936), 71. I have silently modernized all thorns and yoghs in this and other texts containing them.

could be regarded in this light'.[123] Restitution, that is to say, need not be directed specifically to the party wronged, but might be fulfilled through the endowing of chantries or other forms of gift to the Church. Thus, while the casuistry of restitution in the *summae* and in other penitential texts was enormously complex (the author of *Jacob's Well* enquired whether, if one had stolen a horse, it was possible, in making restitution of the value, to deduct one's costs in pasture and feeding and curing the animal of any sickness?[124]), the question of how to *prove* to whom restitution was due was not an issue. It is a matter of emphasis, of course, but it could be said that performing restitution to one's local church, rather than to individuals wronged, runs somewhat counter to any idea of the sacrament of penance as involving either 'truth and reconciliation' or 'an annual settlement of social accounts'. Whether or not that is so, it was to this aspect of restitution that St German objected, noting in *A treatise concernynge the division betwene the spirytualtie and temporaltie* (1532), that priests were widely perceived to be

more diligent to enduce the people to suche thynges, as shall brynge riches to the churche, as to gyue money to trentals, and to founde chaunteries and obites, and to obteyene pardons, & to go upon pylgremages and suche other: than they be to enduce them to the *payment of theyr dettes to make restitutions for such wronges as they haue done or to doo the werkes of mercy to their neyghboures*.[125]

In response to More's accusation that he had by this argument denigrated the value of obits (annual offices for the dead), trentals (a set of thirty requiem masses for the dead), and chantries (endowments for priests to sing daily Mass for the dead), St German insisted that he was in no way opposed to them, except in so far as they had displaced the primary obligation of restitution, on which forgiveness depends:

And if it be said, that men be so loth to haue their wronges knowen, that they wyl in no wise make restitution: it may be answered, that though some percase be so harde harted . . . yet it is not like that all men wolde be so, if they had the good charitable counsayle in that behalfe: but if the spiritual counsayle wyl enclyne more to trentals, obytes, makynge of chaunteries, and such other . . . the due examination that is requisite for making of restitutions, may lightly be forgotten . . . For though prayers be right expedient and helthfull to the soule: yet they serue not in al

[123] Eamon Duffy, *The Stripping of the Altars* (New Haven and London: Yale University Press, 1992), 356.　　　　　　　　　　　　　　　　　[124] *Jacob's Well*, ed. Brandeis, 205.
[125] Christopher St German, *A treatise concernynge the division betwene the spirytualtie and temporaltie*, in *The Yale Edition of the Complete Works of St. Thomas More*, ix. 178; my italics.

cases, as to discharge debtes or restitutions, where there is inough to paye them with.[126]

Although he was later to espouse some of the tenets of the Reformers, St German here takes pains to avoid the gesture of unmasking Catholic ritual as some kind of ruse. More's representation of him as the saboteur of Masses for the dead is, he insists, a deliberate missing of the point. St German is clear that the issue is not almsgiving, but 'the due examination that is requisite for making of restitutions', that is, the examination of *evidence* for the existence of a moral obligation to repay.

The trouble, of course, was that the common law was not equipped to enable the conscientious performance of restitution; nor, in fact, did St German believe that any coercive system—any legal system—should enforce conscience. Nevertheless, St German's *Doctor and Student* confronted the danger to the soul perpetuated and encouraged by the mechanical rigidity of the common law. The most obvious way in which the common law actively encouraged men to ignore the imperatives of conscience had to do with its inflexibility with regard to other than written evidences in cases of contracts, bargains, or agreements. In the predominately oral culture in which most fifteenth-century English people lived, many formally binding agreements to exchange property, marry, pay money at a future date, and so forth were made by way of witnessed oaths, sealed with drinking together or exchanging pledges or other rituals. The King's courts of common law, as we have seen, however, would not give an action of debt unless the creditor could show evidence in writing (a 'speciality') of the agreement to pay, or a 'quid pro quo', something the debtor had received in exchange. Conversely, if the debtor who had been bound in a written obligation, paid off his debt and took no written receipt or 'acquittance' of his payment, he could be obliged, in common law, to pay again.[127]

After preparing the ground with several chapters on theological derivation of temporal law from eternal law and on the exposition of the grounds of English common law, St German staged a series of questions in which the theologian challenged the lawyer to defend the common law's failure to conform with divine justice. The first of these concerns the tyranny of written evidence: the Doctor invoked the all-too-familiar case—implied in the dispute at the opening of *Love's Labour's Lost*—of the debtor bound in a written obligation who, having paid but failed to get

---

[126] St German, *Salem and Bizance*, in *The Yale Edition of the Complete Works of St. Thomas More*, x. 345.
[127] See Baker (ed.), *Reports of John Spelman*, ii. 37–9; Barbour, *History of Contract*, 25–40.

a written receipt, might be legally obliged to pay again. How, the Doctor asked, can it be said that the law 'standeth with reason or conscyence' in such a case?[128] Petitions in Chancery in the fifteenth century give some sense of the somewhat demonic operations of the common law in this respect. Sometime after 1432, for example, John Pottok petitioned in Chancery for relief when he sold 'certeyns goodis and catalles' to one Harry Brome by way of a third party, Margrete Wylton, for ten pounds. Harry was bound in an obligation to pay Pottok for the delivery of the goods, but Margrete somehow 'lost the forsayd obligacion', and Harry must have seen his opportunity to refuse to pay. Pottok begged the Chancellor to consider that 'be cause the sayd obligacuon is loste' he had 'no remedie atte the comune lawe to recover the sayd some', unless Harry were subpoenaed to appear in Chancery to be examined on his conscience in the matter.[129]

The Doctor's question was thus far from theoretical: it came directly out of the everyday experiences of late fifteenth-century parishioners and neighbours engaged in informal bargains and exchanges, experiences which led them to petition in Chancery in the hope of relief, or to take their actions for breach of verbal contracts to the Church courts to be adjudicated as spiritual offences or sins of perjury. In the second half of the fifteenth century the consistory courts at Canterbury were enormously busy with cases of this nature.[130] In confronting these issues of conscience with which the law was so ill-equipped to deal, St German's dialogue absorbed and displaced the authority of the priest in confession by appropriating his penitential language and concerns, and adapting these to the evidential limitations and concerns of public accountability that define the positive law. Since restitution was necessary for salvation, the Doctor's first question to the Student on the case of the debtor who took no acquittance confronts not only the problem of injustice in this world, but the danger of damnation. Thus, in response to the Doctor's challenging question of the debtor who has faithfully paid but taken no acquittance, the Student defends the common law insistence on proof, but the dispute ushers in a theoretical exposition, by the Doctor, of conscience and equity. The Doctor's explanation of equity, which occurs in chapter 14 of St German's dialogue, derives indirectly from the passage in Aristotle's *Nicomachean Ethics* in which Aristotle declares it

---

[128] St German, *Doctor and Student*, 77.   [129] Barbour, *History of Contract*, 186–7.

[130] Houlbrooke, 'Decline of Ecclesiastical Jurisdiction'; Brian L. Woodcock, *Medieval Ecclesiastical Courts in the Diocese of Canterbury* (Oxford: Oxford University Press, 1952), 89–92; R. H. Helmholz, 'Assumpsit and *Fidei Laesio*', *Law Quarterly Review*, 91 (1975), 406–32.

right, when a case arises the particular circumstances of which have not been anticipated by the general words of the positive law, to 'rectify the defect by deciding as the lawgiver would himself decide if he were present on that occasion'.[131] Equity, as many commentators have noted, thus becomes a hermeneutic principle with the law itself; when faced with a general rule which in a particular case will produce a decision 'agaynste the lawe of god', the law is permitted to interpret the general rule in the light of these unforeseen circumstances.[132]

St German's insistence on the capacity of the law to respond equitably to the exigencies of particular circumstances went with a denial of the identification of the canon law as the administration of the law of God over inward guilt. In what seemed like a perfectly conventional definition, his Doctor asserted, among the reasons for the law of God, the Thomist commonplace that 'man may only make a lawe of suche thynges as he maye Iuge vpon and the Iugement of man may not be of inward thinges but only of outwarde thynges', and that the law of man may not, in any case, punish all offences, 'for yf all offencis shuld be punysshed the common welth shuld be hurte as it is of contractes'. It cannot be denied, St German's fictional Doctor went on, 'that as longe as contractes be sufferyd many offences shall folowe therby, & yet they be sufferyd for the common welthe'.[133] But these very arguments had been, in the thirteenth century, part of the theological justification for the superiority of private confession over the manifest proofs of *judicium Dei*.[134] In their Thomist deployment, then, they had identified the administration of the law of God with the confessor's power to inquire of 'inward things', and to assign penance for secret offences. St German completely reversed this identification. First, he asserted that 'all the lawes Cannon be not the lawes of god', for some of them are concerned with the 'polytycall...conversacyon' or transactions of the people.[135] And later, in his second dialogue, his common law Student explicitly opposes the

---

[131] Aristotle, *Nicomachean Ethics*, trans. H. Rackham (London: Heineman, 1952), 5. x. 5, 315–17.
[132] St German, *Doctor and Student*, 97. See Rueger, 'Gerson's Concept of Equity and Christopher St German'; John Guy, 'Law, Equity and Conscience'; Richard Schoeck, 'Strategies of Rhetoric in St German's *Doctor and Student*', in *The Political Context of Law*, ed. R. Eales and D. Sullivan (London: Hambledon Press, 1985). Norman Doe, *Fundamental Authority in Late Medieval Law* (Cambridge: Cambridge University Press, 1990), 133–54, seems to me to underestimate St German's innovation.
[133] St German, *Doctor and Student*, 25; Saint Thomas Aquinas, *The Treatise on Law (Being Summa Theologiae, I-11, qq 90 through 97)*, ed. and trans. R. J. Henle, SJ (Notre Dame, IN: University of Notre Dame Press, 1993), 170–1.
[134] Bartlett, *Trial by Fire and Water*, 74–5.   [135] St German, *Doctor and Student*, 23.

argument, taken directly from the *summa confessorum*, that a promise is binding in canon law if the promissor intended to be bound by it. 'No accyon', says the Student,

can lye agaynste hym upon suche promises for yt ys secrete in hys owne conscyence whether he entendyd for to be bounde or naye. And of the entent inwarde in the herte: mannes lawe cannot Juge and that ys one of the causes why the lawe of god ys necessary (that is to saye) to Juge inwarde thynges and yf an accyon sholde lye in that case in the law Canon: then shulde the lawe Canon Juge uppon the inwarde intente of the herte whyche can not be as me semeth.[136]

There could scarcely be a more direct denial of the traditional identification of canon law with the law of God. It had been the theological emphasis on the importance of intention in establishing guilt that had, in the thirteenth century, led to the identification of the Church's confessional jurisdiction as a more appropriate judge of 'interior movements, that are hidden' than the criminal ordeal.[137] Now St German was explicitly identifying canon law as 'mannes lawe', incompetent to judge upon 'the inwarde intente of the herte'. St German's critique thus places intention beyond canon law's private, penitential jurisdiction, but within the common law's publicly accountable jurisdiction by way of the flexible interpretative principle of equitable reconstruction. Again and again in *Doctor and Student*, in discussions of conditional enfeoffment, of recoveries of entailed lands, and in many other contexts, St German asserts the secrecy and illegibility of our inward intentions to one another, and proposes the use of equitable interpretation in compensating for this defect in human law.[138] Moreover, St German's insistence on the spiritual courts' inability to act coercively without 'suffycyent prouffe' because, as his Latin text says, 'in a coercive system the same judgement must be given as to things which cannot be proved as things which have been disproved', has the effect of denying the spiritual judge the right to act on his private knowledge.[139]

St German's common law casuistry of restitution implicitly questioned that doctrine of the fungibility of *poena* which enabled the thought that

---

[136] St German, *Doctor and Student*, 230.   [137] Bartlett, *Trial by Fire and Water*, 80.

[138] See, e.g., *Doctor and Student*, ch. 24, p. 143, in which the issue turns on the intent of the parties in a conditional enfeoffment, and ch. 26, pp. 156–61, in which the Doctor challenges whether the fictitious strategies used to recover entailed lands are conscionable, and the Student replies by imputing a corrupt intention to the makers of the Statute of Westminster (1285), with which the law of entail originated. The Doctor replies that it is perilous 'to Iuge for certayne' that the intention behind the statute was corrupt, since 'there are many consyderacyons' to prove its being composed with good intention.

[139] St German, *Doctor and Student*, 108–9.

Purgatory pains constitute a form of restitution to wronged neighbours, since they 'shall be to the releasynge of other paynes and punyshmentes that thy neighbour ought to have for other offencys which he hath done agaynes god'.[140] It prepared for the later sixteenth-century rise of the action of *assumpsit* which, resembling more the spiritual action of *fidei laesio* than the common law writ of debt, was brought upon the promise to pay implied by a debt, and so required evidence of motive.[141] Given the transformation of political and religious discourse in the seventeenth century by this legal conception of contract as hypothesizing the intentions of another, St German's innovation here should be seen as far-reaching.[142] Indeed, he might well be said to have established the common law, rather than confession, as 'the guardian of the nation's soul' in matters of restitution.[143]

St German and More also clashed revealingly over the differences between Roman canon law and common law procedure with regard to witness testimony in heresy and felony trials respectively. Once again, St German's concern was with the means by which a coercive legal system presumes to detect, or prove, matters which are 'secrete' in man's 'owne breste', and over which 'none can be his iuge but god'.[144] *Ex officio* proceedings in heresy trials permitted the judge to proceed against a suspect by virtue of his office, without, as in common law felony trials, an indictment brought by a presenting jury. The accused was not told the names of those who bore witness against him. The papal decree *Ad abolendum*, issued in 1184, provided for the episcopal examination of suspects under oath, and stipulated that suspects whose guilt was not established by this examination must not be absolved without purgation.

---

[140] John Rastell, *A New Boke of Purgatorye* (1530), in *The Pastyme of the People and A New Boke of Purgatory*, ed. Albert J. Geritz (New York and London: Garland, 1985) 481. The importance of the Reformers' questioning of the possibility that pain might operate economically, as part of the reciprocal justice of restitution, does not seem to have been sufficiently discussed in historians' accounts of debates over Purgatory. John Frith challenged Rastell devastatingly on this issue; see John Frith, *A Disputation of Purgatory* (1533), in *The Works of the English Reformers*, ed. Thomas Russell, 3 vols. (London, 1831), iii. 127. Peter Marshall, *Beliefs and the Dead in Reformation England* (Oxford: Oxford University Press, 2002), is very interesting on fear and commemoration, but has nothing to say about justice and restitution; yet these were topics that concerned such writers as Simon Fish, John Rastell, and Hugh Latimer ('Purgatory's iniquity hath set aside restitutions and brought poor Christians to extreme beggary': *Sermons of Hugh Latimer*, ed. George Elwes Corrie (Cambridge: Cambridge University Press, 1844), ii. 238.   [141] Simpson, *History of the Common Law of Contract*, 326.

[142] See, e.g., Luke Wilson, *Theaters of Intention: Drama and Law in Early Modern England* (Stanford, CA: Stanford University Press, 2000), 78; Victoria Kahn, *Wayward Contracts* (Princeton: Princeton University Press, 2004).

[143] Peter Goodrich, 'Salem and Bizance', in *Law in the Courts of Love* (London and New York: Routledge, 1996), 9–28, at 17.

[144] St German, *Salem and Bizance*, in More, *Complete Works*, x. 355.

On 'vehement suspycyons wythout wytnesses', as Thomas More affirmed, a man might be not only 'put to hys purgacyon', but 'to penaunce also yf he fayle therof'.[145] Such penance, at the ordinary's discretion, might take the form of works which declared the abjuration of any suspected heretical beliefs: 'And yet for the ferther purgacycon of such suspicion, the ordynary myght also enioyne hym some certayn thynges to do, suche as maye declare the more clereli, y^t he is not of such mind/as . . . the doynge of some suche thynges as those heresyes did stande agaynste.'[146] For the heresy suspect to be assigned, on occasion, penance of this nature was not any worse, More insisted, than the felony suspect who might have to wait, in fetters, while the Justices issued a writ '*de gestu et fama*'. At gaol delivery sessions there might be felony suspects who had been arrested but not formally accused (neither indicted nor appealed). In such cases, the Justices of gaol delivery would order the Justice of the Peace to make a public inquiry '*de gestu et fama*', of the deeds and reputation of the suspect, to see whether anyone wished to indict him. If no prosecutor appeared, he was freed on finding surety or after his good fame had been attested.[147] More argued to St German that the shame and physical pain of such a felony suspect was just as great as any shame suffered by an unaccused heresy suspect: the felony suspect 'cometh to the barre as openly as the tother to the consystorye | and somtyme hys feters waye a good pyece of a fagotte on the tothers sholdre'.[148] The heretic bore a faggot (symbolic of the fire that would burn him should he relapse) when performing penance. The felony suspect wore fetters, like those we can see being worn by a prisoner holding his hand up at the bar in an illumination showing the Court of the King's Bench *c*.1450 (Fig. 3).[149] The fetters on the legs of the felony suspect which seem to suggest his guilt before it has been proved are no less shameful, argues More, than the faggot borne by the heresy suspect. St German's objection to the parallel, however, is an objection to the likening of proof to penance. The fetters were not like the faggot; nor was waiting in prison for gaol delivery and the Justice's inquiry *de gestu et fama* analogous to the performance of penance; for when such an

---

[145] More, citing his *Apology* in the *Debellation of Salem and Bizance*, in *The Yale Edition of the Complete Works*, x. 111.

[146] Ibid. 116. [147] Bellamy, *Criminal Trial*, 103–4.

[148] More, quoting his *Apology* in *Debellation*, in *Complete Works*, x. 121.

[149] For an account of this illumination, see G. R. Corner, *Observations on Four Illuminations representing the Courts of Chancery, King's Bench, Common Pleas, and Exchequer*, temp. *Hen. VI*.; repr. from *Archaeologia*, 39, for the Masters of the Bench, Inner Temple, 1909, where the depicted practice of chaining prisoners at the bar is corroborated with reference to Sir Thomas Elyot's 1534 story of Prince Hal's assault on Chief Justice Gascoigne for arraigning one of his men.

Figure 3. Court of King's Bench *c*.1450, from Inner Temple MS 1888. Reproduced with permission from the Masters of the Bench of the Inner Temple.

inquiry had been made, and nothing found, the felony suspect would be not only freed, but 'delyvered as a manne proved to be of good honestie, and to be clered bi his neighbours, of that he was suspected of', whereas 'when he is purged upon the suite *Ex officio*, or for suspicion of herisie, he is put to penance by thordinarie, as a man suspected, wherof he is not clered, and so shalbe taken amonge his neighbours, as a man worthye to do that penance for his offences'.[150] The distinction here is telling: it is hard, under a penitential jurisdiction, for suspects to emerge as innocent, since penance itself (unless it is secret) declares guilt.

In this extending of the ordinary's discretion to permit him to require that the suspect do 'some certayne thynges' for penance, More seems to have been following the collection of English canons made by William Lyndwood in 1433.[151] Lyndwood's *Provinciale* (as his collection was known) included a canon against heretics and schismatics, in which the text's stipulation of purgation (*purgatio*) for suspected heretics was extensively glossed in the notes as 'penitential pains' (*poenae penitentiales*). Lyndwood treats the case of the preacher suspended in his diocese for 'errours or heresyes, whyche it is pretended that he hath preached, affirmed, or thought'. The suspicion of heresy attaching to such a preacher must be 'clensed and washed away (*purgaverit*) at the just arbitrement' of his bishop.[152] The relevant word is '*purgaverit*', glossed in the 1483 and 1679 Latin editions thus:

Purged. Here note, that those who are not condemned of heresy, but are suspected of it, may be enjoined penitential pains, by which such a suspect will purge his innocence. And the injunction of such purgations is left to the arbitration of the bishop, or inquisitor . . . And here penances (*poenae*) are numerous. Of which one is the abjuration of heresy . . . another penance might be imprisonment, or internment in a monastery . . . to build a church, or hospital, or provide marriages or dowries for virgins, or discharge the penance financially, or restore usury, or do some sumptuous work of piety. (My translation)[153]

More's and Lyndwood's 'interpretation of *purgatio* to mean *poenae*', comments Guy, 'is striking. For it could be considered a denial of due process of law if, by way of *canonical* purgation, a suspect who could not be proved guilty had first to swear not that he was innocent of heresy but that he

---

[150] St German, *Salem and Bizance*, in More, *Complete Works*, x. 358.

[151] Guy, 'Legal Context of the Controversy', in *The Yale Edition of the Complete Works of St Thomas More*, x. pp. liii–lv.

[152] William Lyndwood, *Constitutions provincialles of Otho and Octhobone Translated into Englyshe* (London: Robert Redman, 1534), fol. 79ᵛ.

[153] William Lyndwood, *Provinciale, seu Constitutiones Angliae* (Oxford, 1679), lib. 5, tit. 5, 'De Haereticis & Schismaticis', 290–1.

renounced the heretical doctrines of which he was accused, and next, at the bishop's discretion, to perform penance.'[154] It is clear that, under these conditions, there is no possibility of a suspect of heresy emerging innocent. For if purgation amounts to a penance which signifies the abjuration of suspected heretical beliefs, then the very instrument of proof has become the mark of guilt before the law and within the community. In the strictest legal sense, too, the assimilation of purgation to penance and abjuration turned mere suspicion into first-time conviction. A first-time offender, found guilt of heresy, was not usually sentenced to be burnt, but More's suspect is already being treated as a convict, and would therefore be liable to be burnt if prosecuted for heresy again.[155]

The difference between More's and St German's positions corresponds to the degree to which the former sees the judge as God's proxy, best equipped by his training in Roman canon presumptions and proofs to assess the likelihood of guilt in the absence of publicly acknowledged testimony, while the latter sees both the witnesses' and the suspect's public accountability, institutionalized in the inquest or jury procedure, as the common law's safeguard against the inadequacy of human law to judge of hidden matters. Judges of the King's Bench, as Baker has written, 'tended to avoid becoming too involved with the variable facts of particular cases; that was a task for the jury'.[156] More had tried to urge the judges to behave more like ecclesiastical or civil law judges, using 'their own discretions' to mitigate the rigour of the common law. He blamed his lack of success in this on the judges' perception that 'they may by the verdict of the jury cast off all quarrels from them selves uppon them'.[157] Exactly this view informs More's conviction that in some instance a heresy suspect may justly do penance 'though he be not proued gylty of the dede' but only 'suspect', because it is 'after tharbitrement of the ordinarye', once the ordinary or ecclesiastical judge has considered 'the qualytees of ye person & cyrcumstances of ye cause'.[158] More's faith in the discretion of the judge trained in the elaborate Roman canon learning of presumptions, *indicia*, and circumstances, derived and codified from Roman forensic oratory, and his corresponding lack of

---

[154] Guy, 'Legal Context of the Controversy', in *Complete Works of St Thomas More*, x. p. lv.

[155] Ibid. p. liv; see John A. F. Thomson, *Later Lollards 1414–1520* (Oxford: Oxford University Press, 1965), 231 and 237–8.

[156] Baker (ed.), *Reports of Sir John Spelman*, ii. 34.

[157] See Bradin Cormack, *A Power to Do Justice* (Chicago: University of Chicago Press, forthcoming); William Roper, *The Life of Sir Thomas More*, in *Two Early Tudor Lives*, ed. Richard S. Sylvester and Davis P. Harding (New Haven: Yale University Press, 1962), 222.

[158] More, *Debellation*, in *Complete Works*, x. 114.

faith in the untrained jury's verdict, emerges obliquely yet tellingly from another point of disagreement between himself and St German over the consistory court's admission of the testimony of perjured witnesses against suspected heretics.

St German objected, in his *Division*, to the witness who was admitted to be sworn again 'contrarye to his fyrst othe' in the same court. More, speaking the Roman canon evidential language of presumptions and considerations, offers to prove to St German that there may be instances, even in felony trials, where the jury is prepared to believe the witness swearing, contrary to his first oath, that the accused is guilty after all. His argument here is intriguing for a number of reasons, not least because it seems to show, contrary to the belief of many historians, that juries did hear evidence at the bar in the first decades of the sixteenth century, and that witnesses testifying for the defence might speak on oath. More seems, at first, to be crediting his hypothetical jurors with a judge-like capacity to deliberate on the probabilities of guilt and innocence by weighing one presumption against another ('presumptions' were not really items of proof, but they aided probability by enabling the canon or civil law judge to assume a general truth for the purposes of investigative inquiry into the circumstances[159]). He acknowledges that the 'cause wherfore a person ones perjured is repelled from beryng wytnesse agayn, is bycause the lawe presumeth that he setteth not so much by an othe, but that his oth notwithstandyng he were likely inough to lye'.[160] This presumption, however, may in some cases be 'countrepaysed' by a contrary presumption, that will, equitably, be 'for that case an excepcyon out of the generall rule'.[161] For example, continues More, it also is a presumption of law that no man will cast away his soul to do hurt to his own body or friend's. If this presumption is admitted, then 'the presumpcyon of hys trouth in his fyrst oth, is taken away by the secunde', because the first risks perjury to preserve his own body or that of his friend, whereas in the second 'yf he were forsworen, it were to theyr bothe harme'.[162] It could, of course, be objected that if this argument were admitted, witness testimony sworn in defence of the accused's innocence would always be presumed false, but that is not actually the most interesting feature of More's manoeuvring here. For what is most striking about his example is the way in which it attributes a discretionary, even equitable capacity to the jury (since More is maintaining the validity of this example for felony trials). However,

[159] On 'presumptions', see Thayer, *Preliminary Treatise*, 314; Macnair, *Law of Proof in Early Modern Equity*, 263; Shapiro, *'Beyond Reasonable Doubt'*, 120–56.
[160] More, *Debellation*, in *Complete Works*, x. 151.   [161] Ibid. 152.   [162] Ibid. 152–3.

when it comes to offering an exemplary felony trial scenario, an extraordinary thing happens. Unable in fact to conceive of a jury actually weighing the arguments for preferring one sworn testimony above another, More imagines a scene that resembles, in its climatic conjunction of inadvertent revelation, inward remorse and penitent confession, something much less like jury trial than like the sacrament of penance. Indeed, More's anecdote, *mutatis mutandis*, resembles in form the familiar penitential anecdotes of the erasure of Tutivillus's false reckoning in the moment of surprised discovery and contrition. 'If two or thre wytnessys', says More,

wold at the barre excuse uppon theyr othes some one man of felony | and afterward whan they were stepped fro the barre happed to be herde rowne and rejoyce to gether, that they had gevyn good evidence for the acquytayle of theyr fellow, with whom them selfe had ben at the same robbery: if they were sodaynly brought agayn to the judges, the jury not yet departed fro the barre | and beynge severally questyoned in that sodayne abashement, seynge y^t god had so uttred theyr falshed, bygan to haue remorce and came forth wyth ye trouth, and agreed in the cyrcymstaunces and told all one tale, confessynge both the prysoner & them selfe gylty, and wold be content to swere that this tale were trew contrary to the othe y^t they sware there byfore: wolde not the judges trowe you geue them the herynge? yes yes I dowte not, and the jury to.[163]

The court, in More's scenario, overhears the witnesses admitting to having lied. As in the Tutivillus anecdotes, this sudden revelation of the falsifying of God's word results in contrition and confession: the witnesses 'come forth' with the truth, erasing the former 'tale', or account. More cannot actually imagine jurors acting as lie-detectors, discriminating, by the weighing of presumptions and circumstances, between evidence that seems likely to be true and that which seems likely to be false. By the end of the sixteenth century, however, thanks in part to St German's theoretical writing, the discretionary capacity of the jury to hear and evaluate evidence was itself being equated, by Lord Justice Coke, with the discretionary capacity of the Lord Chancellor.[164]

---

[163] Ibid. 153–4.

[164] See Bernadette Meyler, 'Substitute Chancellors: The Role of the Jury in the Contest between Common Law and Equity' (10 Feb. 2006), Cornell Legal Studies Research Paper No. 06–007. Available at SSRN: http://ssrn.com/abstract=882829. I am grateful to Bernadette Meyler for sharing her important work with me before it was published.

2

Rethinking Foucault: The Juridical Epistemology of English Renaissance Drama

Beyond Spectacle versus Discipline

For the whole of the first chapter, nothing was said about Michel Foucault's highly influential genealogy of modern Western discipline as part of a single 'epistemological-juridical formation'.[1] Foucault saw Western humanism, with its development of analytical discourses for the construction and exploration of 'psyche, subjectivity, personality, consciousness etc.', as the direct legacy of the early modern state's appropriation, for the purposes of the criminal prosecution by which it legitimized itself, of investigatory techniques and anathematic rituals developed by the medieval Church for the production of the soul. The soul, he wrote, 'is the element in which are articulated the effects of a certain type of power and the reference to a certain type of knowledge' as well as 'the machinery by which the power relations give rise to a possible corpus of knowledge'.[2] Later, in a pair of lectures on the 'hermeneutics of the self', Foucault defined as a subset of the state's 'techniques of domination' over individuals a particular group of techniques which he called 'techniques of self'. He defined 'government' as the interaction between structures of domination and the techniques people used to conduct themselves. The Christian practice of confession, he went on to show, may be distinguished from apparently similar Stoic practices of self-examination and moral accountancy by the way in which Christian confession involves 'a dramatic manifestation' of renunciation, 'the revelation of the truth

---

[1] Michel Foucault, *Discipline and Punish*, trans. Alan Sheridan (Harmondsworth: Penguin, 1977), 23.   [2] Ibid. 29.

about oneself cannot be dissociated from the obligation to renounce oneself'.[3] The argument of these late lectures thus locks neatly into the historical thesis of *Discipline and Punish* in which Foucault had earlier traced an unbroken line from the twelfth-century Church's establishment of confessional and inquisitorial techniques of juridical investigation through the early modern arrogation of such techniques to the power of the sovereign state, to the modern disciplinary effects of humanistic discourse.[4] Summarizing the thesis, he wrote: 'To declare aloud and intelligibly the truth about oneself—I mean, to confess—has in the Western world been considered for a long time either a condition for redemption of one's sins or as an essential item in the condemnation of the guilty.'[5] Recent law-and-literature work has taken up, whether explicitly or not, the thinking behind this aphorism. Matthew Senior's *In the Grip of Minos: Confessional Discourse in Dante, Corneille, and Racine* (1994) is an authoritative study of literary form and confessional culture both before and after the Council of Trent, but is decidedly less convincing on *Hamlet* than on *Phèdre*.[6] Peter Brooks's stimulating *Troubling Confessions: Speaking Guilt in Law and Literature* (2000) likewise does not distinguish between European and Anglo-American legal systems, tracing a direct path from the provisions of the Fourth Lateran Council in 1215 to police interrogation in contemporary America. Brooks explicitly wants to link 'the image of the penitent with the priest' with 'the criminal suspect locked in the interrogation room'.[7] While there are many contexts in which the similarities between legal and theological confession are more important than their differences, I will argue in this chapter that our understanding of specific developments in dramatic narrative in Reformation England is, on the whole, hindered by the Foucauldian genealogy. Foucault's model, as I will show, assumes that the criminal law must, in the early modern period, directly appropriate the Church's 'techniques of the self' as well as the Church's 'techniques of domination'; it takes over, that is to say, the investigative methods of the Church's penitential jurisdiction as well as secularizing the anathematic rituals by which it expels heresy. There is no doubt that the Tudor state did both, to some extent: the official dismemberment of the bodies of those convicted for treason, much quoted

---

[3] Michel Foucault, 'About the Beginnings of the Hermeneutics of the Self', *Political Theory*, 21, no. 2 (May 1993), 198–227, at 203, 221. [4] Ibid. 225.
[5] Ibid. 201.
[6] Mathew Senior, *In the Grip of Minos* (Columbus, OH: Ohio State University Press, 1994).
[7] Peter Brooks, *Troubling Confessions* (Chicago and London: University of Chicago Press, 2000), 2–3.

hue and cry, a criminal had not been tracked down and apprehended.[13] What, then, happens to a Foucauldian reading when we acknowledge the traces of a communal justice system informing the representation of Hamlet's own investigation? Such an acknowledgement would also involve recognizing that the activity of lay detection figures, in such revenge tragedies as *Hamlet*, not simply as a subject of mimetic representation, but as a hermeneutic principle, an aspect of *plot*, on which the intelligibility and credibility of dramatic action and of character depends.

Without, then, denying that Foucault's analysis has made the violence of the Renaissance theatre newly legible, I want in this chapter to argue for the value of shifting our attention from the Renaissance theatre's visual impact (its 'stagings', 'spectacles', or 'displays' of violence) in order to think, instead, about the forensic rhetoric of plot. I want, further, to suggest that even in revenge tragedy, the bloodiest of genres, the shaping epistemology of plot is not that of Foucault's 'spectacle of the scaffold', but is, rather, derived from the common ground which English dramatists perceived to exist between the forensically based plots of Latin intrigue comedy and the popular practices of detection and evidence evaluation that defined their own culture of trial by jury. In the final stages of my argument I will show how *Titus Andronicus*, a play once likened to 'a broken down cart, laden with bleeding corpses from an Elizabethan scaffold', is actually a perfect example of how Elizabethan revenge tragedy is self-consciously plotted to distinguish the participatory, open, and adversarial jury trial from the inquisitorial system Foucault described.[14]

The connection I am proposing between English revenge tragedy and the detective plot is not completely without precedent in critical discourse, but it has not been developed in ways which take seriously the idea that a participatory justice system might have had an impact on dramatic epistemology, and vice versa. In 1923 T. S. Eliot observed that the element of plot in plays such as Shakespeare's *Hamlet* and Kyd's *Spanish Tragedy* seemed to point less to their supposed Senecan sources than to the plots of modern detective drama, but he did not speculate as

[13] See Cynthia B. Herrup, *The Common Peace* (Cambridge: Cambridge University Press, 1987), 70; Joan Kent, *The English Village Constable 1580–1642* (Oxford: Clarendon Press, 1986), 26; Marianne Constable, *The Law of the Other* (Chicago: University of Chicago Press, 1991), 13–14; Michael Dalton, *The Countrey Justice* (London: John More, 1635), 133.

[14] *Titus Andronicus*, ed. John Dover Wilson (Cambridge: Cambridge University Press, 1948), p. xii.

to the cause.[15] More recently John Kerrigan has explored links between the tracking motifs of tragedy, revenge drama, and detective fiction from Sophocles to Sherlock Holmes, suggesting that all these genres express a universal expiatory impulse towards retribution. However, although Kerrigan's sense of the Sherlock Holmesian affinities of Elizabethan revenge tragedy is informed by work on the links between the poetics of Greek tragedy and Greek forensic oratory, he warns against applying the Greek parallel directly to sixteenth-century England: 'Greek legal process', he writes, 'had for centuries before *The Orestia* more closely resembled TV drama than did, for instance, the assize courts known to Kyd (who was by training a legal scrivener).'[16] Perhaps; yet the Athenian legal system did resemble that of sixteenth-century England inasmuch as cases were often decided by a panel of lay judges, or *dikasts*—a kind of jury.[17] And it is the jury trial, according to Carol Clover, which is the key to understanding the extraordinary generativity of plot and plotting strategies in twentieth-century popular genres, such as the TV drama to which Kerrigan likens the forensic plots of Greek tragedy. Clover emphasizes the jury trial's characteristic appeal, through the oral presentation of evidence in the courtroom, to the evaluative ingenuity and generic expectations of the audience-as-jury.[18] What seems helpful about Clover's model, by contrast with Kerrigan's, is the way in which it links the investigative energy of the plot or narrative structure of the film or drama to an emotional and intellectual appeal to the audience *as lay judges*, thus throwing the emphasis simultaneously on to the audience's intellectual capacity to puzzle out what the plot presents as 'evidence' and on its ethical arbitration of what that evidence implies. Sixteenth-century English revenge tragedy, while not presenting us with competing narratives of the facts as such, nevertheless makes a similar open-ended appeal to our capacity as equitable moral

---

[15] T. S. Eliot, 'Introduction', in *Seneca His Tenne Tragedies translated into English* [1581], ed. Thomas Newton (London: Constable and Co. Ltd., 1927), p. xxiii.

[16] John Kerrigan, *Revenge Tragedy* (Oxford: Clarendon Press, 1996), 27 and 59–87. On connections between Greek tragedy and Greek legal process, see Kathy Eden, *Poetic and Legal Fiction in the Aristotelian Tradition* (Princeton: Princeton University Press, 1986).

[17] See Sally C. Humphreys, 'The Evolution of Legal Process in Ancient Attica', in *Tria Corda* (Como: Edizioni New Press, 1983), 229–51, which discusses the same passage in the *Iliad* to which Kerrigan refers for his sense of the drama of Athenian legal process; see also the definition of 'dikasteria' (popular court) as being made up of 'jurors' in *The Oxford Classical Dictionary*, ed. Simon Hornblower and Anthony Spawforth, 3rd edn. (Oxford: Oxford University Press, 1996), 452.

[18] Carol J. Clover, 'Law and the Order of Popular Culture', in *Law in the Domains of Culture*, ed. Austin Sarat and Thomas R. Kearns (Ann Arbor: University of Michigan Press, 1998), 97–119; see also *idem*, 'God Bless Juries!', in *Refiguring American Film Genres*, ed. Nick Browne (Berkeley: University of California Press, 1998), 255–77.

arbiters of the case.[19] As Joel Altman says of Hieronimo in Kyd's *Spanish Tragedy*, only the theatre audience is finally in a position to 'judge him in the light of all the circumstances', and thereby to 'show compassion for the cause'.[20] Compassion for Hieronimo's cause, incidentally, is necessarily also awareness of the need for regime change. Likewise, in the last scene of *Titus Andronicus*, Lucius addresses a 'gracious auditory' of Roman senators, telling them of the wrongs that have driven Titus to murder their emperor and empress, while Marcus, Titus's brother and a Roman tribune, asks them to 'judge what cause had Titus to revenge'.[21] Here, as in Horatio's charge to tell Hamlet's story, the theatre audience assumes the position of the 'people' who are to be judges of all the circumstances that led to the regicidal massacre and, as such, to participate in an act of critical judgement that has both moral and political dimensions. What are the implications of such an appeal to the audience? In order to find out, we have to start by revisiting Foucault's political anatomy of early modern penal practice, so as to compare the epistemological foundations of criminal jurisdiction in early modern France and England.

The Roman Canon System of Proof in Foucault

Foucault's governing metaphor of the scaffold as spectacle or theatre—the political spectacle of intense pain which reaffirms the body of the King and hence the body politic—has, I have already suggested, become routinely used in the criticism of the English Renaissance tragedy. Yet, in Foucault's argument, the ordinary spectacle of penal violence is integrally related to *a specific system of evidence evaluation* which, in its underlying logic, bears no relation to the English understanding of evidence or of what constitutes or who decides the 'truth' of what happened in a criminal case.

When critics of English Renaissance drama cite Foucault's 'famous description of punishment', focusing on his pronouncements that 'public torture and execution must be spectacular', they seem to forget that public

[19] For an example of a scandalous reading of *Hamlet* as open-ended about the question of whodunit, see W. W. Greg's 'Hamlet's Hallucination', *Modern Language Review* 12 (1917), 393–421. Greg argued that the insensibility of Claudius to the dumb show's enactment of his alleged crime proved that Claudius was innocent, and that Hamlet had hallucinated the ghost. John Dover Wilson's agitation at Greg's 'specious paralogism' resulted in the writing of *What Happens in Hamlet* (Cambridge: Cambridge University Press, 1935).

[20] Joel B. Altman, *The Tudor Play of Mind: Rhetorical Inquiry and the Development of Elizabethan Drama* (Berkeley: University of California Press, 1978), 281–2.

[21] *Titus Andronicus*, ed. Jonathan Bate (London: The Arden Shakespeare, 1995), 5. 3. 95, 124. Further references to the play in this edition are given in the text.

torture was only half the story.[22] In fact, the *spectacle* of punishment in which the condemned body participates acquires its meaning in Foucault's account only in relation to the regulated *secret* administration of torture prior to the sentence. The tortured body affirms 'open for all to see, the truth of the crime', because that truth has already been arrived at according to 'rigorous rules' and 'formal constraints' governing the professional judges' weighing, in secret, of different kinds of evidence, of which a confession extracted under torture was one.[23] These procedures, as Foucault explains, had been defined in the Middle Ages and elaborated by Renaissance civilians: they are known to legal historians as the 'Roman canon system of evidence', for they derive from ecclesiastical inquisitorial tribunals. The Roman canon system was established as part of the penal code in France a century after the abolition of the judicial ordeal, and was further codified in the Ordinance of Blois (1498), the Ordinance of Villers-Cotterets (1539), and, after our period, but within the period Foucault treats, the criminal ordinance of 1670.[24] Briefly, its main features were that it was an inquisitorial system—that is to say, it did not depend on criminal accusations being made by injured parties in the community—and it was operated in the name of the Crown, by professional judges. From preliminary investigation, through examination of the accused, confrontation, examination of defence witnesses, *'question extraordinaire'*, or torture, to the conviction, the process was entirely conducted in secret.

Foucault's account, stressing the symmetry and interdependence of public spectacle and secret examination of evidence, dwells less on the stages of preliminary inquiry, accusation, and confrontation, than it does on the theory of legal proofs that dictated the judge's procedure from stage to stage. Foucault describes, vividly, the meticulous 'penal arithmetic' which the Roman canon system adapted from Roman orators' discussions of 'artificial proof'.[25] According to this arithmetic, as Barbara Shapiro has written,

---

[22] See, e.g., Daryl W. Palmer, 'Histories of Violence and the Writer's Hand', in *Reading and Writing in Shakespeare*, ed. David M. Bergeron (Newark, NJ: University of Delaware Press, 1996), 82–115, at 83.   [23] Foucault, *Discipline and Punish*, 36–7.

[24] See Adhémar Esmein, *Histoire de la Procédure Criminelle en France* (Paris: L. Larose et Forcel, 1882); John H. Langbein, *Prosecuting Crime in the Renaissance* (Cambridge, MA: Harvard University Press, 1974), 129–313; Barbara Shapiro, *Probability and Certainty in Seventeenth-Century England* (Princeton: Princeton University Press, 1983), 173–8; Langbein, *Torture and the Law of Proof*; Lisa Silverman, *Tortured Subjects* (Chicago: Chicago University Press, 2001).

[25] Foucault, *Discipline and Punish*, 37.

two unexceptional witnesses constituted a full proof, one doubtful and one unexceptional witness, added up to something more than a half proof, but not a full proof. Other types of evidence, such as 'common fame' or private, as opposed to public, documents, also were considered half-proof... In criminal causes, one witness—no matter how good or how reliable—could never result in conviction. Without a confession, two witnesses were absolutely essential. In this way the law encouraged and, indeed often required, the torture of the accused in order to produce a confession.[26]

As one of Foucault's sources, Adhémar Esmein, observed in his 1882 study, the aim of the process was to devise a set of mechanical rules for weighing the evidence regardless of the opinion of the judge: '*mis en face de ces preuves*', Esmein writes, '*il doit nécessairement condamner; peu importe dans l'une ou l'autre hypothèse sa conviction intime... Le judge est comme un clavier, qui répond inévitablement lorsqu'on frappe certaines touches*'.[27] Once the proofs added up, there was no possibility of contradictory evidence of the accused's innocence, of the so-called '*fait justificatif*' weighing against conviction.[28] Foucault sums up the paradoxical tendency of this process to the extraction of confession through torture: 'Written, secret, subjected, in order to construct its proofs, to rigorous rules, the penal investigation was a machine that might produce the truth in the absence of the accused. And by this very fact, though the law strictly speaking did not require it, this procedure was to tend necessarily to the confession.'[29] It is, of course, this secretly produced confession, 'complement to the written, secret preliminary investigation', which Foucault analyses at length as the coerced, ritualized production of an authenticating guarantor of the rightness of the conviction, in the form of both torture and public execution. Hence it is that he insists on the distinction between the unrestrained torture of modern investigations and this torture, which 'occupied a strict place in a complex penal mechanism', a two-part evidentiary mechanism for producing truth.[30]

English Jury Trial: Witness Testimony as 'Evidence' rather than 'Proof'

That the sixteenth-century English system of criminal justice in no way resembled this 'penal mechanism' has not deterred the application of

---

[26] Shapiro, *Probability and Certainty*, 174.   [27] Esmein, *Histoire*, 261.
[28] Langbein, *Prosecuting Crime in the Renaissance*, 238; Esmein, *Histoire*, 147.
[29] Foucault, *Discipline and Punish*, 37.   [30] Ibid. 39.

Foucault's model of the juridical production of the French monarch's power to its English counterpart. And this is not surprising. For while, as was mentioned in Chapter 1, the abolition of judicial ordeal in England in 1215 resulted not, as in France, in the extension of the Roman canon inquisitorial system to criminal procedure, but in the establishment of trial by jury, other points of similarity between the French and English penal systems have seemed to override this difference. Foucault himself notes that, perhaps because of the role model of jury trial, England was 'one of the countries most loathe to see the disappearance of the public execution'.[31] And, in any case, what Renaissance critics have learned from Foucault is how to read accounts of public executions as dramatic texts.[32] There are no transcripts of what took place at the ordinary jury trial for felony (though we have records of treason trials in the *State Trials*), and there has been a corresponding tendency to underestimate the impact of the jury trial's diffusion of certain habits of thought and practice through the culture.[33] J. S. Cockburn's publication of indictments recorded from the assize courts of the Home Circuit for the reigns of Elizabeth and James in the ten volumes that make up the *Calendar of Assize Records* (1975–82), along with Cockburn's articles analysing his findings, has surely done much to deter taking jury trial in the sixteenth and seventeenth centuries seriously. Cockburn's reservations about the possibility of meaningful evaluation of evidence taking place in jury trial are many, and are reiterated in various places. I will take up his arguments at a later stage, but for the moment it is enough to note that he has, in addition to quoting very selectively from the contributions to the debate over the role of the jury in the late seventeenth century, used statistics derived from records of jury service and from the indictments to paint a very bleak picture of an institution in decline: an institution incapable of acting independently to find the facts in criminal cases, and increasingly intimidated by a powerful judiciary.[34] John Langbein's *The Origins of Adversary*

---

[31] Ibid. 14.   [32] See Cunningham, 'Renaissance Execution', 210–11.

[33] As far as I know, the record of only one felony trial appears in the *State Trials*: that of John Udall. See *The Trial of Mr. John Udall, a Puritan Minister, at Croydon Assizes, for Felony, 24 July, 1590, 32 Eliz.*, in *A Complete Collection of State Trials, and Proceedings for High Treason, and Certain Other Misdemeanours; commencing with the Eleventh year of the reign of King Richard II and ending with the Sixteenth Year of the Reign of King George III* (Dublin, 1793), i. 186–209.

[34] See J. S. Cockburn, 'Early Modern Assize Records as Historical Evidence', *Journal of the Society of Archivists*, 5 (1975), 215–31; *idem*, 'Trial by the Book? Fact and Theory in Criminal Process', in *Legal Records and the Historian*, ed. J. H. Baker (London: Royal Historical Society, 1978), 60–70; *idem*, *Calendar of Assize Records* (London: Her Majesty's Stationery Office, 1985), Introduction; *idem*, 'Twelve Silly Men? The Trial Jury at Assizes, 1560–1670', in *Twelve Good Men and True*, ed. J. S. Cockburn and Thomas A. Green (Princeton: Princeton University Press,

Criminal Trial would seem to support Cockburn's view, since its sketch of the criminal trial in the sixteenth and seventeenth centuries stresses the speed of the arraignments, the lack of provision of defence counsel for the accused, and the lack of any rules of evidence.[35] Even Langbein's earlier work on Justices of the Peace has been interpreted as proving that jury passivity increased. In this ground-breaking work, John Langbein analysed the so-called Bail and Committal Statutes of Mary Tudor's reign, 1555 and 1556 respectively, which required Justices of the Peace to take pre-trial examinations of felony suspects before either granting them bail or imprisoning them.[36] It seems that Justices of the Peace, along with bailiffs and mayors, were already fairly routinely examining suspects and taking written depositions from witnesses prior to the trial much earlier than 1555, however. J. G. Bellamy finds corroboration of such practice being 'well established and sophisticated' from the papers of Thomas Cromwell in the 1530s and from Thomas More's writings, and Edward Powell's work on the early fifteenth-century criminal trial argues that Justices, constables, and bailiffs probably provided evidence at the bar when juries were not drawn from the vicinity of the offender.[37] Even if the statutory requirement of pre-trial examination was not quite as revolutionary in its effects as Langbein originally maintained, however, it does seem to have acted as an important catalyst in the shaping and development of the jury's already emergent role as evaluators of evidence, rather than ethical witnesses.[38] Nevertheless, Elizabeth Hanson has used

1988), 158–81. For examples of Cockburn's misleading use of quotations as evidence of jury inadequacy, see 'Twelve Silly Men?', 159. Here he cites (1) an insinuation that juries were illiterate from a pamphlet by Sir Samuel Starling, the Lord Mayor of London, who was responding hostilely to the jury that had conscientiously acquitted the Quakers Mead and Penn in 1671 (on this see Thomas Andrew Green, *Verdict According to Conscience* (Chicago and London: University of Chicago Press, 1985), 228–9); (2) the Jesuit Robert Parsons's 1590 description of English jurors as 'silly', an adjective which did not, at that time, mean foolish, but rather 'unlearned', 'unsophisticated' (*OED*, 'silly' *a.*, 3a); (3) Zachary Babington's 1677 description of the composition of juries as a 'scandal', a criticism which occurs in a pamphlet otherwise devoted to upholding the importance of the open evaluation of evidence by the trial jury; see n. 69 below.

[35] John H. Langbein, *The Origins of Adversary Criminal Trial* (Oxford: Oxford University Press, 2003).   [36] Langbein, *Prosecuting Crime in the Renaissance*.

[37] J. G. Bellamy, *The Criminal Trial in Later Medieval England* (Stroud: Sutton Publishing, 1988), 119; Edward Powell, 'Jury Trial at Gaol Delivery in the Late Middle Ages: The Midland Circuit, 1400–1429', in *Twelve Good Men and True*, J. S. Cockburn and Thomas A. Green, 78–116.

[38] Langbein, *Prosecuting Crime in the Renaissance*, 118–25. J. S. Cockburn attacked Langbein's view in 'Early Modern Assize Records' and 'Trial by the Book?'. However, Cockburn's suggestion that 'the Marian legislation ... quickly proved an unattainable ideal' ('Early Modern Assize Records', 227), seems to be contradicted by manuscript records of justices taking examinations. See, e.g. R. D. Hunt (ed.), 'Henry Townsend's "Notes of the office of a Justice

Langbein's earlier work, and Cockburn's critique of it, to argue that the effect of the Marian statutes was to deprive the jury entirely of its role in producing, through the verdict, an account of the truth as they saw it. The legislative force granted to pre-trial investigations by Justices of the Peace, Hanson writes, made them 'into sorts of Crown prosecutors'. 'In short,' she concludes, 'the production of an account of a crime was now supposed to be in the hands of the investigating justice rather than the jury.'[39]

Why, then, make an issue of the limited application of Foucault's model of the production of knowledge/power to the English judicial system? Precisely because, for all its inadequacies, the English jury system implied a completely different epistemology: one which, I think, came to be integrally associated, in the wake of the Marian Bail and Committal Statutes, with the very rhetorical structures of probability on which dramatists were beginning to rely for composing plot and character. As I shall argue, the developments in pre-trial investigation which Elizabeth Hanson's argument finds to be producing the equivalent of France's top-down model of state control over criminal investigation may be interpreted quite differently, especially in relation to the plotting of dramatic narrative and the representation of criminal justice on the stage.

In order to understand the distinctive epistemologies of jury trial, as opposed to trial by the Roman canon law's system of proof, we need to start with the difference between the ways each system approached the 'witness'. In the Roman canon system, as we've seen, a witness was part of the tariff of *proof*. In the German *Carolina*, for example, it is stipulated that 'When a crime is proved with at least two or three credible good witnesses, who testify from a true knowledge, then there shall be ... judgement of penal law according to the nature of the case.'[40] In English jury trial, however, nothing bound the jury to accept the testimony of witnesses. This freedom, which originated in the idea that the jury's verdict came from their own knowledge of the facts, modulated into unlimited discretion in the evaluation of evidence given by witnesses. In the last chapter we saw how Christopher St German and Thomas More compared and contrasted canon law and common law proceedings against heretics and felons, respectively. In the course of this debate, St German was concerned to distinguish the witness 'in the spyrytuall courte, that shall acquyte or condempne the parties' from 'suche witnes,

of the Peace'', 1661–3', *Worcestershire Historical Society*, n. s., 5 (Leeds: W. S. Manley and Sons Ltd., 1967), Appendix B, and n. 48, below.

[39] Elizabeth Hanson, 'Torture and Truth in Renaissance England', *Representations*, 34 (Spring 1991), 53–84, at 62, 54.   [40] Langbein, *Prosecuting Crime in the Renaissance*, 284.

as be sometyme broughte into the kyngis courtis, to giue evidencis to an enquest'. The crucial distinction turned on the word 'evidence'. In common law, St German went on, 'the jurie be not bounde alwey to folowe tho wytnes...For their saying there, is but as an evidence, which the jurie shuld not be bounde to beleue, but as the truthe is.'[41] When St German made the point, he was not necessarily defining the juror's role as that of an evaluator of evidence presented in court; he imagined that a jury's knowledge of the facts might come from sources outside the courtroom. But his definition made room for the gradual development of the jury's already emergent evidential role. It became commonplace to define the witness's testimony in jury trial as 'but evidence to a jury'.[42] In 1607, James VI and I signed a proclamation which declared that the law of the realm placed such confidence in jurors 'as it doeth not absolutely tye them to the evidences and proofes produced, but that it leaveth both supplie of Testimonie, and the discerning and credit of the Testimonie, to the Juries consciences and understanding'.[43] Here the transitional quality of the jury's role is clearly registered: it may, in its self-informing capacity, be responsible for 'supplie of Testimonie', but it may also evaluate 'the evidence and proofes produced'. Remarkably, too, James dignified the jury's role by aligning it with the most famous judgement in all Scripture, the judgement of Solomon: 'For even that Judgement which was given by a King in Person, and was so much commended in the Scriptures, was not any learned exposition of the law, but a wise sifting and examination of the fact, where testimonie was obscure, and failed.'[44]

Over the course of the sixteenth and seventeenth centuries, however, jurors were gradually becoming more and more reliant on testimony presented in court. Legal historians refer to the jury's becoming 'passive', but contemporaries naturally did not characterize their role in this way. Steve Hindle quotes Sir Francis Willoughby urging trial jurors in the 1580s 'not to look *upon* evidences only, but to look *into* them', hardly an instruction to be passive.[45] Langbein proposed that the requirement

---

[41] Christopher St German, *Salem and Bizance* [1533], in *The Yale Edition of the Complete Works of St. Thomas More*, x, ed. John Guy, Ralph Keen, Clarence H. Miller, and Ruth McGugan (New Haven and London: Yale University Press, 1987), 361.

[42] See, under 'jury', Thomas Blount, *Nomo-Lexicon, A Law Dictionary* (London, 1670). See also Barbara Shapiro, *A Culture of Fact* (Ithaca, NY, and London: Cornell University Press, 2000), 11.

[43] 'A Proclamation for Jurors', Hampton Court, 5 Oct. 1607, in *Stuart Royal Proclamations*, ed. James F. Larkin and P. L. Hughes (Oxford: Clarendon Press, 1973), i. 167–71.

[44] Ibid. 168.

[45] Steve Hindle, *The State and Social Change in Early Modern England, c.1550–1640* (Basingstoke: Macmillan Press, 2000), 129.

that Justices of the Peace examine suspects and bind witnesses to testify tended to organize the oral production of evidence ready for the trial.[46] From 1557 onwards, chapters on 'Evidens' appear in books on criminal procedure, such as Staundforde's *Les Plees del Coron* (1557) and Pulton's *De Pace Regis et Regni* (1609).[47] The wording of indictments and records of Justices taking recognizances make it clear that the witnesses were bound over to bring evidence before the jury.[48] Hanson argues that the rise of pre-trial investigation by Justices of the Peace is, like the sudden and transitory appearance of torture as part of political criminal procedure in this period, symptomatic of a more general 'rise towards hegemony in this period of... "analytico-referential discourse"': discourse that assumes that truth is an objective condition, external both to the mind that perceives it and the language that describes it'.[49] This formulation, looking forward to the triumph, at the end of the seventeenth century of a scientific discourse of 'facts' as objectively knowable truths, elides the rhetorically based discourse of probability from which the scientific discourse of fact emerged. Though Hanson argues that the 'developing practices of criminal investigation' in the period 'began to make both the facts of the crime and the guilt of the perpetrator objects of mystery and methodical discovery', this argument occludes the participation of lay jurors in the finding of 'fact' which, *pace* Hanson's use of the term, was not thought of as an object of methodological discovery, but a contentious or conjectural issue. A 'fact' was a deed allegedly done. So, as Barbara Shapiro puts it, ' "[f]act" in the legal context did not mean an established truth but an alleged act whose occurrence was in contention'.[50] Hanson's lack of interest in the dialogic process by which legal 'truth' was supposed to emerge is clear from her glossing of the word 'boult': 'boult', she says, means 'sift' and is a synonym for 'try'. However, sixteenth-century uses of the word 'boult' suggest a definitive connection between 'sifting' and *pro-et-contra* argument, as when Sir Thomas Smith writes, in explanation of having composed his *Discourse of the Commonweal* dialogue-wise: 'that kind of reasoning seems to me best for boulting out of the truth which is used by way of dialogue or colloquy, where reasons be made to and fro, as well

---

[46] Langbein, *Prosecuting Crime in the Renaissance*, 118–25.

[47] Ibid. 122; Sir William Staundforde, *Les Plees del Coron* (London: Richard Tottell, 1583), fols. 163–4^v; Ferdinando Pulton, *De Pace Regis et Regni* (London, 1609), fols. 204^v–6.

[48] See Granville Leveson-Gower, esq., 'Note Book of a Surrey Justice', in *Surrey Archaeological Collections*, vol. 9 (London: Surrey Archaelogical Society, 1888), 161–232, at 177; *William Lambarde and Local Government*, ed. Conyers Read (Ithaca, NY: Cornell University Press, 1962); Cockburn, *Calendar of Assize Records*.

[49] Hanson, 'Torture and Truth', 54.   [50] Shapiro, *Culture of Fact*, 15.

for the matter intended as against it'. Similarly, Sir Matthew Hale writes in praise of jury trial, as opposed to Roman canon trial by witnesses, 'that by this Course of... open Examination, there is Opportunity for... any of the Jury... to propound occasional Questions, which beats and boults out the Truth much better than when the Witness only delivers a formal Series of his knowledge without being Interrogated'.[51]

Poetic Invention and Legal Concepts of Probability

For my purposes, the most significant consequence of the statutory requirement that Justices take pre-trial examinations is the way in which that requirement focuses attention on the rhetorical probability of any given narrative of the facts. Examining suspects and binding witnesses to give evidence to the jury meant that Justices were required to be aware of problems of coherence, consistency, and motivation, indeed of the *arguability of likelihood* in any case. Thus in 1609 the Surrey Justice of the Peace Bostock Fuller recorded examining Thomas Kyllock's having accused Edward Rogers, 'uppon a verye slyght suspicion of ffelonye of stealing of a horse', which, he says, 'being examined on bothe sydes before me hathe noe probabilytye & the sayde Thomas dothe now relin-quyshe his accusacon in that kynde & dothe onely accuse him of suspicion for being in an Alehouse at Blechingly in suspicious manner'.[52] In Lancashire in 1682 the coroner Richard Fleetwood, investigating the death of a bastard child, took an information from the physician, Thomas Worthington. Worthington informed on oath that, having stayed with the mother, Margaret Greene, during a period of sickness, he noticed 'severall symptoms' which, corroborated by 'the Relation he had from Margrett Greenes mouth', caused him think that a poison administered to her by the child's father 'might in all Reason and probability' have been 'of furtheraunce to the death of the sayd child'.[53] The fact that Justices and coroners routinely took such examinations after 1557 meant that they were necessarily made aware of the resemblance between their analysis of evidential probability and the rhetorical techniques of probable argument disseminated by such texts as Cicero's *De inventione* and Quintilian's *Institutio oratoria*. These treatises were translated and adapted to the uses of

[51] Hanson, 'Torture and Truth', 53; *A Discourse of the Commonweal of this Realm of England*, attrib. to Sir Thomas Smith, ed. Mary Dewar (Charlottesville: University of Virginia Press, 1969), 13; Sir Matthew Hale, *The History of the Common Law of England*, ed. Charles M. Gray (Chicago and London: University of Chicago Press, 1971), 164.
[52] Leveson-Gower, 'Note Book of a Surrey Justice', 182.   [53] PRO, PL 27/1.

rhetoric generally, though in fact they were specifically concerned with forensic rhetoric, with establishing a case for the guilt or innocence of the defendant in a legal case.[54] Both Cicero's and Quintilian's work stress that the orator's goal is the probable or plausible narration of facts in the lawcourts, and both devote a considerable amount of space to the analysis of techniques of proof, which are very nearly coextensive with what we think of as rhetorical invention. Quintilian divides his technical or artificial proofs into *signa aut argumentis, aut exemplis* ('signs, arguments or examples'), and signs are further divided according to their degrees of certainty (e.g., pregnancy is a certain sign of intercourse, but blood stains may be the sign of slaying a victim or of a nosebleed). Arguments include enthymemes, but also the 'places' of argument (*argumentorum loci*), which may be attributes either of the fact (such as cause, time, place, occasion, means) or of the person (such as birth, nationality, sex, fortune, kin, disposition, habits, friends, and so forth). Here Quintilian's treatment overlaps with Cicero's discussion of inference (*coniectura*) or suspicion (*suspicio*) in book 2 of *De inventione*, which concerns what in common law is the 'issue of fact', which Cicero calls the 'conjectural state of the case'. Cicero suggests the usefulness of these forensic strategies to poets and dramatists. He writes, for example, of the importance of establishing the credibility of an impulse, if one is arguing that the accused did something on impulse.[55]

It is crucial that we appreciate how quickly these techniques were disseminated in sixteenth-century England, and not just in Latin, or to an elite. Quintilian's arguments about proof entered schoolboy consciousness through Erasmus's *De copia*, whence they influenced vernacular writing.[56] Grammar schoolboys read the plays of Terence with commentaries that analysed their comic deceptions according to Quintilian's schematization

---

[54] For example, explicitly forensic material from Cicero's *De inventione* finds its way into Juan Luis Vives, *De consultatione*, 'Of Counsel'; see Juan Luis Vives, 'De consultatione', in *Opera in duos distinctos tomos* (Basel, 1555), sigs. N5ʳ–O5ᵛ, where Vives's source is Cicero, *De inventione*, 2. 4. 16. Ann Moss finds *De inventione* influential for Renaissance thought generally, in *Printed Commonplace Books and the Structuring of Renaissance Thought* (Oxford: Clarendon Press, 1996); on the transmission of *De inventione* in the Middle Ages and Renaissance, see John O. Ward, 'From Antiquity to Renaissance: Glosses and Commentaries on Cicero's *Rhetorica*', in *Medieval Eloquence*, ed. James J. Murphy (Berkeley: University of California Press, 1978), 25–67.

[55] Quintilian, *Institutio oratoria*, book 5. In the translation by Donald A. Russell in 5 vols. (Cambridge, MA: Harvard University Press, 2001), this book appears at ii. 322–519. Cicero, *De inventione*, trans. H. M. Hubbell (Cambridge, MA: Harvard University Press, 1949), II. v. 16; II. ix. 28–9; II. ix. 31; II. x. 32; II. xii. 38; II. xii. 42.

[56] Desiderius Erasmus of Rotterdam, *On Copia of Words and Ideas*, trans. Donald B. King and H. David Rix (Milwaukee, WI: Marquette University Press, 1999), 57–68.

of proofs; some of those same schoolboys went on to write vernacular drama, others went on to work in the courts, or served as jurors.[57] English Justices of the Peace responded to the new duties imposed on them by the Bail and Committal Statutes by turning to the very same discussions of artificial proof. William Lambarde's 1581 *Eirenarcha*, a popular and much-reprinted manual for Justices of the Peace, was expanded in its 1588 edition to include a much fuller discussion, in book 2, chapter 7, of the examination of suspects for felony, including a table of the 'causes of Suspition', which, as Barbara Shapiro explains, is an easy-to-follow diagram of Cicero's discussion of the conjectural state of a case.[58] As Shapiro notes, schemes similar to Lambarde's are found in Richard Cromption's enlargement of Fitzherbert's *L'office et aucthoritie des justices de peace*, in Thomas Wilson's *Arte of Rhetorique*, and in Michael Dalton's *The Countrey Justice*.[59]

Jury Trial: Hearing and Judging Witnesses on Both Sides

The question that necessarily arises at this point concerns the gradually increasing accessibility of this discourse of suspicion and probability to the jury, who were judges of the fact. Here I need to return to Cockburn's influential arguments, which, insisting that juries were the passive instruments of the judiciary, incapable of exercising judgment, have clearly caused literary critics to ignore the possibility that participation in the justice system diffused concepts of fact finding and evaluation of narrative through the culture. Cockburn focuses on what can be learned about jury trial from the records of Home County indictments preserved in the Public

[57] See Marvin T. Herrick's account of Jodocus Willichius's commentary on *Andria* 359–69, in *Comic Theory in the Sixteenth Century* (Urbana, IL: University of Illinois Press, 1950), 182–3.

[58] See Barbara Shapiro, 'Classical Rhetoric and the English Law of Evidence', in *Rhetoric and Law in Early Modern Europe*, ed. Victoria Kahn and Lorna Hutson (New Haven: Yale University Press, 2001), 54–72, at 62–6. Shapiro is slightly misleading when she says that 'William Lambarde's popular manual of 1581 provides the "Causes of Suspicion" in a Ramist-style diagram', because the diagram does not appear in the 1581 edition. See William Lambarde, *Eirenarcha, or of the office of the Justices of the Peace, in foure bookes* (London: Ralph Newberry, 1592), 217. Prefacing the diagram, he writes: 'Touching the points that may ingender Suspition...I take it not unserviceable to insert here, such a Briefe (or minute) thereof as I haue collected out of Cicero, and others, whereunto all the rest (which all the wit of man may inuent) will easily be referred.'

[59] Sir Anthony Fitzherbert and Richard Crompton, *L'office et aucthoritie de justices de peace* (London: Richard Tottell, 1584), ed. P. R. Glazebrook (London: Professional Books Ltd., 1972), fol. 75, '*Causes de Suspicion de Felony & Murder*'...: 'Ceux sont escries in le Lieux de Arte de Rethorike, compose per Master Wilson, fol. 17'; see Thomas Wilson, *The Arte of Rhetorique* [1553], ed. G. H. Mair (Oxford: Clarendon Press, 1909), 86–92.

Record Office (now the National Archives). Indictments, however, give a slightly misleading impression of criminal process as an official top-down form of prosecution by the Crown. Early modern lawyers theoretically distinguished between the ancient 'appeal' of felony, which they defined as instigated by the victim, 'an accion of Revenge', as the Recorder of London put it in 1607, and indictment, which was technically the Crown's prosecution of felons by way of Justices of the Peace.[60] In practice, however, as Cynthia Herrup and Malcolm Gaskill have amply shown, indictments were also the result of community detective work and communal participation with part-time officials (the headborough and petty constable). A statutory watershed, as far as encouraging victims to bring complaints that might lead to indictments, was 21 Henry VIII c.11, which offered restitution to the victim; previously only through appeal had victims been able to recover damages.[61] Herrup and Gaskill examine records of examinations and informations taken by Justices rather than the indictments examined by Cockburn.[62] These tell the story of neighbours raising the hue and cry, or fetching a constable with a warrant to search premises, or persons suspected of harbouring stolen goods.[63] Sometimes these conflicts were settled without trial; a suspect found by a neighbour with stolen goods might simply confess and return the goods, or a Justice of the Peace might (as we have seen) find from his examination that the accusation

[60] Sir Henry Montague quoted in *The Parliamentary Diary of Robert Bowyer, 1606–1607*, ed. David Harris Willson (Minneapolis: University of Minnesota Press, 1931), 317. On the distinction between appeal and indictment, see J. H. Baker, *An Introduction to English Legal History*, 2nd edn. (London: Butterworths, 1979), 413–14.

[61] Bellamy, *Criminal Trial*, 111, 119.

[62] See Herrup, *Common Peace*, 67–8: 'Since by the seventeenth century private complaints in criminal matters (appeals) had been virtually replaced by public accusations (indictments), public officials should have been in charge of investigations. However, while some part in detection was played by constables, observing, investigating and accusing suspects seem to have remained as much a private concern as governmental duty.' Malcolm Gaskill, *Crime and Mentalities in Early Modern England* (Cambridge: Cambridge University Press, 2000), 21–2, 238–9.

[63] Herrup, *Common Peace*, 67–87; Gaskill, *Crime and Mentalities*, 250–62. Examples of victims and neighbours taking the initiative in detecting suspects can be found in printed accounts of murders, such as *The Horrible Murther of a young boy of three years of age, whose Sister had her tongue cut out: and how it pleased God to reveale the offendors, by giving speech to the tongueless Childe* (London: Ed Alde, 1606), 6; *A true and faithful Relation of that Horrrible Murder committed upon the Body of Mr. John Neill, Late Stationer and Merchant of Glasgow in Scotland, on Feb. 26, 1656* (London: James Cottrel, 1656), 3–4. *Treason and Murther: Or, The Bloody Father-in-Law, Being a True and Perfect Relation of a Horrible Murther, committed at HAM, neer Stratford in Essex, on the Wife of James Alsop, by her Husbands Father and Brother . . . March 25* (London, 1673), 6–7. Examples are also to be found in MS records of examinations by Justices. A typical example is PRO ASSI/15/2/62–4, which concerns a theft in Staintondale in Yorkshire, 1688. The couple who had been robbed had 'in suspicon' a former visitor to their house, and, accompanied by a constable, pursued and found him asleep on the road to Scarborough, with the goods in his pockets.

then, Babington's criticism of the grand jury is not proof that the petty, or trial jury, was thought incapable of judging evidence; it is, rather, proof that both grand jury and trial jury were thought capable of this, but that only the trial jury had access to witnesses of both sides, to a full, public debate, and to hearing the accused speak.

A main plank in Cockburn's case against the possibility that petty juries were capable of judging evidence is his finding of numerous inconsistencies in the surviving indictments for the Home Circuit. He notes a dramatic case in 1616 in which a man was convicted at the Sussex Assizes on an indictment alleging simple larceny at Horsham, Sussex, when a clerk's note on the indictment read, 'it appeared upon evidence that this was robbery upon the highway in Surrey', a much more serious offence, and less likely to be regarded with clemency by the jury.[71] However, the discrepancy between indictments and what emerged as evidence in the oral trial does not seem necessarily to invalidate the jury's consideration of evidence. Zachary Babington said endorsing the indictment as *billa vera* meant only endorsing 'that which for substance seems to them (*prima facie*) to be a probable truth ... although they have no proof of all the Aggravations and Circumstances that attend the Fact', because this evidence may appear upon 'the further enquiry of another Jury'. Babington quotes Sir Edward Coke's important distinction between indictment and oral trial: '*An Indictment is no part of the Tryal, but an Information ... For by Law the Tryal in that case is not by Witnesses, but by the Verdict of Twelve men, and so a manifest diversity between the Evidence to a Jury, and a Tryal by a Jury.*'[72]

Another of Cockburn's arguments against the jury's ability to exercise responsible judgment is based on the speed of felony trials. Sir Thomas Smith's *De Republica Anglorum* suggested that only two or three prisoners were tried before a single jury, but Cockburn finds that that number grew between 1559 and 1588, to reach a maximum, on average, of eight, before it began again to decline. On the strength of such figures, he concludes, there is 'no way in which meaningful jury discussion could have taken place'. Thomas Green, however, points out that jurors did not deliberate after each case, but towards the end of a two- or three-hour period of testimony; for the few difficult cases, he concludes, there may

---

[71] See Cockburn, 'Early Modern Assize Records', plate 3; *idem*, 'Trial by the Book?', 61–3; 'Introduction', 77–84.

[72] Babington, *Advice to Grand Jurors*, 123–5, 113–14, 136. Cockburn refers to 'Sir Edward Coke's characteristic sophistry' on this point ('Early Modern Assize Records', 221), but since Babington was a clerk of assize, and actually drafted indictments, it is to be supposed that he knew about the practice, as well as the theory.

have been ample time.[73] William Walwyn, defending jury trial against Henry Robinson's proposal to do away with it in 1651, argued, against Robinson's objection that keeping deliberating jurors without victuals increased the possibility of false verdicts, argued that 'they have had time enough at Trial . . . to be fully satisfied from the examination of Witnesses, in the right state of the Cause; which then they are to look to, and to clear all their scruples by what questions they please . . . before they discharge Witnesses'.[74] There are instances of the jurors retiring to deliberate, and then returning to ask further questions concerning the facts. A manuscript report of a case at the Old Bailey in 1616, in which a servant was arraigned for having taken diverse belongings from her mistress and placed them in a trunk, records that 'the jury in this case departed from the bar and returned and asked the advice of the court, whether it was proved that the trunk was removed out of the house for any of this time'.[75] Clearly, the jury wanted, in spite of the evidence for felonious intent, to argue that the case was not one of burglary on the grounds that nothing was actually removed from the house. They were, then, deliberating on the evidence.

The Old Bailey cases recorded in this manuscript, probably written by the young barrister Arthur Turnour, are revealing in relation to another of Cockburn's arguments, which is that the jury—which he describes as 'illiterate, impressionable, inexperienced'—was increasingly, in this period, intimidated by the Bench, and so could not have given verdicts based on their own judgment of the probabilities. Cockburn himself offers statistics to show that jury literacy increased rapidly during the seventeenth century.[76] Evidence for the intimidation of juries, however, cuts both ways. If, as Cockburn argues, jurors were being sent to Star Chamber from the 1580s and through James's reign for finding fact contrary to the judge's view of the evidence, then this in itself is not evidence of jury passivity, but evidence of an ongoing struggle between bench and jurors, between the official definitions of culpability, and the views of

[73] Cockburn, 'Twelve Silly Men', 179; also Cockburn, 'Introduction', 110–11; Green, *Verdict According to Conscience*, 150–2, n. 179.

[74] William Walwyn, 'Juries Justified; or, a Word of Correction to Mr. Henry Robinson', in *The Writings of William Walwyn*, ed. Jack R. McMichael and Barbara Taft (Athens: University of Georgia Press, 1989), 443.

[75] 'Le jury en cest cas depart de le barr et reviendront et demand le advise del court, entant que ne fuit prove que le truncke fuit remove hors del meason al ascun temps' (J. H. Baker, 'Criminal Justice at Newgate 1610–1627', *Irish Jurist*, 8 (1973), 307–22, at 313. The reports begin in Law French, and then shift into English.

[76] Cockburn, 'Twelve Silly Men', 178, 162–3.

the community.[77] Thomas Green's *Verdict According to Conscience* narrates a shift in the means used by juries to 'nullify', as he puts it, the
rigour of the official law on homicide. Throughout the medieval period, patterns of jury acquittal suggest a discrimination, which anticipated
the later legal distinction between murder and manslaughter, between
homicides who had offended against the standards of the community and those of a less serious nature. Transformations in the sixteenth
century, particularly the gradual shift from a self-informing jury to a
trial based on evidence, increased the scope for judicial instruction of
juries, as well as for judicial intimidation, making this kind of jury discretion more difficult to exercise without an evidential basis. However,
developments which led to the decision in *Bushel's Case* (1671), that a
judge may not punish or threaten to punish any juror for his verdict,
tell a tale not of jury passivity, but of case after case of confrontation
between jury and bench over the implications of the evidence. Moreover,
although *Bushel's Case* emerged from confrontation between judge and
jury over the political trial of the Quakers William Mead and William
Penn, the history of judicial intimidation leading up to it included cases of homicide, in which juries were said to have encroached on the
judge's privilege of finding law rather than fact, because they brought
a verdict of death *'per infortunium'*, or by misadventure, when the judge
would have it murder. In other words, the question of the jurors' fact
finding involved inferences about intent, and it was, as Green writes,
'this problem that lay at the heart of future tensions between judge
and jury'.[78] (It is also worth noting that one of the arguments made
by Chief Justice Vaughan in *Bushel's Case* testifies to the continuance
of the jury's 'self-informing' role: Vaughan argued that fining a jury for
bringing a verdict against the evidence should be illegal, because the jury
might have private knowledge of the falsity of the evidence presented in
court.[79])

When considerations of intent mitigate decisions about guilt, what is
taking place (as the reading of Christopher St German in the last chapter
has shown) is equitable judgment, judgment based on the hypothetical
reconstruction of intention from the available evidence. As Bernadette
Meyler has shown, seventeenth-century debates on the role of the jury

---

[77] Cockburn, 'Introduction', 70–2.

[78] Green, *Verdict According to Conscience*, 120 and *passim*. See esp. pp. 200–49, and Green's
comments on Cockburn's statistics on jury acquittals of non-clergiable highway robberies,
which Green sees as evidence of jury discretion, since the Bench was rarely reluctant to send
offenders to the gallows (151 n. 179).   [79] Ibid. 237–40.

increasingly ascribed to it the conscionable, equitable role once ascribed to the Lord Chancellor in Chancery.[80] Although the history of jury trial through the late sixteenth and seventeenth centuries was indeed a history of attempted intimidation by and conflict with the Bench, it is important to see that the theoretical space for exercising judgment that was opened up by the development of jury trial was a space that had the potential to become politicized in the period of the English constitutional revolution (1688–9), in the wake of a series of treason trials of infamous procedural corruption. While there is no case for arguing that jury trial was always or even ever a bastion of Whiggish 'liberty', there is a case for taking seriously the way in which narratives of intimidation and resistance drawn from records of famous sixteenth- and seventeenth-century jury trials became part of a discourse of judicial participation as political responsibility. Moreover, this discourse of political responsibility was grounded in the concept of everyday fact finding in trials as an exercise in the evaluation of evidential circumstance. '[I]s it not every Day's practice', asked John Hawles in his 1680 treatise, *The Englishman's Right*, 'that when Persons are indicted for *Murther*, the Jury does not only find them *guilty* or *not guilty*, but many times, upon hearing and weighing of the Circumstances, brings them in either *guilty* of *Murther, Manslaughter, per Infortunium*, or *se defendendo*, as they see Cause? Now do they not herein complicately [*sic*] *resolve* both Law and Fact?'[81] For Hawles in 1680, the routine practice of juries in 'weighing of the Circumstances' was proof that they were capable of not giving credit too easily to unconscionable and perjured prosecution witnesses, or being baffled by barristers presenting to them 'a common innocent Act...clothed and disguised in the indictment with the name of Treason'.[82] Evaluating the intention behind the legal 'fact' or act committed had become a political responsibility.

Holger Schott has recently argued that early seventeenth-century juries did not really evaluate narratives, because pre-trial investigation largely determined the outcome of the trial. High acquittal rates are 'only superficially a counter-argument' to the notion of the predetermined trial outcome, he argues, because Justices of the Peace preferred to have juries decide on innocence or guilt, and so would allow suspects to go to trial that

---

[80] Bernadette Meyler, 'Substitute Chancellors: The Role of the Jury in the Contest between Common Law and Equity', (10 Feb. 2006), Cornell Legal Studies Research Paper No. 06–007. Available at SSRN: http://ssrn.com/abstract=882829.
[81] Sir John Hawles, *The Englishman's Right* (London: A. Shuckburgh, 1764), 13–14, 15–16.
[82] Ibid. 17.

a modern-day police force would release.[83] These conclusions, however, necessarily derive largely from a careful and persuasive analysis of Coke's notebooks, which reveal the pre-trial determination of the outcome of the Earl of Essex's trial for treason. What is at stake politically in the outcome of a treason trial is, of course, incomparably higher than anything imaginable in a routine provincial case of felony. It seems to me less likely that Justices of the Peace would have had as strong motives for determining the outcome of ordinary felony cases, and in any case, as Sir Matthew Hale wrote, the trial was supposed to give 'Opportunity for . . . any of the Jury . . . to propound occasional Questions', an opportunity that would not even be mentioned if trial outcomes were regularly predetermined by the documents generated by the pre-trial investigation.[84] Finally, if some manuscript informations and examinations in the National Archives from the second half of the seventeenth century do indeed look as if the Justice is building up a case for the prosecution just as many others seem to record competing accounts of the facts from witnesses. For the purposes of my argument, however, the point is that these participatory procedures permitted lay people to become acquainted with ways of thinking about how to present or evaluate narratives as evidence at the same time as some popular drama was (as we shall see) encouraging the development of a similar kind of awareness.[85]

It has been asserted in some modern accounts of early criminal procedure that the common law did not allow defence witnesses, but, as Langbein has recently pointed out, this is a misconception probably based on incidents reported in Nicholas Throckmorton's and John Udall's trials (1554 and 1590 respectively), when judges refused the defendant's requests to have their witnesses heard. In these instances the judges acted illegally. Throckmorton and Udall knew the common law: the only restriction was that defence witnesses could not be sworn, and this restriction in itself 'was criticized at least from the time of Coke'.[86] Sir Henry Townsend

[83] Holger Schott, 'The Trials of Orality in Early Modern England' (Ph.D. dissertation, Harvard, 2004).   [84] Hale, *History of the Common Law of England*, 164.

[85] An example of an MS which reveals a Justice taking informations that record competing versions of events is PRO ASSI 45/15/2, which records a case in Cumberland in 1688 involving the death of Lancelot Graham from wounds given him by one William Palmer, after both had been drinking together. Palmer maintains that he drew his sword in self-defence; witnesses inform variously as to who drew first; one maintains that Palmer rode away on his horse, and others testify to the seriousness of Graham's condition, and others again to the copious amounts of drink consumed by both parties. It would be hard to tell from these informations which way the verdict would go in a trial.

[86] See Langbein, *Origins of Adversary Criminal Trial*, 52–6 and n. For a convenient modern edition of Throckmorton's trial, see Annabel Patterson (ed.), *The Trial of Nicholas Throckmorton*

suggests that unsworn defence witnesses were routinely heard, and asked to take their testifying seriously: 'The Judges usualy heare evidence on the behalf of the prisoner', wrote Townsend, under the heading 'Evidences' in his copy of *The Complete Justice* (1637), 'but not upon oath, yet with a chardg to speake the truth as before God on oath…and then leave the same to the jury.' On the same page, Townsend quoted Sir Edward Coke's criticism of the rule against sworn testimony on behalf of the accused: 'To say truth, we never find in any Act of Parle, Author, Book-case or Record that in Criminall cases the party accused should not have witnesses sworn for him: And therefore there is not so much as *scintilla juris* against it.'[87] Reports of cases show that juries acquitted on the basis of unsworn evidence, if it explained the facts credibly. In a case before the Southwark Assizes in 1678, the jury acquitted a waterman for the murder of one of his fellow tradesmen. It appeared that, in a quarrel over a fare, the accused struck the other on the ear, 'as 'twas proved…so fatally, that the fellow sickned and shortly after died'. Sworn testimony of the blow as cause of death notwithstanding, the jury found the waterman not guilty on the grounds of 'no murderous intention appearing'. The waterman's own unsworn account and the jury's sense of the probabilities in this case must have persuaded them.[88]

The 1607 Commons debate over the proposal to allow sworn witnesses for the defence as well as the prosecution in trials on the English–Scottish borders provides support for the prevalence of the view that jurors should bring their verdicts on the basis of as much evidence as possible, rather than on the basis of pre-empting credibility conflicts by selecting witnesses or discounting unsworn testimony.[89] Anxiety over the radical proposal in the bill that accused felons should be able to call sworn witnesses in trials on the borders prompted an amendment from the House of Lords (delivered by Francis Bacon) to the effect that jurors should be empowered

---

(Toronto: Centre for Reformation and Renaissance Studies, 1998). For Udall's trial, see *A Complete Collection of State Trials…To which is prefixed a new preface by Francis Hargrave, esq.*, 5th edn. (Dublin, 1793), 186–209.

[87] Bodleian MS Eng. Misc. e. 479, fol. 105ᵛ. This is an octavo volume of *The Complete Justice* interleaved with Henry Townsend's MS notes, taken between 1661 and 1663. The Coke quotation comes from an earlier printing of Sir Edward Coke, *The Third Part of the Institutes* (London, 1669), 79. See also 'Henry Townsend's "Notes of the office of a Justice of the Peace"', 1661–3', 95.

[88] *The Proceedings at the Assizes in Southwark for the County of Surrey on Thursday the 21 March and not ended till Tuesday the 26 of the same month, 1678* (London, 1678), 7.

[89] The debates in the Commons leading up to the Act which allowed sworn defence witnesses in border trials (4 Jac. 1, c.1 §6 (1606)) are recorded in *Parliamentary Diary of Robert Bowyer 1606–1607*, 308–19, 323–30, 333–4, 350–1, 353–6, 358–62.

to refuse to hear a witness if they regarded him as unfit to give sworn evidence.[90] The response to this amendment by those who were for the granting of sworn witnesses to accused felons makes interesting reading. Henry Yelverton, for example, argued that jurors should not prejudge witness testimony: '*Sicut audio sic iudico* saieth Christ so it is not the sight but the hearing of a witnesse that must lead the Jurors, wherfore I am against that clause.'[91] Sir Anthony Cope, likewise, argued, 'That all witnesses should be herd, and not to leave power to the Jurors to accept or reject a witness. He shewed that Deuteronomy wee must search before wee iudge which cannot be but by hearinge witnesses.'[92] Cope went on to distinguish between a juror and a jury trial witness in such a way as to anticipate Jeremy Bentham's much later insistence that the exclusion of testimony worked against the discovery of the truth:

Three differences he madd between Jurors and witnesses, Jurors ought to be without 3 exceptions viz. he must not false in woord and deede: 2do. not furious and revengefull, 3° not corrupt: And theis are not requisite in a witnesse for his testimony is but to enforme the Jury, who may beleave as they see cause for if they find by circumstances that a bad fellow saieth true they may beleeve him *et contra*.[93]

The sixteenth and seventeenth centuries were a period of transition, when both popular modes of collaborating with officials of the law and the popular experience of hearing and evaluating testimony in oral trial were changing. But there is no need to imagine jurors in this period as incapable of disbelieving sworn testimony or evaluating conflicting narratives. In 1533 it was already possible to think that jurors were not bound to judge according to the oaths of testators, or according to numbers of testators (as the judge did in civil and ecclesiastical law). By 1607, it had become possible to argue that jurors should hear as much testimony, sworn and unsworn, as possible, so that they might 'find by circumstances' which person or which narrative was to be believed.

The Displaced Jury Trial in *Titus Andronicus*

Literary critics, no less than legal historians, have tended to characterize the period prior to the eighteenth century as one in which there was little

[90] *Parliamentary Diary of Robert Bowyer*, 326.   [91] Ibid. 355.
[92] Ibid. 359. Bacon objected to Cope's argument, supporting the exclusion of unfit witnesses with the argument that Satan was forbidden to testify to Christ's divinity (p. 361).
[93] Ibid. 359. For Bentham's views, see Christopher Allen, *The Law of Evidence in Victorian England* (Cambridge: Cambridge University Press, 1997), 52–6; William Twining, *Theories of Evidence* (Stanford, CA: Stanford University Press, 1985), 19–108.

or no concept of the explanatory force of circumstantial narrative, and one in which, legally speaking, proof by oath, confession, or eyewitness testimony dominated. The genre associated with the eighteenth-century legal privileging of circumstantial narrative (and with Jeremy Bentham's critique of the oath) is, of course, the novel.[94] I have tried to suggest that the emergent epistemology of jury trial differed in significant ways from the epistemology of the inquisitorial trial described by Foucault in *Discipline and Punish*, and that already, as early as the late sixteenth century, it provided a legal context in which concepts of narrative probability and the circumstantial coherence of the alleged 'facts' had begun to displace other forms of proof. Chapters 3 and 4 will offer an account of how Latin models of narrative and intrigue drama were adapted by sixteenth-century dramatists in ways which fostered a comic awareness of the evidential and mimetic power of narrative, as opposed to sworn or eyewitness testimony. Before I undertake such a thoroughgoing analysis of the relationship between dramatic mimesis and classical forensic rhetoric, however, I want to demonstrate in a more impressionistic way just how an awareness of the legal contexts I have been describing can illuminate the narrative structure, or the temporal shape, of early Shakespearean drama.

For this purpose, I will offer a reading of Shakespeare's *Titus Andronicus* as a play which presents political tyranny as the refusal of an open hearing of the evidence, which in turn precipitates an alternative, *pro-et-contra* inquiry into the signs and probabilities by the revenge hero/dramatic plot. The example of *Titus Andronicus* might seem perverse, given the play's tendency to be read, by critics as far apart ideologically as Francis Barker and John Dover Wilson, as continuous with and exploitative of the hangman's trade, rather than as taking a critical interest in the political importance of participation in the criminal justice system.[95] Even more recently, Karen Cunningham's Foucauldian reading of *Titus* has developed her analysis of Marlowe's drama in similarly arguing that Shakespeare's mutilated bodies work to unsettle the Tudor monarchies' uses of spectacular public executions to uphold their own authority and truth.[96] My suggestion, however, would be that these interpretations give us no insight into why

---

[94] See Alexander Welsh's excellent study, *Strong Representations* (Baltimore and London: Johns Hopkins University Press, 1992).

[95] *Titus Andronicus*, ed. Dover Wilson, p. xii; Francis Barker, 'A Wilderness of Tigers', in *The Culture of Violence* (Chicago: University of Chicago Press, 1993), 143–205, at 169–79.

[96] Cunningham, ' "Scars Can Witness" ', proposes a similarity between the Tudor state execution and the early medieval trial by ordeal, arguing that Shakespeare reveals that the meanings of mutilated flesh are more ambiguous than Tudor monarchs would like. However, she does also note in her perceptive discussion that the 'archaic solution' of ordeal is rejected 'and replaced in the play's final scene by a rhetorical mode that is closely linked to trial by

the play's action follows the precisely plotted temporal sequence that it does. The play's plot, in other words, is conceived as an adaptation of the error-based plot of Roman comedy to the form of a jury trial.[97] The errors of a comic plot become deceptions as to the facts of a recent homicide, and the middle acts of the play represent the characters trying to reason out, from the uncertain, ambiguous probabilities of evidence, what the true facts are.

I have already mentioned that the schoolroom analysis of Roman New Comedy tended to emphasize characters' uses of probable reasoning from uncertain signs. Sir Thomas Smith's *De Republica Anglorum*, written in Toulouse, emphasizes as the main distinction between the English 'common' and French 'civilian' systems the fact that in the English system the '*indices* or tokens which we call in our language evidence' are heard 'openly, that not only the xij, but the Judges, the parties and as many as be present may heare what ech witnesse doeth say'. Smith explicitly likens this 'strange' openness of trial to the original republican context of forensic oratory: 'Although this may seem strange to our civillians now', he writes, 'yet who readeth *Cicero* and *Quintilian* well shall see there was no other order or maner of examining witnesses or deposing among the Romans in their time.'[98] Now, *Titus Andronicus* is also concerned with the difference between republican and imperial governments, especially as distinguished by their systems of justice.[99] It used to be thought that the play's anachronistic inclusion of both republican and imperial institutions was attributable to its general incompetence, but the republican/imperial contrast plays out tellingly in the course of the tragedy as the distinction between an open, participatory justice system and one which, like the Roman canon law system, precludes public inquiry and treats artificial proofs as incrementally adding up to guilt. After presenting Rome's rapid fall into imperial, hereditary rule through Titus's crucial misjudgement in Act 1, Scene 1, Shakespeare sets in motion a version of the erotic intrigue plot typical of Roman New Comedy as a plot of incrimination, in which the villains employ a rhetoric of probability to frame the guilt of the Andronicii family. The subsequent refusal, by Rome's emperor, to

jury' (p. 76). My position would be that Lavinia's mutilations are not forms of trial by ordeal, and the play's emplotment throughout corresponds to the epistemology of trial by jury.

[97] See Joel Altman, *The Tudor Play of Mind* (Berkeley: University of California Press, 1978), 130–47, and Lorna Hutson, *The Usurer's Daughter* (London: Routledge, 1994), 163–87.

[98] Sir Thomas Smith, *De Republica Anglorum*, ed. Mary Dewar (London: Cambridge University Press, 1982), 99–100.

[99] T. J. B. Spencer, 'Shakespeare and the Elizabethan Romans', *Shakespeare Survey*, 10 (1957), 32.

allow for an open examination of the deceptive evidence is followed by scenes of an extraordinary mixture of pathos teetering on the brink of farce, in which Lavinia's mutilated and speechless person embodies the uncertainty of evidence as to the question of her condemned brothers' guilt. The slow and painful attempts of Marcus, Titus, and young Lucius to interpret Lavinia's signs are a displaced form of inquiry into the evidence denied by official justice, the outcome of which inquiry is communicated to the wider Roman world by the corroborating proof represented by Aaron's paternity of Tamora's child.

The play's action as Roman New Comedy, as I see it, begins in what I would call the opening of Act 2 (though Bate's new Arden Edition makes this scene continuous with Act 1), a scene in which Tamora's sons Chiron and Demetrius threaten one another as competitors for the love of Lavinia, Titus's daughter, while Aaron, their mother's lover, fashions the sons' libidinous rivalry as instrumental to his own stratagem. This scene represents a new departure, the introduction of a distinctly *comic*, bustling energy, the kind of energy we associate with intrigue. It follows the play's sombre, stately, but nonetheless eventful opening, in which Titus, returning victorious from war with the Goths to bury twenty-one of his twenty-five sons in the family tomb, has also sealed Rome's terrible political fate by choosing as Rome's emperor Saturninus (and with him the principle of primogeniture) instead of Bassanius, who stood for the principle of popular election. Bassanius's betrothal to Titus's daughter, Lavinia, then hinders Saturninus, who wished to acknowledge Titus's support by the usual means of marrying his daughter and allying the Andronicii with the imperial throne. In the ensuing tussle over who should marry Lavinia, Titus's political fortunes take a decisive turn for the worse when Saturninus, in anger, turns to woo Tamora, Queen of the Goths, as his empress. As Titus had pitilessly ordered the slaughter of Tamora's eldest son in the first moments of the play, this sudden elevation of the Queen of the Goths bodes nothing but ill for his entire family. His lack of judgement and misplaced trust in authority is once again shown, however, in his readiness to believe that her intercessions with her husband on his behalf are made in good faith, and he invites Saturninus and Tamora to join his family in a hunting party. So when Tamora's lover, Aaron the Moor, remains on-stage to comment on these violent reversals of political and family fortune after the rest of the cast has left, we have the sense, I think, not of the continuation of a scene, as Bate's stage directions would suggest, but of the play's shift into a new discursive mode. And it is this new mode, I would argue, which, as it turns out, is signposted for us as a gruesome, tragic-farcical version of the erotic intrigue plot of Roman New Comedy.

The scene in which Tamora's sons Chiron and Demetrius suddenly, and without motive or dramatic preparation, express love for Lavinia, bears a close structural resemblance to other English Renaissance imitations of the initiation of Terentian plots of seduction. In such scenes the association between the erotic impulse and the prudential, paralogistic course of deception on which the lovers thereafter embark is expressed structurally in the deliberative dialogue between the lover and his intimate friend or servant, and lexically in various metaphors of deceptive vision and blindness. For example, in Shakespeare's *Taming of the Shrew*, the servant Tranio shapes the erotic trance of his master Lucentio into an awareness of the need to assume a disguise in order to have sexual access to Bianca, the object of his affections. 'If you love the maid | Bend thoughts and wits to achieve her' (*The Taming of the Shrew*, 1. 1. 178–9), he advises, and proceeds to outline their predicament. Lucentio catches on quickly with a scheme to gain access to Bianca alone, and 'now 'tis plotted', concludes Tranio (1. 1. 188). In *Titus Andronicus*, Aaron replies to Chiron's protestation, 'Aaron, a thousand deaths would I propose | T'achieve her whom I love', with a similarly practical question: 'T'achieve her how?' (1. 1. 580). In truly comic plots (the dialogue between Pyrocles and Musidorus in Sidney's *Old Arcadia* is another example) the deceivers are, of course, young lovers, and the deceit, while its object is the satisfaction of forbidden desire, is not murderously criminal, or at least not intentionally so. But for all its generic difference, *Titus* employs the same Terentian shorthand to set up its paralogistic criminal plot. Aaron's preparation of what Sidney had called 'the ground-plot'[100] of a rhetorical invention comically realizes the spatial metaphor. We see him digging, burying gold under a tree. This gold is, itself, an artificial proof: an *indicium* or probable sign, which will help to incriminate the innocent. Aaron's excavations recall the current spatial sense of 'plot', a word which recurs in these scenes: 'you do but plot your deaths', he had earlier advised Chiron and Demetrius, when dissuading them from seeking to make love to Lavinia at court (1. 1. 577). 'The forest walks', he goes on to suggest to them, 'are wide and spacious, | And many unfrequented plots there are, | Fitted by kind for rape and villainy'

---

[100] Sidney writes that in poetry, the narration is 'but a ground-plot for a profitable invention'; see Philip Sidney, *A Defence of Poetry*, ed. Jan Van Dorsten (Oxford: Oxford University Press, 1966), 53. On the relationship between the rhetorical and spatial senses of 'plot' and 'plat' in this period, see Lorna Hutson, 'Fortunate Travelers', *Representations*, 41 (Winter 1993), 83–103.

(1. 1. 614–16). 'Plot' thus fluctuates between spatial and rhetorical senses, and even in its spatial sense is endowed with agency in providing
opportunity for deception and for lack of evidential traces: being 'unfre-
quented', the forest's spaces present a contrast with the palace's plenitude
of 'tongues, of eyes, and ears': these plots are 'ruthless, dreadful, deaf and
dull' (1. 1. 627–8).

Act 2's woodland location is thus encoded as 'plot' and as a 'plotted'
series of events which work to suppress sensory perception, to make the
sight 'dull', just as Terentian rhetorical emplotments of disclosure work,
through the uses of artificial proof, to beguile the expectations of the
audience, and to make them believe what is not before their eyes. Thus
Tamora, having praised the forest clearing in which she meets her lover
as a *locus amoenus*, a place designed for amorous encounter, is quickly
persuaded by him to shift from the delights of *eros* to the uses of inference,
and her subsequent description of the same place as a 'barren detested
vale' forms part of a *tour de force* of probable reasoning in which she accuses Bassanius and Lavinia of having lured her to that spot with intent to
torture her, and enjoins her sons to avenge this wrong. The forest plot, in
this curious way, literalizes the Terentian transformation of seduction into
paralogism; we, as audience, have no way of knowing whether it is 'really'
a delightful or a detestable place. Analogues in earlier and contemporary
plays abound: in John Foxe's Terentian play *Titus et Gesippus*, for example,
when Titus's wily servant Phormio promises to think of a stratagem to
ensure Titus's appropriation of his best friend's *fiancée*, he says he will
look up his places of dialectic, for 'everyone's eyes must be blinded' by
rhetorical invention.[101] In *The Taming of the Shrew*, Lucentio describes his
plot to possess Bianca as a series of 'counterfeit supposes' which 'bleared'
the eyes of their fathers (5. 1. 107). Similar metaphors of sightlessness per-
meate the rape and murder scenes of *Titus*. After Chiron and Demetrius
have killed Bassanius, dumping his body into the stage's pit, and dragging
Lavinia off-stage, we see Aaron leading Lavinia's brothers Quintus and
Martius to the same pit, with promise of finding game. Quintus's apprehension is expressed as defective vision: 'My sight is very dull, whate'er
it bodes' (2. 2. 195). A similar non-naturalistic myopia causes Martius to
fall, conveniently, into the very pit where the corpse of Bassanius lies.
This is, again, an almost comic literalization of the brothers' readiness

---

[101] *Titus et Gesippus*, 1. 4. 20, in *Two Latin Comedies by John Foxe the Martyrologist*, ed. and
trans. John Hazel Smith (Ithaca, NY: Cornell University Press, 1978), 72–3. This play will be
discussed in detail in Ch. 4.

to 'fall in' with Aaron's plans, to capitulate to the plotted opportunity of the time and place. Neither brother exhibits any power of resistance. When Martius asks his brother to pull him out, Quintus again grants premonition more power than vision: 'My heart suspects more than mine eye can see', he replies. The discovery of the dead Bassanius, fulfilling the brothers' sense of foreboding, causes Quintus, too, to fall into the same trap.

The emperor Saturninus arrives, promptly brought by Aaron to the scene. The Terentian comic plot, with its sequence of artificial proofs designed to blind the fathers and enable rape or consensual adultery, becomes here a test of the father's—for which read here the magistrate's—capacity for just judgement. In this regard, Saturninus represents, as Heather Kerr has written, 'the dangers inherent in a civil law procedure', which treats artificial proofs not as probabilities, but as part of a penal arithmetic, adding up to certainty.[102] Tamora's production of the letter—earlier described by Aaron as 'this fatal-plotted scroll' (2. 2. 47)—which appears to incriminate the brothers by referring to the bag of gold hidden under the elder tree, prompts comparison with Kyd's *Spanish Tragedy*. In Kyd's play, Hieronimo, having found the body of his son, receives a letter which claims to inform him (truly, as it happens) of the murderer's identity. Hieronimo, a judge, refuses to credit the letter too quickly: 'be not credulous', he warns himself, resolving that he will 'by circumstances try' the letter's testimony, for it may have been written to 'entrap' him (3. 2. 48). Saturninus, however, crassly fails to examine the letter he receives. For him it functions not as an *indicium*, a probable sign needing further interrogation, but 'as an inartificial proof'.[103] He deems no further trial necessary: the brothers will be dragged 'from the pit unto the prison', there to languish until 'we have devised | Some never-heard-of-torturing pain for them' (2. 2. 283–5). The syntax of the next exchange between Saturninus and Titus emphasizes the way in which the emperor's actions pre-empt the time and space of trial and uncertainty, in which evidence might be questioned, doubts aired, different hypotheses advanced. Titus kneels before Saturninus and begs, 'That this fell fault of my accursed sons, | Accursed if the fault be proved in them—' (2. 2. 290–1); but the provisional, conditional quality of the curse is refused by the emperor: '*If* it be proved? You see it is apparent', he insists (2. 2. 292).

---

[102] See the excellent analysis by Heather Kerr, 'Aaron's Letter and Acts of Reading', *AUMLA: Journal of the Australasian Universities Language and Literature Association*, 77 (1992), 1–19. Kerr's analysis of this episode in *Titus Andronicus* is the only one I have come across which engages with the play's highly self-conscious rhetoric of probability.   [103] Ibid.

It turns out that Titus himself found the letter—an incriminating detail which he freely admits:

> I did, my lord, yet let me be their bail,
> For by my father's reverend tomb I vow
> They shall be ready at your highness' will
> To answer their suspicion with their lives.
>
> (2. 2. 295–8)

Here Titus is invoking not Roman legal practice, but the discretion of Justices of the Peace in granting bail to felony suspects on examination, though in fact Justices of the Peace were not permitted to grant bail to suspects in murder cases. In refusing the request, however, Saturninus pre-empts not only probable examination, but trial itself, for he denies the conceptual space of 'suspicion' which Titus has proposed:

> Thou shalt not bail them. See thou follow me.
> Some bring the murdered body, some the murderers.
> Let them not speak a word: *the guilt is plain*;
> For, by my soul, were there worse end than death
> That end upon them should be executed
>
> (2. 2. 99–103; my italics)

The horrors of Saturninus's reign are encapsulated in this: that mere suspects should be named murderers and sentenced to a 'worse end than death', without a moment's thought given to open trial.

The extent of that horror is made emblematically apparent in the next moment of the play, as Chiron and Demetrius bring Lavinia on-stage, *'her hands cut off and her tongue cut out, and ravished'*. The young men taunt her with her inability to reveal their criminality: 'So, now go tell, and if thy tongue can speak, | Who 'twas cut out thy tongue and ravished thee'; 'Write down thy mind, bewray thy meaning so...' (2. 3. 1–4). There could not be a clearer, nor cruder, symbolism of the previous scene's pre-emption of the possibility of disclosure. Critics have been troubled by the metaphorization of the violence done to Lavinia in what is, in fact, Marcus's extraordinarily humane and humanizing speech on encountering her in the woods.[104] Much more troubling, surely, is the jarring violence of the allegorical representation of evidence itself.

---

[104] See, e.g., Heather James's comments on this speech in her excellent 'Cultural Disintegration in *Titus Andronicus*', in *Violence in Drama* (Cambridge: Cambridge University Press, 1991), 123–40, at 129.

sand. She scrawls the word '*Stuprum*' (sexual defilement) and the names of Chiron and Demetrius. The language and action that have intervened since Marcus's accurate surmise of the Philomel-like quality of Lavinia's ordeal has highlighted, in a quasi-allegorical way, the process of trial and the radical uncertainty of knowledge of the 'fact' during that process.

Once Lavinia's signs have become intelligible thus, the fact has, unofficially, been proved, and the guilt of Tamora's sons is no longer obscure to the Andronicii family and their supporters. It is still, however, only unofficial knowledge and, as such, is extremely dangerous in imperial Rome. The play now begins to move towards a more manifest proof of the erotic intrigue within which, as we have seen, was implied the whole plot of the Andronicii's downfall. Only at this point does it become obvious why Shakespeare chose to imagine Tamora's lover as a Moor. In the scene after Lavinia's revelation of the names of the rapists, Titus sends, by way of young Lucius, a message to Aaron and Tamora's sons revealing a knowledge of their guilt. Simultaneously, and without any preparation whatsoever, a nurse brings on-stage Tamora's newly born baby. The appearance of this baby is described as an issue: 'a joyful issue', according to Aaron, but the nurse replies that it is a 'black and sorrowful issue'. Now, an issue, as Thomas Blount's law dictionary of 1670 put it, '[H]ath divers applications; sometime being used for Children begotten between a Man and Wife;…some for the point of a matter depending in Suite, whereupon the Parties joyn, and put their Cause to the Trial of Jury'. But Blount insists on the identity of these different significations: 'in all these, it has but one signification, which is an effect of a Cause preceeding; as Children are the effect of the Marriage; [and]…the point referr'd to 12 Men is the effect of pleading'. In Shakespeare's punning conception here, the baby's colouring will clarify the issue before the jury in the last act. Paternity in this instance is not, as the old wisdom goes, the paradigmatic form of conjectural or uncertain knowledge, but a manifest, *inartificial proof*: The baby proves Aaron's liaison with Tamora, which, as we saw, also generated their plot. Hence it is that when Aaron brilliantly declaims on the inferiority of whiteness in a speech defending the life of his son, he characterizes whiteness as the colour which betrays guilt inadvertently, by blushing, while his son's complexion announces frankly to his father and to the rest of the world, 'Old lad, I am thine own' (4. 2. 123). The preservation of Aaron's son's life is crucial to the ensuing communication of the facts of his and Tamora's guilt beyond the immediate circle of the Andronicus family in Rome, to Lucius and the Goth army, and finally, to the 'gracious auditory' of the Roman citizens in the final speeches of the play.

In his essay on the occlusion of violence in the new historical 'poetics of culture' and in Renaissance tragedy, Francis Barker picked out a curious and chilling incident from Act 4 of *Titus Andronicus*, in which a rustic figure, referred to in speech headings only as 'the Clown', happens to cross paths with Titus and some of his friends and kin. Titus in his assumed or real derangement of mind has persuaded his friends to help him shoot arrows into the air bearing letters to the Olympian gods with complaints about the departure of Justice from Rome. In the exchange between Titus and the Clown we learn that the latter is taking pigeons to the tribunal plebs to settle a legal dispute between his uncle and one of the emperor's men. Titus asks the Clown to take a supplication to the emperor for him, and he wraps a knife in it, instructing the Clown to hold the knife 'like an humble suppliant' (4. 4. 116). What happens when the Clown has audience with the Emperor, and presents him with Titus's letters is, as Barker puts it, stunning. The Clown is 'simply taken away to execution. Without cause given.'[106] It is the uncanny, enigmatic quality of the horror here that prompts Barker to trawl through the numbers of hangings recorded in the indictments of the Home Circuit Assizes for the years of Elizabeth's and James's reigns. The resulting statistics of deaths are indeed sickening, but it seems to me that Barker is mistaken in arguing that they gloss the otherwise unintelligible incident of the Clown's arbitrary execution in the play. Barker says that the incident 'lacks credence according to the positive norms of behaviour in the play'; but, as I have tried to show, behaviour in the play is not grounded in naturalistic representations of individuals, but gives emotional credibility to what are, in fact, emblematic dramatizations of political ideas about justice. In this sense, the arbitrariness of the Clown's being sentenced to death is far from unintelligible. His death sentence is given moments after Saturninus has complained that Titus's letters sent to the gods are politically motivated: 'What's this but libelling against the senate | And blazoning our injustice everywhere? | A goodly humour, is it not, my lords? | As who would say, in Rome no justice were' (4. 4. 17–20). Of course there is no justice in Rome, and the Clown's being held responsible for the message he has carried from Titus is a vivid example of how Saturninus's reign of terror maintains itself by silencing voices of opposition.

The Clown's message from Titus enrages Saturninus, and provokes him to reiterate that Titus's sons died 'by law for murder of our brother'; he next wants Titus to be dragged 'by the hair' before him, no doubt to

---

[106] Barker, 'A Wilderness of Tigers', 165–8.

be dispatched after the manner of the Clown, but after the subsequent arrival of news that the Goths are on the march, with Titus's banished son Lucius in command, his plan changes. Saturninus fears Lucius, because the citizens of Rome favour him; for this reason, Tamora proposes that she try to 'enchant the old Andronicus', hoping thereby to persuade him to intercede with his son for Rome's safety. Tamora, of course, does not at this point know what the audience know, which is that the child of which she has just been delivered is still alive and with Aaron on the outskirts of Rome. It is this child—proof of their collaboration in stratagems as well as sex—that forms the centre of the next scene, in which Aaron is brought by a soldier of the Goths before their commander, Lucius. Lucius threatens to kill the child, but Aaron bargains for its life, offering a frank confession of the all the facts of Bassanius's murder and his sister's rape. By this device, Lucius is put in possession of the crucial knowledge he lacked in Act 3, Scene 1; he spares the lives of Aaron and the child in order to have them as corroborative witnesses. In the final scene, after Titus has ingeniously managed to slit the throats of Chiron and Demetrius, baking them in a pie to be served to their mother, and then killing both Lavinia and Tamora, it is Lucius who, having killed Saturninus, proceeds to interpret the scene of slaughter to the Roman people:

> Then, gracious auditory, be it known to you
> That Chiron and the damned Demetrius
> Were they that murdered our emperor's brother,
> And they that ravished our sister;
> For their fell faults our brothers were beheaded
>
> (5. 3. 95–9)

Lucius, as he himself admits, digresses into a justification of his own joining with the Goths, but Marcus picks up the address to the jury:

> Now is my turn to speak. Behold the child:
> Of this was Tamora delivered,
> The issue of an irreligious Moor,
> Chief architect and plotter of these woes.
> The villain is alive in Titus' house,
> And as he is to witness this is true,
> Now judge what cause had Titus to revenge
> These wrongs unspeakable, past patience,
> Or more than any living man could bear.
> Now you have heard the truth: what say you, Romans?
>
> (5. 3. 118–27).

'Behold the child' is as much as to say, 'here is the issue before you'. Once again, the literalization of metaphor edges towards farce: one is reminded of Laurence Sterne's account of the decline of eloquence since the days when Roman orators wore capacious mantles, enabling them to pop out, at the critical moment, the required material proof: 'a scar, an axe, a sword, a pinked doublet... but, above all, a young infant royally accoutred'.[107] But if the image borders on the absurd, its audacious embodiment of the intellectual structures of forensic reasoning, like other, more brutal, embodiments in the play (Lavinia's mutilation, the brothers' falling into the pit), assumes an awareness of both the poetic and political importance of questions of evidential probability, and of the link between judicial and political participation. And perhaps the most significant effect of the construction of the play's narrative around the motif of a displaced trial is the emergence, in Acts 3 and 4, of a profound sense of the pathos of human beings' opacity to one another, a sense which encourages critics and producers to disregard the play's outrageous implausibility in the interests of breathing interpretative life into the *dramatis personae* as characters. And so, as we shall see, out of the forensic structure of the Renaissance detective plot emerges not Sherlock Holmes, but *Hamlet*.

[107] Laurence Sterne, *The Life and Opinions of Tristram Shandy* (Harmondsworth: Penguin, 1967), 196.

3

Judicial Narrative and Dramatic Mimesis

The Story So Far

In Chapter 1 we saw that although the anticipation of post-mortem trial and judgement dominates the late medieval dramatic depiction of human life, such drama is nevertheless not concerned at all with questions of evaluating evidence. Chapter 2 distinguished common law conceptions of proof from those obtaining in the Roman canon system influentially described by Foucault, and explained how the task of the jury became increasingly identified with the evaluation of evidence in a slow transition which extended from the beginning of the fifteenth to the end of the seventeenth century. The jury's task was increasingly conceived as 'a wise sifting and examination of the fact, where testimonie was obscure', in the words of James's proclamation of 1607.[1] That this aspect of popular participation in the system of justice was perceived by contemporaries as being related, in some way or other, to understanding the action of a play was suggested by the chapter's concluding interpretation of Shakespeare's *Titus Andronicus*, which showed how the scene-by-scene ordering of the action follows an identifiable evidential logic. At this stage of my argument, however, much still remains mysterious about the relationship between this evidential plot and sixteenth-century popular legal culture. How typical is the example of *Titus Andronicus*? And if it is representative of a larger body of drama which can be proved to be plotted likewise, why would this be so? Why should late sixteenth-century English dramatists want to exploit forensic models of narrative? Clearly, their purpose

---

[1] 'A Proclamation for Jurors', in *Stuart Royal Proclamations*, ed. James F. Larkin and P. L. Hughes (Oxford: Clarendon Press, 1973), 167–71, at 168.

was not, as it would be for writers of nineteenth- and twentieth-century detective fiction, to create a hermeneutic puzzle. In the case of *Titus*, there's no whodunit: the audience knows all along the identities of the murderers and rapists. Yet there is, as we saw, a significant *political* charge in the play's representation of resistance to tyranny as participation in the work of justice. As we saw, too, this choice of plot enables distinct kinds of *emotional* effect. Uncertainty about a legal issue of fact shapes the tragic plight of the civic-minded Titus, who, throughout the excruciating and emotionally pivotal first scene of Act 3, remains unsure whether his sons are indeed guilty and so deserving of punishment by the state, or not. This early use of evidential uncertainty adumbrates Shakespeare's later interest in the rich potential for arousing strong feeling (both comic and tragic) offered by emphasizing characters' partial, uneven, and often merely conjectural knowledge of one another's thoughts and hidden actions. In *Titus* the tyrannical suppression of judicial process unexpectedly—though characteristically—turns the detective process inward. Lavinia's painful, pitiful struggle to be understood, and her kinsmen's well-intentioned attempts to construe the meaning of her signs, make the brutal, scarcely credible extremities suffered by the Andronicii resonate with the audience's experience of the more banally wretched failures in understanding that beset our attempts to communicate with one another.

The next two chapters will be concerned with developing these observations by showing that the forensic quality characteristic of the plot of *Titus Andronicus* is indeed representative of a richly significant but almost entirely overlooked element of the transformation of vernacular dramatic writing between 1560 and 1600. An account of this transformation makes a contribution towards our understanding of the still very mysterious and imperfectly understood transition in dramatic writing which occurred between the 1570s and the 1590s. There are many strands to this story; recently, for example, Edward Gieskes has begun to trace the way in which plays of the 1570s and 1580s respond to and innovate within what he calls the 'crafts tradition' of sixteenth-century theatre, making this tradition of theatre-as-craft as significant and as dramaturgically intelligible as the better-documented 'literary tradition'.[2] The strand of the story that I wish to tease out and examine in the next two chapters, however, is part of the familiar story of the literary transformation wrought by Renaissance humanism, albeit with a new emphasis on the relation of that literary

---

[2] See Edward Gieskes, *Representing the Professions* (Newark, NJ: University of Delaware Press, 2006), 162–214.

but disappeared. The idea that the ordering of scenes and the selection and disposition of narrative elements might contribute in crucial ways to dramatic mimesis at the height of the English Renaissance appears to have dropped somewhere below the current critical radar.[7] At the same time, however, what unites the diversity of current cultural-historical approaches to dramatic mimesis in the English Renaissance is precisely the assumption that mimesis, construed as lifelikeness, or likeness to an essential and unvarying 'nature', is an illusion.

So why would questions of narrativity, of plot, have ceased to be relevant for a culturally and historically inflected criticism, seeking to expose the essentialist illusion of mimesis? The reasons are not immediately obvious or easily summarized, but in order to argue for the importance of a forensic conception of narrative to the mimesis of English Renaissance drama, a preliminary sketch is required. In the interests of clarity and brevity, I will divide current cultural-historical approaches to Shakespeare into three kinds (though, of course, the distinctions are by no means absolute and are introduced here for purely pragmatic reasons).

The first—which we might call, after Leah Marcus, 'unediting', or, after Margreta de Grazia, 'unmodernizing' Shakespeare—involves a materialist exposition of the extent to which 'our' Renaissance, and 'our' Shakespeare in particular, is the product of textual mediation at every level, and is hence largely a product of the eighteenth and nineteenth centuries. Practitioners in 'unediting' textual criticism of this kind have innovatively and resourcefully challenged the traditional divide between literary critics and editors, effectively transforming Shakespeare criticism. Their work disrupts readers' expectations of the canonical literary text's mimetic coherence by drawing attention to the way in which it has been shaped and reshaped by the material contingencies of transmission.[8] It is conceived both as a tribute to and exposure of the far-reaching material and ideological legacy of the editing work devoted to Shakespeare since the eighteenth century, and it reacts particularly strongly against the scientific aspirations of the so-called New Bibliography of the early twentieth century, which

---

[7] An exception is Alistair Fowler, *Renaissance Realism* (Oxford: Oxford University Press, 2003), though Fowler's study approaches the mimetic realism of Renaissance narrative exclusively by analogy with what he calls 'Renaissance picturing of the world' (p. v), making use of revisionary histories of perspective. See my review of Fowler, 'An Earlier Perspective', *Times Literary Supplement*, 30 May 2003.

[8] See, e.g., Stephen Orgel, 'The Authentic Shakespeare', *Representations*, 21 (1988), 1–25; Margreta de Grazia, *Shakespeare Verbatim* (Oxford: Clarendon Press, 1991); Leah S. Marcus, *Unediting the Renaissance* (New York: Routledge, 1996); Laurie E. Maguire, *Shakespeare's Suspect Texts* (Cambridge: Cambridge University Press, 1996); Andrew Murphy (ed.), *The Renaissance Text* (Manchester: Manchester University Press, 2000).

rigorously strove to uncover the immaterial form of authorial intention from such obscuring errors of transmission as might result from printing house and prompt copy. Thus, while the focus of 'unediting' criticism is still often the vexed question of the relation of variant texts—particularly, the relation of the so-called Bad Quartos to the more authoritative texts of the First Folio (1623)—its object is less to decide on authoritative readings or on definitive bibliographical narratives of how the variants came to be, as to expose the ideological stakes of these contested readings, and to show how conjectural narratives of the provenance of Shakespeare's texts take on a moralizing, mimetic life of their own, making villains of 'piratical' printers and unscrupulous players.[9]

How does the question of Renaissance dramatic mimesis figure in this kind of criticism? Generally speaking, the idea of 'mimesis' or likeness to life as a standard by which to measure the authentically 'Shakespearean' has been (quite properly) discarded, and in its place it is suggested that the notion of dramatic 'character' in particular is an anachronism, a by-product of editorial attentions and of the gradual emergence of more private, novelistic contexts for the consumption of Renaissance texts in the eighteenth and nineteenth centuries. Randall McLeod, for example, draws our attention to the link between nineteenth-century character criticism and eighteenth-century editing practices, targeting Alexander Pope's editorial claim that allocation of speeches in the plays is made easier by the fact that 'every single character in Shakespear is as much an Individual, as those in Life itself'.[10] Exemplifying just how unstable are the attributions of speeches and assignments of speech tags in pre-eighteenth-century Shakespeare, McLeod concludes unassailably that these speeches could not be said to be 'unmediately *mimetic* or redolent of the *personal* character of Life itself', and that, indeed, speeches in Shakespeare's text as often served the functions of indicating time, or creating ambience, or serving 'to open or close a scene in a *play*'.[11]

To McLeod's argument it could be objected that what is not being answered is the question of what prompts an editor or reader in another period to find lifelikeness amidst the unintelligible signifiers of obsolete cultural codes and practices. A range of scenic and dramatic functions are likewise competently served by speech tags in the plays of any number of Shakespeare's contemporaries and even some of his predecessors. In

---

[9] See Maguire, *Shakespeare's Suspect Texts*.

[10] Randall McLeod [Random Cloud], '"The very names of the Persons"', in *Staging the Renaissance*, ed. David Scott Kastan and Peter Stallybrass (New York: Routledge, 1991), 88–96, at 88.   [11] Ibid. 96.

other words, the uneditors' assault on eighteenth-century editors or on New Bibliographers for reading Shakespeare mimetically and for assuming mimesis to be a product of authorial intention has exposed the historical and cultural contingency of the 'mimetic prejudice' that first prompted editorial attention to Shakespeare, but has not been able to account for it entirely.[12]

More recently, Lukas Erne has offered an explanation for the emergence of character-centred readings of Shakespeare which turns on the difference between earlier printed Quartos and the texts of the First Folio, but without reintroducing the New Bibliographers' qualitative and moralizing distinction between them. Re-evaluating the evidence for the widespread assumption that dramatists and players were indifferent or even hostile to the publication of play texts, Erne argues that the 1590s saw the emergence of the idea of the press and stage as equally desirable means of publicizing and disseminating plays, and that the difference in length between some Quarto and Folio variants of the same play by Shakespeare testifies to Shakespeare's own readiness to exploit literary demand. Invoking Walter Ong's distinction between oral and literate expectations of character to explain how the characterizations of dramatis personae in the longer, 'literary' texts differ from those in the shorter stage abridgements, Erne finds that Ong's ' "flat" character, the type of character that never surprises the reader', which 'derives originally from primary oral narrative', is consistent with the kind of characters that we find in the shorter Quartos of Shakespeare's plays, whereas Ong's ' "round" human character...—deeply interiorized in motivation, powered mysteriously but consistently' conforms to the way in which complexity and ambiguity is made room for in the longer Quarto and Folio variants of the plays.[13]

Erne's is an original and suggestive hypothesis. His contention that the longer, more 'literary' versions of Shakespeare's plays are the ones which offer hints of interiorized motivation and 'rounded' character, however, still begs the question of the provenance of this mimetic technique. One of Erne's own examples might be alleged to show that the distinction cannot simply be ascribed to the difference between a text designed for reading and one designed for performance. Gertrude in modern editions of *Hamlet*, as Erne notes, is one of the those figures 'whose "motivations"

---

[12] This phrase is Christopher Prendergast's; see *The Order of Mimesis* (Cambridge: Cambridge University Press, 1986), 15.

[13] Lukas Erne, *Shakespeare as Literary Dramatist* (Cambridge: Cambridge University Press, 2003), 241.

can and have been subject to extensive analysis', as opposed to 'Gertred' in
Q1 of *Hamlet*, whom Erne invokes to exemplify how the 'short, theatrical
texts repeatedly flatten out the complex, "life-like" characters...into
"mere types", the villainous king, the loyal mother Gertrude'.[14] But in
its comparative unambiguity, the character of 'Gertred' in Q1 is actually
closer to that of Geruth in the fifth history of the fifth volume of Francois
Belleforest's *Histoires Tragiques* (1572) than it is to Q2 or F of *Hamlet*.[15]
As Belleforest's *histoire* was designed for print consumption, just as Erne
persuasively contends that the longer versions of Shakespeare's play texts
were, mimesis of character cannot be said to be an effect solely of designing
a text for literary consumption. Indeed, it is remarkable that it is the *plays*
of the English Renaissance that have always seemed more novelistic to
later readers than the prose fictions from which they frequently derived
their plots. It is easier, as generations of character critics have proved,
to understand *Romeo and Juliet* or Webster's *Duchess of Malfi* or even
Heywood's *A Woman Killed with Kindness* in a novelistic way than it is to
read William Painter's *Rhomeo and Julietta* (translated from Bandello and
Boaistuau) or Painter's *Duchess of Malfy* (from Bandello via Belleforest) or
Painter's and Geoffrey Fenton's *Salibeme and Angelica* (Heywood's source)
thus.[16] The reasons for this, I want to suggest here, have something to
do with the way in which English Renaissance writers responded to the
(neoclassically inspired) mimetic demands of scenic continuity, dramatic
urgency, and immediate on-stage intelligibility even though they rejected
the limited time-space of strict neoclassical poetics.

Another kind of cultural criticism which has aimed to expose the
essentialist and humanist assumptions informing mimetic and characterological interpretations of Shakespeare is British cultural materialism. Alan

[14] Ibid. 237–41. On the difference between 'Gertred' in Q1 and 'Gertrude' in Q2/F, see also Dorothea Kehler, 'The First Quarto of *Hamlet*', *Shakespeare Quarterly*, 46, no. 4 (1995), 398–413.

[15] Though Geruth admits to Amleth that she knew of the murder and excuses herself for marrying Fengon by explaining that she had no choice, given the treachery of the courtiers, while Gertred in Q1 swears to Hamlet, 'I never knew of this most horride murder', each representation has in common with the other what Lukas Erne describes as an 'explicit and wholehearted allegiance to her son', in contradistinction to Gertrude in Q2 and F, 'whose motives and allegiances are far from clear'. See Erne, *Shakespeare as Literary Dramatist*, 239; François de Belleforest, *Le Cinquiesme Tome des Histoires Tragiques* (Paris, 1572), fols. 162–3, and *The Tragicall Historie of Hamlet Prince of Denmarke*, ed. Graham Holderness and Brian Loughry (Hemel Hempstead: Harvester Wheatsheaf, 1992), 81, 88.

[16] See William Painter, *The Palace of Pleasure*, ed. Joseph Jacobs (New York: Dover Publications, 1966, republication of 1890 edn.), iii. 80–124, 3–43; Geoffrey Fenton, *Certain Tragicall Discourses written out of French and Latine* (London: Thomas Marshe, 1567). I have discussed narrative in Belleforest, Painter, and Fenton in Lorna Hutson, *The Usurer's Daughter* (London: Routledge, 1994), 87–151.

Sinfield's *Faultlines* and Catherine Belsey's *The Subject of Tragedy* both, in different ways, explicitly called into question the tendency to interpret the dramatis personae of Renaissance plays as coherent 'characters' showing 'development' and speaking from fully imagined psychological depths.[17] Both Sinfield and Belsey essentially argue that 'character' is the product not of coherence and depth, but of discontinuities in codes that make up the legibility of the speaking subject, and of the perceived 'surplus' of information that these generate. Belsey sees the theatre of the English Renaissance as the product of a transient moment of convergence of two distinct theatrical modes: the emblematic mode of late medieval morality drama, which puts the signified allegorically on display, and the emergent illusionist mode of Restoration theatre, which 'isolates the world of the fiction from the world of the audience, and shows the first as an empirical replica of the second'.[18] Roland Barthes's exposure of the 'deceptive plenitude' of the reader's subjectivity as ultimately nothing more than 'the generality of stereotypes' woven from the codes of cultural representation clearly informs Belsey's analysis of liberal humanist criticism as finding 'its own reflection, its own imaginary fullness' in the dramatic speeches of a theatre in transition from emblematic to empirical mode.[19] Perceiving 'a silent self anterior to the utterance' is what we do when we try to make sense of speeches in Renaissance drama; we might equally, Belsey argues, read in them a set of quasi-allegorical or emblematic codes which generally convey the condition of fallen humanity and do not give us access to the fictional character's imagined wholeness and selfhood.[20]

Belsey attempts to undo a critical tradition of interpreting the literary instantiation of cultural codes in psychological terms as evidence both of individuality and of the transhistorical universality of 'human nature' more generally. Her method works especially well in opening up for analysis the points at which traditional readings of soliloquy as thought-process rely on essentialist assumptions about gender. But while Belsey, like Sinfield, shows how liberal humanist readings of sixteenth-century plays can be disrupted, her account of the historical transition from emblematic to empirical styles of dramatic representation is inadequate to the task of explaining why liberal humanist critics wanted to read Renaissance drama mimetically in the first place. She limits herself, essentially, to a

---

[17] Alan Sinfield, *Faultlines* (Oxford: Oxford University Press, 1992), 52–79.

[18] Catherine Belsey, *The Subject of Tragedy* (London: Methuen, 1985), 23.

[19] Roland Barthes, *S/Z*, trans. Richard Miller (New York: Hill and Wang, 1974), 10; Belsey, *Subject of Tragedy*, 51.　　　　　　　　　　[20] Belsey, *Subject of Tragedy*, 48–9.

brief demonstration of the transition from the emblematic staging of the *Castle of Perserverance*, *c*.1430, to the perspective scenery of Davenant's *Siege of Rhodes* in 1661, as if narrative realism were explicable in terms of the advent of perspective.[21] Moreover, her confinement of interest to the relations between the subject of enunciation and the subject of utterance—in other words, what 'I' seem to be declaring in relation to 'myself'—produces a misleading impression that the mimesis of character in Renaissance drama is entirely a product of the development of soliloquy. Since soliloquy is only one part of a very complex unfolding of rhetorically connected speeches designed to produce the effect of a causally motivated sequence of actions, a demonstration of the disruption of the speaking subject in soliloquy is not necessarily an exposure of the mimetic illusion of character.

Most influential of all the cultural-historical approaches to Renaissance dramatic mimesis, of course, has been New Historicism. With New Historicism, the concept of 'representation' was substituted for that of 'mimesis' or 'imitation', thus helping to discredit the old idea that literature was imitative of or replicated an anterior and unvarying or 'natural' social order. The concept of 'representation' brought the imitative practices of art into alignment with the work of culture (language, social practice, ritual) more generally. Stephen Greenblatt's introduction to *Shakespearean Negotiations* (1988) encouraged us to rethink mimesis spatially rather than temporally. An object performed one sort of cultural work when represented in one institutional space (say, in a church), and another when removed to the institutional space of theatre. The rhetorical figure of *enargeia*, the most vividly illusionistic of figures, he famously redefined as the textual trace of the 'social energy' generated by these movements of cultural exchange. The venerable Platonic image of mimesis as reflection was likewise redefined.[22] Greenblatt argued reflection itself was believed, in the sixteenth century, to involve exchange: 'Both optics and mirror lore in this period suggested that something was actively passing back and forth in the production of mirror images, that accurate representation depended on material emanation and exchange.'[23] From here it was a short step to a typology of forms of theatrical mimesis, or exchange (by appropriation, by purchase,

---

[21] Ibid. 19–24.

[22] Stephen Greenblatt, *Shakespearean Negotiations* (Oxford: Clarendon Press, 1988), 7. For recent explorations of the meaning of Plato's use of the mirror metaphor, see Christopher Janaway, *Images of Excellence* (Oxford: Clarendon Press, 1995), 113–29, and Stephen Halliwell, *The Aesthetics of Mimesis* (Princeton: Princeton University Press, 2002), 118–47.

[23] Greenblatt, *Shakespearean Negotiations*, 8.

by symbolic acquisition, and so forth), and to the aphorism, 'Mimesis is always accompanied by—indeed is always produced by—negotiation and exchange.'[24]

Defining mimesis so decisively in terms of the fungibility and availability of objects or subjects of cultural representation, Greenblatt certainly heightened awareness of representation's cultural consequences.[25] At the same time, however, he deflected attention from the formal contribution to mimesis made by processes of selection and ordering in temporal and causal sequence. Plots—the why, where, when, how, and who of fictional representation—were assumed, by the Greenblattian typology of mimesis as cultural acquisition, to be to some extent ready-made. Their mode of acquisition was designated as purchase: 'the playwright or the company did pay for the books used as sources', but this designation itself seemed to exist more for the sake of rhetorical contrast with other more interesting modes of acquisition (such as the symbolic acquisition of charismatic religious practices) than as a way into thinking about the modifications needed to produce prose narratives as culturally intelligible sequences of action on the English Renaissance stage.

Yet attending to the way in which the (editorially mediated) literary text negotiates with, and invokes, the codes and stereotypes of a given culture need not necessarily involve a neglect of the *temporal* and *narrative* aspects of mimesis. If a form of representation involves narrative, as Renaissance drama does, there is no obvious reason why we should not ask how narrative itself, or the selection and sequence of represented actions, contributes to and reproduces, or transforms, the *doxa*, or the stereotypes of a particular culture.[26] From Greenblatt's modification of the Platonic figure of the mirror, then, we might productively turn to Paul Ricoeur's meditation on Aristotle's forging of an equivalence, in chapter 6 of the *Poetics*, between *mimesis*, or representation, and *muthos*, or plot.

In *Time and Narrative* Ricoeur observed that Aristotle's definition of tragedy as 'the imitation of an action' (*mimēsis praxeōs*) mutated in chapter 6 of the *Poetics*, via the subordination of 'character' to action, into an equivalence between 'the imitation of an action' and 'the organization of the events' (*tōn pragmatōn sustasis*), or their emplotment (for which

---

[24] Greenblatt, *Shakespearean Negotiations*, 12.

[25] This, of course, is why New Historicism could be accused of replicating the very cultural work of literary 'representation' itself, making 'victims' of those for whom it claimed to speak. See Walter Benn Michaels, 'The Victims of New Historicism', *Modern Language Quarterly*, 54, no. 1 (1993), 111–20.   [26] As, indeed, Barthes's *S/Z* shows.

Ricoeur's word is *intrigue*).[27] Or, as Stephen Halliwell translates the passage from *Poetics* 6:

Since tragedy is the representation of an action, and is enacted by agents, who must be characterised in both their character and their thought (for it is through these that we can also judge the qualities of their actions, and it is in their actions that all men either succeed or fail), we have the plot structure as the mimesis of the action (for by the term 'plot structure' I mean the organisation of the events).[28]

Aristotelian dramatic mimesis is thus identified with the poet's ability to organize and motivate the action persuasively, to produce the sequence of events as both plausible (not overdetermined by plot requirements) and intelligible. The quasi-equivalence of mimesis and emplotment was noted by commentators on the *Poetics* at the turn of the sixteenth century. Daniel Heinsius pointed out that Aristotle used the term *muthos* (translated as *fabula*) both as '*materia tragoediae*', the material which tragedy sets out to imitate, and as its arrangement, '*tum illius actionis dispositione*', the organization of that action (*tōn pragmatōn sustasis*).[29] Likewise, Ricoeur stresses that Aristotelian unity has to do not with the represented action's imagined duration, or with the unity of chronology, but with the organizational capacity to produce causal or apparently causal motivation within the sequence. Thus, mimesis as *muthos* or emplotment involves the imbuing of an apparently natural temporal sequence with a heightened sense of causality: 'To make up a plot is already to make the intelligible spring from the accidental . . . the necessary or probable from the episodic.'[30]

To think of dramatic mimesis as the composition of events into an intelligible yet apparently natural sequence is to recognize the extent to which the mimetic prejudice—the kind of reading which takes its point of departure from the persuasive reality of the actions and characters represented—is concerned with inferring motives and causes for the action as it unfolds. Of course, as has often been pointed out, the process of determining causes and (in particular) inferring human motives for action involves audience and readers in precisely that work of recognizing and reproducing cultural stereotypes that theorists have identified as the repressive and policing effect of mimesis.[31] But in turning our critical

[27] Paul Ricoeur, *Time and Narrative*, trans. Kathleen McLaughlin and David Pellauer, i (Chicago and London: University of Chicago Press, 1984), 32–5.

[28] Stephen Halliwell, *The Poetics of Aristotle* (London: Duckworth, 1987), 37.

[29] Daniel Heinsius, *De Tragoediae Constitutione Liber* (1611) (New York and Hildesheim: Georg Olms Verlag, 1976), 33.   [30] Ricoeur, *Time and Narrative*, 41.

[31] See, e.g., Prendergast on Roland Barthes, *Order of Mimesis*, 6.

attention exclusively to the question of whether the mimetic illusion can be disrupted, or whether (to put it in words more familiar since New Historicism) the mimetic 'recording' of subversive voices is always contained by the authoritarian project of dramatic mimesis itself, we need to pay some attention to nature of the work of inference, to the very habit of discriminating between likelihoods, and hunting for causes, that Aristotelian *muthos* or emplotment encourages in the audience/reader. Ricoeur, for example, follows those theorists of historical narrative who argue that history's intelligibility resides in the connections established between events, 'or on the judicatory act of grasping together', of making such connections.[32] Thus, for Ricoeur, the answer to the question of what kind of causality determines the organization of events in dramatic plots, or in narrative, is not limited to the culture's familiarity with a certain typology of plots. Rather, it is clear that the play's or story's invitation to the audience or reader to perform the 'judicatory act of grasping together' itself cultivates not only the disposition to identify and recognize, but *the habit of sceptical inquiry into likelihood*, which tends to discriminate between identifications and recognitions.

Bradley's *Shakespearean Tragedy*: Circumstantial Narrative and Character Criticism

A habit of sceptical inquiry into probability or likelihood is not, as one might first imagine, limited to that kind of eighteenth-century criticism that found Shakespeare's plays 'improbable' to the extent that they were irregular with regard to the neoclassical unities.[33] For if the *acme* (or *nadir*) of the mimetic or characterological approach to Shakespeare is universally agreed to be A. C. Bradley's post-nineteenth-century *Shakespearean Tragedy* (1904), it is not hard to see that Bradley's mimetic project itself takes the form of subjecting details of the plot's indicators of timing and causality to a quasi-forensic inquiry into what these reveal about the psychological and moral condition of the characters. Bradley's book was the culmination of a trend of such inquiry, which itself emerged from the Romantics' defence of Shakespeare's plays from eighteenth-century neoclassical strictures, epitomized in Coleridge's observation that Shakespeare's 'irregular' plots

---

[32] Ricoeur, *Time and Narrative*, 41.

[33] See Douglas Patey, *Probability and Literary Form* (Cambridge: Cambridge University Press, 1984), 77–83, 122–3. See also Margreta de Grazia, 'When did *Hamlet* Become Modern?', *Textual Practice*, 17, no. 3 (2003), 485–503.

interest us for the sake of the characters, and not vice versa.[34] It is a short step from arguing that plot interests us for what it reveals about character to Bradley's contention, in his lecture on *Hamlet*, that 'the only way ... in which a conception of Hamlet's character could be proved true, would be to show that it, and it alone, *explains all the relevant facts* presented by the text of the drama'.[35] The legal resonance of Bradley's term, 'the relevant facts', is not accidental. As Alexander Welsh has shown, Bradley drew on an evolving legal conception that the strongest, most convincing proof resided neither in oath, nor in witness testimony, nor in confession itself, but in the corroboration of detailed facts in a coherent, circumstantial narrative.[36] Welsh explains that the key to the new faith in circumstantial evidence lay in the recognition that whereas oath-takers might risk perjury, and testators bear false witness, the detailed corroboration of incidents and circumstances told a story that was difficult to falsify; the facts, as it were, 'spoke for themselves' by corroborating one another. As James Fitzjames Stephens put it, 'a consideration of the degree to which circumstances corroborate each other, and of the intrinsic probability of the matter sworn to, is a far better test of the truth than any oath can possibly be'.[37] There is a rhetorical advantage, as Welsh observes, in the belief that indirect evidence emerging from a circumstantial narrative has more evidential weight than direct testimony, since the auditor or reader of such narratives may be flattered into conviction by the very work of drawing inferences from what appear to be raw data.[38] Finally, the problem of proving motive, or intention, seemed to be especially intractable by the older means of oath and testimony, whereas circumstantial evidence, as writers as far apart as Edmund Burke and Jeremy Bentham alike conceded, was relevant to the inferential discovery of what Bentham called 'facts of a psychological kind'.[39]

Bradley, as Welsh shows, produces a reading of circumstantial evidence in Hamlet's defence, focusing on 'the main fact, Hamlet's inaction', with which critics had seen fit to charge him. Welsh sees Bradley's innovation within this critical debate as his perception that the charge of delay was largely made on the basis of the hero's own testimony against himself

---

[34] Leo Salingar quotes Coleridge to this effect (*Shakespeare and the Traditions of Comedy*, 19); see also de Grazia, 'When did *Hamlet* Become Modern?', 491.

[35] A. C. Bradley, *Shakespearean Tragedy* [1904], with a foreword by John Bayley (Harmondsworth: Penguin, 1991), 127; my italics.

[36] See Alexander Welsh, *Strong Representations* (Baltimore and London: Johns Hopkins University Press, 1992).

[37] Quoted ibid. 11.   [38] Ibid. 10.   [39] Ibid. 37–9.

weave of scene and speech, that it proceeded to analyse the temporal sequence represented in the play as if the sequence itself gave some indication of the imagined duration necessary for such events to have taken place.

The desire to reconstruct the 'real' sequence of the action—the raw *fabula* behind the *sjuzet*, or the *histoire* behind the *récit*—is, as we have seen from Welsh's reading of Bradley, not only a profoundly mimetic response to the text of a play, it is also a forensic one. That is to say, the mimetic legacy of such criticism—the way in which it rounds out the life and interiority of Shakespeare's dramatis personae—is a product of its forensic or detective-like habit of subjecting imagined events to the interrogating and sceptical pressure of reconstruction as a circumstantial narrative. Thus, as Jones puts it, double-time theories arose because no other explanation 'could possibly account for the *facts*' revealed by critical scrutiny. And, indeed, with reference to the extreme case of *Othello*, John Wilson, *alias* Christopher North, summed up the perceived critical problem of the play's temporal mimesis if it were a legal case:

Verdict: DESDEMONA MURDERED BY OTHELLO ON THE SECOND NIGHT IN CYPRUS.

Verdict: DESDEMONA MURDERED BY OTHELLO HEAVEN KNOWS WHEN.[46]

The question that arises from all this, of course, is whether nineteenth- and twentieth-century legalistic readings of Shakespeare's plays as sources of circumstantial evidence of timing and character are merely the product of accumulated mimetic prejudice fuelled by novelistic expectations, or whether we should see in them a critical response to a fundamental characteristic of Shakespeare's neoclassical strategies of emplotment. Bradley himself, for one, was convinced that Shakespeare planted the evidence: 'What do these facts mean?', he wrote with reference to Falstaff's character, 'Does Shakespeare put them in with no purpose at all...? It is incredible.'[47] The proposal I want to put forward in the rest of this chapter is more or less in accord with Bradley's. I will argue that Shakespeare did indeed deliberately plant evidence of time, place, circumstance, and motive in the sense that among his strategies for ensuring intelligibility and dramatic continuity while giving an impression of longer duration was included a classical understanding of narration as the judicial presentation of the facts at issue, or under dispute.

[46] Wilson, 'Dies Borealis, no. 6', 498, 505.
[47] Bradley, *Oxford Lectures on Poetry*, 266–7, quoted by Welsh, *Strong Representations*, 122.

Judicial *Narratio* and Renaissance Dramatic Mimesis

In classical judicial oratory a *narratio* was defined as a preliminary exposition, designed to be persuasive, of the facts in dispute.[48] By choosing to narrate these disputed facts in a certain way, the orator tried to predispose the judge and jury to accept the arguments or proofs he would subsequently present in defence of his client's innocence, or in prosecution of another's guilt. Thus, although this classical rhetorical theory of narrative stresses qualities which would almost seem to deny its status as art (its composition should, says Quintilian, be unobtrusively pleasing; its art should be *'occulta'*, or hidden; its language *'cotidianis'*, or everyday; its elements should cohere as if naturally), the practical judicial context from which it emerges reveals how high are its artistic stakes.[49] To narrate successfully is to make use of the compositional virtues of brevity, clarity, *enargeia*, circumstantial specificity, etc., in order to overcome a certain scepticism, a certain anticipated judicial resistance to the way in which the narrator wants to present the events alleged to have taken place.

All that Quintilian and Cicero say about judicial narrative, then, tends in the same direction as Ricoeur's commentary on the relationship of the logical to the chronological in the Aristotelian concept of plot. The virtues of judicial *narratio* are conceded to be three, and sometimes five: brevity, clarity (or 'openness'), and probability (or 'credibility'), to which Quintilian adds 'vividness' (*enargeia*) and, when appropriate, 'grandeur' (*magnificentia*).[50] These virtues are each discussed in terms which stress their seductive unobtrusiveness, their apparent fidelity to an anterior reality. Thus Cicero says that the effect of transparency or openness is achieved if the chronological order of events in time is preserved.[51] Quintilian advises finding within incidents the elements of natural sequence and coherence, so that the listening judge will find himself anticipating the consequences as the narrative proceeds. The places from which arguments of proof will subsequently be derived—person, motive (*causa*), place, time, means, and opportunity—can all be hinted

---

[48] Cicero writes: *'Narratio est rerum gestarum aut ut gestarum expositio'* ('Narrative is an exposition of events that have occurred or are supposed to have occurred') (*De inventione*, trans. H. M. Hubbell (Cambridge, MA: Harvard University Press, 1949), 1. 27). Quintilian adds the goal of persuasion: *'Narratio est rei factae aut ut factae utilis as persuadendum expositio'* ('A Narrative is an exposition, designed to be persuasive, of an action done or deemed to be done') (*Institutio oratoriae*, trans. Donald A. Russell (Cambridge, MA: Harvard University Press, 2001), 4. 2. 31).   [49] Quintilian, *Inst.* 4. 2. 117; 4. 2. 58; 4. 2. 53.
[50] Cicero, *De inv.* 1. 28; Quintilian, *Inst.* 4. 2. 31–2, 61–5.   [51] Cicero, *De inv.*, 1. 29.

at by the selection and ordering of narrative elements; Quintilian talks of 'sowing seeds' (*semina . . . spargere*) of these proofs.[52] Narrative is thus conceived with exceptional single-mindedness as the art of making 'the intelligible spring from the accidental', as Ricoeur's gloss of Aristotle has it.[53]

In the sixteenth century in England, *narratio*, or narrative, was one of the skills taught through reading and composition, but the way in which it was taught—the elements that schoolboys were asked to identify when reading narrative, and to include when composing it—was directly derived from writings on classical judicial oratory. There is no doubt that well-educated Renaissance writers were skilled in imitating judicial *narratio* as part of a classically conceived forensic oration: *Ane Detectioun of the duinges of Marie Quene of Scottes* (1571) attributed to George Buchanan uses narrative thus to persuade of Mary's guilt in Darnley's death, just as Philip Sidney has Philanax compose a powerful narrative of the (extremely unclear) facts to persuade the Arcadian court of Pyrocles' involvement in the murder of Basilius in the *Old Arcadia*.[54] But the specifically legal derivation of the pedagogy of narrative was more widely diffused than these examples might suggest. Renaissance grammar schoolboys learned about narrative from the elementary reading and composition exercises in Aphthonius's *Progymnasmata*, which, as Peter Mack has recently shown, they read in a Latin edition enriched by the commentaries of Reinhard Lorichius. In the section on narrative, Lorichius refers to its use 'within the classical four-part oration to set out the circumstances of a case', and adds the example of the *narratio* from Cicero's famous (though unsuccessful) defence of Milo from charges of murder.[55] Lorichius's mnemonic setting out of the topics of *narratio* likewise derives from judicial rhetorics. 'Narrative', he writes, is 'concerned with circumstances which are listed in this little verse: who, what, where, with what help, why, how, when. It can be made more copious if you amplify and dwell on the circumstances

---

[52] Quintilian, *Inst.* 4. 2. 53–6.   [53] Ricoeur, *Time and Narrative*, 41.

[54] See George Buchanan (attrib.), *Ane Detection of the duinges of Marie quene of Scottes* (London: John Day, 1571). The *narratio* implicating Mary in Darnley's murder is at sigs. A2ʳ–F4ʳ, and is followed, as in classical judicial oratory, by the proofs, 'Ane oratioun, with declaration of evidence against Marie the Scotishe Quene, quhairin is by necessarie argumentis plainely provit that sche was giltie and privie of the sayde murder', sigs. F4ᵛ–O1ᵛ. On the authorship of this text, see James Emerson Phillips, *Images of a Queen* (Berkeley: University of California Press, 1964). For Philanax's convincing *narratio* of Pyrocles' guilt, see Philip Sidney, *The Old Arcadia*, ed. Katherine Duncan Jones (Oxford: Oxford University Press, 1985), 334–8.

[55] Peter Mack, *Elizabethan Rhetoric* (Cambridge: Cambridge University Press, 2002), 27, 36–7.

and carefully describe the time, the place, the manner, the instrument and lastly the reason (*causa*) for which something was done.'[56]

The topics of *quis, quid, ubi, quibus auxiliis, cur, quomodo, quando*, are recognizably related to the proofs, or topics of suspicion, listed by Cicero as arising from 'the act itself' in what is called a 'conjectural issue' or issue of fact: these include *locus, tempus, occasio, facultas* (place, time, occasion, and feasibility or means). As we have seen, Quintilian to some extent breaks down the distinction between the narrative and the proofs by saying that the narrative's apparently natural sequence and coherence should be composed out of the 'seeds' of these proofs, anticipating their fuller development.[57] Following Cicero's *De inventione*, Lorichius links narrative closely to the plots and characters of Terentian comedy (Cicero quotes from Terence's *Andria* and from *Adelphoe* in his discussion of narrative), and glosses the traditional virtues of narrative—'*claritas*', '*brevitas*', '*probabilitas*'—with reference to Cicero and Quintilian.[58]

We have seen how a modern critic of the novel, Alexander Welsh, defined the emergence of the probative power of circumstantial narrative as an Enlightenment phenomenon, as distinct from the earlier English legal practice of reliance on proof by oaths and witnesses, and as distinct from the classical rhetorical tradition of Cicero and Quintilian, for whom, he proposed, 'methods of proof and narrative might seem distinct'.[59] However, the more one looks at the way in which a judicial oratorical tradition is diffused into English legal practice (through justicing handbooks) and into habits of fictional and dramatic composition (Sidney's *Old Arcadia*, for example, is both a prose fiction and a 'five-act' Terentian tragicomedy), the more it seems as if a sophisticated attitude to the capacity of narrative to contribute to judicial probability, by making 'the intelligible spring from the accidental', might already have been well in place and ready to be exploited in vernacular drama by the late sixteenth century.

---

[56] *Aphthonii Sophistae Progymnasmata . . . cum luculentis & utilibus in eadem scholijs Reinhardi Lorichii Hadamarii* (London: Thomas Marsh, 1583), fol. 17ʳ⁻ᵛ; the translation is Mack's, *Elizabethan Rhetoric*, 37.   [57] Cicero, *De inv.* 2. 38–40.

[58] *Aphthonii . . . Progymnasmata*, fol. 17ᵛ; Lorichius follows the first book of George of Trézibond's *Rhetoricorum libri V* (*c.*1434) and Cicero, *De inv.* 1. 27, where Cicero defines narrative, divides it into three kinds (an exposition of the case, a purposeful digression, written for pleasure and exercise), and then, dividing these further into classes of narrative dealing with persons and events, defines the latter as *fabula*, *historia*, and *argumentum*. The last, as Lorichius notes, is a fictitious narrative which could have happened, like the plots of comedy; to exemplify this definition, Cicero quotes from Terence, *Andria*, 51. On narratives of persons, Cicero gives Terence's *Adelphoe*, 60–4, as exemplary, and Lorichius again quotes from Cicero, *De inv.* 1. 27.   [59] Welsh, *Strong Representations*, p. x.

Before we move on to the uses of the judicially derived *narratio* in dramatic mimesis, however, two further related points about its characteristics need to be made. These are that the coherence of judicial *narratio* is linked to the ways in which circumstances and motives might be thought to knit together, and that this coherence, in turn, renders intelligible a set of facts which are in themselves *incoherent*: generated by dispute over facts, narrative is what produces the facts *as facts*, so to speak. On this point it is instructive to look at the way in which the Latin legal rhetorics teach the distinction between an issue of law and one of fact. The former is one in which the facts are agreed and the dispute is over their justification. The textbook example of such an issue is taken from tragedy: Orestes' killing of Clytemnestra. In contrast to Orestes and Clytemnestra, the issue of fact is no less inevitably exemplified by the question 'Did Ulysses kill Ajax?'[60] This latter example seems to have come from a now lost tragedy by Pacuvius in which Ulysses was found by the body of Ajax with a blood-stained sword. Quintilian cites the example as a counter to those who would argue that narrative is unnecessary. This is not so, says Quintilian,

for the accuser does not simply say: 'You killed him'; he narrates (*narrat*) to prove it. To take an example from tragedy. When Teucer accuses Ulysses of murdering Ajax saying that he was found in a lonely place near the lifeless body of his enemy, holding a bloodstained sword, Ulysses' reply is not only that he did not commit the crime, but *that he had no quarrel with Ajax*, there was simply a rivalry in honour between them; and he then goes on to explain how he came to the lonely place, saw the lifeless body, and withdrew the sword from the wound.[61]

From the textbook example of Ulysses and Ajax we see how narrative was understood to be primarily generated by controversy as to what had happened in a specific time and place (Ulysses being found with a blood-stained sword in a lonely place, next to the corpse of his rival) and, at the same time, how it was thought to persuade by excavating a remoter past (a history of motive, character, and relationship) in order to narrate, or make intelligible, a more immediate and specific sequence of events which might otherwise more probably point towards guilt (in this case, the sequence that led Ulysses to be holding the sword). The exemplary *narratio* included in sixteenth-century editions of Aphthonius—Cicero's *Pro Milone*—demonstrated these characteristics to Renaissance students

---

[60] Cicero, *De inv.* 1. 11; see also 1. 93 and the exercise in [Cicero], *Rhetorica ad Herennium*, trans. Harry Caplan (Cambridge, MA: Harvard University Press, 1954, repr. 2004), 2. 19. 28: '*Causam ostendemus Ulixi fuisse quare interfecit Aiacem*' ('We shall show that Ulysses had a motive in killing Ajax').   [61] Quintilian, *Inst.* 4. 2. 13–14; my italics.

with exceptional clarity. For in his defence of Milo in 52 BC from the charge of having murdered Clodius, Cicero had to counter the glaringly suspicious fact that Clodius had died a violent death on the Appian Way after an encounter with Milo, whose retinue of armed slaves (including gladiators) numbered more than 300, in contrast to Clodius's mere twenty-six.[62] All the circumstantial details of Cicero's narrative, then, are devoted to encouraging the jury to infer that it was Clodius who set out with an intention to ambush Milo and kill him, not the other way around. Quintilian uses *Pro Milone* as instruction in the placing of imperceptible hints as to whether actions are motivated or unpremeditated. Cicero, he writes, 'very advantageously anticipates everything that shows that it was Clodius who lay in wait for Milo, and not Milo for Clodius'.[63] The first part of Cicero's narrative persuades us of Clodius's political motives for wanting Milo dead, while a brilliant detail from the narrative of the fateful day implies, by contrast, Milo's lack of concern for planning and timing, as it describes the leisurely, feminine preparations for departure in the Milo household. 'Milo', writes Cicero, 'having been in the Senate all day until the sitting ended, came home, changed his shoes and clothes, and waited a little while his wife got ready—you know what women are.' Quintilian exclaims:

How leisurely, how unpremeditated are Milo's actions made to seem! The most eloquent of orators achieves his end not only by the details with which he prolongs the delays and the slow proceedings of the departure, but by the common, everyday language (*verbis etiam vulgaribus et cotidianus*) and well concealed art (*arte occulta*). If these things had been put any other way, the sound of the words would itself have aroused the judge to keep a sharp eye on the advocate.[64]

Renaissance readers were well aware that the 'facts' of what happened on the Appian Way were not as Cicero narrated them; an alternative account by Quintus Asconius Pedianus was usually bound with Cicero's speeches in the sixteenth century.[65] This alerts us to the possibility that the unobtrusively mimetic power of *narratio*—its capacity to produce 'fact' as such—was more readily appreciated in the sixteenth century than it is now. If this was indeed the case, judicial *narratio* is likely to have been thought to function especially effectively as one of the strategies which enables scenic continuity in five-act drama by allowing for the

---

[62] Cicero, *Defence Speeches*, trans. D. H. Berry (Oxford: Oxford University Press, 2000), 164.
[63] Quintilian, *Inst.* 4. 2. 57.   [64] Ibid. 4. 2. 58.
[65] See, e.g., *In omnes M. Tullij Ciceronis orationes doctissimorum virorum lucubrationes...adiectis Q. Asconij Pediani commentarijs* (Venice, 1547).

impressionistic rendering of off-stage events, or of events immediately past. It is probable that its contribution to the mimetic realism of Renaissance drama has been overlooked because of its very effectiveness. We are inclined to forget how much is not actually staged in a Renaissance play, because the *enargeia*, or vividness and presence, of various characters' narrations of events that take place elsewhere gives us the impression, especially as readers, of a reality as immediate as that which we imagine to take place on-stage. Audiences and readers alike delight, for example, in Hotspur's lord 'Fresh as a bridegroom, and his chin new reap'd ... like a stubble-land at harvest-home', who, while taking snuff from a 'pouncet-box', found fault with Hotspur's soldiers because they would 'bring a slovenly unhandsome corse | Betwixt the wind and his nobility' (*1 Henry IV*, 1. 3. 29–69). Yet this vivid, unforgettable creation is sparked into life in a lengthy narration explicitly designed as Hotspur's judicial defence against the accusation that he denied the King his prisoners. The 'certain lord', 'perfumed like a milliner', who provoked Hotspur's rage by talking 'like a waiting-gentlewoman | Of guns, and drums, and wounds, God save the mark!', is none other than a brilliant mitigating circumstance rhetorically invented by Hotspur (which, incidentally, rather belies the latter's subsequent characterization by Hal as the taciturn Northerner readier to kill Scotsmen than speak two words to his wife).

In discussions of Senecan declamatory drama, the *enargeia* of narrations of off-stage events tends to be linked to ekphrasis and with epideictic rhetoric (the rhetoric of display).[66] But in Quintilian's discussion of narrative, the Greek word *enargeia* is glossed as the Latin *evidentia*, meaning distinctness or clarity.[67] *Enargeia*, in other words, is linked to the etymology of the English legal concept of 'evidence'. 'Evidence' is that which emerges from the skilful narration of disputed facts in such a way as to make them seem coherent and self-evidently true; as Quintilian says, he who would obscure something, and present false statements as true, needs to make his narrative as *plainly evident* or perspicuous as possible, '*evidentissima*'.[68] *Enargeia* or *evidentia* understood thus resembles the 'judicatory act of grasping together' that defines the intelligibility of narrative, and is particularly related to making what is fictive seem plainly true.

---

[66] See Terence Cave, 'The Mimesis of Reading in the Renaissance', in *Mimesis*, ed. John D. Lyons and Stephen G. Nichols, Jr. (Hanover, NH: University Press of New England, 1982), 162–3; Roland Barthes, 'The Reality Effect', in *The Rustle of Language*, trans. Richard Howard (Oxford: Blackwell, 1986), 143–4.

[67] '*Sunt qui adiciant his evidentiam, quae ἐνάργεια Graece vocatur*' ('Others add vividness, which the Greeks call enargeia' (Quintilian, *Inst.* 4. 2. 63, discussing the virtues of *narratio*).

[68] Quintilian, *Inst.* 4. 2. 65.

Renaissance dramatists could not help but be aware of the judicial contexts from which their understanding of narrative, and its uses for dramatic continuity, emerged. They had all been to grammar school: Cicero's narrative exonerating Milo from the murder of Clodius was as familiar to them as any standard elementary text book example could be, and they knew perfectly well how unlikely to be true Cicero's version of events, with its deceptively artless 'everyday language', actually was. Indeed, we get some sense both of Cicero's reputation as a master of forensic rhetoric and of the associations between forensic skill and eye-deceiving illusion from the episode in Nashe's *Unfortunate Traveller* in which Erasmus requests the conjurer Cornelius Agrippa to show him Cicero delivering his famous speech defending Roscius Amerinus against a charge not only of murder but of parricide. Cicero duly appears by magic and 'declaimed verbatim the forenamed oration' so effectively that, as Nashe's narrator slyly notes, 'all his auditours were readie to install his guiltie client for a God'.[69] Nashe's nervous joke here draws on an association between skill in forensic rhetoric and a power to deceive the senses that occurs throughout English Renaissance drama. In Cyril Tourneur's *The Atheist's Tragedy* (1609), the atheist's device to fake the death of the virtuous Charlemont and so acquire his inheritance takes the form of having his 'instrument', Borachio, disguise himself as a soldier and deliver a detailed circumstantial narration of the slaughter of Charlemont at the siege of Ostend, while the atheist himself supplies sceptical questions which enhance the narration's credibility.[70] In *Othello*, famously, Iago follows Quintilian's advice of using ambiguous signs to 'thicken other proofs', and offers a vivid but entirely fictitious account of overhearing Cassio muttering in his sleep as part of the 'imputation and strong circumstances | Which lead directly to the door of truth' (3. 3. 411–36). Thus, where Welsh's Enlightenment thinkers see circumstantial narratives as empirically faithful to the 'facts', and as such, a legal and moral solution to the falsifications of human testimony and perjury, their Renaissance equivalents see *narratio* and circumstantiality as the product of the skilful artifice of forensic rhetoric, and hence more productive of illusion and ambiguity than objectively investigative and revelatory of truth. So it is that where Renaissance dramatists draw playful or tragic attention to the

[69] Thomas Nashe, *The Unfortunate Traveller*, in *The Works of Thomas Nashe*, ed. Ronald B. McKerrow (repr. from the original edition with supplementary notes by F. P. Wilson), 5 vols. (Oxford: Basil Blackwell, 1966), ii. 252.

[70] Cyril Tourneur, *The Atheist's Tragedy*, 2. 1. 38–105, in *Four Revenge Tragedies*, ed. Katharine Eisaman Maus (Oxford: Oxford University Press, 1995), 269–71.

powerfully mimetic effect of narrations which permit competing interpretations of the same circumstances, a later critical tradition will read
the wealth of circumstantial detail and inferential possibility generated
by such narratives and the habits of sceptical scrutiny they anticipate
and provoke as evidence of the feelings, desires, and repressions of the
characters created by the dramatist.

Narratio and Mimetic Illusion

Judicial *narratio* was understood by the most skilled dramatists to be the
key to the production of mimetic illusion in drama. George Gascoigne's
imitation of Ariosto's *I Suppositi*, performed at Gray's Inn as early as 1566,
will be the subject of detailed analysis in the next chapter, but it enters the
discussion here as a good first example of how judicial *narratio* establishes
an early form of what we might call 'the Bradley effect'—that is, the
illusion that the figures we see and hear before us are immersed in complicated relations extending back into the recent and the remoter past.
The complicated situation which we are already in the midst of at the
opening of Gascoigne's *Supposes* involves a rather scandalous love affair
which has been going on for some time between a young daughter of a
Ferrarese merchant and a servant of her father's household. Issuing out of
one of play's 'houses' on to the stage which represents the street outside,
the daughter's nurse, Balia, who is complicit in the affair, reassures her
charge with fine irony that they may now speak freely of her secret liaison,
because here, on-stage, 'is no body', whereas the imaginary interior of the
house backstage is crammed with spies, 'the cupbords them selves have
eares'.[71] This is a brilliant opening exposure of the theatre's illusory mimesis of place the novelty of which perhaps needs stressing. David Bevington
recognizes in it Gascoigne's adherence to classical models, commenting
that the *Supposes* characters 'pretend that no audience exists', but he sees
this as an undramatic, 'literary' departure from the vital interlude tradition of actor–audience communication. Luke Wilson gives more credit to
consciousness of dramaturgical novelty registered in Gascoigne's English.
With the phrase 'Here is nobody', he points out, 'the actors are not behaving as though there's no one there, but . . . are making a point of telling the

---

[71] George Gascoigne, *Supposes*, in *A Hundreth Sundrie Flowres*, ed. G. W. Pigman III (Oxford:
Clarendon Press, 2000), 1. 1. 1–4. Further references to act, scene, and line numbers of this
edition are given in the text.

mere indication of these two confessions amounts, as Philanax knows, to a potent indication of the probability of their guilty confederacy: 'What is to be thought passed between such virtuous creatures, whereof the one hath confessed murder and the other rape, I leave to your wise consideration', as he says.[80] Yet as readers, we know that to recount the 'facts' would actually involve a much more complicated and improbable story than the one Philanax makes the evidence tell. *We* know, for example, that Gynecia was wearing Pyrocles' Amazonian robes as part of a complicated double-crossing bed trick, whereby Pyrocles would ensure (more in order to realize his own sexual dreams than for virtue) that neither Basilius nor Gynecia could realize their dreams of committing adultery with him. Our knowledge of this, we had been encouraged to think, was part of our recognition of the generic affinities of Sidney's narrative—we knew, or thought we knew, that we were safely in the territory of amorous intrigue, in which titillating situational absurdities, such as the perversity of Basilius's and Gynecia's simultaneous lust for the same beautiful androgyne, could have no serious repercussions. Sidney, however, in an innovative and unnerving juxtaposition, perceives the inherent affinities of Roman New Comedy and Ciceronian forensic oratory, setting up his amorous intrigue perfectly as the disputed 'facts' of a murder case. Such a generic blending makes us realize acutely the fragile, precarious bases of what we confidently thought was our 'knowledge' about other peoples' actions and motives, for the most profoundly disturbing effect of Philanax's narration is its comparative credibility. The narrator of *Arcadia* may label Philanax's speech 'malice', but it nevertheless has more *prima facie* likelihood than the story we have followed as readers through 'books' or 'acts' 1 to 4. Moreover, Philanax's explicitly forensic modes of reasoning make us sharply aware of his own uncertainties and the sincerity of his attempt to discover by inference who might have murdered his master. Philoclea is so shocked to hear mention of her father's death that Philanax, on questioning her, 'easily acquitted her in his heart of the fact', but finding that Pyrocles, too, 'named Basilius unto him as supposing him alive', Philanax in his case infers that Pyrocles does this out of 'cunning' rather than 'ignorance'.[81] The point here is not whether or not Philanax can be accused of prejudice against Pyrocles, the foreign rapist; rather, it is that this pre-novelistic prose fiction adumbrates the nineteenth-century

---

[80] 'Intimation' is a sixteenth-century rhetorical term for a 'way of amplifying...that leaves the collection of greatness to our understanding'; see John Hoskyns, *Directions for Speech and Style*, ed. Hoyt T. Hudson (Princeton: Princeton University Press, 1935), 25.

[81] Sidney, *Old Arcadia*, 264, 261–2.

novel's interest in representing the opacity of persons to one another to the extent that it perceives the affinity of the neoclassical dramatic plot with classical forensic oratory.

Shakespeare's early drama responds to this intertwining of formal and ethical investment in the judicial probability of narrative. The 1594 Quarto of *2 Henry VI*, known as *The First Part of the Contention of the two famous houses of York and Lancaster*, features a speech for Queen Margaret which, though a fraction of the length and complexity of the same speech in the Folio text, nevertheless hints at the blend of forensic and mimetic skill that will characterize the later version. In both speeches there is a remarkable awareness of the way in which judicial *narratio* vividly produces a sense of a continuous past leading up to the present moment. Yet in this instance we know well that this is a rhetorical trick, that the past being described is fictive, for the speech is designed to initiate a judicial process against Humphrey, Duke of Gloucester, to arouse suspicion about his behaviour. Margaret's is a narrative of Humphrey's gradually increasing disdain and aloofness only recently noticed by her. Nothing but her speech establishes that sense of a perceptible change in Humphrey's habitual action. The impression we get from the ordering of scenes in the play scarcely corresponds: Humphrey is authoritative from the opening of the action, when Margaret arrives in England, but is hardly likely to have become more haughty and imperious in the period of his wife's having been tried and sentenced to do public penance in the streets. Yet this is what Margaret insinuates:

> The time hath bene, but now that time is past,
> That none so humble as Duke Humphrey was:
> But now let one meete him even in the morne,
> When every one will give the time of day,
> And he will neither move nor speake to us.
> See you not how the Commons follow him
> In troupes, crying, God save the good Duke Humphrey,
> And with long life, Jesus preserue his grace,
> Honouring him as if he were their King.
> Gloster is no little man in England,
> And if he list to stir commotions,
> Tys likely that the people will follow him.
> My Lord, if you imagine there is no such thing,
> Then let it pass, call it a womans feare.
> My Lord of Suffolke, Buckingham and Yorke,
> Disprove my Alligations if you can,

> And by your speeches, if you can reprove me,
> I will subscribe and say, I wrong'd the Duke.[82]

In the Folio text, Margaret's speech has much more *enargeia*; she speaks of Humphrey becoming 'insolent of late'; where once he was 'upon his Knee' everytime she glanced at him, now 'He knits his Brow and shewes an angry Eye' (F 1301, 1305, 1309). But even in the Quarto the idea of Margaret's forensic skill is clearly present in the detail of Humphrey's departure from the etiquette of daily greeting 'even in the morne, | When every one will give the time of day'. It is this detail, with its unobtrusive, everyday language that works in the fashion of Cicero's description of Milo's leisurely departure from Rome, to suggest that what the speaker relates are, quite simply, the facts, the way things are. This is a speech for the prosecution, designed to suggest that Humphrey harbours ambitious and treasonous thoughts; Margaret produces what she herself says are these 'allegations', causes of suspicion which now need to be disproved. But it is also this kind of speech, with its suggestion of what the mid-Victorian critics would call 'long time' or 'protracted time', that adumbrates the fully illusory effects of the later comedies and tragedies.

Other early plays likewise show Shakespeare's alertness to the uses of judicial *narratio*. In the last chapter I noted briefly that Tamora in *Titus Andronicus* recasts events which have just passed, telling a story of herself as victim so as to provoke her sons, in her defence, to kill Bassanius. This is a particularly striking example of the forensic orientation of *narratio*, since the fictive sequence of events related by Tamora is a distorted account of a scene which the audience has just witnessed. Shakespeare, in other words, foregrounds the virtuoso mimetic power of judicial *narratio*, since to be prompted into asking what 'really' happened in the scene we have just witnessed, in contrast to what Tamora says about it, is to become aware of how our sense of its empirical reality (for example, whether the woodland plot is sunny or gloomy) is the effect of the play's mimesis.

Thus, in Act 2, Scene 2, Tamora's amorous advances towards Aaron in the Ovidian woodland are deflected by Aaron into a plot to murder Bassanius, legally frame Lavinia's brothers for the murder, and silence the sole witness to all this, Lavinia. Aaron concludes his sketchy instructions to Tamora with the injunction that she 'be cross' with Bassanius, while

---

[82] *First Part of the Contention*, ll. 991–1006. For the Folio text, see *The Norton Facsimile of the First Folio of Shakespeare*, prepared by Charles Hinman with a new introduction by Peter Blayney (New York: W. W. Norton, 1996), ll. 1299–1335.

135

he, Aaron, will 'go fetch thy sons | To back thy quarrels'.[83] Tamora has no trouble stirring up the antagonism of Bassanius and Lavinia. On the pre-planned entry of Chiron and Demetrius, however, cued by Demetrius's asking why she looks so pale, she embarks on an astonishingly lurid *narratio* in which she casts herself as the victim of the most unlikely ambush and torture by her slanderers:

> Have I not reason, think you, to look pale?
> These two have 'ticed me hither to this place:
> A barren, detested vale you see it is;
> The trees, though summer, yet forlorn and lean,
> O'ercome with moss and hateful mistletoe;
> Here never shines the sun, here nothing breeds
> Unless the nightly owl or fatal raven.
> And when they showed me this abhorred pit,
> They told me here at dead time of the night
> A thousand fiends, a thousand hissing snakes,
> Ten thousand swelling toads, as many urchins,
> Would make such fearful and confused cries
> As any mortal body hearing it
> Should straight fall mad, or else die suddenly.
> No sooner had they told this hellish tale,
> But straight they told me they would bind me here
> Unto the body of a dismal yew
> And leave me to this miserable death.
> And then they called me foul adulteress,
> Lascivious Goth, and all the bitterest terms
> That ever ear did hear to such effect.
> And had you not by wondrous fortune come,
> This vengeance on me had they executed.
> Revenge it as you love your mother's life,
> Or be ye not henceforth called my children.

$$(2.\ 2.\ 91–115)$$

The immediate effect of this extraordinary performance is the death of Bassanius, since Demetrius responds instantly by stabbing him. But why the elaborate narration? Demetrius and Chiron might have been imagined capable of vengefully killing Bassanius on being told of the actual taunting which he and Lavinia inflicted on their mother at lines 55–88. Tamora's

---

[83] Shakespeare, *Titus Andronicus*, ed. Jonathan Bate (London: The Arden Shakespeare, 1995), 2. 2. 48–54. Further references to act, scene, and line number in this edition will be given in the text.

narratio ostentatiously stages its own rhetorical triumph as a triumph of mimesis. After all, this same 'barren detested vale' where 'never shines the sun', whose fearful sounds apparently drive the hearer fatally insane, was moments ago described by Tamora as full of melodious bird-song, cooling wind, and cheerful sunshine (2. 2. 12–15). How credulous are Chiron and Demetrius? Can't they see what is really there? But of course—and this is the point of what Tamora's *narratio* says about Shakespearean dramatic mimesis—what is really there and what has really been there is only what the words persuade us to see.

Judicial *Narratio* and Character Criticism: 'How was this seal'd?' (*Hamlet*, 5. 2. 48)

At this point readers might well object that all that I have said has little to do with the mimesis of *character* in Renaissance drama and in Shake-spearean drama in particular. And yet judicial *narratio*, as Renaissance schoolboys were taught it, was designed to produce a particular telling of events that made sense as evidence of *motivation*, and hence of 'character'. In the schoolboy text of *Pro Milone* Cicero's narrative begins not with the events on the Appian Way, but with signs from months before that Clodius desired Milo's death (although, as we have seen, it was terribly unlikely that Clodius had in fact planned to murder Milo). So one of the things the narrative of *Pro Milone* does is to produce Clodius's fictive 'character', though this is not its purpose. Likewise, in contradistinction to recent critical arguments that 'character' and 'psychological depth' are modernizing excrescences grafted on to a sixteenth-century dramatur-gy which was essentially driven by collaborative, actor-based practices of appealing to popular tastes, I will conclude this chapter by showing how mimetic uses of judicial *narratio* in *Hamlet* and *2 Henry IV* produce characterological readings of Shakespeare in the nineteenth century.

The position I want to challenge here is exemplified by Margreta de Grazia's recent contention that the precocious modernity of *Hamlet* is a nineteenth-century invention, deriving from nothing in Renaissance poetics, and from nothing that might be intelligible to an early modern audience or readership of Shakespeare's rewriting of Kyd's play.[84] De Grazia suggests that Shakespeare's *Hamlet* was 'old on arrival', a recycling of Kyd's earlier variant on 'the Senecan formula of murder, madness

---

[84] De Grazia, 'When did *Hamlet* Become Modern?'.

and revenge', popular more for the 'hyperactivity' that linked Hamlet with the 'clown of medieval folk tradition' than for any introspective consciousness.[85] As distaste for Shakespeare's barbarity and Gothicism is well documented from the Restoration onwards, de Grazia asks what produced the transformation of *Hamlet* from old-fashioned revenge play to icon of modernity. She notes that while eighteenth-century criticism is preoccupied with Shakespeare's neglect of the neoclassical unities of time, place, and action, a shift in response is perceptible with Nicholas Rowe's 1709 edition which defended the superiority of Hamlet's characterization to that of Orestes in Sophocles' *Electra*. In the ongoing debate over the Orestes/Hamlet parallel, alternative criteria for judging Shakespeare's artistry emerge. Whereas Orestes is seen to be a mere instrument of the classically unified plot, Hamlet's hesitations (he does not, unlike Orestes, kill his mother) define him as a 'character'.

The hint that Hamlet's hesitations enable him to transcend plot is fully developed, as de Grazia shows, by Coleridge, who went on to redefine what had been perceived as Shakespeare's barbaric ignorance of the unities of time and place as his 'psychological' dramatic method of transcending temporal and spatial constraints. He characterized Shakespeare's dramatic method as one in which the mind, perceiving 'the most remote and diverse things in time, place and outward circumstance' was able nevertheless to bring those things 'into striking mental contiguity and succession'.[86] As de Grazia dryly notes, this psychological 'method' of Shakespeare's turns out to be also 'peculiarly characteristic of Hamlet's mind'. She describes how Coleridge quotes 'a long passage from Act IV... in which Hamlet narrates to Horatio his adventures at sea, reporting how aboard ship he discovered the King's commission ordering his execution and replaced it with a forged commission commanding instead the execution of its two bearers'.[87] Coleridge generalizes on Hamlet's whole character from his symptomatic reading of this speech. It's important, for Coleridge, that the speech is a narrative, because this shows at one level how methodical Hamlet's mind is: the events 'with the circumstances of time and place, are all stated with equal compression and rapidity', notes Coleridge, 'not one introduced which could have been omitted without injury to the whole process'.[88] This methodical grasp of causality is typical of the mind 'which has been

---

[85] De Grazia, 'When did *Hamlet* Become Modern?', 485–6.

[86] Samuel Taylor Coleridge, *Lectures and Notes on Shakspere and Other English Poets*, ed. T. Ashe (London: George Bell and Sons, 1904). See also S. T. Coleridge's *Treatise on Method*, ed. Alice D. Snyder (London: Constable and Co. Ltd., 1934), 26–36, at 31.

[87] De Grazia, 'When did *Hamlet* Become Modern?', 493.   [88] Coleridge, *Lectures*, 503.

accustomed to contemplate not things only...but likewise and chiefly the relations of things'.[89] However, the same habit of perceiving relation can injure intelligibility: Hamlet omits 'one material circumstance' from his narrative, which obliges Horatio to ask for clarification: how was the forged commission sealed? The omission of this vital detail Coleridge interprets as exemplary of Hamlet's 'mind, ever disposed to generalize, and meditative to excess', going on to interpret his wilder, 'antic' speeches as 'the side-effect of excessive thought'.[90] So, de Grazia concludes, Coleridge's Kantian reading measures the distance *Hamlet* has travelled since its antiquated folk-theatre origins: 'The antics that in 1600 were a throwback to popular stage traditions are in 1800 instantiations of recent "mental philosophy". Old theatrical stunts are taken for newly identified psychological symptoms of a mind diseased by "surplus meditation".'[91]

De Grazia's reading of Coleridge's response to *Hamlet* is illuminating, but its 'unmodernizing' consequences seem to me exaggerated. It does not follow that because Coleridge read Hamlet's omission of the detail of the forged seal symptomatically, the detail had no mimetic purpose, or that other speeches are explicable as 'old theatrical stunts'. In making his case for Q1 as a shortened, stage version of *Hamlet*, and Q2 and F as longer, literary versions, Lukas Erne notes that the scene in which Hamlet narrates his forging of the commission to kill Rosencrantz and Guildenstern is part of a diffuse set of materials conveying the off-stage events of the sea voyage which, in Q1, are condensed and presented more economically and less ambiguously.[92] But this does not mean that the scene was not written and conceived at the turn of the seventeenth century, nor that its conception as a *narration* is egregious.

For *Hamlet* is clearly a play concerned at both a formal and an ethical level with questions of evidential probability, and there seems reason to suppose that its source—Kyd's play of *Hamlet*—hinted at similar concerns. After all, Hieronimo in *The Spanish Tragedy* refuses to accept the evidence of a letter he receives, saying that he will 'by circumstances try | What I can gather to confirm this writ', before acting upon it, just as Shakespeare's Hamlet wants 'grounds | More relative' on which to credit the evidence of the ghost.[93] The first two acts of *Hamlet* establish the constraints upon Hamlet's own process of enquiry into the nature of the ghost's evidence

---

[89] Ibid. 502.

[90] De Grazia, 'When did *Hamlet* Become Modern?', 493; Coleridge, *Lectures*, 506–7.

[91] De Grazia, 'When did *Hamlet* Become Modern?', 493.

[92] Erne, *Shakespeare as Literary Dramatist*, 236–9.

[93] Kyd, *The Spanish Tragedy*, 3. 2. 48–9, in *Four Revenge Tragedies*, ed. Katharine Eisaman Maus (Oxford: Oxford University Press, 1995).

by depicting Polonius (Corambis in Q1) as a typical *senex* preoccupied, in the forensic manner of Terentian comedy, with policing the effects of his children's amorous intrigues on the family's honour. We infer mimetically from Laertes' and Polonius's advice to Ophelia in Act 1, Scene 3, a circumstantial recent past in which Hamlet has courted her affections. Once we imagine Laertes dispatched to Paris, however, Act 2 opens with Polonius instructing Reynaldo (Montano in Q1) to 'make inquire' not into his daughter's, but into his son's conduct, and to report the evidence back to him.[94] Polonius's behaviour seems here to be modelled on that of perhaps the most well-known stage *senex* of Roman comedy, Simo in Terence's *Andria*, whose report of the results of his own enquiries into his son's possible misconduct at a brothel was twice quoted by Cicero as exemplary of the virtues of forensic *narratio*.[95] In the seventeenth century the minister Richard Bernard made Terence's Simo sound very much like Polonius: Bernard's Simo says he 'made inquirie' of the page boys of his son's fellow brothel-frequenters, asking them what his son did there.[96] Scafuro observes how Simo imagines himself as prosecution in a case against his own son: 'he must be able to formulate a charge that can stand up to any argument offered by the defense', hence his 'inquiries into his son's conduct... ready with deductions and theories constructed from circumstantial evidence'. Comic though this is all supposed to be, she concludes, 'Such a forensic habit might be devastatingly effective' in policing young men's lives.[97]

In Shakespeare's tragedy of intrigue, Polonius's sinister exaggeration of the forensic disposition underlying the play's comic antecedents creates the claustrophobic effect of which Hamlet himself complains ('Denmark's a prison' (2. 2. 243)). It is an effect of excessive inferential detective work, an overdetermined 'mimetic prejudice', as it were, at work in everyone's but Horatio's responses to Hamlet's words and actions. If we don't see the results of Polonius's methods on Laertes, that is because we see, instead, how they affect Hamlet himself: the play is, in part, the story of that effect, played out in what de Grazia calls Hamlet's 'antics'.

---

[94] *Hamlet*, ed. Harold Jenkins (London: Methuen, 1982), 2. 1. 4. Further references to act, scene, and line number of this edition are given in the text. For the equivalent scene in Q1, see *Tragicall Historie of Hamlet Prince of Denmark*, ed. Graham Holderness and Bryan Loughry (Hemel Hempstead: Harvester Wheatsheaf, 1992), 46–8, 55–7.

[95] See *The Woman of Andros*, in *Terence*, trans. John Barsby (Cambridge, MA: Harvard University Press, 2001), 75–95; See Cicero, *De inv.* 1. 27; 1. 33–4, and, for comment, Scafuro, *Forensic Stage*, 357–74.

[96] Richard Bernard, *Terence in English* (London: John Legatt, 1629) 9.

[97] Scafuro, *Forensic Stage*, 362.

Later in the same scene in which Polonius dispatched Reynaldo to cast suspicion on Laertes, Ophelia comes on and, as previously instructed by her father, offers evidence of Hamlet's love for her in the form of a vividly enargeitic narration of his bursting, doublet unbraced and stockings ungartered, into her closet while she was sewing. Polonius does not hesitate to construe this narrative as evidence that the cause or motive of Hamlet's madness is love, and to propose further trials of his hypothesis to Claudius and Gertrude. The latter's employment of Rosencrantz and Guildenstern to investigate from outward signs of speech and behaviour just what is going on in Hamlet's 'inward man' (2. 2. 6) curiously anticipates the character criticism that would, after Coleridge, predominate in readings of the play. That is to say that the modern critical sense that there is something within Hamlet to investigate is, at least in part, an effect of Hamlet's speeches having been conceived as consciously anticipating and resisting just such forensic inferential activity, such a mimetic prejudice. A verbal echo links Polonius to the common English Renaissance variant on the evidence-gathering *senex*—the figure of the jealous merchant husband. When Polonius asks Hamlet, 'Will you walk out of the air, my lord?', and Hamlet replies, 'Into my grave?', Polonius reflects, 'Indeed, that's out of the air—How pregnant sometimes his replies are!' (2. 2. 206–9), echoing Thorello, in Jonson's earlier play of *Every Man in his Humour* (in which Shakespeare acted), where this jealous husband figure exercises a similar interpretative virtuosity in response to his wife's casual asking if he would come in out of the air: 'How simple, and how subtle are her answers!', comments the tormented Thorello to himself.[98] These processes of evidence gathering, of course, reflexively stage and anticipate modern critical character criticism, but are complicated in that they also circumscribe and endanger Hamlet's own sceptical enquiries into the nature, first, of the apparition Horatio has seen and, subsequently, of what he learns from it. So in all three variant texts the play moves forward as a sequence of sceptical enquiries into likelihood. Unusual care has been taken, in the emplotment of *Hamlet*, to exploit the potential inherent in dramatizing a number of issues (including the murder, the state of Hamlet's mind, the degree of Gertrude's complicity) as uncertain *issues of fact* rather than, as in the example of Orestes, an ethical issue of which the facts are already certain.

[98] Harold Jenkins comments on this echo in his edition of *Hamlet*, 467. *Every Man In* was played by the Lord Chamberlain's Men in 1598; see Ch. 7, p. 310.

If we return, at this point, to Hamlet's narration of the forged commission to Horatio (which, in modern editions, comes in Act 5, Scene 2), it's important to note that Coleridge does not select this speech alone, but as a contrast with a speech from *2 Henry IV*, Mistress Quickly's 'relation of the circumstances of Sir John Falstaff's debt to her'.[99] Coleridge uses Quickly's torrent of circumstantial detail ('Thou didst swear to me upon a parcel-gilt goblet, sitting in my Dolphin chamber, at the round table, by a sea-coal fire, on Wednesday in Whitsun week, etc.') to prove that hers is a mind which can only organize impressions according to their contiguity in time and place, and not according to any other relation. Hamlet's mind, we recall, is by contrast so ready to organize the relations 'which past or pressing events and objects bear to general truth', that he overlooks 'that other relation in which they are likewise to be placed to the apprehension and sympathy of his hearers' and so omits the detail of how the forged commission was sealed. Mistress Quickly, in other words, has no sense of arranging the circumstances of a past event with regard to enhancing the rhetorical probability of her narrative, while Hamlet's philosophical tendencies dispose him to overlook pragmatic rhetorical concerns.

Both Mistress Quickly's and Hamlet's narrations are, of course, judicial in conception. Mistress Quickly's speech is a comic variant on the forensic arguments of Ovid's *Heroides*, where abandoned mistresses protest that their erring lovers promised, or at least intended, to marry them.[100] Falstaff is in debt, living off the credit of his (mistaken) great expectations of promotion on Hal's ascent to the throne, and Quickly has entered an action against him, opportunity for much comic sexual innuendo. As John Barrell has brilliantly written, the contrast that Coleridge stages between Hamlet's and Quickly's styles is made as part of his development of a 'gendered notion of syntax' which ascribes to the methodical and masculine intellect 'the habit of foreseeing, in each integral part, or (more plainly) in every sentence, the whole that he intends to communicate'.[101] Quickly's sentences display no such syntactical evidence of masculine foresight, 'no deferment, no suspense, no eventual revelation that, though we might have been lost, she was always present in the sentence, actively foreseeing its development and the final assertion of its unity'. The whole sentence,

---

[99] Coleridge, *Lectures*, 501; *idem*, *Treatise on Method*, 27–8.

[100] Lorna Hutson, 'The "Double Voice" of Renaissance Equity and the Literary Voices of Women', in *"This Double Voice"*, ed. Danielle Clarke and Elizabeth Clarke (London: Macmillan, 2000), 142–63.

[101] John Barrell, 'Masters of Suspense: Syntax and Gender in Milton's Sonnets', in *Poetry, Language and Politics* (Manchester: Manchester University Press, 1988), 44–78, at 72–3.

Barrell goes on, 'exists for no other purpose that Coleridge can see than to disperse goodwife Keech among the circumstantial, with the effect that the speaking subject is also thus dispersed, and becomes evermore an object determined by a memory which recalls everything except the point of speaking at all'.[102] Yet, as we have seen, Hamlet is also riskily not quite in control, as Coleridge thinks, of the impression his syntax is making on his audience. Though 'the events, with the circumstances of time and place, are all stated with equal compression and rapidity' in his mind, Hamlet, 'ever disposed to generalize', omits a 'material' circumstance. In Hamlet's case, however, this 'excess of method', as opposed to Quickly's absence of method, serves to prove that Hamlet cannot be charged with the fault of speaking in a self-serving way, to prove his own case, which is exactly what Quickly's desperate attempt to reconstruct the circumstances that would bear witness to Falstaff's promise betrays her in the act of doing.

Yet what is so marvellous about Hamlet's speech, in fact, is that its apparently inadvertent omission of a material circumstance works decisively in his rhetorical favour, if we imagine the impression his speech makes in relation to the facts—effectively resulting in the murder of Rosencrantz and Guildenstern—that he is relating. If Mistress Quickly's narration comically discredits her by simultaneously revealing her desire to make the case and her incompetence in doing so (Falstaff quickly denies her version of the 'facts', and discredits her as a witness, insisting to the Lord Chief Justice that 'this is a poor mad soul, and she says up and down the town that her eldest son is like you'), the impression Hamlet gives of having a mind with a 'tendency of omission' regarding 'the mere facts of the question' is, by contrast, greatly to his credit in preventing a sense that he is arguing his own case. Coleridge was focusing, like Polonius or Claudius, on what Hamlet's words could tell us about Hamlet's 'inward man', and so could not see that the omission of the seal did not injure but contributed to the effects of probability and mimetic reality aimed at by the scene's conception as Hamlet's narrative to Horatio. The reality of the 'facts', as we have seen, emerges in a judicial concept of *narratio* under the pressure of sceptical circumstantial enquiry, whether actual or anticipated by the orator. Gascoigne's Balia interrogated the improbability of Polynesta's tale of master–servant disguise ('Are there no other *Sicylians* heere...which may discover them?'), just as Hamlet examined Horatio's unlikely tale of having seen a ghost, 'Armed at point exactly, cap-à-pie', looking just like

---

[102] Ibid. 73.

Hamlet's father. 'Arm'd, say you?', asks Hamlet, 'From top to toe?' . . . 'Then saw you not his face?' (1. 2. 224–8). Moments like these are part of advocate–jury logic underlying the dramatic use of *narratio*, and in Renaissance dramaturgy they work as surrogates for audience scepticism, helping to produce an impression of circumstantial fullness, of narrative detail that could go on being unfolded beyond the immediate needs of the scene and the play. Horatio's question 'How was this seal'd?' enables a fleshing out of the circumstantial, unpremeditated quality of Hamlet's action, for it prompts Hamlet to return to his earlier, self-exonerating association of his own improvisational genius with the intervention of providence in a just cause ('Our indiscretion sometimes serves us well | When our deep plots do pall; and that should learn us | There's a divinity that shapes our ends' (5. 2. 8–11)). In response to Horatio's enquiry about the seal, Hamlet recalls this comforting sentiment: 'Why, even in that was heaven ordinant. | I had my father's signet in my purse' (5. 2. 48–9). Horatio's question, then, affords an opportunity for a further hint, in the manner of Cicero's description of Milo's leisurely departure, of that improvisatory quality, that crucial lack of premeditation, that might distinguish an imagined jury's verdict on his desperately ingenious response to being 'benetted round with villanies', from their verdict on his having, in cold blood, plotted Rosencrantz's and Guildenstern's murder.

Christopher Prendergast has associated the claustrating order of mimesis—the readiness of codes and stereotypes to be recognized in the inferring of 'realistic' or plausible causes and motives—with the practice of lawcourts in assigning guilt: 'one area', as Prendergast writes, 'in which legal debate is regularly contaminated by enthymemic reasoning, or rather by its ideological transformation, is in its deliberations on the question of "motive"'.[103] Denmark may be a prison because a similar 'claustrating order' is dramatized from the outset of the play in a court in which Polonius's forensic work of inferring guilt and construing motive to political advantage is ubiquitously delegated and even posthumously operative. Conceived in resistance to these imprisoning conditions (which are also the conditions of mimesis), Hamlet's relationship with Horatio is marked by the former's constant anticipation of having his 'cause' or motives publicly misinterpreted and misconstrued after the fact. So even before we hear Hamlet narrate the circumstances of his murder of Rosencrantz and Guildenstern to Horatio, his opening words in the scene suggest another long, unheard relation, full of crucial distinctions: 'So

---

[103] Prendergast, *Order of Mimesis*, 47–8.

much for this, sir. Now you shall see the other. | You do remember all the circumstance?' (5. 2. 1–2). The point of charging Horatio's memory, and of ensuring that he has the circumstantial details right, will, of course, emerge in the final scene, when Hamlet, dying, surveys the slaughter and (we imagine) anticipates the questions that will arise after his death at the sight of the baffling double regicide. To Horatio he says, 'Horatio, I am dead, | Thou livest. *Report me and my cause aright* | To the unsatisfied' (5. 2. 342–5; my italics). We do not, then, need to decide between a modernizing psychological or characterological reading of *Hamlet* and an 'unmodernizing' reading of its primitive, folk-drama logic. Hamlet's interiority is compelling not because he states in soliloquy that he has 'that within which passeth show', but because many of his speeches to other characters in the play are reflexively marked by resistance to the same forensic habit of inference that had already, as early as 1600, come to be associated with the mimesis of dramatic narrative.

145

4

From Intrigue to Detection: Transformations of Classical Comedy, 1566–1594

In the last chapter we saw that the humanist pedagogy of narrative owed much to classical forensic rhetoric, and that vernacular dramatic texts from the 1560s onwards began to play with the mimetic possibilities offered by the powerful capacity of forensic, circumstantial narrative to make us (or other characters) believe in the 'facts' as related. The chapter also touched on the question of an affinity between the genre of the forensic narration and that of classical intrigue comedy which, from Philip Sidney's skilful blending of the two, we can see was clearly recognized and exploited by writers of the period. This chapter will explore the question of that affinity in much more depth, focusing on the fate of the most significant and controversial of the English experiments in neo-classical comic drama, George Gascoigne's *Supposes*, which was written for a legally trained audience at the Gray's Inn revels of 1566. The 1560s and 1570s, the period of *Supposes'* first performance and first appearance in print, coincides with a time of intense concern, evinced in Parliamentary debates and legislation, with monitoring the administration of justice in the localities, and with making local judicial institutions more accountable to the centre.[1] Not coincidentally, this period also sees the beginnings of what Barbara Shapiro has described as the 'migration' of Roman canon and civil conceptions of evidential standards of probability into the common law procedures of pre-trial examination and grand jury

---

[1] See Steve Hindle, 'County Government in Early Modern England', in *A Companion to Tudor Britain*, ed. Robert Tittler and Norman Jones (Oxford: Blackwell, 2004), 98–115, esp. 104–11; see also Frederic A. Youngs, Jr., 'Towards Petty Sessions', in *Tudor Rule and Revolution*, ed. D. J. Guth and J. W. McKenna (Cambridge: Cambridge University Press, 1982), 201–16, esp. 208–10.

investigation.[2] Shapiro's migration of evidential concepts may itself be taken as symptomatic of the intensification of governmental and judicial activity at all levels of society, involving not just professionals, but amateur officers and lay people. For it is not in books for professionals, but via self-help manuals designed to aid untrained Justices of the Peace and conscientious jurors that these Roman canon concepts of probability first enter English common law procedure.[3] Steve Hindle, who has given a comprehensive account of the increase of lay participation in judicial governance beginning in this period, quotes Sir Francis Willoughby telling trial jurors in the 1580s that 'the trueth lieth hid in evidence as fier in ashes & he which will find fier must stirre ashes'.[4] This chapter will show how the diffusion of the sense that one was doing one's civic duty by 'stirring the ashes of evidence' was to affect the vernacular reception of classical and neoclassical comedy in the 1560s and 1570s, and was to bring about its peculiarly English transformation into the materials for a tragicomic drama of evidence gathering, inference work, and detection.

'Circumstance and oaths': Evidence in *The Comedy of Errors*

The main concern of this chapter is the legacy of George Gascoigne's work as a transformer of the classical and neoclassical comic tradition into a complex moral detective drama which would be adapted to a variety of romance, chronicle history, and tragic forms. One approach to making the argument for Gascoigne's legacy is by way of Shakespeare's *Comedy of Errors*, which, though existing only in the 1623 Folio text, has been identified fairly certainly with 'a Comedy of Errors (like to Plautus his *Menaechmus*)' played by 'the players' at Gray's Inn as part of their Christmas revels on 28 December 1594.[5] Gascoigne's influence on *The Comedy of Errors* has not gone completely unnoticed, but I want to argue that it is not simply a question of Gascoigne's being a 'lively' vernacular

---

[2] Barbara Shapiro, *'Beyond Reasonable Doubt' and 'Probable Cause'* (Berkeley: University of California Press, 1991), 114–85.

[3] For example, in William Lambarde's *Eirenarcha* (London: Ralph Newberry, 1592); Dalton's *The Countrey Justice*, (London: John Moore, 1635); and Richard Bernard, *A Guide to Grand Jurymen* (London: Felix Kingston for Ed. Blackmore, 1627).

[4] Steve Hindle, *The State and Social Change in Early Modern England, c.1550–1640* (Basingstoke: Macmillan, 2000), 129.

[5] See *The Comedy of Errors*, ed. Charles Whitworth (Oxford: Oxford University Press, 2002), Appendix B, 183–7.

medium for the unproblematic transmission of the *commedia erudita* conventions of plots based on mistaken identity.[6] Such assessments treat Gascoigne's *Supposes* in isolation both from its own fate as a text which had to undergo revisions as a result of the objections of the High Commission on its first appearance in print in 1573, as well as from Gascoigne's own later reworking of the play's plot structure in a tragic and didactic neoclassical play called *The Glasse of Government* (1575). This latter play inspired George Whetstone's attempts at neoclassicism in *Promos and Cassandra* (1578), a play which was in turn rewritten by Shakespeare as *Measure for Measure* in 1604. To understand Shakespeare's *Comedy of Errors*, and many other aspects of the mediated neoclassicism and forensic rhetoric of Shakespeare's dramaturgy, we need to acknowledge not just *Supposes* in isolation, but *Supposes* as two kinds of cultural event: first, as a performance at Gray's Inn in 1566, and then as a printed text in 1573 to which the author was obliged to make minor but highly significant revisions in 1575. Before we consider *Supposes*, however, let us, if possible, take an estranging look at Shakespeare's *Comedy of Errors* itself.

The Comedy of Errors is universally acknowledged to be Shakespeare's closest imitation of New Comedy, but in its opening dilemma it departs very strikingly from anything in Plautus or Terence. Instead of the usual narration of an amorous intrigue that has reached crisis point, we start with a distinctly improbable narrative alleging extenuating circumstances and spoken before a judge who has already pre-empted what rhetorical power it might have by sentencing the accused. In a strange reversal of judicial process, the Duke asks Egeon, to 'say in brief the cause' of his offence *after* he has told him, 'by law thou art condemn'd to die' (1. 1. 25, 28).

How is the sentence of death lifted? It is well known that Shakespeare makes much of the reputation of Ephesus as the sinister habitation of conjurers and magicians, of 'jugglers that deceive the eye, | Dark-working sorcerers that change the mind' (1. 2. 98–9). But, of course, it is not by such eye-deceiving or mind-altering magic that Egeon's execution comes to be averted, unless we include in our definition of magic the 'conjuring' of Renaissance dramatic mimesis. The idea that Shakespearean dramatic mimesis is best explained by analogy with the prosopoetic magic of conjuring informs much recent criticism. Stephen Greenblatt began work on *Hamlet and Purgatory* (a book which includes a chapter

---

[6] As is suggested, e.g., by Harry Levin, 'Two Comedies of Errors', and David Bevington, 'The Comedy of Errors in the Context of the Late 1580s and Early 1590s', both repr. in *The Comedy of Errors*, ed. Robert S. Miola (New York: Routledge, 1997), 119–20 and 337.

on ghosts and uncanny resemblances throughout Shakespeare) with 'the notion of writing a book about Shakespeare as a Renaissance conjuror', by which term he meant 'someone who has the power to call forth or make contact through language with things—voices, bodies, spirits—that are absent'.[7] Charles Whitworth's recent Oxford edition of *Comedy of Errors* notes the importance of the concept of 'conjuring' in this early specimen of Shakespeare's dramatic writing, calculating that 'the words *conjure* and *conjurer* occur six times in *Errors*, more than in any other play'.[8] But the analogy between Shakespearean mimesis and conjuring may cause us to overlook an important aspect of what it is that actually produces the emotional credibility of the dénouement in this staged narrative of hallucinatory mistakings. As I suggested in the previous chapter, the mimesis of English Renaissance drama—by which I mean drama affected, as all English drama was by the 1590s, by the popularization of classical models of plot—depended not just on moments of vivid linguistic representation of things absent, but on the anticipation and representation of a habit of sceptical, forensic enquiry into likelihood, or on what we might call the strategic exploitation, or rhetorical invention, of 'suspicion'. In Gascoigne's *Supposes*, Balia's questioning the probability of Polynesta's tale that her lover is a heir in disguise ('Are there no other *Sicilians* heere...which may discover them?') functions, as does the pathos of Polynesta's father's inability to believe her story ('would god it were true that *Polynesta* told me ere while; that he who hath deflowred hir, is of no servile estate, as hitherto he hath been supposed...Well, I will goe examine hir againe, my minde giveth me that I shall perceive by hir tale whether it be true or not') as constitutive of what Leo Salingar calls the 'artificial order of time' in English neoclassical drama.[9] For the 'artificial order of time' is less an artificial temporal order *as such* than a presentation of the uneven distribution of knowledge between characters about one another and about what exactly has happened. That is to say, what is in question is not whether a play renders time impressionistically or precisely, but whether it offers scope for characters to offer accounts of events of which others lack knowledge. It is this explicit unevenness of knowledge, and the constant quasi-forensic enquiries, examinations, and conjectural reconstructions that characters

---

[7] Stephen Greenblatt, *Hamlet in Purgatory* (Princeton: Princeton University Press, 2001), 3.

[8] Shakespeare, *Comedy of Errors*, ed. Whitworth, 41.

[9] George Gascoigne, *Supposes*, 1. 1. 98–9, 5. 6. 33–5, in *A Hundreth Sundrie Flowres*, ed. G. W. Pigman III (Oxford: Clarendon Press, 2000). Further references to line and scene numbers from this edition are given in the text. See also Leo Salingar, *Shakespeare and the Traditions of Comedy* (Cambridge: Cambridge University Press, 1974), 76.

engage in as a result, that actually structure the fictional representation of time and of persons in a way that corresponds to our own daily experience.

What this means in relation to *Comedy of Errors* is that the prominence of the play's vocabulary of sorcery and conjuring is best made sense of in relation to an equally prominent strand of legal vocabulary associated with attempts to verify and render probable accounts of the apparently impossible things that characters have seen and heard. For it's a remarkable fact that the whole of Acts 4 and 5 of the *Comedy* are given over to the exchange of passionate, oath-bound testimony of what the senses seem to have perceived—'Witness you', Adriana begs the assembled crowd on seeing Antipholus appear from the Phoenix, when she believes she has stowed him safely in the abbey, 'That he is borne about invisible' (5. 1. 186–7). The vocabulary of Acts 4 and 5 is nothing if not *testamentary*. The word 'perjured' occurs twice, 'witness' occurs four times, versions of 'swear' and 'forswear' appear seven times, and there is no less frequency of phrases indicating oaths ('God doth know' (4. 4. 65), 'sooth to say' (4. 4. 69), 'Perdie' (4. 4. 71), 'Sans fable' (4. 4. 73), 'So befall my soul' (5. 1. 208–9), 'Ne're may I look on day nor sleep on night' (5. 1. 210–11), 'I never saw the chain, so help me heaven' (5. 1. 268)), and of phrases insisting on first-hand, ear- and eye-witnessing ('These ears of mine…did hear thee' (5. 1. 26), 'I will be sworn these ears of mine | Heard you confess' (5. 1. 260–1)).

What seems astonishing here is Shakespeare's bold confrontation of the inherent improbability of the 'real' explanation for all the confusion by casting the events of the first three acts as sources of disputed *eyewitness* testimony, as empirically probable evidence. And it is this fictitious evidential conflict that interrupts an apparently inexorable temporal progress—the passage of Egeon to his death—when the Duke decides to hear and 'determine' (as in law French 'terminer') Adriana's cause first, before seeing (albeit reluctantly) to the execution of Egeon according to Syracusan law (5. 1. 167). For it is in the course of determining the cause between husband and wife, Antipholus and Adriana, that we have the recognition scene, which absolves everyone involved in the testimonial conflict, proving no one to have been perjured, no one forsworn, no one to have borne false witness (except for one, and her falsehood goes benignly unnoticed[10]).

---

[10] This is, of course, the courtesan, who invents the story of Antipholus taking away her ring 'all in rage', at 4. 4. 137.

Turning Acts 4 and 5 into a dispute over the evidence for what has actually taken place in the previous three acts is so audacious because (of course) the so-called *real* or empirically 'probable' explanation for occurrences otherwise explained as jugglers' or conjurers' tricks is itself the most improbable affront to credulity of all. Indeed, the improbabilities of 'what *really* happened' are so numerous that to list them is tedious: not one, but *two* sets of identical twins; these different sets of twins coincidentally born on the same day, in the same place; each set of brothers being given (most improbably) the same *name* as his twin; two perfectly symmetrical packages of parent, son, and servant twin being rescued, separately, from a shipwreck, each losing touch with the other; the father then apparently being indicted and condemned according to the same law against stranger merchants that in Gascoigne's *Supposes* is offered as the most blatant of confidence tricks to fool only men 'of small experience' travelling to foreign towns (*Supposes*, 2. 1. 131). The idea that one would render a story based on such a tissue of unlikelihoods credible by casting it as the resolution of a dispute over evidence and likelihood is amazing. Yet that is exactly how Acts 4 and 5 of *Comedy of Errors* works.

So, when Adriana pleads with her neighbours and the audience to witness that Antipholus is borne about invisibly, by magic, we know he isn't; but the 'real' explanation for how her husband can emerge from one place, having been 'stowed' in another, is no less improbable a yarn than Fortunatus's cloak of invisibility. Jonson's famous comment to Drummond that he had 'had ane intention to have made a play like Plaut' Amphitrio, but left it of, for that he could never find two so like others that he could persuade the spectators they were one', should alert us to the point here: the improbable indistinguishability of the twins is an achievement of Shakespeare's plot, it is not its precondition.[11] A very general resemblance between the actors playing the Antipholi and the two Dromios comes to seem, in the course of the play, like confusingly identical looks, and, conversely, productions which have one person play both twins (Danny Sheie at Santa Cruz in 1988, Ian Judge at Stratford in 1990) seem to make audiences uncomfortable.[12] Peter Holland, reviewing Ian Judge's production, found the decision to have Graham Turner double as both Dromios, and Desmond Barrit as both Antipholuses destroyed the emotional effect of the play. 'We know', he wrote,

---

[11] Jonson, *Conversations with Drummond*, 420, in Ben Jonson, *Complete Works*, ed. C. H. Herford and Percy Simpson, i (Oxford: Clarendon Press, 1925), 144.
[12] Miola (ed.), *Comedy of Errors*, 33–4.

how the play will end . . . but along the way we end up nearly as confused as the characters. When both Dromios are played by the same actor the audience's ability to be confused . . . is simply evaded, evaded because the audience comes to follow actor, not rôle, Graham Turner, not Dromio . . . The history of the characters is replaced by the history of the performance.[13]

Holland's astute comment reveals how much Shakespeare's evidential shaping of the plot contributes to the sense of the characters having 'histories' and lives of their own. For if we acknowledge that the persuasion of likeness that Jonson sought in vain can only be an effect of audience desire, it's clear that in *Comedy of Errors* this desire is deliberately intensified by the structuring of the two final acts as an evidential dispute. As Holland notes, our knowledge of how the play is going to end does not pre-empt our experience of perplexity during the scenes of rapidly alternating Antipholus and Dromio twins. But the resolution of this perplexity would feel mechanical were it not that in the scenes of dispute between the neighbours and merchant community of Ephesus about exactly who owed, and who received, a chain, who saw whom reviled by his wife, shut out of his house, etc., we become drawn into the almost hypnotically creative power of forensic *narratio* cast as sincere, impassioned, domestic misunderstanding.

When the Duke enters with Egeon of Syracuse ominously, *'bare-head, with the* Headsman and other Officers', he is interrupted by two long narrations, one spoken by Adriana, impeaching her husband, and one by Antipholus of Ephesus, accusing her. Each of these narratives, though perfectly reasonable as an account of the day's crazy events, acquires its plausible coherence from the mutual suspicion which we infer from the couple's interpretation of the day's mystifying contradictions, supplemented by the glimpse we have had of the tensions of their domestic life (sketched in the Erasmian exchange between Adriana and Luciana in Act 2, Scene 1, and developed in the detailed consequences of the Ephesian twin's exclusion from his house—his vengeful bestowing of the chain on the courtesan, for example, and Luciana's advice to his twin to be 'secret-false' in his conduct of his affairs (3. 2. 15)). Adriana's narrative assumes that the afternoon's wild happenings are the result of her husband's sudden descent into lunacy: 'this ill day | A most outrageous fit of madness took him' (5. 1. 138–9). The key to this is plotted a few scenes earlier, when the courtesan, worried that she is going to come off worse by forty ducats (the worth of a ring which she gave to Antipholus in

---

[13] Peter Holland, 'Ian Judge's Stratford Production, 1990', in *Comedy of Errors*, ed. Miola, 564.

expectation of his giving her the gold chain originally meant for his wife), decides that she'll tell Adriana a lie about how Antipholus came by her precious goods. 'My way', she resolves,

> is now to hie home to his house,
> And tell his wife that, being lunatic,
> He rush'd into my house, and took perforce
> My ring away.

(4. 3. 92–5)

The courtesan's improvised falsehood takes hold and exacerbates misunderstanding; Adriana hires Pinch to exorcize her husband, and her husband assumes Pinch's confederacy in a plot to banish him earlier that day. A passionate altercation follows, which resolves nothing. To the Duke, Adriana tells a story which coheres neatly round the falsehood she's been told:

> May it please your Grace, Antipholus my husband,
> Who I made lord of me and all I had
> At your important letters—this ill day
> A most outrageous fit of madness took him,
> That desp'rately he hurried through the street—
> With him his bondman, all as mad as he—
> Doing displeasure to the citizens
> By rushing in their houses, bearing thence
> Rings, jewels, anything his rage did like.

(5. 1. 136–44)

The courtesan's little fib, designed to strengthen her claim to the ring and prevent the inference of a liaison between herself and Antipholus, swells unintentionally here into a tabloid story of crazed, random violence. Adriana then implies subsequent events by it: her husband's breaking free from Pinch's custody is typical of the unusual strength commonly ascribed to lunatics, fitting seamlessly into the narrative: 'I wot not by what strong escape, | He broke from those that had the guard of him' (5. 1. 148–9). Antipholus of Ephesus counters with his own *narratio*, carefully establishing his sanity and sobriety, and invoking neighbour-witnesses (unfortunately less credible in that he also thinks them 'perjured') to testify to his explanation for the day's events. In his view, all can be explained as the work of a conspiracy between his prostitute wife and her pimp or client, the mountebank Pinch, working in league with a gang of undesirables who have clearly plotted to take over his household by having him certified as out of his wits:

> My liege, I am advised what I say
> Neither disturbed with the effect of wine,
> Nor heady-rash, provok'd with raging ire,
> Albeit my wrongs might make one wiser mad.
> This woman lock'd me out this day from dinner;
> The goldsmith there, were he not pack'd with her,
> Could witness it, for he was with me then,
> Who parted with me to go fetch a chain,
> Promising to bring it to the Porpentine,
> Where Balthazar and I did dine together.
> Our dinner done, and he not coming thither,
> I went to seek him. In the street I met him
> And in his company that gentleman.
> There did that perjur'd goldsmith swear me down
> That I this day of him receiv'd the chain,
> Which, God he knows, I saw not; for the which
> He did arrest me with an officer.
> I did obey, and sent my peasant home
> For certain ducats; he with none returned.
> Then fairly I bespoke the officer
> To go in person with me to my house.
> By th' way, we met
> My wife, her sister, and a rabble more
> Of vild confederates.

(5. 1. 214–37)

The famous description of Pinch follows, the luridness of which owes much to Antipholus's sexual disgust, made explicit at 4. 4. 61–5, that this 'companion with the saffron face', is his wife's lover, busy with her indoors at lunchtime, while he stood humiliated in the street. As in *Titus Andronicus*, a legal model of evidential uncertainty acquires a compelling pathos as mistaken inferences and failures to make sense of the facts are so clearly shaped by the creative powers of intense emotional vulnerability.

In the last chapter I suggested that character criticism, which took for granted work done on Shakespeare's complex interweaving of protracted and accelerating time schemes, responded mimetically and forensically to uses of narrative that were themselves consciously employing forensic strategies for mimetic ends. An engaging appreciative essay written in 1842 by Charles Knight enacts this process for *Comedy of Errors*. For Knight, character becomes Shakespeare's ingenious solution to the problem of distinguishing between identical twins, which he perceives as an empirical difficulty. He praises the play's beautifully managed plot for immersing the audience in confusion, but suggests that this very perplexity prompts the same audience to look for differences of personality in the twins. An autobiographical anecdote serves to exemplify the process. He tells of his own acquaintance with a pair of adult twins, one a resident of his home town and the other a stranger, visiting for a day. He and his wife mistook the stranger for their neighbour, and were for a time puzzled, until the stranger's 'total ignorance of the locality' gave him away. But in any case, continued Knight, small differences of gesture and manner soon became apparent, and, 'if we had known them at all intimately, we probably should have ceased to think that outward points of identity were even greater than points of difference. We should, moreover, *have learned the difference of their characters'* (my italics). So, he concludes, 'the spectator of The Comedy of Errors will very soon detect the differences of the Dromios and Antipholuses, and . . . while his curiosity is kept alive by the effort of attention which is necessary for this detection, the riddle will not only tease him, but its perpetual solution will afford him the utmost satisfaction'.[14]

Knight's delightful insight shows appreciation of how an embedded intrigue plot structure (even when there is no intrigue) provokes the work of detection which in turn constitutes character as its effect, but even this reading underestimates how creative the structure is. Knight sees the 'effort of attention' necessary for the 'detection' of differences of character as unmotivated by anything other than the confusions wrought by physical likeness. The process of detection, however, is what whets the audience's desire to see the 'intricate impeach' dissolve in the revelation of the 'real' existence of two brothers called Antipholus. It is this desire alone that sustains the emotional conviction of twinship and of the family's 'reunion' when the non-identical actors playing the four twins finally appear all together on the stage. As Jonson knew, you can never just *find* 'two so like others' that you 'could persuade the spectators that they were one'; such a persuasion of eyewitness proof has to result from the emotional work of the plot (and, as we will later see from *Jacke Jugeler*, the dramatic illusion of the double in this generic tradition does not work unless there is a plot). In this way, then, the play's forensic or legal enquiry into the purely *imaginary* villanies, lewdnesses, and betrayals with which characters are charged has prompted us, the

---

[14] *The Pictorial Edition of the Works of Shakespeare*, ed. Charles Knight, 7 vols. (London: Charles Knight and Co., 1842), i. 257–8.

audience, to infer more inward and psychological causes for the nature of those imaginings, which, in turn, precludes our sceptical dismissal of the romance dénouement, grounding it firmly in our sense of what is emotionally credible. Greenblatt's comment that in *Errors* there are 'no ghosts…only perplexing, unnerving resemblances that *turn out to have an entirely naturalistic explanation*' (my italics) overlooks the way in which a 'naturalistic explanation' was itself, at the time, the product of the '*arte occulta*', the hidden art of a way of telling a story, the credible narrative order, which Latin writers on forensic rhetoric linked to the order of comedy.[15]

Two things, then, are remarkable about *Comedy of Errors*, especially when we remember that it is the first English neoclassical comedy to be played at Gray's Inn, thirty years after George Gascoigne's *Supposes* was performed there in 1566. The first is that, developing, as we shall see, what was a mere hint in Gascoigne's play, Shakespeare's play goes out of its way to transform the intrigue structure which defines neo-classical comedy into a projection of the characters' imaginations: no one has actually deliberately got up to any intrigue (except, arguably, the courtesan). The second, related point involves the mimetic effects of this transformation. Intrigue plots generally foster mimesis by inviting detective work on the part of readers and audiences: when we try to follow the intricacies of a deception, we have to remember specific indi-cations of time and place in enough detail to give these fictional indices what Barthes calls a 'reality effect'. Such fictional circumstantiality, such detailed inventions of time, place, and motive already derive, as we have seen, from forensic models, but when Shakespeare transforms their uses as elements of intrigue into the elements of paranoia (conspiracies and plots imagined by the 'victim'), he makes their inherently forensic qualities explicit. That is to say, the paranoid imaginings which lend urgency and warmth to the dispute over what really happened can be understood as the turning inward of intrigue, or the reshaping of intrigue into a judicial enquiry into the imagination of its own criminal and spiritual dimension. But what is most odd about this inward turn is that while Shakespeare exploits the emotional intensity of subjecting the adulteries and perjuries of intrigue to a more serious, judgemental scrutiny than comic conven-tions usually allow, he at the same time refuses the inevitably tragic consequences of such a spiritually judgemental perspective by making

---

[15] Greenblatt, *Hamlet in Purgatory*, 161; Quintilian, *Inst.* 4. 2. 58. In his book on *narratio*, at 4. 2. 53, Quintilian writes, 'There is also a pattern of events which is credible, like that which is found in comedy or mime.'

the hurts inflicted—adulteries, false witnessing, broken promises—purely imaginary. Shakespeare, then, seems not only to be redeeming the mimetic potential of the intrigue plot from some earlier taint of criminality, but to be deriving the plot's mimetic potential from processes of suspicious imagination and detection. But if this is so, where did the taint of criminality come from? Why might a Plautine plot like that of *Menaechmi* or *Amphitruo* be associated, by Tudor writers, with judicial enquiry into crime? This chapter will be concerned with answering that question by exploring the mid-sixteenth-century English reception and imitation of Roman intrigue comedy in the context of men's growing awareness of and concern with questions of 'governance', or the administration of justice at a local level.

Prologue: Transformations of Governance, 1570–1600

The importance of Roman New Comedy for the development of English drama has not been neglected critically, as the studies of Salingar, Altman, and Miola, to name only a few, bear witness.[16] However, the generic pervasiveness of New Comedy's influence on the 1590s genres of chronicle history and revenge tragedy has been underestimated. This may be partly because the association of Seneca with tragedy, and Plautus and Terence with comedy, has tended to override critical consciousness that the native tradition of interlude tends to alternate comic and grave action, so that the absorption of strategies of representation from classical and neoclassical drama on the public stage is likely involve a breaking down of the strict tragic/comic division and a diffusion of intrigue elements, including forensic *narratio*, into the mixed, episodic structures already familiar to audiences.[17] Recently, Subha Mukherji's work on the uses of artificial proof in tragicomedy and in what used to be called 'domestic tragedy' has begun to show that the rhetorical legacy of New Comedy extended well beyond English comedies of disguise and mistaken identity, but the pervasiveness and importance of that legacy still remain to demonstrated.[18]

---

[16] Salingar, *Shakespeare and the Traditions of Comedy*; Joel B. Altman, *Tudor Play of Mind* (Berkeley: University of California Press, 1978); Robert S. Miola, *Shakespeare and Classical Comedy* (Oxford: Clarendon Press, 1994).

[17] Altman's excellent study, e.g., divides the comic, inventive influence of Terence from the declamatory influence of Seneca (*Tudor Play of Mind*, 130–96, 229–321).

[18] Subha Mukherji, *Law and Representation in Early Modern Drama* (Cambridge: Cambridge University Press, 2006), 45–54 and *passim*. Mukherji develops arguments about the uses of artificial proof in comedy from Altman's *Tudor Play of Mind*, from Terrence Cave's *Recognitions*

The beginnings of the story of New Comedy's effects on developments in English drama in the latter half of the sixteenth century are complicated and obscured by a question of historical chronology which involves developments in both literary/dramatic and political/judicial realms of cultural activity. The decades in which a Roman-style intrigue model of neoclassical comedy might have taken hold in English-language literary circles were the 1560s and 1570s: precisely those decades which saw the first, and most politically involved, phase of the translation and imitation of Seneca, the model throughout Europe for neoclassical tragedy.[19] However, the very same concern with questions of governance which prompted attempts to render Seneca into the vernacular also led to a distrust of vernacular renderings of Plautus and Terence. For while Seneca's plots are based in a rhetoric of deliberation, offering models of how constitutional questions ought to be approached, the plots of Plautus and Terence, by contrast, are grounded in forensic rhetoric, offering models of the uses of evidence. In them amorous adolescents, wily slaves, and suspicious fathers endlessly summon one another to court, gather witnesses, and assemble arguments of proof, in order to achieve their ends. Their techniques were perfectly recognizable to sixteenth-century lawyers as what are known, in arts of rhetoric, as 'artificial proofs'.[20] 'Artificial proofs' were gaining a new currency as the basis of copious rhetorical invention generally; but as we have seen, they already had a long legal history, having been codified in Roman canon law as fractions in the calculation of the 'full proof' needed for conviction.[21] Classical comedy, with its repertoire of forensic arguments, could be seen to be very relevant, in a technical sense, to the success of good governance, since that success depended on the ability not only of Justices of the Peace, but of ordinary trial jurymen, to evaluate evidential narratives and decide which was most probable. Nevertheless, the plays of Terence and Plautus, though far more prominent in grammar school curricula than Seneca, were not translated and hardly imitated during the 1560s and 1570s.[22] For whereas Seneca's tragic plots might show

(Oxford: Clarendon Press, 1988), and from my *The Usurer's Daughter* (London: Routledge, 1994).

[19] See Jessica Winston, 'Seneca in Early Elizabethan England', *Renaissance Quarterly*, 59, no. 1 (2006), 29–58.   [20] See Ch. 2, p. 00.

[21] See Shapiro, *'Beyond Reasonable Doubt'*, 116–20; Alessandro Giuliani, 'The Influence of Rhetoric on the Law of Evidence and Pleading', *Juridical Review*, 62 (1969), 216–51.

[22] T. Howard-Hill, working from the British Library Catalogue, counts twenty-one Latin editions of Seneca's ten attributed plays extant by 1589, with English translations being published from 1559 to 1581. Of Plautus's twenty plays, there were thirty-seven editions by 1578, though vernacular translations did not, on the whole, appear until the eighteenth century. Of Terence's six plays, however, 117 editions were published *before the end of the*

'the just revenge and fearful punishments and horrible crimes... in these our myserable daies', the comic plots of Terence and Plautus presented near-crimes and legal scams as triumphantly successful, thus seeming to endorse a view of judicial procedure as purely strategic, without moral authority or divine sanction.[23] And whereas Seneca's deliberative rhetoric, offering arguments on either side of the case, might present a model of how important constitutional questions ought to be approached in the new political nation, the forensic strategies employed by the wily slaves and amorous adolescents of Roman intrigue comedy seemed dangerously akin to an abuse of the techniques of assessing proofs and weighing up presumptions that defined the discretion of judges in the various equity or ecclesiastical courts and, increasingly, of juries in the common law. Roman intrigue comedy, then, seemed to call into question the possibility of distinguishing evidential procedures in law from mere rhetorical conjuring tricks precisely at a time of acute consciousness of problems of administering justice and enabling moral self-governance in the localities.

Jessica Winston has, in a couple of important and related articles, re-examined the significance of the almost forgotten 'first phase' of the translation and imitation of Seneca at the Inns of Court from 1559 to 1581, broadening and complicating our understanding of these writings as political interventions. Specifically, whereas readings of Thomas Sackville and Thomas Norton's *Gorboduc* have become ever more narrowly topical in recent years, Winston convincingly demonstrates that *Gorboduc*'s political significance must be read much more broadly as being concerned with the relationship between the governmental institutions—monarch, Privy Council, and Parliament—involved in decision-making processes. In this sense, the play both argues for, and participates in, that 'expansion of the political nation' that historians agree to have taken place in the course of Elizabeth's reign. Such an expansion, as Winston argues, 'involved not just the growth of the English bureaucracy, but also an altered understanding of the sorts of people and institutions that could legitimately contribute to conversations about the governance of the realm'.[24]

---

fifteenth century, another 198 editions by 1540, and another 335 by 1600, averaging five editions a year from 1470 onward. Again, as with Plautus, vernacular versions were slower to appear, the first complete plays of Terence in English being Richard Bernard's 1598 translation. See 'The Evolution of the Form of Plays in English during the Renaissance', *Renaissance Quarterly*, 43, no. 1 (1990), 112–45.

[23] Alexander Neville, *Oedipus* (1563), quoted by Winston, 'Seneca in Early Elizabethan England', 48.

[24] Winston, 'Expanding the Political Nation', *Early Theatre*, 8, no. 1 (2005), 11–34, at 17, 27.

Winston's choice of word, 'governance', should alert us to another aspect of this Elizabethan expansion of popular civic consciousness, an aspect which makes the relevance of classical models of comic plot, with their unmistakable structural affinities with judicial rhetoric, much clearer. For, as the work of Steve Hindle, Anthony Fletcher, Keith Wrightson, Patrick Collinson, and A. Hassell Smith has shown, the reign of Elizabeth, especially from 1570 to its end, was remarkable for seeing the beginning of an unprecedented transformation of relations between central government and the localities, which can be conveniently referred to as a transformation in forms of 'governance'. Anthony Fletcher's *Reform in the Provinces* describes the 'increase of governance' as 'a general quickening of the tempo of local administration', the key to which was the linking of Justices, constables of hundreds, and parish officers in effective channels of communication through the holding of regular petty sessions.[25] Hindle's general synthesis and analysis of this work on early modern local administration explains that the term 'governance' refers to 'the conflation of judicial and administrative functions within early modern government'. It includes, among its aspects, the already well-known centralizing tendencies of Tudor government, but also the much less well-known (or at least not understood to be *political*) relations between central government and local officers (Justices of the Peace, ecclesiastical judges, constables, and churchwardens), and, finally, the growth in civil litigation and in people's readiness to use local judicial institutions (criminal and spiritual) as forms of protection and remedy.[26]

This much expanded understanding of what constituted the 'political nation' in the late sixteenth and early seventeenth centuries should help us understand that dramatic representations of private litigious activity and of local processes of detection and judicial administration (processes that do not explicitly concern monarch and 'matters of state') were seen by contemporaries, especially in the difficult early decades of Elizabeth's reign, as just as *political* as Senecan tragedy. Concern about the

---

[25] Anthony Fletcher, *Reform in the Provinces* (New Haven: Yale University Press, 1986), 116–42. Though Fletcher's focus is the seventeenth century, he notes that some counties were more precocious in these matters than others: Essex high constables held petty sessions from the 1560s, and Cheshire Justices mention the practice in 1572 (ibid. 123–4). See also, for William Cecil's influence, Youngs, 'Towards Petty Sessions', esp. 208–11.

[26] Steve Hindle, *State and Social Change*, 3. See also Fletcher, *Reform in the Provinces*; Patrick Collinson, 'The Monarchical Republic of Queen Elizabeth I' (1986) and '*De Republica Anglorum*: or, History with the Politics Put Back' (1989), both in Collinson, *Elizabethans* (London: Hambledon, 2003), 1–58; Keith Wrightson, 'Two Concepts of Order', in *An Ungovernable People*, ed. J. Brewer and J. Styles (London: Hutchinson, 1979), 21–46; A. Hassell Smith, *County and Court* (Oxford: Clarendon Press, 1974).

representation of law in classical and neoclassical comedy was especially acute in these decades, when men close to the government (and, in those decades, these *were* the men who were writing plays) were responding to the legacy of rapidly alternating regimes and the lack of either a conscientious, educated clergy or similarly qualified commission of peace. The Parliaments of the 1560s and 1570s are known among literary scholars for being primarily concerned with the question of succession, but they were no less concerned with questions of local government and the reform of the local administration of the law. When Sir Nicholas Bacon made his opening speech to Parliament in the fifth year of Elizabeth's reign, 1562, he identified, among problems most urgently requiring debate and solution by the assembly, the related questions of church discipline and the reformation of ecclesiastical laws, and the question of the local administration of justice. For the first, he proposed 'the deveidinge of everye of the dioceses accordeinge to their greatnes into deaneryes . . . and the committeinge of thease deaneryes to men well chosen (as I thinke commonly they be not); and then the keepinge of certen ordinarye courtes at theire prescripte tymes for the well executeinge of thease lawes of discipline', with the 'severe' oversight of 'inferior ministers' by bishops and chancellors. For secular administration of local justice, Bacon envisaged something similar. Justices of the Peace were commonly negligent and corrupt, he pointed out, and suggested that there should be

throughoute the realme a trienniall or byenniall visitacion in his nature made of all the temporall officers and ministers that by vertue of theire office have in chardge to see to th'execucion or lawes. By this I meane that the Queene should make choise every second or thirde yeare of certaine experte and proved persons, to whom commission should be graunted to trye out and examine by all meanes and wayes the offences of all such as have not seene to the due execucion of lawes accordeinge to the offices and chardges committed to them by the prince . . . Of effecte much like this, and to like ende, was the visitacion of the Churche first devised . . . and whether the old commissions of *oyer* tended somewhat to this ende I doubte.[27]

While Bacon's suggestion of a bi- or triennial royal commission to examine the Justices of the Peace wasn't implemented as such, his pinpointing of the crisis in local judicial administration was accurate, and its resolution did come about by a variety of initiatives which all tended, as Bacon envisaged, to strengthen the allegiance of local justices to central

---

[27] *Proceedings in the Parliaments of Elizabeth I*, ed. T. E. Hartley (Leicester: Leicester University Press, 1981), 82–3.

government, and to ensure their commitment to carrying out conscientiously the administrative and judicial duties imposed on them. Among these were Bacon's own introduction, in the same year, of the Star Chamber charge to circuit judges travelling to the localities to sit at the courts of assize. After the 1560s these circuit charges increasingly came to be used both as vehicles of propaganda for government policy and as a means of monitoring the conscientiousness of local magistrates, since judges were required to report the names of negligent Justices back to the Privy Council.[28] In addition, Sir Nicholas Bacon's suggestion that secular local government learn from the ecclesiastical courts bore fruit when, as Lord Chief Justice, Sir John Popham started the practice of requiring circuit judges to liaise directly with high constables of parishes and towns.[29] Practices like these, justified on the grounds of the inefficiency of local magistrates, were supplemented by the Privy Council's increasing strategic management of appointments to the Commission of the Peace. As the office of Justice of the Peace was unsalaried, the burden of appointment to the Commission of Peace was itself the appointment's reward and this, paradoxically, enabled pressure from central government. In Elizabeth's reign, recognition that local administration was defective and needed reform was strongly advocated by Sir Nicholas Bacon, Lord Burghley, Sir John Puckering, and Sir Thomas Egerton. Burghley initiated a systematic collection of information about particular Justices of the Peace, 'purging' corrupt Justices from the Commission.[30] Assize judges and, latterly, clerks of the peace were expected to act as spies on Justices of the Peace, and report Justices and constables who failed to report or punish faults; however, in practice, Justices could not be forced into action, and local administration and law enforcement required their conscientious co-operation. Both Justices and constables exercised discretion in what they would or would not pursue as larceny or felony, upholding, as Keith Wrightson has written, two different concepts of order, and mediating, as Fletcher writes, between 'the national legislative ideal and ambivalent local realities'.[31] Not unrelated to this increase in

---

[28] Hindle, *State and Social Change*, 6; Louis A. Knafla, *Law and Politics in Jacobean England* (Cambridge: Cambridge University Press, 1977), 146.

[29] Roger Wilbraham, 'The Journal of Sir Roger Wilbraham, Solicitor-General in Ireland and Master of Requests for the Years 1593–1616', ed. H. S. Scott, *The Camden Miscellany*, 10 (London: Royal Historical Society, 1902), 20; Fletcher, *Reform in the Provinces*, Hindle, *State and Social Change*, 7.   [30] Fletcher, *Reform in the Provinces*, 5–11.

[31] Ibid. 55–67, at 65. Fletcher cites the case of Bostock Fuller, whom we met in Ch. 2, examining the victim of the theft of a hatband, who did not want to pursue it as felony, so 'we all agreed to leave it' (ibid. 63). Hindle, 'County Government', 101–3, explains how Justices were motivated by fear of being dropped from the Commission. See also Wrightson,

magisterial conscientiousness was the unprecedented rise, in the decades 1570–1600, of levels of educational attainment among both clergy and Justices of the Peace.[32] In tandem with this, levels of popular participation in judicial proceedings, both secular and ecclesiastical, intensified. More people had recourse to binding their neighbours to keep the peace, as well as to other forms of legal remedy.[33] Levels of responsibility assumed by the inferior officers of both secular and ecclesiastical administration (constables and churchwardens) increased, and the secular and ecclesiastical officers worked together on various issues of common parish and local welfare.[34] Finally, the exponential growth both of civil litigation in property issues and of popular initiative in binding neighbours to keep the peace, bringing complaints to Justices, and initiating suits in the ecclesiastical courts are themselves manifestations of the social broadening and deepening of levels of involvement in processes of local governance.[35]

Having some awareness of the transformation in local governance and civic consciousness which took place in the latter decades of Elizabeth's reign helps us both to appreciate what was at stake in the first phase of the imitation of classical comedy by men like John Foxe, Nicholas Udall, George Gascoigne, and George Whetstone, and to understand how these imitations themselves were part of this ideological transformation. It also helps us begin to see why 1590s dramatic genres such as Shakespearean romantic comedy, chronicle history, and Jonsonian humours comedy

who gives an example of a constable attempting to distinguish degrees of culpability, though overridden by a clerk of peace ('Two Concepts of Order', 31–2). See also John P. Dawson, 'The Privy Council and the Private Law in the Tudor and Stuart Periods: I', *Michigan Law Review*, 48, no. 4 (1950), 393–428, at 400–3, who compares developments in England with those in France in the same period.

[32] The average percentage of JPs who attended universities increased, in six counties, from 5 to 61 per cent between 1562 and 1636. See Fletcher, *Reform in the Provinces*, 36–7. For a similar rise in the clergy's educational attainments, see Rosemary O'Day, *The English Clergy* (Leicester: Leicester University Press, 1979), 126–43.

[33] Hindle, *State and Social Change*, 94–115.

[34] See the example of William Lambarde's entry for 24 Dec. 1583, when he and another Justice of the Peace took order for the punishment of Abigail Sherwood, for bearing a bastard child, but 'as touching the reputed father . . . left the decision thereof to the ecclesiastical trial, for that she herself confessed she had been carnally known of many men' (cited in J. H. Gleason, *The Justices of the Peace in England 1558 to 1640* (Oxford: Clarendon Press, 1969), 12). See also Ronald A. Marchant, *The Church under the Law* (Cambridge: Cambridge University Press, 1969), 235, and Martin Ingram, *Church Courts, Sex and Marriage in England, 1570–1640* (Cambridge: Cambridge University Press, 1987), 29–31.

[35] See Christopher W. Brooks, *Pettyfoggers and Vipers of the Commonwealth* (Cambridge: Cambridge University Press, 1986); Hindle, *State and Social Change*, 94–115; Cynthia B. Herrup, *The Common Peace* (Cambridge: Cambridge University Press, 1987); Ingram, *Church Courts*, 28, 32–4.

involve so many comic scenarios of conscientiously litigious subjects bringing imagined malefactors and breachers of the peace to constables, Justices, and officers of the law: Mistress Quickly bringing an action of debt against Falstaff, Cob binding Bobadil to keep the peace, Don Armado having Costard arrested by Constable Dull, the Hostess planning to fetch the thirdborough to eject a drunken Christopher Sly who proposes to 'answer him by law' (Induction, 14), are only the first that spring to mind. And beginning to recognize how varied are the generic uses of such legal scenarios in the dramatic genres of the 1590s brings us to the development of another proposition broached in the last chapter. This is the proposition that, although Seneca was more overtly prominent as a dramatic model in the 1560s and 1570s, it was the comedies of Terence and Plautus (and because of, rather than despite, their admonitory and civic reworking in the 1570s) that were recognized as more useful for the purposes of achieving circumstantial verisimilitude and a convincing dramatic mimesis of time and place. T. S. Eliot indicated as much when, in an introduction to the *Tudor Translations* edition of the Inns of Court Senecan translations of the early 1560s and 1570s, he deplored the unmimetic quality of Senecan tragedy: 'In the plays of Seneca, the drama is all in the word, and the word has no further reality behind it', he complained. The dramatic situation lacked substantiality, characters had no inwardness, 'no private life'.[36] This, he intuited, had something to do with the lack, in Senecan drama, of an element found in abundance in English tragedy: the element of 'plot':

'Plot' in the sense in which we find plot in the *Spanish Tragedy* does not exist for Seneca at all. He took a story perfectly well known to everybody, and interested his auditors entirely by his embellishments of description and narrative, and by smartness and pungency of dialogue; suspense and surprise attached solely to verbal effects. *The Spanish Tragedy*, like the series of Hamlet plays, including Shakespeare's, has an affinity to our detective drama. The plot of Hieronymo to compass his revenge by the play allies with it a small but interesting class of drama which certainly owes nothing essential to Seneca: that which includes *Arden of Feversham* and *The Yorkshire Tragedy* ... In *Arden of Feversham*, the wife and her conspirators stab the husband to death upon the stage—the rest of the play being occupied by a primitive but effective police inquiry into the evidence.[37]

It was Eliot's brilliant hunch that what distinguished English tragic forms from the form of Senecan tragedy was an underlying plot structure not

---

[36] T. S. Eliot, 'Introduction', in *Seneca His Tenne Tragedies translated into English* [1581], ed. Thomas Newton (London: Constable and Co. Ltd., 1927), p. viii. [37] Ibid. p. xxxiii.

unlike the inferential double narrative of detective fiction, in which the scene of a crime is gradually reconstructed.[38] But, in seeming to find a native source for this plot structure in non-classical plays based on real-life crimes, he overlooked the fact that even these apparently empirical accounts of the effectiveness of the justice system owed something, in their 1590s dramatic form, to the previous decades' ideological transformation of the litigious plots of Roman New Comedy into plots of popular forensic detection. Precisely to the extent, moreover, that the deliberative rhetoric of Senecan tragedy seemed to have 'no further reality behind it', the forensic rhetoric typical of Roman New Comedy seemed to be able to invent a deceptively real—visible, tangible, credible—world. It was for this reason that early imitators were both drawn to, and troubled by, the comic uses of such forensic rhetoric, and it is to these comic uses in Plautus and Terence that we now turn.

Phormio: Forensic Disposition and Mimetic Power

As we have seen, plays of the 1590s and 1600s make the assumption that vivid circumstantial narrations—which are also the tools of forensic enquiry—can, like theatre, make people seem to witness what has never happened and see what isn't there. Why do these late sixteenth-century plays assume an association between judicial process and dramatic mimesis or dramatic illusion? The origins of this association lay in the comedies of Plautus and Terence, read and performed as these were throughout the sixteenth century at grammar schools and universities. As we have begun to see in the previous chapter, it is hard to exaggerate the prominence of legal scenarios and references to litigation and forms of proof in Roman New Comedy; indeed, historians of Roman law draw heavily on Plautus and Terence for evidence of legal practice in the mid-Republic period.[39]

---

[38] See, on the novel, Alexander Welsh, *Strong Representations* (Baltimore and London: John Hopkins University Press, 1992). On detective fiction, see Régis Messac, *Le 'Detective Novel' et l'influence de la pensée scientifique* (Paris: H. Champion, 1929); Ronald R. Thomas, *Detective Fiction and the Rise of Forensic Science* (Cambridge: Cambridge University Press, 1999); Lawrence Frank, *Victorian Detective Fiction and the Nature of Evidence* (New York: Palgrave Macmillan, 2003). On the way in which detective fiction is taken to be paradigmatic of novelistic form, see Laura Marcus, 'Detection and Literary Fiction', in *The Cambridge Companion to Crime Fiction*, ed. Martin Priestman (Cambridge: Cambridge University Press, 2003), 245–67.

[39] For example, J. M. Kelly, *Roman Litigation* (Oxford: Clarendon Press, 1966), 62–4; other examples are given in Adele C. Scafuro, *The Forensic Stage* (Cambridge: Cambridge University Press, 1997), 6.

In Plautus and Terence, characters *use* the law, or use the threat of legal action, as a means to achieve their desires. This accounts, as Adele Scafuro argues, for the theatricality, the role-play, of much of the communication between characters. Characters develop 'forensic strategies' in their inter-actions with one another, calling witnesses to ensure the legal force of their actions, acting as arbitrators, offering slaves for examination under torture, as legally admissible evidence to prove their confidence in their own case.

Typically, in the plays of Plautus and Terence, young men and wily slaves strategically engage legal procedure, or the threat of it, as part of a plot to extract a beautiful young woman from the clutches of a pimp, or slave-dealer, and/or to ward off the consequences of paternal displeasure with the amorous affair. Thus, for example, in Plautus's *Poenulus* ('The Carthaginian'), Agorastocles, lovesick for Adelphasium, plans to frame the pimp, Lycus, in whose possession Adelphasium languishes. He gathers witnesses, and dresses his bailiff, Collybiscus, as a Carthaginian stranger, supplying him with cash so that he can go to the pimp and request a good time. The idea is that once the disguised Collybiscus, being unrecognizable by the pimp as one of Agorastocles' men, is safely in the pimp's house, Agorastocles will be able to take the unsuspecting Lycus to court for the legal offence of 'concealing his man and his money', and so, 'when he comes to court the praetor will adjudge his entire establishment to you', as Agorastocles' slave, Milphio, triumphantly puts it.[40]

Threats of going to court, and preparations, such as gathering witnesses or requesting slaves to be examined under torture (the only way in which slaves' evidence was legally admissible), also frequently form a part of these adolescent plots. In Plautus's *Mostellaria*—which inspired Jonson's *Alchemist* and from which Shakespeare derived the names Tranio and Grumio for *The Taming of the Shrew*—a house is turned over by young men and slaves to drinking and debauchery while their father and master, Theopropides, is away on business. When Theopropides arrives back unexpectedly early, the clever Tranio obscures the truth from him by various inspired lies: first, he tells his master that the house has been barred up because it is haunted, as the site of a former murder; second, he tells him that, in his absence, his son has bought for him the next-door neighbour's house, which explains why he owes so much money.

---

[40] Plautus, *Poenulus*, 185–6: '*ubi in ius venerit,* | *addicet praetor familiam totam tibi*', in Plautus, *Works*, trans. Paul Nixon, 5 vols. (London: William Heinemann Ltd., 1932), iv. 18–19.

When Theopropides finds out, first, that the house's former owner denies there having been any murder, and then that the next-door neighbour denies having sold his house, preparations for evidence to decide these questions legally immediately ensue, with the wily Tranio taking the lead in suggesting that Theopropides should take his neighbour to court, in spite of the fact that he knows that the evidential disputes have arisen as a result of his lies.

Scafuro tends to write about these pervasive scenarios involving threats of legal action and anticipations of legal consequences as depicting 'self-help' remedies, which resolve themselves in out-of-court settlements instead of in judicial action. But if we see these plays not as empirical replicas of what people would really do, but as rhetorical fictions, we can see that the dramatic effect of what Scafuro calls 'out of court' settlement is to diffuse the rhetorical work of evidence gathering and proof through every aspect of dramatic action, so that it is, indeed, forensic rhetoric which shapes and drives the plays forward. Thus, for example, in Terence's *Adelphoe*, one young man, Aeschines, is thought to have betrayed his pregnant girlfriend, Pamphilia. Pamphilia's mother and her slave, Geta, ask Hegio, their kinsman, to act for them legally, and Hegio accordingly confronts Aeschines' father, Demea, charging his son with rape. Demea asks if he's quite sure of his facts, and Hegio replies: 'The girl's mother will vouch for it, and then there's the girl herself, and the sheer facts of the case. And besides, there's Geta here, who's honest and resourceful, as slaves go... take him up, tie him up, interrogate him.'[41] All these proofs are, as Scafuro points out, 'inartificial', or *atekhnoi*—eyewitness to the rape, the mother, the maid, and the pregnancy itself ('the sheer facts of the case'), as well as the testimony of the slave, willing to undergo torture.[42] But precisely because we understand these proofs in Hegio's speech to take effect merely as warnings to Demea of the strength of the family's legal position, their dramatic effect is not 'atechnic', but decidedly artful and rhetorical, simultaneously furthering Hegio's case and the action of the play.

The most important feature of the representation of litigiousness in Roman intrigue comedy for our purposes, however, is a quality which Scafuro does not discuss: the plays' reflexive identification of forensic strategy and mimetic power. The plays of Terence and Plautus triumphantly draw attention to the resemblance between their characters' sometimes downright fraudulent uses of law and the power of the comic plot itself to

[41] Terence, *Adelphoe* ('The Brothers'), 478–83, in *Terence*, ed. and trans. John Barsby (Cambridge, MA: Harvard University Press, 2001), ii. 305.
[42] Scafuro, *Forensic Stage*, 105–11.

persuade an audience to applaud its absurdly contrived romance for a probable fiction. Dramatic mimesis is thus, in Roman intrigue comedy, explicitly associated with forensic expediency. Take, for example, Terence's play called *Phormio*. This brilliant, hilarious comedy opens with one slave, Geta, asking another, Davus, to return some money he lent him. Geta then explains the reason why he needs to call in his debts: his master's son, Antipho, is getting married. It turns out to be a long story, which Geta narrates to Davus in detail. The master, Demipho, has been away on business, and Antipho's brother, Phaedria, has fallen in love with a singing-wench, which meant that Antipho and Geta had to hang about the dancing school where Phaedria met his girlfriend, with nothing much to do. One day, when they were waiting at a barber's shop near the dancing school, they heard tell of a beautiful girl lamenting alone over her dead mother, with no one, neither kinsman, lover, nor friend, no one but her frail old nurse to assist her with the burial. Antipho and Geta rush out to see this maiden, who is indeed very beautiful, and the next day Antipho asks the nurse if he may 'take his pleasure on her'.[43] But the old woman denies him, since the girl is of good parents and a citizen of Athens. Davus interrupts the story at this point: would Antipho's father have given him leave to marry the girl, if he had been home? Geta's reply is heavy with sarcasm: would he give him leave to marry a penniless brat? What, Davus asks, did you do, then? So Geta comes to the crux of the story, and introduces the parasite, Phormio (I continue in the words of Richard Bernard's school text translation first published in 1598):

What would come of it? there is a certaine Parasite called *Phormio*, an audacious fellow, I would his necke were broken...There is a law, saith he, that damsels left fatherlesse and motherlesse, should marry to the next of kin, and this selfe same law doth command those of the next kindred to marry them: now therefore I will say you are her kinsman, and will enter an action against you in her behalfe and I will make as though I were a friend of the maid's father: and we will come before the Judge and I will devise all these things to tel who was her father, who her mother, and how she comes to be your kinswoman: which shall bee good and profitable for me. For I shall surely overcome, when you shall refell none of

[43] I quote from the translation for schoolboys made by Richard Bernard, which was first published in 1598. See Richard Bernard, *Terence in English* (London: John Legatt, 1629), 379. Further references to this edition will be given by page number in the text. Bernard's text alternates Latin and English versions of a scene, and prefaces each Latin and English scene with an 'argument'. Bradin Cormack and Carla Mazzio comment on the form of Bernard's English Terence in *Book Use, Book Theory, 1500–1700* (Chicago: University of Chicago Library, 2005), 55.

these. Your father, it may be, will be present, processes wil be out against me, care I anything for that? we shall surely carry away the wench. (pp. 373–4)

What then?, Davus asks, and Geta concludes: 'The young man was persuaded to it; it is done, the matter is come to the issue, and we are cast, and he hath married her.' 'O, *Geta*', replies Davus, sympathetically, 'what will become of thee?'

I have dwelt on the first scene of Terence's *Phormio* at such storytelling length to emphasize the fact that the action so far has consisted of one long circumstantial *narratio*: there has been no staged activity for the whole of Act 1, Scene 2, only narration. Awareness of this fact helps us understand how Tudor readers of Terence would appreciate the resemblance between Geta's opening *narratio*, which establishes for us the mimetic reality of the past leading up to the moment of the play, and Phormio's courtroom perjury. For Phormio's plan depends on being able to *narrate* a convincing story of the girl's and Antipho's consanguinity: to 'devise', as he says, 'how she comes to be your kinswoman'. The legal situation presented here—which was just as unfamiliar to Terence's own Roman audience as it was to a sixteenth-century readership—derives from the Greek laws concerning *epikleroi*, or heiresses without fathers and brothers (Terence's play is based on one by the Greek Apollodorus). According to the Greek law that protected poor *epikleroi*, nearest male kin would be obliged to marry them or to provide them with dowries.[44] So Phormio's ingenious solution to Antipho's problem of desiring an orphaned girl, who is nevertheless apparently a citizen (though we don't know, as yet, who her father is), is to bring an action on the basis of epiklerate laws, prosecuting Antipho for failing to protect his kinswoman, and obliging him to marry her. It is worth noting, too, that Bernard uses common law equivalents for a legal language in Terence's text which was based on Greek practice: for '*Ego . . . tibi scribam dicam*', a phrase based on Greek practice, which Bernard did not expect his students to know, he gives 'I will enter an action against you'; he translates '*refellere*' as 'refell', a commonly used term in the sixteenth and seventeenth centuries meaning 'to refute' or 'to prove false or untenable'. For '*ventumst*', 'it was come', Bernard gives, 'the matter is come to the issue', locating Phormio's action precisely in common law practice.[45]

---

[44] See Scafuro, *Forensic Stage*, 69–71, 282–3. See Barsby's translation, *Phormio*, 125–7, in *Terence*, ii. 23–5 and 25 n. Barsby notes: 'This is an Athenian law, not Roman, and Terence has no doubt spelled it out for the sake of the Roman audience.'

[45] The phrase '*dicam scribere*' meant 'to write out an action', 'to sue', but as there was no procedure for initiating a suit by a written indictment in Roman law, the phrase seems

As the plot unfolds, Phormio's audacity in basing this legal action on an invented story of kinship is thrown into ever more desperate crisis, requiring all concerned—Geta, Antipho's brother Phaedria, and Phormio himself—to improvise increasingly ingenious frauds and forensic strategies to prevent the lie from being discovered. In the first phase of the crisis, Demipho, Antipho's father, returns from his travels. Antipho weakly runs away, leaving Geta and Phaedria to orchestrate a forensic defence of Antipho's failure to defend himself in court. Phaedria takes the task upon himself creditably, pleading that one of Phanium's kin may have plotted to 'intrap' Antipho with this legal action, in which case he is not to blame (p. 383). Demipho then reprimands Geta, but Geta reminds him that slaves are not permitted by law to plead, so he can't help Antipho in court. 'The lawes', he says, 'permit not any man servant to plead (*causam orare*) nor to bear witnesse' (p. 383). Eventually, Demipho ferrets out that the legal action was brought at Phormio's initiative, and demands to meet him—but not before furnishing himself with some friends (*advocati* in Latin, and in Bernard's translation, 'friends' and 'advocates') to 'be present at the handling of this matter', that is, to be his legal *witnesses*, should Phormio try anything on (pp. 365, 383).

The first scenes of Act 2, in which 'Phormio *is here brought on to defend the fact*' are a *tour de force* of comic improvisation and forensic rhetoric (p. 385). Phormio, meeting Demipho, immediately goes on the offensive, and asks whether Demipho is actually daring to deny that the young woman (whose name is Phanium) is kin to him? Does he actually deny, Phormio asks, on a note of rising incredulity, knowing her father, one of his oldest friends? Ah, says Phormio, thus it goes, 'this old man during that time did tell me how that this *Demipho* made small reckoning of him, beeing his neere kinsman: but what a man did hee thus lightly account of? The honestest man that I euer knew in my life' (p. 389). Geta brilliantly plays along with Phormio, pretending to defend Demipho (his master) from Phormio's insults and attacks. But Demipho is not fooled: if Phormio is such an old friend of this neglected kinsman of his, he asks, perhaps he can tell Demipho his name? For a terrible moment, Phormio forgets the name of Phanium's father (though he has mentioned it a few moments before). Phormio prevaricates, playing for time, but Demipho gets angry: 'Thou makest me mad, tell me his name.'

to be a Greek borrowing, based on *diken graphesthai*, 'to have a private suit written down'. See Scafuro, *Forensic Stage*, 95–6. Bernard offers his students a marginal note to help with the phrase, explaining that '*dicam*' is a noun; see *Terence in English*, 371. For 'refell', see *OED* n. 1.

P[HORMIO]. His name, forsooth, that I will...Alas, I am undone. In good sooth I have quite forgot it.

D[EMIPHO]. Ha, what saist thou?

P. *Geta*, call me to minde, if thou remembrest, that which I told thee long since: and nay, I will not tell you: as though you knew it not, you doe it to try me.

D. Do I make a triall of thee?

G[ETA]. *Stilpho.*

P. And verily what need I tell his name? He is called *Stilpho*.

(p. 389)

The comic routine plays on a familiar gag: the liar needs a good memory, and nothing is funnier than the fraudster who momentarily forgets a detail of his story, and has to be reminded of it by his sidekick in a loud stage-whisper. But Phormio's momentary lapse draws our attention to the reflexive contribution of his kinship fraud to the mimetic power of the plot as a whole. For at this point, obviously, Phormio, like the audience, is under the impression that Phanium is not really related to Antipho, and that honest Stilpho is a person whose kinship with Demipho has been invented, from start to finish, by Phormio and Geta so as to enable Antipho to achieve his desires. But as the plot unfolds, we find out, gradually and indirectly, the reason why Demipho's brother, the father of Phaedria, who is called Chremes, has always spent so much time away—on business, as he claims—on the isle of Lemnos. His wife, Naustrata, is puzzled and annoyed that his long sojourns in Lemnos don't seem to increase their revenues from the farms and rents that her father left them both there. What can he be up to? In Act 5, Scene 1, Phanium's nursemaid catches up with Chremes and reveals all: she calls him 'Stilpho'. It turns out that Chremes is a bigamist, and that his second marriage, in Lemnos, was to Phanium's mother, who came to Athens to seek him, where she died (we connect this with Geta's narrative at the beginning). So Phormio's lie was not a lie after all: Demipho is Stilpho's brother, and Antipho would have been, in fact, obliged to marry his cousin Phanium according to epiklerate law.

Phormio thus unabashedly celebrates what Terence Cave has called the scandal of Aristotelian poetics: the creaking contrivances by which art brings about its 'recognitions' of legitimate kinship ties and identifications. Aristotle, Cave explains, writes as if dramatic narratives should ideally make moments of recognition the result of a logical sequence of cause and effect, uncontaminated by the fallibility and contingency of the hermeneutic process (the tracking and interpreting of material signs and traces on which all reading depends). Inferential detective work, or what Cave, following Ginzburg, calls 'cynegetic' processes of reasoning, enters Aristotle's scheme as the possibility of false inference (paralogism) that ushers in fears of 'catastrophic transgressions: incest, parricide, expropriation, fraud, the passing off of an illegitimate child as a true heir'.[46] Whereas such fears may be played out in tragedy (*Oedipus* is the obvious example), comedy thrives on contrivance, and on flaunting the indistinguishability of legitimate proofs (of marriage, kinship, paternity) from cleverly contrived tall stories. In *Phormio*, we cannot help but notice that the plausibly indirect means by which Terence leads to us to 'realize' that Chremes and Stilpho are the same person is no different from the plausible fashion according to which Phormio promises to 'devise all these things to tel who was [Phanium's] father, who her mother, and how she comes to be your kinswoman' when he speaks 'before the Judge' (pp. 373–4). If, for Cave's 'cynegetic paradigm' we substitute the term used in the English translation of Carlo Ginzburg, the 'evidential paradigm', the intimate, if disavowed, relationship between Aristotelian poetics and detective work becomes clearer. And, as Cave puts it, it is in plays like *Phormio* that 'the parallel between the characters' plot (*fallacia*) and the author's plot (*fabula*) is repeatedly made explicit', so that the relationship of poetic proof to Aristotelian paralogism or false inference 'is here performed as a comic principle'.[47]

Anxieties of Evidence: John Foxe's *Phormio* (1544)

The plays of Plautus and Terence, then, shamelessly draw attention to the ease with which the most cherished proofs of legitimacy, kinship, and identity might be falsified, and they link such falsification to the mimetic success of the dramatic narrative itself. But in England they did not, in the sixteenth century, draw these links to the attention of those who were not in the process of learning Latin (Bernard's 1598 translation was aimed at Latin learners). Both the relative numerousness of editions of Terence and Plautus compared with those of Seneca, and the relative tardiness of Terentian and Plautine translations compared with Senecan translations, suggest that there was something deliberate in the confining

---

[46] Cave, *Recognitions*, 252.

[47] Ibid. 256–7. Cave cites Ginzburg's essay in Italian as 'Spie. Radici di un paradigma indiziario', which is translated by John and Anne Tedeschi as 'Clues: Roots of an Evidential Paradigm', in Carlo Ginzburg, *Myths, Emblems, Clues* (London: Hutchinson Radius, 1990), 96–125.

of the forensically derived mimetic power of Roman comedy to morally regulated educational contexts. But the earliest Latin imitation of Roman New Comedy by an English author shows unmistakably that its mimetic power was, indeed, identified with its forensic rhetoric.

In 1544, the young John Foxe, chafing at the prospect of the celibate life of an Oxford don, decided to advertise himself for a tutoring job by writing a play which demonstrated, as fully as anyone could wish, the relationship between comic intrigue and judicial proofs. This comedy, *Titus et Gesippus*, features the two exemplary friends made famous by Boccaccio's story, but refashions their story as part Roman New Comedy intrigue, part Roman civil law investigation, featuring (quite unlike vernacular interludes of the same period) real evidential uncertainty, and a careful and explicit weighing of different arguments of proof.

In Boccaccio's story of Titus and Gisippus, Titus falls in love with the bride promised to Gisippus, and Gisippus, as proof of his friendship, agrees that Titus and he should change places at the wedding, so that Titus can, clandestinely, become the husband of Gisippus's promised bride.[48] Foxe, however, clearly a little uncomfortable with the questionable morality of this device, invents a character—'Phormio', servant to Titus—whose role is simply to think up this scheme, and so deflect our discomfort with its dubious legitimacy away from either of the young gentlemen, Titus and Gesippus. Foxe stresses the relationship between a knowledge of the artificial proofs of classical forensic rhetoric and the capacity to dazzle and deceive the eyes. When Titus explains to Phormio that he is dying of love for his best friend's bride, the latter replies, '*Ego consulam locos meos dialecticos*' ('I will consult my dialectical "places"'), a phrase which Foxe's modern translator glosses as 'the grounds of proof in argument'. Later, he soliloquizes on the difficulty of deceiving bride and bridegroom's kin during the wedding ceremony: 'Everyone's eyes must be blinded', (*Populo universi oblinendi oculi*) he says.[49] But when he consults his places of dialectic, he hits, at once, on 'the place of similitude'

[48] See the eighth novella on the tenth day of Giovanni Boccaccio, *Decameron*, ed. Antonio Enzio Quaglio (Milan: Garzanti, 1974), ii. 887–905, and Sir Thomas Elyot's English version in *The Boke named the Gouernour*, introduced by Foster Watson (London: J. M. Dent, 1907), 166–83. In Boccaccio, Gisippus performs the public ceremony, and Titus is substituted for the bedroom ritual, but in Elyot's version Titus goes through both public ceremony and bedroom ritual. For this and other reasons, John Hazel Smith, translator and editor of *Titus et Gesippus* in *Two Latin Comedies by John Foxe the Martyologist* (Ithaca, NY: Cornell University Press, 1978), 15–17, thinks Foxe likely to have known the story only through Elyot, and not Boccaccio.
[49] Foxe, *Titus et Gesippus*, in *Two Latin Comedies*, 1. 1. 58; 1. 4. 20. Further references to act, scene, and line in this edition are given in the text.

(1. 4. 29). The dramatic image is both of an orator inventing an argument and of a schemer hatching a scheme—exploiting the idea of the friends' similitude to deceive the wedding guests is, of course, a 'crime' (*facinus*), as Phormio acknowledges (1. 4. 10); but, in explaining his device to Gesippus, his recollection of his own literary antecedents reminds us that such 'crimes' are the basis of comic plots: 'Menaechmus is no more like Menaechmus than you two are like each other in every way...Titus will go into Sempronia in your clothing, and I will be your Phormio' (1. 9. 50–5).

If Foxe's invention of Phormio-as-plotter signals awareness of the shared space between forensic rhetoric and a villainous capacity to deceive the eyes, another sign of such awareness comes when Gesippus, thinking how to justify the fact to his father, considers to himself how important in such matters is the forensic 'order of telling' (*re explicandi ratio*). For, as Gesippus says, 'In every circumstance, the way something is explained is very important, because what generally matters is not what's committed, but in what order it is transmitted to a judge' (2. 5. 11–14). Gesippus, then, already positions himself both as criminal and advocate, identifying the common ground between them as their common perception that what matters is not the way things are *done* (*gestae*), but how they are explained (*digestae*) to the judge (2. 5. 12).

As with the last two acts of *The Comedy of Errors*, so it is the last two acts of Foxe's comedy that make most explicit the perceived association between the recognitions of Roman New Comedy and the strategies of forensic rhetoric. In Foxe's play these are organized around the trial of Gesippus for murder. This extraordinary situation comes about, as it does in Boccaccio's story, as a result of Gesippus's family's anger with him for colluding in the scheme to have Titus act as his substitute on his wedding day. Titus has already left with his bride for Rome, so Gesippus is left alone to try and justify the scheme, and, failing to placate his father, he is thrown, penniless, out of the house. He wanders to Rome, hoping for help from Titus. However, Titus (now a consul) does not recognize Gesippus, merely seeing him as an example of the problem of urban vagrancy for which, as local magistrate, he now feels responsible. Gesippus, in despair, contemplates suicide, but exhaustion overtakes him, and while he lies asleep in the road, he is spotted by a cutthroat called Martius, who is in flight from having attacked a farmer and left him for dead. The murderer, taking Gesippus's little knife, plants on him his own bloody dagger, to 'fasten all the suspicion on him' (3. 2. 13–14). The broad outline of this action—Gesippus's framing for murder and going on trial before Titus, who recognizes his friend, and decides, out of friendship, to confess to the murder himself, provoking an awestruck confession from the real murderer—comes from Boccaccio's and Sir Thomas Elyot's prose versions of the story. What Foxe does with these elements, however, is to emphasize, at every possible juncture, the slippery, *pro-et-contra* deceptiveness of the merely probable arguments for and against Gesippus's guilt. So, first, he creates a scene (Act 4, Scene 1) in which it is the real murderer, Martius, who raises the hue and cry, urging citizens to help him track the killer with hunting dogs. The search leads directly to Gesippus and the bloody weapon. Martius then takes the lead in accusing Gesippus, and bringing the prisoner bound into the presence of the consuls, Fulvius and Titus. When Titus asks the citizens to produce their testimony, Martius answers first, cleverly manipulating the part taken by other citizens in the search for and apprehension of Gesippus. Had he alone discovered Gesippus with the knife, he would not have brought an action of murder, he claims, but with so many witnesses, the crime is 'manifest' (4. 3. 8 and 4. 3. 41). 'Manifest' is a technical term in Roman canon or civil law for proof meeting a standard which, though not as conclusive as the full complement of two eyewitnesses and/or a confession, might nevertheless secure conviction where such full proofs were lacking.[50] Though the consuls question the other witnesses, establishing that nobody saw him actually attack the farmer, they get nowhere with questioning Gesippus, who speaks ambiguously and uncertainly. Foxe then introduces the romance motif of Titus's beginning to recognize Gesippus as Fulvius interrogates him according to the rhetorical topics or places of *patria* and *cognatus*, native land and kin (4. 3. 33–7). Given Gesippus's ambiguous answers, Titus 'suspects', but does not know what to make of the whole thing (4. 3. 38–9). He begs Fulvius for a reprieve, and then, privately, sends Phormio to see if he can recognize his old friend in gaol; once again, as Terence Cave has reminded us, 'recognition' is not a simple process of seeing, but a complex forensic process of gathering and corroborating information.[51] Titus asks Phormio to find out 'his name, his parents, the reason he ran away' (4. 5. 43). Though both of them soon realize that the accused is indeed Gesippus, no new proof is forthcoming to overturn the conviction of his guilt.[52] Titus embarks on a desperate strategy: he will claim to

---

[50] Shapiro, *'Beyond Reasonable Doubt'*, 120.   [51] Cave, *Recognitions*, 10–24.
[52] John Hazel Smith, assuming that the last scenes turn entirely on the question of Gesippus's identity, does not seem to realize that even once Gesippus has been 'recognized', he is still under presumption of guilt for the murder.

be the murderer. Fulvius, perplexed, refers the question to the people of Rome. *'Populus Romanus'*, a Roman citizen, answers that they do not know, except that they found this thief sleeping with a bloody dagger (5. 2. 46). All at once, Titus hits on ('finds', or 'invents') a brilliant strategy for undermining this evidence of Gesippus's guilt:

Well, Fulvius, from the fact that they surprised him in his sleep, nothing is more certain than that he is not guilty. A wakeful conscience will not readily let those who are guilty of crime fall asleep, certainly not on a road, much less a public way. Then again, if this was his weapon, where is its sheath? Why didn't he throw the dagger away? And why didn't he clean it? (5. 2. 47–54)

Titus's ingenious argument relies on the commonplace association of a guilty conscience with lack of sleep (we are most familiar with its deployment throughout *Macbeth*, though Foxe might have known it from Cicero).[53] He then develops the commonplace through what Quintilian calls a comparative argument, from lesser to greater: if it is known that guilty people cannot rest in bed, how could this man sleep in the road (*in via*), let alone on a public road (*via publica*)?[54] Titus, then, has found his argument, just as Phormio found his, by mentally consulting his 'dialectical places', where he would have found the 'place of comparison', closely related to Phormio's 'similitude'. But not only Titus: Foxe himself, it turns out, must have plotted this aspect of his play around Titus's invention of this probable argument, for where Boccaccio has Gisippus falling asleep in a cave, and Sir Thomas Elyot (whom Foxe probably used) has him taking refuge in a barn, only Foxe's Gesippus falls asleep in the middle of a public highway.[55] The change was obviously motivated by the need to have Titus invent a probable counter-reading of the witness testimony that made the crime otherwise seem so 'manifest'. In a literal sense, then, the action of the play is driven by the need to have

---

[53] For example, Cicero in his defence of Roscius of Amerinus from the charge of parricide, tells the story of the sons of Titus Cloelius of Tarracina, who were found sleeping in the same room where their father was discovered in bed with his throat cut. They were acquitted on the argument that 'people who have committed a horrible crime like that are incapable of sleeping in peace'. Cicero then went on paint a vivid picture of the torments of conscience. See Cicero, *Pro Roscio Amerino*, ed. and trans. John Henry Freese (Cambridge, MA: Harvard University Press, 1934), xxiii. 64–5, pp. 176–9. The passage was well known. Lambinus's edition of Plautus glosses Tranio's remark, 'nothing is worse than a guilty conscience', in *Mostelleria* ('The Haunted House'), 543, with this reference to Cicero, *Pro Roscio Amerino*. See *M. Accius Plautus ex fide, atque auctoritate complurium librorum manuscriptorum opera Dionys. Lambini . . . emendatus* (Lutetiae: apud Ioannem Macaeum, 1577), i. 552.   [54] Quintilian, *Inst.* 5. 10. 87.
[55] See Giovanni Boccaccio, *The Decameron*, trans. G. H. McWilliam (Harmondsworth: Penguin, 1972), 790; Elyot, *Gouernour*, 180–3.

the characters—especially Phormio, Martius, and Titus—engage in the invention of suspicion. And finally, too, Gesippus's innocence is proved by another one of Titus's arguments (the 'public way' argument being mainly useful in opening up the question of what the testimony of the eyewitnesses actually proves). Fulvius is for a while embarrassed by the riches of two confessions, as Titus and Gesippus compete for the final sacrifice of friendship, each claiming to have been the murderer; his mind is 'caught in uncertainty' (5. 2. 57). He decides to refer the matter to the Senate, but it turns out to be otherwise engaged, investing in Fulvius an arbitrary power to investigate and act in the case. Luckily, Martius has been stricken by remorse of conscience, and is ready to absolve both Titus and Gesippus, but Fulvius is not satisfied (though legally, he might be) by Martius's confession. Martius, having confessed, says that he substituted his dagger for Gesippus's little knife. Fulvius asks to see if the knife in Martius's possession will fit into Gesippus's sheath; it does (5. 5. 25–30). While this 'visible' (*spectabile*) proof seems an old contrivance, like the necklaces and rings of romance, it is clear from Foxe's careful portrayal of the reasoning process that led to its final deployment (in Titus's sceptical 'if this was his weapon, where is its sheath?') that it, too, is a product of a rhetorical art—indeed, of the art of inventing suspicion.

Legal Enquiry in Mid-Tudor Comedy: *Jacke Jugeler, Gammer Gurton's Needle, Roister Doister*, and *Nice Wanton*

Foxe's *Titus et Gesippus* remained in Latin and in manuscript until 1978. John Hazel Smith speculates on the possibility of a performance at Magdalen in 1545, but this would, of course, have been in Latin, as were performances of Plautus and Terence in schools and at the universities during the sixteenth century.[56] There were not many signs prior to the performance of Gascoigne's *Supposes* in 1566 of a burgeoning vernacular drama based on the forensic rhetoric of Roman New Comedy. Such explicit vernacular imitations of Roman New Comedy as have survived, however, clearly conceive of the genre's mimetic or illusion-producing power as very closely bound up with evidential procedures.

Mimetic failures are as instructive in this regard as successes. The anonymous *Jacke Jugeler* (c.1562), for all its charming evocation of bourgeois

[56] See Alan H. Nelson, *Early Cambridge Theatres* (Cambridge: Cambridge University Press, 1994).

social life in mid-Tudor London, does not (perhaps deliberately) produce the illusory mimesis of a self-contained story that we associate with Roman New Comedy. The play takes its 'ground' from Plautus's *Amphitryon*, from the opening scene in which Mercury assumes the form of Sosia, Amphitryon's slave, in order to bar Sosia from the house in which Jupiter, in the form of Amphitryon, is making love to the latter's wife (this is also, of course, the basis for Act 3, Scene 1, of *The Comedy of Errors*).[57] Jacke Jugeler, the Mercury figure (called 'the Vyce' in the cast list) manages, as in Plautus's play, to convince Jenkin Careaway, the Sosia figure, that he, Jugeler, is really Careaway because he can give a perfect, blow-by-blow account of the circumstances of the latter's movements and activities since five o'clock that day (in *Amphitryon*, the equivalent proof is offered when Mercury gives Sosia a perfect account of Amphitryon's prowess at the battle against the Teleboians, even down to the detail of the spoils taken[58]). In *Jacke Jugeler*, however, what the 'cursed' and 'ungracious' lad Jenkin has been doing since 5 o'clock is itself a catalogue of the idle misdemeanours which have prevented him from going to fetch his mistress to supper as he was entrusted to do (ll. 114–15). It at first seems a fault in the English play that it gives no thought to the question of how Jack Jugeler—whoever he is—manages to know so much about Jenkin, or to look, dress, and sound exactly like him. The fault, however, may be a part of a different design, involving something like the spiritual and penitential way of thinking about evidence explored in Chapter 1. For Jacke Jugeler informs us that Jenkin, having been sent on an errand to fetch Mistress Boungrace (the name means a veil to keep the sun off the face, suggesting the finicky fastidiousness of women of her class), has not only dallied in playing dice and picked a purse to finance the game, but has also, in an encounter with costard wife, snatched her apples and put them up his sleeve (ll. 132–69). When we meet Jenkin, he plans, rather ingeniously, to employ these very apples as part of a cleverly contrived excuse for his tardiness to Mistress Boungrace: woven into a convincing piece of false witness involving her husband's multiple infidelities, the apples are to be presented to Mistress Boungrace as compensatory gift from her own gentleman lover, whom Jenkin is supposed to have met by the way (ll. 250–305). Jenkin, however, is quite discomfited by his encounter with Jacke Jugeler,

---

[57] See *Jacke Jugeler*, l. 64, in *Four Tudor Comedies*, ed. William Tydeman (Harmondsworth: Penguin, 1984). Further references to *Jacke Jugeler* in this edition will be referred to by line number in the text.

[58] See Plautus, *Amphitryon*, ll. 401–22, in *Works*, trans. Paul Nixon (London: William Heinemann, 1928), 43–5. In the sixteenth century, Plautus's *Amphitryon* included further scenes of evidence evaluation which modern editions omit.

who not only tells him in perfect circumstantial detail the whole story of his dicing and thieving and apple filching on the way to fetch Mistress Boungrace, but, in conclusion, produces the very apples in question, as an inartificial proof, from up his own sleeve (ll. 528–35).[59] Disoriented and in doubt as to his own history and identity, Jenkin Careaway then miserably fails to remember his excuse to Mistress Boungrace, and concludes by informing against himself in order to prove to his master that his double, his other self, really exists. Master Boungrace, understandably, thinks the idiot Careaway, babbling about having been beaten up by someone looking exactly like him, must have been confused by his own shadow. Careaway, however, incautiously replies that the double cannot have been his shadow, because it 'tolde me all that I have done | Syth five of the cloke this afternone' (ll. 895–6). In response to his master's enquiry as to more information about the activities in question, Careaway finds himself openly *confessing* to the playing and filching of apples, all of which he had devised an elaborate and convincing story to hide (ll. 899–903); as Tydeman notes, 'his act of self-betrayal under pressure is a moment of true comic revelation'.[60] Jacke Jugeler, then, as his name (meaning 'conjurer') might suggest, has functioned a little like Tutivillus in fifteenth-century literature and drama. Instead of helping the New Comedy hero to contrive a convincing proof with which to face the *senex*, this devilish, eavesdropping and evidence-gathering Vice figure has prompted a 'Mankind' or 'Youth' figure to confess openly to his misdeeds (although to put it this way perhaps exaggerates the moral element of the play, which seems on the whole more sympathetic to the Careaways of this world than the Boungraces).

The forensic affinities of *Gammer Gurton's Needle* (*c*.1562–3) are much more obvious. This brilliant Cambridge play, as Joel Altman says, 'orchestrates the search into a series of confrontations' that begins 'with a conjuration and ends with a formal legal inquiry'.[61] William Tydeman speaks of the play's 'tough Terentian structure'.[62] For the author of *Gammer's Gurton's Needle*, it seems clear, legal enquiry and tough Terentian structure went hand in hand. When Gammer Gurton loses her needle, Hodge, whose breeches need mending if he is ever to get anywhere with courting Kristian Clack, asks Diccon the Bedlam to help find it. Diccon, for his own devious reasons, tells Gammer that he 'durst be sworne' that

---

[59] As William Tydeman notes, it is never explained how Jugeler came by clothes identical to Jenkin's, or how he provides himself with these apples (*Four Tudor Comedies*, 374, 376).
[60] Ibid., 20.   [61] Altman, *Tudor Play of Mind*, 153.
[62] *Four Tudor Plays*, 27 and 211–12.

he has seen the local alewife, Dame Chat, stoop to pick up Gammer's needle, while to Dame Chat he tells an entirely different tale of Gammer's malice and her maid's slander (2. 4. 524). After being worsted in a violent confrontation with Dame Chat in Act 3, Scene 3, Gammer decides to call in the curate, Dr Rat, for arbitration. Dr Rat's weary entrance, complaining of having to 'trudge about the towne... | Here to a drab, there to a theefe' about matters 'not worth a halfpenyworth of ale', contrasts with the conscientious zeal of later magisterial figures, and, indeed, his methods of evidence evaluation hilariously backfire.[63] Hodge attempts to explain all to the learned doctor, but his account completely fails to mention how it is that he and Gammer come by their certainty of Dame Chat's guilt. Dr Rat astutely enquires, and Diccon is brought in as eyewitness and asked by the Doctor to swear to having seen Dame Chat with the needle in question, but Diccon, ingeniously protesting that witnesses need the protection of anonymity (a valid argument in ecclesiastical law), suggests instead that Dr Rat attempt to catch Dame Chat red-handed by climbing in at a back entrance of her house: there, he says impressively, 'ye shall take the drab with the neele in her handes' (4. 2. 879). Meanwhile, however, Diccon warns Dame Chat of an impending burglary by Hodge, and Dr Rat, inevitably, ends up with a broken head for his pains. The real 'formal legal inquiry' then begins, in Act 5. Dr Rat brings his complaint to a bailiff, who, as was common in the early sixteenth century, presides over a pre-trial examination.[64] The bailiff finds Dr Rat, on his own evidence, to be more in fault: 'The women they did nothing, as your words make probation | But stoutly withstood your forcible invasion', he comments (5. 1. 919). However, Dame Chat is called, and the stage direction has Rat *showing his broken head* as evidence. Chat rightly retorts: 'Bicause thy head is broken, was it I that it broke?', and charges Hodge with breaking and entering her house (5. 2. 970). Hodge reluctantly appears, and the bailiff, inspecting his head, finds it whole and concludes that he did not break into Chat's house; gradually this officer of the law establishes the lack of fit between Gammer's charges against Chat and Chat's complaints against Gammer

---

[63] See *Gammer Gurton's Needle*, 4. 1. 724–5, in *Four Tudor Comedies*, ed. Tydeman. Further references to act, scene, and line number of the play in this edition are given in the text.

[64] See J. G. Bellamy, *The Criminal Trial in Later Medieval England* (Stroud: Sutton Publishing, 1988), 119. The date of the play is uncertain, but based on its reference to the 'King' at l. 1181 and evidence for its authorship by William Stevenson, fellow of Christ's College, Cambridge, 1551–4 and 1559–61, Tydeman suggests a composition date in the early 1550s (*Four Tudor Comedies*, 212).

('Thus in your talke and action, from that you do intend | She is whole five mile wide', he comments (5. 2. 1102–3)). Diccon's mischief making is thus finally discovered. Dr Rat charges the bailiff to arrest the Bedlam Diccon, but the bailiff protests against 'a spiritual man...so extreame', and all ends merrily (5. 2. 1187).

Gammer Gurton's Needle light-heartedly explores the dangers of too easily crediting witnesses who do not want their identities known, a question which, as we saw in Chapter 1, was passionately debated between Thomas More and Christopher St German as a conflict of principle and procedure in canon and common law. The play is even more buoyantly confident than Foxe's *Titus et Gesippus* in aligning the forensic use of artificial proofs that defines Terentian plot structure with a just evaluation of the uncertainties of the evidence. Nicholas Udall's *Ralph Roister Doister* (*c*.1552), on the other hand, indicates the dangerous suggestiveness of artificial proof, and eschews any identification of its comic ending with forensic enquiry. In Udall's play the widow Custance, promised to merchant Gavin Goodlucke, but wooed with letters and tokens by the absurd braggart Doister and his mischievous companion, Merrygreek, realizes to her cost that her stalwart attempts to resist her wooers will not prevent their courtship counting as evidence against her. When Goodlucke's trusted factor, Sim Suresby, braves a tempest to return to his master's betrothed, and check that all is well with their pre-contract, Custance is appalled to find herself being accosted yet again by Doister and Merrygreek, the latter of whom refers, with deliberately compromising effect, to a love-letter, and a 'ryng and tokens' sent to her by Doister. Suresby, standing by, changes perceptibly in his demeanour towards her, refusing to drink with her ere he departs, and angrily rebutting her suggestion that he should carry 'a token' to his master from her: 'No tokens this time, gramercies! God be with you!', he says, curtly taking his leave.[65] Subha Mukherji has discussed the evidential status of rings and other 'tokens' as legal proofs of matrimony in canon law and in the tragicomic drama of the early seventeenth century—in *Cymbeline*, for example, where Iachimo's proofs against Imogen involve 'the combined operation of tokens and narrative *enargeia*'. But a 'token' was also a general English word for the rhetorically manipulable 'signs', 'indications', and 'traces' (*signum, indicium, vestigium*) from which, according to Quintilian's discussion of artificial proof, inferences could be drawn and forensic arguments made. Sir Thomas Smith

---

[65] Nicholas Udall, *Ralph Roister Doister*, in *Four Tudor Comedies*, ed. William Tydeman, 4. 3. 1440. Further references to act, scene, and line number of the play in this edition will be given in the text.

referred to '*indices* or tokens, which we call in our language evidence against the malefactor', and in *Gammer Gurton's Needle*, Dame Chat blesses the 'good token' or dispute-settling evidence of Hodge's head.[66] In *Roister Doister* the epistemological indeterminacy of 'tokens' as *indicia* or signs is treated with less equanimity than in *Gammer Gurton*. Whereas the bailiff in *Gammer Gurton* was able to infer from the indicative lack of fit between Chat's charge against Gammer's 'lying tongue' and Gammer's against Chat's 'fals faith and troth' that neither in fact broke troth or swore falsely, Suresby falsely infers from uncertain signs or tokens in *Roister Doister* that Custance's faith is suspect: she *may* have broken her troth. 'Sym Suresby', Custance rightly worries, 'shall suspect in me some point of naughtinesse' as a result of Doister's attentions (4. 3. 1392). Suresby indeed reports the evidence back to Goodlucke, but advises him to 'examine the matter' before condemning his fiancée (5. 1. 1843). As in other New Comedy imitations, Act 5 is thus given over to the trial and examination of evidence, only in this instance Udall eschews any public and dramatic use of probable arguments and inferences as part of the trial process. Gawyn Goodluck does not believe Custance's protestations of having resisted Doister's courtship: 'Yea, Custance, better (they say) a badde scuse than none', he says guardedly (5. 3. 1874). Luckily, Goodlucke agrees to abide by the testimony of a faithful male friend, Tristram Trusty, who 'was privie bothe to the beginning and the ende' of the Doister affair. Let him, says Custance 'be the Judge, and for me testifie' (5. 2. 1877). Trusty's role as surrogate for the audience, who have been throughout witness to Custance's fidelity, precludes the problems of proof explored in Foxe's play. Trusty's bearing witness on Custance's behalf takes place inaudibly and off-stage, in an imagined private conference between the two men which is supposed to occur between the end of Act 5, Scene 2, and the beginning of Scene 4. Goodlucke's and Custance's readiness to provide themselves with neighbour-witnesses and advocate-friends recalls the forensic disposition of Terentian and Plautine characters who tend to act similarly 'with a view to foreseeable legal consequences'.[67] There is no doubt, however, that Udall's comedy fights shy of exploring, in the explicit manner of Foxe's Latin play, the relationship between this drama's mimetic and forensic energies.

These three explicitly neoclassical comedies emerge, as far as we know, from school and university contexts, and may reasonably be dated to the

---

[66] Mukherji, *Law and Representation*, 53. Quintilian, *Inst.* 5. 9. 9; Sir Thomas Smith, *De Republica Anglorum*, ed. Mary Dewar (Cambridge: Cambridge University Press, 1982), 114.
[67] Scafuro, *Forensic Stage*, 31.

1550s.[68] A different, concurrent tradition of theatre which also concerns itself with the representation of judicial process but to very different effect is the tradition of the mid-Tudor moral interlude. David Bevington couples together *Jacke Jugeler* and the anonymous *Nice Wanton* as 'boys' courtly theater', but tonally and structurally the plays could hardly be more different, the only indirect hint of neoclassical influence in the latter being detectable in the derivation of two of the women characters' names—Xantippe and Eulalia—from Erasmus's quasi-Terentian colloquies.[69] It is, however, extremely instructive to compare the Terentian drama of the 1550s with moral interludes of the same period on the question of how each genre represents judgment and the administration of justice. In the Terentian drama, as we have seen, questions of evidential uncertainty are inescapable: they pervade the drama, whether or not it is explicitly concerned with the courtroom. By contrast, moral interludes of the mid-Tudor period, such as *Nice Wanton*, frequently have an explicit interest in representing courtroom procedure and in drawing attention to possible malpractice within judicial systems; but they show no interest at all in representing the forensic processes of evaluating evidence.[70]

Yet this is not to say that the moral interlude was without strategies for performing the deception of judgment. The genre developed, as John Alford has written, a 'verbal and visual rhetoric of masquerading', whereby figures representing sins or vices impersonate their virtuous counterparts (so 'Pride' can call himself 'Worship', and so forth), requiring the audience to attend carefully to the signs of moral identity.[71] *Nice Wanton*, in keeping with the social turn of Tudor moralities, employs the figure of the Vice

---

[68] *Gammer Gurton* was played at Christ's College, Cambridge, before 1575; Tydeman suggests a date of composition between 1551 and 1554, when William Stevenson, a candidate for the play's authorship, was presenting plays at Christ's as a fellow of the college. Udall's *Roister Doister* may have been presented to Edward VI at Windsor while its author was canon there in 1552 (it must antedate the 1553 publication of the 3rd edn. of Thomas Wilson's *Rule of Reason*, which includes the mispunctuated letter from 3. 4). See *Four Tudor Comedies*, ed. Tydeman, 23–4, 212. W. H. Williams, 'The Date and Authorship of *Jacke Jugeler*', *Modern Language Review*, 7 (1912), 289–95, notes an entry for the play in the *Stationers' Register* in 1562, and finds parallels (not all convincing) with *Roister Doister* which suggest a date of composition *c*.1552.

[69] *A Preaty Interlude called, Nice Wanton* (London: John King, 1560); David M. Bevington, *From Mankind to Marlowe* (Cambridge, MA: Harvard University Press, 1962), 31–2. For the Erasmian names, see the dialogue 'Marriage' in Erika Rummel (ed.), *Erasmus on Women* (Toronto: University of Toronto Press, 1996), 131–44.

[70] It seems likely that *Nice Wanton* dates from the reign of Edward VI. See *The Tudor Interludes*, ed. Leonard Tennenhouse (New York and London: Garland Publishing, 1984), 1–39.

[71] John A. Alford, ' "My Name is Worship" ', in *From Page to Performance* (East Lansing, MI: Michigan State University Press, 1995), 151–77, at 157.

masquerading not as an abstract virtue, but as a figure of social authority: an officer of the law. The play tells the harshly admonitory story of two young people who, indulged by their mother, Xantippe, shun education and turn to a life of Iniquity—literally, since this is the name of the Vice, and the girl, Dalia, becomes Iniquity's mistress, while her brother, Ismael, follows him into dicing and robbery. Eulalia, a virtuous, humanist-style wife, warns Xantippe that Ismael is 'suspected lyght-fyngered to be'.[72] The suspicion turns into an indictment, and a judge—who announces himself as 'Daniel'—comes on to try the case: 'I tary for the verdite of the quest ere I go', he says; 'Go, baily; know whether they be agreed or no . . . I wold hear what they say' (ll. 346–9). But the bailiff is none other than Iniquity in masquerade. Before going to fetch the foreman of the jury, he tries to influence the judge to set him free 'for my sake', because he 'is come of good kynne'; he offers twenty pounds and 'a right faire horse, | Worth ten pound' for the release of the prisoner (ll. 353–8). All this, the stage direction says, '*He tellet[h] him in hy[s] eare, that all may heare*'.

The judge, unmoved, proceeds against the prisoner, charging the jury in procedurally accurate terms:

> Where Ismael was indited by xij men
> Of felony, burglary and murder,
> As thinditement declareth how, where and when,—
> Ye heard it read to you lately, in ordre,—
> You, with the rest,—I trust, all true men—
> Be charged with your othes to give verdyte directly
> Whether Ismael therof be guilty or not guilty.
>
> (ll. 374–80)

Inevitably, 'one for the quest' declares him 'most gilty' (l. 381). We are likely, especially after considering the sophisticated dramatizations of forensic arguments and evidence evaluation in Terentian drama, to find this dramatization of the inscrutable jury trial impoverished and intolerably harsh. However, the dramatic and moral proof made here has clearly been that of the judge's uprightness in 'tarrying' for the verdict of the jury rather than yielding to the iniquity of special favour and bribes: 'justice' here is identified with impartially following procedure. The play's lack of interest in the processes by which the facts against Ismael were established and evaluated by pre-trial examination and contrary witness

---

[72] *A Preaty Interlude Called, Nice Wanton*, in *Specimens of Pre-Shakespearean Drama*, ed. John Matthews Manly (Boston, 1897), i. 463, l. 116. Further references to line numbers in this edition are given in the text.

testimony is an effect of its preference for the satirical and morally testing rhetoric of masquerade, the use of the Vice as impersonator, over the neoclassical plays' uses of forensic strategies, or artificial proofs. It is genre, rather than popular legal culture, that is responsible for this choice of representative strategies. In the next section we will see what happened to the neoclassical use of forensic arguments as mimetic resources in the reforming decades of the 1560s and 1570s, when 'a general quickening of the tempo of local administration' forced awareness of the problems of evidence evaluation in a participatory justice system to the forefront of the consciousness of men involved in government.

Gascoigne's *Supposes* on Stage (1566) and in Print (1573–5)

The 1560s and 1570s, when George Gascoigne was writing drama for performance and publication, were decades during which there was much discussion about how justice should be locally administered and ecclesiastical laws (if at all) reformed. The figures prominently involved in this discussion were frequently the very same men who were, at one time or another, associated with experimentation in the imitation of classical dramatic genres. We may begin with a collaboration between two prominent experimenters in neoclassical dramatic writing: John Foxe and Thomas Norton (the latter secure of a place in English literary history as the co-author of *Gorboduc*). In the years prior to 1571, Foxe and Norton were liaising on the preparation for publication of a text of the proposed reformation of English ecclesiastical laws which had been worked on intensely by various committees up until 1552.[73] After Edward VI's death, Mary Tudor had reinstated the pre-Reformation *status quo* on English canon law, and a new edition of William Lyndwood's 1430 *Provinciale*, with its provision for mandatory confession and aggressive insistence on clerical legal privilege, was issued.[74] At the beginning of Elizabeth's reign, some sort of administrative reform of ecclesiastical discipline in the parishes seemed pressing as part of a more general need to

---

[73] See Gerald Bray (ed.), *Tudor Church Reform* (Boydell Press: Church of England Record Society, 2000), pp. lxxviii–lxxix. See also James C. Spalding, *Reformatio Legum Ecclesiasticarum* (Kirkville, MO: Sixteenth Century Journal Publishers, 1992), and Leslie Raymond Sachs, *Thomas Cranmer's 'Reformatio Legum Ecclesiasticarum' of 1553 in the Context of English Church Law from the Later Middle Ages to the Canons of 1603* (Washington: Catholic University of America Press, 1982).

[74] STC 17112. 5. William Lyndwood, *Constitutiones Angliae prouinciales* (London: Thomas Marshe, 1557).

reform local governance: Lord Keeper Bacon set the agenda for Parliamentary discussion in his opening speech of 1562, and various disciplinary issues discussed in Convocation became bills in Parliament.[75] It was in this context that Foxe and Norton began their work. In 1571, Foxe was living with the printer John Daye (who also in that year reissued *Gorboduc* as part of a collection of Norton's works), working to produce a published text of the manuscript drafts of the *Reformatio*. Foxe received from Norton (who was Cranmer's son-in-law) various Edwardian manuscripts for legal reform, one of which was MS Harleian 426, Cranmer's draft of the *Reformatio Legum Ecclesiasticarum* which had failed to become law in 1552.[76] Interestingly, many of the changes made in Cranmer's own hand to this draft concerned the question of judicial discretion in weighing presumptions and circumstances to arrive at a probable judgment when no full proof could be had. Thus, for example, in chapter 49, 'Of Presumptions', Cranmer added an entire paragraph expressing confidence in the judge's ability to judge probably. 'If the proofs of the defendant and the acts do only conclude presumptorily,' Cranmer inserted, 'it is the duty of the judge, having diligent consideration of the circumstances, to judge thereupon.'[77] In chapter 41, 'Of Proofs', the committee's draft reads: 'Therefore whether trials are held by way of witnesses, instruments, presumptions, [*indications* **judgments** *or* [**and**] report, a wise judge (who has an important part to play in this, we think)', and Cranmer adds, '**will easily figure out (after weighing of the circumstances of the matters and persons) how much of what each one says is to be believed**' (*facile existimabit, pensatis rerum et personarum circumstantiis, quatenus cuique credendum sit*).[78] Foxe made additions to this manuscript in his own hand, too, so that in a real sense his work on the reformation of ecclesiastical legal governance was continuous with his thinking through classical comedy.

An older Parliamentary historiography assumed that the attempt to revive the *Reformatio* in the Parliaments of the 1560s, and especially in 1571, was initiated by 'Puritan hot-heads' who favoured a Genevan model of government; but it now seems clear that its revival was primarily worked on and debated by those who wanted to achieve its ends through collaboration between the established religious hierarchy,

---

[75] Norman Jones, 'An Elizabethan Bill for the Reformation of Ecclesiastical Law', *Parliamentary History*, 4 (1985), 171–87, at 178–9; *Proceedings*, ed. Hartley, 82.

[76] Bray (ed.), *Tudor Church Reform*, pp. lv–lix.

[77] *Reformatio Legum Ecclesiasticarum*, trans. ibid. 650–1.

[78] Ibid. 562–3. The words in bold translate those inserted by Cranmer.

the Privy Council, and the Commission of the Peace.[79] The work of Foxe and Norton and others on the committee appointed to discuss the reformation of ecclesiastical law in 1571—which included William Fleetwood, Sir Thomas Smith, Norton, and Christopher Yelverton—needs to be seen, then, in the larger context of a longer-term transformation of working relations between the Commission of the Peace and the responsibilities of ecclesiastical courts over the jurisdiction of morals and belief.[80]

For a vivid illustration of just how involved these men were in actively debating questions of ecclesiastical reform in the context of local governance generally, we may turn to the anonymous Parliamentary journal kept from 2–21 April 1571. On 6 April the journalist records the opening of a discussion on the reformation of ecclesiastical laws in which Norton spoke of Foxe's having worked on 'a booke newly imprinted to be offered to that House, which he did there and then shew forth'.[81] On the very same day, and apparently immediately thereafter, another debate took place on a bill requiring all subjects to come to divine service once a quarter. Responsibility for the enforcement of this and similar measures to ensure religious uniformity would oscillate, in future legislation, between quarter sessions and church courts.[82] On this occasion, the anonymous journalist recorded that William Fleetwood of the Middle Temple argued that the statute should not be enforced by professional informers. Sir Thomas Smith argued that the bishops should oversee it, and Sir Owen Hopton, Justice of the Peace for Suffolk, was of the opinion that 'the presentation of such defaults should not depend upon the relacion of the church wardens, who being simple men and fearful to offend, would rather daunger of periurie then displease some of their neighbours. He offered for proofe experience.'[83] In this one brief cameo of the debate we see precisely how those technical questions of 'governance' to which Fletcher, Hindle, Hassell Smith, and others have drawn our attention were at the forefront of men's minds: whether professional

---

[79] N. Jones, 'Elizabethan Bill for the Reformation of Ecclesiastical Law', 175.

[80] For the committee, see Bray (ed.), *Tudor Church Reform*, pp. lxxviii–lxxix, who thinks that the committee never met. On the question of division of responsibility between Justices of the Peace and ecclesiastical judges in decisions concerning paternity of bastards, see above, p. 163 and n. Cases of bastardy and disputed paternity were clearly among the most common cases in which the judge's skill in weighing presumptions would be called upon, as the *Reformatio* suggests.

[81] *Proceedings*, ed. Hartley, 201. Hartley lists among the candidates for this journal's authorship Sir Francis Knollys, Thomas Wilson, William Fleetwood, and Thomas Norton; these men are all mentioned by name, but this 'is no automatic disqualification' (p. xvi).

[82] Hassell Smith, *County and Court*, 133–7. [83] *Proceedings*, ed. Hartley, 201–2.

informers or voluntary officers, whether lay or ecclesiastical, should be responsible for enforcing attendance at church. Similar questions were being debated throughout the decade. In 1577, for example, Norton wrote to Sir Francis Walsingham at the latter's request, advising against paid informers as executers of penal statutes, nor allowing 'the lawe to be Courtiers merchandise', suggesting rather the appointment of commissions of 'men of the best credit and note of uprightness in every shire' to 'examine the qualitie of every such offence, with all the circumstances both of facte, and of the state and manner of the offender'.[84] Norton's proposals here were not original, but derived from the kind of scheme for more efficient administrative oversight of local government first mooted by Sir Nicholas Bacon 1562. The point for us to note, however, is that this and similar debates about local responsibility for the enforcement of statutes, which were live from the early 1560s through the 1570s, focused on the problems of failure of due process through fear or favour, and saw as a solution to such problems the employment of men of substance and credit, skilled in the examination of facts and circumstances. These skills, of course, were identical to those exhibited by characters in the forensically driven plots of classical and neoclassical comedy.

The participants in these discussions were experienced in both Roman canon and common law courts of justice, and were as such key agents of what Barbara Shapiro has described as the institutional 'migration' of evidential concepts from the Roman canon system into the English procedures of examination and evidence evaluation used by Justices of the Peace and grand and petty juries.[85] Each sat on many different kinds of tribunal. Thomas Norton was an attorney for the Stationers' Company, and in the 1580s was appointed remembrancer to the Lord Mayor of London (a sign of the increasing responsibilities of civic governance). William Fleetwood was recorder of London, and he and Sir Owen Hopton often sat together on sessions of oyer and terminer in the Guildhall and in Star Chamber and on the Court of High Commission of 1572 and 1576.[86] Fleetwood also wrote, in 1577, a manual for Justices of the Peace which,

---

[84] See Thomas Norton, *Instructions to the Lord Mayor of London, 1574–5: Whereby he is to govern himself and the City*. Together with a Letter from him to Sir Francis Walsingham, respecting the disorderly dealings of promoters. In *Illustrations of Old English Literature*, ed. J. Payne Collier (London: Privately Printed, 1866), iii. 1–23, item 8. On this correspondence, see Michael A. R. Graves, *Thomas Norton* (Oxford: Blackwell, 1994), 132.

[85] Shapiro, *'Beyond Reasonable Doubt'*, 119–243.

[86] On Norton, see Graves, *Thomas Norton*, and Marie Axton, 'Norton, Thomas (1530/2–1584)', in *Oxford Dictionary of National Biography* (Oxford: Oxford University Press, 2004).

in anticipation of Lambarde's, was composed to rectify the increasingly urgent problem that 'many in the Commission of Peace, have not been students of the Laws of this Realm'.[87] Sir Thomas Smith was a civil lawyer, who wrote authoritatively, in *De Republica Anglorum*, about the procedures of English common law; he was also a member of the Middle Temple, where his portrait now hangs, and a member of the Court of High Commission in 1572 and 1576. Christopher Yelverton of Gray's Inn would become a Justice of the King's Bench in 1602, and sit on the High Commission in 1601.

These men had more in common than their shared legal and administrative experience. Most of them were, surprisingly enough, also associated in one way or another with avant-garde developments in neoclassical dramatic poetry. Foxe's Terentian writing has been discussed. In 1560 Jasper Heywood's preface to his translation of Seneca's *Thyestes* grouped Sackville, Norton, and Yelverton together as Inns of Court poets:

> There Sackville's Sonnets sweetly sauc'd and featly fined be;
> There Norton's ditties do delight; there Yelverton's do flee
> Well pur'd with pen...[88]

Yelverton wrote an epilogue for George Gascoigne and Francis Kinwelmarsh's *Jocasta* (Gray's Inn, 1566) as well as contributing to the multi-authored *Misfortunes of Arthur* at Gray's Inn in 1587/8.[89] In 1575, Gascoigne would dedicate an entirely new experiment in neoclassical forensic drama to Sir Owen Hopton, and in 1578 George Whetstone

On Fleetwood see Christopher W. Brooks, 'Fleetwood' [Fletewoode], William (*c*.1525–1594), *lawyer and antiquary'*, in *Oxford Dictionary of National Biography* (Oxford: Oxford University Press, 2004); *The House of Commons 1558–1603*, ed. P. W. Hasler, ii. members D-L (London: HMSO, 1981), 133–8; Thomas Wright (ed.), *Queen Elizabeth and her Times, A Series of Original Letters Selected from the Inedited Private Correspondence of the Lord Treasurer Burghley, the Earl of Leicester, the Secretaries Walsingham and Smith, Sir Christopher Hatton*, 2 vols. (London, 1838). For Hopton's and Fleetwood's presence on the High Commission in 1572 and 1576, see Roland G. Usher, *The Rise and Fall of the High Commission* (Oxford: Clarendon Press, 1913), 350.

[87] William Fleetwood, *The Office of a Justice of Peace together with instructions, How and in what manner Statutes shall be expounded* [written 1577] (London, 1657), sig. A6ʳ. For the date of Fleetwood's writing of this book, which remained in manuscript until 1657, see his letter to Burghley, 'Peradventure your Lordship would knowe how myself is occupied. I am in very deed, my Lord, at presente, at the request of dyvers of my frends, setting down an order how justices of peace shall use themselves in theire offices...Thus most humblie I take my leave of your Lordship. At Bacon Howse, in Foster-Lane in London this 30 July, 1577' (Wright (ed.), *Queen Elizabeth and her Times*, ii. 64).

[88] Jasper Heywood, *Thyestes*, ed. Joost Dalder (London: Ernest Benn, 1982), 11.

[89] Gascoigne, *Hundreth Sundrie Flowres*, ed. Pigman, 139–40; Marie Axton, *The Queen's Two Bodies* (London: Royal Historical Society, 1977), 153.

dedicated his self-consciously neoclassical comedy on the administration of justice, *Promos and Cassandra*, to William Fleetwood.[90]

They were also among the men likely to have been present on the night of the first performance of George Gascoigne's *Supposes* in 1566.[91] Katherine Duncan-Jones has argued that Philip Sidney was probably present that night, too, which is suggestive, in view not only of Gabriel Harvey's marginal cross-referencing of the intrigue plots of *Supposes* and *Arcadia*, but also in relation to *Old Arcadia*'s criticism of negligent Justices of the Peace, which Blair Worden has linked to the influence of Norton's writings and the Parliamentary debates of the 1560s and 1570s.[92]

What might these men, whose interest in rhetoric and poetics was inseparable from their religio-political concerns with justice, have seen, on that evening of the Gray's Inn Candlemas revels, in Gascoigne's play? Versed in Terence and Plautus, they would, of course, have relished the play's brilliantly tight intrigue plot, and laughed at its gags and routines.[93] Ariosto's minor characters—servants, parasites, old crones—specialize in a much riper, broader line of sexual and scatological insult than audiences brought up on Shakespeare imagine to be the norm for the period, and Gascoigne enjoyed adding lewdnesses of his own: 'arskisse', for example, for Ariosto's '*Rosorastro*'.[94] But, whether or not they had read Ariosto's play, they would also have noticed that Gascoigne's version of it departs in significant ways from the Roman New Comedy tradition. As is usual in New Comedy, the legal scam perpetrated by the amorous intriguers is identified with the 'argomento' or argument (a word which

---

[90] See George Gascoigne, *The Complete Works*, ed. John W. Cunliffe, 2 vols. (Cambridge: Cambridge University Press, 1910), ii. 3; George Whetstone, *Promos and Cassandra*, in Geoffrey Bullough (ed.), *Narrative and Dramatic Sources of Shakespeare*, ii. (London: Routledge, 1968), 442.

[91] Katherine Duncan-Jones thinks that Philip Sidney was also present at Gray's Inn that night; see *Sidney*, 48.

[92] Ibid.; Blair Worden: 'The shepherds are supposed to do, and have failed to do, 'justice'[s] work, the work, among England's landowners, of J.Ps. In that respect they correspond to, and share the failings of, England's J. P. class (the class that is answerable to the monarchy for local government, but does not form policy, or shape conflicts of power, at the centre' (*The Sound of Virtue* (New Haven: Yale University Press, 1996), 200 and 203–4). Worden refers to the words of Sidney's Arcadian satirist Mastix, who says of Arcadia's 'greatest shepherds' (the magistracy) that 'Sport it is to see with how great art | By justice' work they their own faults disclose' (*Old Arcadia*, 69).

[93] William Fleetwood, e.g., quoted Terence in Parliament in 1571; see *Proceedings*, ed. Hartley, 233.

[94] See Gascoigne, *Supposes*, 2. 4. 79 in *Hundreth Sundrie Flowres*. In Ariosto's prose *Suppositi*, this is 'Rosorastro' or 'Arosto'; in his verse *Suppositi*, it is 'Rospo, o Grosco'; see Ariosto, *I Suppositi* (in prosa), 2. 3. 89, (in versi) 2. 4. 832, in *Le Comedie*, eds. Angela Casella, Gabriella Ronchi, Elena Varasi, *Tutte le Opere Di Ludovico Ariosto*, iv (Milan: Mondadori, 1974).

signified both plot and a form of artificial proof) of Ariosto's play.[95] But in Terence and Plautus this identification of the characters' trickery with the author's plot is never conceived as subversive of an ideal of civic justice, because no such ideal, no sense of the 'city' as a contemporary political community, is ever evoked (Roman comedy is set in a fictive 'Athens'). The Italian humanist tradition of neoclassical theatre in Ariosto's time, however, was nothing if not preoccupied with the *città ideale*. Prevailing trends of theatre architecture and scene painting in Florence and Rome were moving towards the use of perspective 'to unify natural and artificial space', transforming 'the theatre into an ideal city in which all the contradictions of the real city were recomposed into the unifying vision of the Court'.[96] Sergio Costola has argued, however, that the scenic conventions of the Ferrarese stage did not follow these trends; the stage was shallow, and the *scena di città* painted for the 1509 performance of Ariosto's *I Suppositi*—as part of Carnival festivities in the Palazzo Ducale which Ariosto himself masterminded—neither adhered to one-point perspective nor represented an ideal city but, rather, depicted the Ferrara outside the place of the performance, replicating the very Palazzo Ducale in which the play took place, as well as Ferrara's Tower of Rigobello, the marketplace, and the merchants' shops. The orator Tomà Lippomano wrote of a later performance of *I Suppositi*: 'The comedy was... such, that it simulated a Ferrara, and in the hall a Ferrara was built, as precise as the real one.'[97] As the painted scene used no unifying perspective, so Ariosto's plot or 'argomento' itself presents Ferrara from a number of perspectives, including that of disoriented strangers to the city who find themselves embroiled in a Ferrara which seems to them populated by rogues, cheats, and false witnesses. Finding their own identities already, in this strange city, laid claim to by others, these visitors to the city look into a surreal representational abyss: perhaps, says one of them (a servant called Lico), there is more than one Ferrara, and 'this isn't the Ferrara where your

---

[95] See Ariosto, 'Prologo', l. 22, in *I Suppositi*, in *Le Comedie*, 197. For a translation, see *The Comedies of Ariosto*, trans. and ed. Edmond M. Beame and Leonard G. Sbrocchi (Chicago: University of Chicago Press, 1975), 53. References to the prose version of Ariosto's play in Italian in the Mondadori edition will appear in the text by way of the title *I Suppositi*, followed by act, line, and scene number.

[96] See Sergio Costola, 'Ludovico Ariosto's Theatrical Machine (Ph.D. dissertation, University of California at Los Angeles, 2002), 85–103; quotation at 57–8.

[97] Ibid. 56, 88–103. Costola writes: 'Instead of positing a privileged beholder gazing at the theatrical scene from afar, the Ferrarese apparatus placed the viewer inside the scene. Thus, the attention was not on a vanishing point which was a reflection of a privileged position in the audience—the sovereign's eye—but a more "democratic" system apt to convey attention to the entire space' (ibid. 103).

son, whom we're looking for, is staying'. A few scenes later, he scathingly casts doubt on a patriotic suggestion that they have recourse to Ferrara's judicial procedures to redress the wrongs the city has done them: 'If all the other witnesses in this city are like this one,' he comments, referring to the Ferrarese citizen who makes the suggestion, 'one can prove whatever one wishes.'[98]

If Ariosto's play, as Costola argues, thus punctures a model of mimesis as idealizing simulacrum of the well-governed city-state, it does so by using the deceptions of New Comedy intrigue to demystify an idealizing discourse which identifies the *città ideale* with the Prince's 'vision' as all-seeing dispenser of justice: 'Ci abiamo e iudici e podestà, e sopra tutti un Principo iustissimo. Non dubitare che ti sia mancato di ragione, quando tu l'abbia' ('We have judges and a podesta, and above all a most just prince. Don't worry; you will have justice if your cause is just'), says the patriotic Ferrarese citizen (*I Suppositi*, 4. 8. 37–9). Moreover, the 'recognition scene', which seems at first to resolve the play's evidential crisis and decorously to draw a veil over the previous act's glimpse into the shortcomings of civic justice, works actually to generate further scepticism about its reliability. In view of the identity frauds that have just been successfully perpetrated in Ferrara, it is hard to feel convinced by the 'manifesti segni' (*Suppositi*, 5. 5. 136) or the 'evident tokens' (*Supposes*, 5. 5. 128) of the mole on the left shoulder, etc. that the lawyer Cleandro/Cleander claims are proof that Dulippo is his long-lost son.

The servant Dulippo, as Costola suggests, functions as an author-surrogate: he is the chief intriguer and author of the *fallacia*, or trick, that works by the same means as the mimesis of Ariosto's *fabula*. The name 'Dulippo' suggests the Latin *dolus*, 'trick, device, fraud' as well as the Italian *doppio*, double. And although the play's resolution turns on the recognition of Dulippo as the son of the play's representative of the justice of Ferrara's civic institutions ('we have a most juste prince, doubt not but you shall have justice' (*Supposes*, 4. 8. 36–7)), Ariosto's prologue explicitly links this 'just' resolution to the deceptions made possible by *suppozioni*, or merely probable, and possibly false, inferences. The play, his prologue announces, is called *Suppositi* because it is full of *suppozioni*, 'As you know, children have been "supposed" [substituted] for one another in the past, and sometimes are today.' As Costola comments, this sentence is laden with innuendo in Italian: ' "*per l'adietro*" means both "in the past" and "from behind", with the latter giving to the rest of the prologue a

---

[98] *Comedies of Ariosto*, ed. Beame and Sbrocchi, 79, 82.

quite explicit double meaning focused on sodomy', which Ariosto helps along by disavowing any relationship between his 'supposes' and 'the lascivious books of Elephantis'. The prologue, as David Posner says, 'offers a new model for the relationship between the play and its audience, one suggesting not the performance of truth but of deception... [its] insistence on the omnipresence of *"suppozioni"* throughout the play certainly suggests to the audience that it ought to watch its back'.[99] Gascoigne, of course, changed the prologue (though he introduced his own sodomitical word-play on 'supposes' and 'suppository' which, at the end of his play, exposes the decorous 'expectation of justice' as a cruder form of punitive desire). Yet Ariosto's prologue was only the most overt of the signals that the play was a consummate 'performance of deception', challenging idealizations of civic justice, and Gascoigne's translation omits none of these signals, stressing throughout the play's subversive references to judicial practice.

The main intrigue of Ariosto's play and Gascoigne's English version is, like *Phormio*, amorous, and concerns, like Foxe's *Titus et Gesippus*, substitution. Erostrato, in love with Polynesta, has changed places with his servant, Dulippo, so as to be able to take service in Polynesta's father's household and see his lover everyday, while Dulippo, pretending to be the Sicilian merchant's son, Erostrato, pursues his master's suit for Polynesta's hand in marriage so as to 'countervaile' the suit of the lawyer Cleander, who, 'by reading, counsailing and pleading', has gathered an enormous fortune, but lacks a son and heir, having lost his only son at the Battle of Otranto (1. 3. 89 and 1. 2. 43–69). As the play opens, the disguised Dulippo has, on his master's behalf, devised a new plot to counter Cleander's marriage suit by faking a better dowry offer (1. 3. 94). Meeting with a rather simple-minded Sienese merchant, Dulippo (believed by the stranger to be the gentleman Erostrato, of course) has told the merchant that he is in danger of his life in Ferrara, because of laws recently passed by Duke Ercole D'Este against the Sienese. He then offered him refuge and a new identity as his own Sicilian merchant father, Philogano, asking him in return to merely sign a fake bond for a dowry of 2,000 ducats a year. Erostrato congratulates his servant on this cunning plan: but what neither expects, of course, is what happens: Philogano himself comes to Ferrara.

So it is that in Act 4—usually the act in which such a crisis occurs—Philogano and his servant Litio, wearied by their long journey from Sicily,

---

[99] Quoted by Costola, 'Ariosto's Theatrical Machine', 176–7 n. See also ibid. 175–6, 179–8.

hammer in vain on the doors of Erostrato's Ferrara lodgings, hoping to find Philogano's son. This is already a striking departure from the tradition of Roman comedy, for although in Roman comedy the unexpected return of the *senex* usually triggers a convulsion of panic-stricken activity as the intriguers revise their plans and move into emergency mode, the panic depicted is more or less comic and is linked to ideas of ingenuity and improvisation. Normally, of course, the senex is returning *home* (see, for example, *Mostellaria*, 2. 2. 440). Ariosto's decision to make Philogano enter Ferrara as a stranger—a Sicilian—has a profound effect on this comic convention. The disorienting experiences of Philogano and Litio in Ferrara suddenly put pressure on the idea, or ideal, of Ferrara as a well-governed *city* whose civic and judicial institutions are accountable when such outrages happen to foreign visitors. It is in the context of witnessing Philogano's experience as a stranger—bullied, abused, and told outrageous lies by a man occupying his accommodation and claiming to be him—that we first meet the citizen (called simply 'Ferrarese' in Ariosto's play, though referred to as 'Ferrarese the Inne keeper' in Gascoigne's) who speaks patriotically for the city's good government, and especially for its judicial system.

So when Philogano, instead of meeting his longed-for son, finds himself, with Litio ('Lico' in Ariosto), trading insults and obscenities with Erostrato's cook, who maintains, brandishing a pestle, that Erostrato's father is already in the house, the effect is much more disturbing than anything comparable in Roman comedy. And the peculiar nature of the disturbance derives from the relationship between the increasingly demented, disorienting evidential contradictions, and the invocation of a Ferrara as a civic ideal. After a dig at the proverbial falsehood of the Ferrarese (in a pun on the Italian *'fe'* or *'fede'* for 'faith'), Philogano's servant, Litio, accuses the bystanding Ferrarese citizen of belonging to a city without due respect for law, where 'officers . . . suffer such faultes to escape unpunished' (4. 6. 8–9). The Ferrarese, stung, replies, 'What knowe the officers of this? thinke you they know of every fault?' (4. 6. 10). Litio's scathing retort—'I thinke they will knowe as little as may be, specially when they have no gaines by it' (4. 6. 12–13)—suddenly introduces a more material, less idealizing, view of the problems of judicial administration. In the Great Hall of Gray's Inn in 1566, these words must have resonated momentarily with those in the audience who were by day preoccupied with the problems of effective detection of 'faultes' by local officers. But it is when the Ferrarese innkeeper attempts to vindicate the honesty of Ferrara by presenting the Sicilian stranger with his son Erostrato that the most marked departure from the Roman comic tradition takes place. In this moment we experience not only an unsettling subversion of the Ferrarese's civic idealism, but, in our sympathy with Philogano, a brush with the everyday possibility of tragedy. The well-meaning but rather naïve Ferrarese innkeeper introduces the disguised Dulippo to Philogano as the old man's son. Philogano, having longed to see Erostrato, suddenly realizes that the man whom all Ferrara takes to be his son is his *servant*, into whose care he had entrusted his son—with dawning horror, he imagines or 'recognizes' this servant as his son's probable murderer: 'Out and alas', Philogano laments,

> he whom I sent hither with my sonne to be his servaunt, and to give attendance on him, hath eyther cut his throate, or by some evill meanes made him away, and hath not only taken his garments, his bookes, his money and that which he broughte out of *Sicilia* with him, but usurpeth his name also, and turneth to his owne commoditie the bills of exchaunge that I have alwayes allowed for my sonnes expenses, Oh miserable *Philogano*, oh unhappie olde man: oh eternall god, is there no judge? no officer? no higher powers whom I maye complaine unto for redresse of these wrongs? (4. 8. 25–34)

No *senex* figure of Roman comedy sounds quite so distraught on discovering how he's been made a dupe in his absence. (Indeed, a nearer comparison might be Gynecia wrongly surmising, in Act 4 of the *Old Arcadia*, that Basilius is dead.) The difference from Roman comedy lies partly in Ariosto's and Gascoigne's exploitation of the horror of surmise: Philogano's imagined scenario of his son's murder would indeed have seemed more likely than the substitution's 'real' explanation of improbable amorous intrigue. Gascoigne himself followed the fictional Philogano in assuming that 'bills of exchaunge' would be motives for murder when he wrote to his friend Bartholomew Withypoll a poem of advice on travelling in Italy. Withypoll was, like Erostrato, the son of a wealthy merchant: Gascoigne warned that his purse lined with 'billes of credite' would be a perilous 'bayte to sette *Italyan* handes on woorke'.[100]

But the other difference from Roman comedy lies in the speech's Christian appeal to judicial authority as God's substitute on earth. As Katherine Maus has argued, sixteenth- and seventeenth-century English writing across the denominational spectrum constitutes human inwardness 'by the *disparity* between what a limited, fallible, human observer

---

[100] 'Gascoigne's councell given to master *Bartholomew Withypoll* a little before his latter journey to Geane' (*Hundreth Sundrie Flowres*, ed. Pigman, 297, ll. 64–6).

can see and what is available to the hypostatized divine observer'.[101] The pathos of Philogano's lament lies in its opening out of this disparity: 'you shoulde', he remonstrates with the Ferrarese innkeeper, 'have feared the vengeance of God the supreme judge (which knoweth the secrets of all harts) in bearing this false witnesse with him, whom heaven and earth do know to be *Dulippo* and not *Erostrato.*' Heaven may know it, and so may God and the audience, but when the Ferrarese reminds them patriotically that Ferrara is ruled by a 'most juste prince' and that a representative of the prince's just rule is Cleander, 'one of the excellentest doctors of law in our citie', this only exacerbates the problem. For, whether we read Ariosto here as decorously attempting to compliment Duke Ercole D'Este or, as Costola persuasively argues, playing '*doloi*', or tricks, the play's idealization of judicial authority and the legal profession can only be undermined by intrigue comedy's conventionally pragmatic conception of law as indistinguishable from intrigue itself—as mere strategy.

As we have seen, Ariosto uses Roman Comedy within an Italian human-ist tradition which increasingly identified both city and theatre as spaces of civilizing spectacle. Although no precisely comparable English theatrical tradition exists, the Inns of Court revels have been extensively analysed as occasions on which gentlemen and aristocrats claimed, through rev-elling and performance, a part in the government of the *res publica*.[102] Architectural innovation testifies to a sense of the significance of the Inns and their members: between 1556 and 1558, the hall of Gray's Inn (where *Supposes* was performed) had been entirely rebuilt, with a grand hammer beam roof and Gothic pendants. Slightly later, Middle Temple Hall was magnificently rebuilt under the supervision of Edmund Plow-den. Both architectural projects derived from the lawyers' own sense of the authority of their profession.[103] These new spaces were ornamented to dignify a legal profession increasingly confident in its own judicial, or decision-making role. A remarkable narrative painting now in the Middle Temple which is likely to have been commissioned by Plowden for the rebuilding of the Hall in about 1570 illustrates this point (Fig. 4). The

[101] Katherine Eisaman Maus, *Inwardness and Theater in the English Renaissance* (Chicago: University of Chicago Press, 1995), 11.

[102] See, e.g., Axton, *The Queen's Two Bodies*; Paul Raffield, *Images and Cultures of Law in Early Modern England* (Cambridge: Cambridge University Press, 2004); Winston, 'Expanding the Political Nation'.

[103] Mark Girouard, 'The Architecture of the Halls of the Inns of Court', unpublished lecture, delivered at The Intellectual and Cultural World of the Early Modern Inns of Court, Courtauld Institute, London, 14–16 Sept. 2006. Raffield also notes the rebuilding (*Images and Cultures of Law*, 43, 74).

Figure 4. Judgement of Solomon, Anglo-Flemish, *c*.1570, Middle Temple Hall. Reproduced with permission from The Honourable Society of the Middle Temple.

painting depicts the judgement of Solomon (1 Kgs 3: 16–28). In it, the two harlots delivered of children stand on either side of the enthroned figure of a youthful Solomon; directly in front of the throne lies the body of the dead child. Across the foreground, raised sword in hand, kneels a man holding the living baby by the ankle. The woman on the left kneels, one arm outstretched and the other raised to her breast, apparently pleading; on the right the other woman stands aloof, apparently unmoved. In the lower left-hand corner, a Latin inscription declares the import of the scene. Here is a translation:

All things indeed establish truth and rejoice in a true discovery; even falsehoods themselves destroy each other with their own weapons. Daniel was able by the evidence afforded by those ashes to detect thy frauds, O Bel, and to annul an unjust judgment by the difference of a tree, the crime being discovered. To thee, O Solomon, is the honour of true justice due by all perplexed mortals. Thou layest bare the inmost senses of the soul, and thou disclosest the secrets of the human heart, and in thy wisdom thou triest with fear the mothers' minds. With thee as judge the innate love of the real parent in its fullness stands revealed, while the false stands confused at the discovered evidences of her fraud. And now whoever holds the reins of justice let him learn this mighty lesson of just decision, and at a distance let him adore the footsteps of the king fully taught of God.[104]

This is a remarkable choice of subject. As we have seen, James VI and I was to use the example of Solomon to dignify the role of the jury in their examination of the fact, 'a matter no less important to the summe of Justice, then the true and judicious exposition of the Lawes themselves'.[105] Earlier, in the 1550s, Cranmer and the Committee for the Reformation of Ecclesiastical Laws had invoked the example of Solomon in their discussion of presumption, arguing that the ecclesiastical judge had discretion, when fuller proofs were lacking, 'to give sentence upon | a | violent presumption', a concept which, by 1628, had entered Coke's *Institutes* as a category of probability that might move a jury to find their verdict.[106] If it is the case that Plowden commissioned the painting, this is fitting. John Baker has identified the publication of Plowden's *Reports* (1571) with

---

[104] This is the modern translation next to the painting in the Middle Temple. The Latin text runs as follows: 'Cuncta fidem vero faciunt, gaudentque reperto, | Et jugulant sese ipsa suis mendacia telis. | Indicio cinerum potuit sic prodere fraudes, | Bele, tuas Daniel; potuit discrimine plantae | Pellere judicio confictum crimen iniquo, | At tibi praecunctis, Salamon mortalibus uni | Justitiae debetur honos; tu pectoris imos. | Rimaris sensus, atque abdita corda recludis | Maternumque sagax animum formidine tentas. | Agnita nativo, te judice gestit amore | Vera parens, fictamaque suae jam dispudet artis | Hauriat hinc legum quisquis molitur habenas | Justitiae Documentum ingens, longeque secutus | Coelitus edocti vestigia regis adoret.' I am grateful to Tarnya Cooper of the National Portrait Gallery, and to Jayne Archer, Elizabeth Goldring, and Sarah Knight, organizers of the conference on 'The Intellectual and Cultural World of the Early Modern Inns of Court', 14–16 Sept. 2006, at which Dr Cooper lectured on the painting, and Dr Mark Girouard gave a lecture on Plowden's supervision of the rebuilding and refurbishment of Middle Temple Hall. It is interesting that the author of this inscription links Solomon's ability to 'detect' which of the mothers spoke the truth with Daniel's detection of the fraudulent god, Bel. Daniel's discovery of footprints in the ashes around the idol is recounted in ch. 14 of the Book of Daniel, and, though rejected as apocryphal in Protestant Bibles, appeared in the original 1611 King James Bible.

[105] *Stuart Royal Proclamations*, ed. James F. Larkin and P. L. Hughes (Oxford: Clarendon Press, 1973), i. 167–71.

[106] See Bray (ed.), *Tudor Church Reform*, 643; Shapiro, *'Beyond Reasonable Doubt'*, 208.

a perceptible shift of emphasis in the common law towards a greater confidence in decision making. But judicial decision making in the common law involved, of course, the fact-finding work of the jury.[107] The painting points to the closeness of the relationship between the concerns of dramatists in exploiting the mimetic effects of probable rhetoric, or 'supposes', and those of lawyers, judges, and jurors in employing the same rhetorical strategies as the means by which to detect frauds and arrive at true judgments.

In this context, the neoclassical mimesis of Gascoigne's comedy, ostentatiously signalled in its opening pretended ignorance of the audience, may well have been recognizable as an aesthetic appropriate to the new jurisprudential emphasis in common law; but if so, there could likewise be no mistaking the comedy's mischievous suggestion that judicial decision making was merely an exercise in supposing. Moreover, the English dramatic tradition was still, in 1566, dominated by the allegorical mode of the moral interlude, so that in some ways the subversive effect of Ariosto's association of judicial practice with the deceptions of '*suppositi*' would be even more striking to an English audience. In Thomas Garter's 1578 English interlude, for example, *The Commody of the most vertuous and Godlye Susanna*, the Judge is about to sentence Susanna to death on the 'evidence of these men', the lascivious elders, whom we have seen elaborately '*kis the Boke*' before telling a very plausible story of having witnessed 'with both our eyes' Susanna's adulterous carryings-on with an entirely fictitious young man. Moments before the Judge's unjust sentence is to take its effect, however, a stage direction tells us '*Here the Judge ryseth, and Susanna is led to execution, and God rayseth the spirite of Danyell.*' Daniel insists on a retrial: 'Go sit in judgement once agayne, the witnesse they have borne, | Is false, and yet their gravity your sences doth subborne.' After a few lines, '*they returne all back to judgement*', and the Judge allows Daniel to take over in causing Susanna's innocence to be proclaimed by the crier. He is apparently untroubled by his own failure to examine the probability of the evidence more closely.[108]

---

[107] See J. H. Baker, 'English Law and the Renaissance', in *The Legal Profession and the Common Law* (London: Hambledon Press, 1988), 461–76, esp. 474–5, and Hutson, 'Not the King's Two Bodies', in Victoria Kahn and Lorna Hutson (eds.), *Rhetoric and Law in Early Modern Europe* (New Haven: Yale University Press, 2001), 169. Baker associates the greater emphasis on jurisprudence, or judge-made law, with Plowden.

[108] Thomas Garter, *The Commody of the moste vertuous and Godlye Susanna, never before this tyme Printed* (London, 1578), sig. E1ʳ–E2ʳ. Bevington, *Mankind to Marlowe*, 63, comments on this 'untheatrical' stage direction, and concludes that Garter's play was never performed, though the title-page does offer suggestions for doubling the actors.

God sees the secrets of men's hearts, and in the native English tradition of interlude which (as George Whetstone complained to William Fleetwood in the same year) 'bringeth Gods from Heaven, and fetcheth Divels from Hel', the stage God can be relied upon to put human judges right when they accept a plausible fiction for true witness testimony.[109] But neoclassical comedy, taking the mimetic power of circumstantial narration more seriously, must acknowledge the fallibility and contingency of judicial investigations of evidence. Though Cranmer might invoke the example of Solomon, judging by presumptions, and assert that the judge learned in civil and canon law 'will easily figure out (after weighing of the circumstances of the matters and persons) how much of what each one says is to be believed', Ariosto's and Gascoigne's plays subvert this confidence. Act 5, Scene 5, begins with Cleander expressing to Philogano his grave doubts about the possibility of proving that Dulippo is not, after all, Erostrato, as well as the near-impossibility of proving that Philogano is, indeed, himself:

Yea, but how will ye prove that he is not *Erostrato*, having suche presumptions to the contrarie? or how shal it be thought that you are *Philogano*, when an other taketh upon him the same name, and for proofe bringeth him for a witnesse, which hath bene ever reputed here for *Erostrato*? (*Supposes*, 5. 5. 1–5)

As Litio had earlier commented, with witnesses like false Erostrato's false father (the Sienese merchant), 'men may go aboute to prove what they will in controversies here' (*Supposes*, 4. 8. 14–15). What happens, of course (given that we know that Erostrato has not been murdered by Dulippo, but lies imprisoned at Polynesta's father's house), is that Cleander's anticipation of the problem, expense, and ultimately ineffective nature of the mode of proof that Philogano proposes becomes redundant as the conjectural work of the dénouement's 'recognition' takes over: Cleander begins to piece together clues and fragments of evidence which suggest that Dulippo is, in fact, the son he lost long ago at the Battle of Otranto. The predictable romance dénouement obviates the need to dwell further on the legal impasse momentarily glimpsed in the discussion of how inadequate Philogano's evidence is, but it no less clearly raises further evidential questions. As Cleander finds out from Philogano that Dulippo's former name, as a foundling, was 'Carino', he immediately claims that 'Carino' was the name of his own son, whom he lost at Otranto. From

---

[109] George Whetstone, 'The Epistle Dedicatorie, to his worshipfull friende, and Kinseman, William Fleetwoode, Esquier, Recorder of London', *Promos and Cassandra* (1578), in Bullough (ed.), *Narrative and Dramatic Sources of Shakespeare*, ii (1968), 443.

the perspective of the strangers to Ferrara, however, this simply looks like another trick: as soon as Cleander asks Philogano for details of Dulippo's origins, Litio is on guard: 'Sir, have I not told you enough of the falshood of *Ferrara*? this gentleman will not only picke your purse, but beguile you of your servaunt also, and make you beleeve he is his sonne' (*Supposes*, 5. 5. 84, 99–101). When Cleander comes to his 'recognition' finale ('What nedeth me more evident tokens? this is my sonne out of doubt whom I lost eighteene yeares since . . . he shuld also have a moulde on his left shoulder'), Litio offers another subversive, Ariostan reminder to the audience that they should watch out behind: 'He hath a mould there in deede', concedes the servant, 'and an hole in an other place too, I would your nose were in it' (5. 5. 132–3). Finally, of course, the suppositional 'proving' of the trickster Dulippo's legitimacy and wealth as the son and heir of the rich lawyer (who has made 10,000 ducats by his ability to handle presumptions and other evidential signs) cancels the shocking transgression of status boundaries implied by the cross-dressing of master and servant, so that all is (supposedly) well. But Damone, Polynesta's father, now realizes that the man he had intended to shackle in chains borrowed from the city's gaol is likewise a gentleman and heir. Damone's final joke addressed to poor old Nevola, his dim-witted servant, mocks the vengeful 'supposes', or the false inferences born of prejudice and desire, which we all too easily mistake for the workings of justice. Nevola (who is called 'Nebbia', or 'fog', in the prose version of Ariosto's play) is instructed, in Act 3, Scene 4, to go 'and seeke maister *Casteling* the jayler' who 'dwelleth by Saint Anthonies gate'. Nevola is to ask the gaoler to lend Damone 'a paire of the fetters he useth for his prisoners' (3. 3. 1–4). Once alone, the servant muses on the cause of this errand, recalling how he 'marvelled alway at this fellow of mine *Dulippo*, that of the wages he received, he could mainteine himselfe so bravely apparalled'. Now, he says, 'I perceive the cause': Dulippo's wardrobe, he thinks, has been financed by Polynesta. With more than a touch of envy, Nevola relishes the thought of Dulippo getting his just deserts with the fetters he himself will fasten on him: 'he was as fine as the Crusadoe, and we silly wretches as course as canvas: well, behold what it is come to in the ende' (3. 3. 11–18). Either Saint Anthony's gate is some distance, or Nevola walks very slowly, for two whole acts later he arrives in the midst of the merry-making with the fetters and bolts Damone asked him to bring. Damone tells him what to do with them: 'Marie I will tell thee Nevola, to make a right ende of our supposes, lay one of those boltes in the fire, and make thee a suppositorie as long as mine arme' (5. 10. 44–6). '[D]oubt you not, but you shall have justice if your cause be just', the Ferrarese citizen had assured Philogano, but just as what Philogano (and the audience) got was not justice but more supposes, so Damone's joke exposes expectations of justice as envious supposes, lewdly transforming the symbols of felony into a final warning to the audience to watch their backs.

The Policing of Supposing: The 1575 *Posies* and Gascoigne's *Glasse of Government*

Viewed from a seat in Gray's Inn Hall, in the legal centre of a city in which 'little comedie[s]' of identity fraud, forged contracts, and clandestine marriages were frequent enough (the lawyers William Fleetwood and Robert Snagge came across one during a vacation reading in Middle Temple in 1575), Gascoigne's *Supposes* probably seemed just scandalous, satirical, and topical enough to be extremely funny.[110] Problems, however, seem to have arisen when Gascoigne attempted to widen his coterie learned audience into a vulgar, unlearned readership. In 1573 Gascoigne published *Supposes* as part of a collection of his writings entitled *A Hundreth Sundrie Flowres*. It is well known that this publication caused some scandal, and that Gascoigne felt it necessary to present a revised edition, *The Posies*, as the fruits of his 'repentance' in 1575. Recently, however, critics have pointed out that the revisions of 1575 do not go much beyond a superficially moralized recasting of the 1573 materials, and that in places Gascoigne even seems to use his revisions to mock the ' "grey heared" censors behind a posture of abject penitence'.[111] A critical rejection of C. T. Prouty's, Richard McCoy's, and Richard Helgerson's biographical readings (which are now routinely and rather unfairly criticized for taking

[110] Recorder Fletewood to Lord Burghley, Bacon House, 8, Aug. 1575: 'Yesterdaye, being Fridaye, betwene five and six of the clock, I being arguing of Mr. Reader's case, and all the whole company being present, as our order is, there cometh into the Temple church a minister, one Tasse, a northern man, servant to my Lord of Warwick, a hosier and his wife dwelling nere Cecille House, and a daughter of Sir Robert Drewye's, and in a secret corner of the church, the minister, without any license or banns asked, was beginning to marry this Tasse and Mrs. Drewrye, and by chaunse my fellow Robert Snagge missing his man, and seking for him in the churche, by chaunse fell upon this solempne marriage. And thereupon he drove them all out of the churche before him, and told me of it, and I sought out this same Tasse, and brought him before the Master of the Rolles and Mr. Hennage, and upon the examination of the matter, it appeared Sir Robert would not give anything to her marriage, because she intended to marrye against his will. Nothing in this little comedie did more offende me, than that they said they did choose rather to marrye in the Temple, because they supposed it to be a lawles churche' (in Wright (ed.), *Queen Elizabeth and her Times*, ii. 20).

[111] Felicity Hughes, 'Gascoigne's Poses', *Studies in English Literature*, 37 (1997), 1–19.

Gascoigne's strategic self-presentation as repentant prodigal at face value), as well as a revisionist criticism of older exaggerations of the efficiency of Elizabethan censorship have led to more tentative interpretations of the meaning of Gascoigne's revisions in the 1575 *Posies*.[112] It is rightly observed that Gascoigne's career was not a failure after 1575 as was formerly suggested, and some critics even argue that Gascoigne's prefatory apology to the High Commission at the opening of the 1575 *Posies* does not prove that his first attempt at printing these works actually offended any of them.[113] In her thesis on Gascoigne, Gillian Austen argues that the High Commission would not have deigned to read Gascoigne's *Flowres*, while Cyndia Clegg contends that if Gascoigne's book really caused offence, the revisions would have been more drastic. And although the evidence shows that Gascoigne's revisions were indeed not acceptable (in 1576 the High Commission ordered Gascoigne's publisher to return fifty copies of Gascoigne's *Posies* to Stationers' Hall), Clegg even takes this as an argument against their censorship. The calling-in of a mere fifty copies, she says, 'points to a considerably less resolute Commission in censorship than has regularly been assumed'.[114]

For our purpose of understanding the legacy of *Supposes* for the subsequent English transformation of intrigue comedy on the popular stage, however, we need to distinguish these questions of the sincerity or otherwise of Gascoigne's moral repentance, and of the High Commission's censoring efficiency, from our question of how Gascoigne's highly subversive comedy was received. Evidence that there was some concern about the moral impact of the play's forensic rhetoric has three sources. The first involves the personnel appointed to the High Commissions of 1572 and 1576 and their links to Gascoigne's later writing. For the second, we have the slight but (*pace* Clegg) highly significant revisions that were made to the 1575 text of *Supposes*. For the third and most telling,

---

[112] For the earlier readings, see Charles T. Prouty, *George Gascoigne* (New York: Columbia University Press, 1942); Richard McCoy, 'Gascoigne's "Poëmata Castrata"', *Criticism*, 27 (1985), 29–55; Richard Helgerson, *The Elizabethan Prodigals* (Berkeley: University of California Press, 1976).

[113] G. W. Pigman includes Gascoigne's prefaces to the revised *Posies* in his edition of *A Hundreth Sundrie Flowres*, 359–69.

[114] See Gillian Austen, 'The Literary Career of George Gascoigne' (D.Phil., Oxon, 1997), 136–7. I have since corresponded with Dr Austen, however, and she is now inclined to revise this view and consider that the High Commissioners did read Gascoigne's book. See also Cyndia Clegg, *Press Censorship in Elizabethan England* (Cambridge: Cambridge University Press, 1997), 54 and 103–22. For the calling-in of the copies of the 1575 *Posies*, see under 'xiij° die Augusti 1576', 'Item receyued into the hall of R Smithe half a hundred of Gascoignes poesies', in *Records of the Court of the Stationers' Company 1576 to 1602 from Register B*, ed. W. W. Greg and E. Boswell (London: The Bibliographical Society, 1930), 86–7.

however, we have Gascoigne's next experiment in adapting the forensic rhetoric of neoclassical intrigue comedy to the moral and civic concerns of the ongoing reformation in local governance. This experiment is the excellently plotted, though unperformably didactic, *Glasse of Government* of 1575.

Clegg, assuming the exclusively religious and doctrinal concerns of the High Commission, has underestimated both the concern with secular literature common to all humanist-trained men and the continuity between personnel sitting in judgment in different types of legal court in the 1570s and 1580s. On the Commissions of 1572 and 1576, both of which seem to have objected to aspects of the 1573 and 1575 editions of Gascoigne's writings, were not only clerics who would have known Terentian comedy well (one of these was Alexander Nowell, Dean of St Paul's, who had been Foxe's Oxford roommate in 1544 when the latter was thinking up *Titus et Gesippus*), but laymen deeply involved in questions of judicial administration, such as William Fleetwood, Sir Owen Hopton, Sir Thomas Smith, and Sir Francis Walsingham.[115] Fleetwood's letters to Burghley in the 1570s and 1580s demonstrate the fluid movement of personnel between different types of court: on one Thursday in 1582 Fleetwood kept two sessions of the Peace, one at Finsbury and one at the Guildhall; after dinner he sat on the High Commission, and when that hearing was over, he was sent for by the Earl of Leicester to discuss a Chancery case. Two days later, he sat at the Middle Temple, hearing a case with Thomas Norton; his lack of leisure, he told Burghley came from the absence of Sir Owen Hopton (whom he refers to as 'Mr. Levetenant'), who would normally share this work with him.[116]

Since Hopton was the dedicatee of Gascoigne's 'reformed' representation of civic justice, *The Glasse of Government*, in 1575, and Fleetwood received the dedication of George Whetstone's thematically similar *Promos and Cassandra* in 1578, it seems quite likely that these men were among those on the High Commission who foresaw problems with a text which encouraged readers to identify judicial procedure so closely with the 'supposes' that enable comic deception. Here the question of whether Gascoigne was 'sincere' or 'ironic' in presenting the revised *Posies* as a repentant text is irrelevant: the point to grasp is that the revisions to *Supposes*—which have so often led to misreading the play—were

[115] On the personnel of the High Commission in 1572 and 1576, see Usher, *Rise and Fall of the High Commission*, Appendix II.

[116] 'Recorder Fletewood to Lord Burghley (MS Lans. 37, 5), Jan. 19, 1582', in Wright (ed.), *Queen Elizabeth and her Times*, ii. 186.

indisputably motivated by Gascoigne's 'concern over reception of the first, and fear for the second' edition, as G. W. Pigman puts it. Clegg has suggested that the prefatory letters to *The Posies* are not evidence of censorship, but should be read as 'an elaborate "devise" that sought to depoliticize its reception', but I am inclined to agree with Pigman's stronger claim: 'The prefatory letters make it abundantly clear that the major motivation for the revisions in *The Posies* was, in fact, external—an only too justified fear of censorship.'[117]

The main difference between the text of *Supposes* in the 1573 *Hundreth Sundrie Flowres* and that in *The Posies* of 1575 consists in the addition to the latter of marginal notes which identify every instance of Aristotelian paralogism or false inference in the dramatic narrative as a 'suppose'. These notes have been regularly assumed by critics to have been part of Gascoigne's original design, and have occasioned pejorative remarks about the essentially 'literary' and 'untheatrical' nature of the classical tradition represented by the play. David Bevington, for example, while conceding that *Supposes* is 'practicable as theater', finds in these marginal glosses evidence that it 'looks back from the literary printed text to the ephemeral phenomenon of performance', and he links this 'literary' quality to the fact that the characters 'pretend that no audience exists'.[118] There is a fundamental confusion here about the nature of the 'literary' and the 'theatrical': in fact, the realism of the dramatic action, confidently expressed in the opening joke that no audience exists, is dependent on the narrative's constant encouragement of inferential activity on the part of the audience and the characters, and it is this inferential activity, this ironic, sceptical *poetry*, that is arrested and closed down by the revised text's marginal notes.

With the revisions to *Supposes*, Gascoigne was obliged to pre-empt the reader's inferential work of distinguishing a character's false inference from what other characters know to have taken place by flagging up every single moment of conjecture on the part of a character with the government health warning of its being '*a suppose*'. If to encourage 'supposes' is, as Gabriel Harvey wrote in appreciation of Gascoigne's prologue, 'To coosen the Expectation', then Gascoigne's marginal annotations killed his supposes dead.[119] Your expectation can hardly be 'coosened' or

---

[117] Pigman, 'Editing Revised Texts', in *New Ways of Looking at Old Texts*, ed. W. Speed Hill (Tempe, AZ: Renaissance Text Society, 1998), 1–9; Clegg, *Press Censorship*, 103.

[118] Bevington, *Mankind to Marlowe*, 37.

[119] *The Posies of George Gascoigne Esquire, corrected, perfected and augmented* (London: Richard Smith, 1575), Bodleian Malone 792, sig. B2ᵛ.

temporarily fooled when the legend 'you are now being fooled' is written all over the dialogue's plausible misleading indirections and deliberate false turns. Take, for example, an early scene in which the disguised Erostrato takes an opportunity to tease his rival in love, Cleander. Cleander and his servant, Carion, have been waiting in the marketplace for Pasafilo, the parasite, who has seen a better opportunity for having a good meal at Damon's house, and has left. Cleander then spies the disguised Erostrato: 'Holde thy peace,' he instructs Carion, 'here is one of *Damons* servaunts, of him I shall understande where he is: good fellow art thou not one of *Damons* servaunts?' (2. 4. 30–2). A marginal note to this line reads: 'An other suppose'.[120] Of course a reader might easily have forgotten (the speech tag reading, as it does, '*Dulippo*') that this is the disguised *Erostrato* approaching Cleander, just as an audience member might forget Polynesta's earlier explanation that this servant's clothes disguise a rich merchant's son. However, as the dialogue proceeds, an audience member or reader will try to grasp what lies behind the apparently gratuitous insulting of Cleander, as Dulippo insinuates first that the lawyer is miserly and has physically repulsive habits, and then, more scandalously, that he wants a beautiful young wife to lure handsome men to his house. It is because the speech gradually reveals itself as probably motivated by the aggressive impulses of sexual rivalry that we 'recognize' the speaker as Erostrato. This is how mimetic reading works: we infer probable motives in such a way as to 'invent' distinctions and subtly distinctive relationships between dramatic characters. Mimetic 'reading' of this kind (which is not just a textual experience, but includes the interpretative hearing and seeing of a performance by theatre audiences) accounts for much of the sophisticated pleasure and comparative naturalism of neoclassical drama (including its Shakespearean development), and is part of what distinguished it so spectacularly in Elizabethan eyes from the moral distinctions implied by disguise in the interlude tradition.[121] And the temporal experience is important: Gabriel Harvey did not say that 'supposes' cozened the audience for good; they only cozen 'expectation'—that is, their purpose is to retard and complicate understanding by making the audience work at understanding the motivations of speech so as to recognize, gradually, who everyone is and what their relations are.

Similar things could be said of every single instance of the word 'suppose' appearing warningly in the margin, but I will give only two more

[120] *Posies of George Gascoigne Esquire*, sig. D1ʳ.
[121] For the moral distinctions implied by disguise in the interlude tradition, see Alford, '"My Name is Worship"', 157.

examples. As I mentioned earlier, Damon's servant, Nevola, thinks, when the liaison between Dulippo and Polynesta has been discovered, that he has now figured out why it is that his fellow-servant was always so well dressed (3. 4. 11–13). His implicit assumption—that Polynesta paid for her lover's wardrobe—is solemnly labelled in the margin 'An other suppose'. So it is, but recognizing this implicitly, without being told, is to 'recognize' or infer a character and class position for Nevola: his mistaken inference suggests an understandable resentment which, for a moment, makes him real to us. All we might gain in terms of the mimetic effect of inferring by ourselves the meaning of Nevola's 'suppose' is lost in the flattening, abstracting effect of the margin's admonitory finger wagging.

Finally, the labelling of 'supposes' closes down the proliferating ironies of the final recognition scene. Litio, characteristically sceptical of Cleander's readiness to recognize Dulippo as his long-lost son, warns Philogano, 'Beware sir, be not to lavishe' (5. 5. 84). But this and the ensuing instances of Litio's doubt, which (as we have seen) comment metadramatically and lewdly on the mimetic contrivance of the whole fiction, are pre-empted by the marginal early warning sign: 'a crafty suppose', which indicates naïvely that in this instance the conjecture is not *true*, thereby losing the level on which it is precisely true, since the play's identification of 'Dulippo' with 'Carino' is, as Litio shrewdly supposes, nothing more than an improbable fiction.

Given the practical involvement of many of the High Commissioners in assessing the probabilities of whether a person's story or alibi was suspicious, or likely to be true, it is striking that all Gascoigne's revisions to *Supposes* are concerned to ensure that the reader is not 'cozened' (not even temporarily, and in the interests of enhanced mimetic effect) in judging which stories are true and which mere 'supposes'. Even more striking, however, is Gascoigne's imaginative application of these revisions in his next and last dramatic work, *The Glasse of Government*. This play was dedicated to Sir Owen Hopton, a veteran of Guildhall sessions of oyer and terminer and privy searches at Burghley's command to keep law and order in London.[122] Though *The Glasse of Government* has been assumed to have been modelled on Dutch 'prodigal son' plays, it has no source or analogue in Dutch Latin drama, and is actually more remarkable for its precise transformation of the classical intrigue plot into a plot in which intrigue is *successfully detected and punished*.

---

[122] See Wright (ed.), *Queen Elizabeth and her Times*, ii. 17, 63, 68, 187.

In this play, moreover, Gascoigne shows his skill in using characters' conjectures and inferences about what has happened in their absence to manipulate emotion, instilling anxiety and eliciting pathos, but he avoids having characters use conjectural arguments with impunity to deceive one another: all deliberately deceptive 'supposes' become clues in a plot of magisterial detection.

It is not until the second half of Act 4 that *The Glasse of Government* introduces the all-important figure of the civic magistrate, the Markgrave of Antwerp, whose opening speech on the burdens of judicial administration sounds just like the oppressed Recorder Fleetwood in the London of the 1570s. 'I am at the least the best parte of an hundred nights a yere abroad in searches, I never reste', wrote Fleetwood to Burghley on one occasion, and on another, he complained of lacking the assistance of 'Mr Levetenant' (Sir Owen Hopton, Lieutenant of the Tower), without whom, he wrote, 'I am so exercised that I have no leasure at all skarse to read a Littleton's case'.[123] The complaints of Gascoigne's Markgrave would therefore sound familiar to Gascoigne's dedicatee, Sir Owen Hopton himself:

Suters at the chamber dore do breake the sweetest sleepe, the rest of the forenoone is lyttle enough for the ordynarie howres of the courtes and decydyng of contentions, at diner you shall hardly dysgest your meate without some sauce of complaynts or informations . . . and the night suffyzeth not to forecast what polityke constitucions are needful to be devised or renewed, for to meete with the dayly practises and inventiones of lewde persones.[124]

The Markgrave's first action is to order his officers to arrest the prostitute, Lamia, along with her bawd, Pandarina, on suspicion of keeping a brothel. But, as Linda Salamon noted, he is initially not able to punish either of these, nor their pimp, Eccho, because 'he makes a great point of *finding direct evidence*, not executing summary punishment'.[125] The play, in fact, adapts the forensic structure of intrigue comedy, transforming the wily slave's heroic improvisation of lies into the heroic magistrate-detective's capacity to gather and evaluate the *evidence* on which to condemn those lies. Intrigue becomes the material on which the retrospective work of detection thrives. Thus, the whole of Scene 4 in Act 5 is taken up with the Markgrave's pre-trial examination of the pimp, Eccho, and

---

[123] Wright (ed.), *Queen Elizabeth and her Times*, ii. 187.
[124] *The Glasse of Government*, in George Gascoigne, *The Complete Works*, ed. John W. Cunliffe (Cambridge: Cambridge University Press, 1910), ii. 67.
[125] Linda Bradley Salamon, 'A Face in *The Glasse*', *Studies in Philology*, 71 (1974), 47–71, at 68.

it is from the reconstructive work of this dialogue in this scene that the impressionistic time indicators of previous scenes acquire greater concreteness and realistic specificity.

The play, as has often been pointed out, dramatizes the moral of Ascham's *Scholemaster* that 'quick wits' in youth often prove less fortunate and profitable than slower-witted youths who learn their moral lessons more thoroughly.[126] To demonstrate this, the play pairs the quick-witted elder sons of two Antwerp burghers whose names are Phylautus ('self-love') and Phylosarchus ('lover of clothes') with the same burghers' two younger, duller sons, Phylomusus ('lover of the muses') and Phylotimus ('lover of honour'). The action opens with the fathers' employment of a schoolmaster, Gnomaticus, to prepare the boys for university, and the first two acts plod somewhat tediously through the tutor's lessons to his pupils, interrupted by a more tantalizing glimpse in Scene 5 of Act 4 of plots afoot elsewhere in the city to lure suitable young men into the prostitute Lamia's net. Already we know which of the boys are likely to be easiest to seduce, and in this sense the plot is, as critics have argued, didactic and predictable, attempting a reduction of literature to precept even at the level of layout on the physical page.[127] But if we look at the play from the point of view of plot structure, focusing on how characters, especially latterly, come by their knowledge of one another, we can see just how ingeniously and influentially Gascoigne worked in this play to adapt what he learned from Ariosto about mimetic power of deception to a similar but less ironically subversive mimesis of *detection*.

For such intrigue as there is in the play exists to promote its own ultimate detection and use as evidence for the prosecution. It is set in motion in Act 2, Scene 3, when Eccho, meeting Gnomaticus, improvises a clever deception to enable the two elder boys to have an afternoon off in which to spend time with Lamia (whom Phylosarchus has already looked at with longing when passing her by in the street). Seeing Gnomaticus, Eccho quickly searches his mind for 'some device to bleare his eyes for a while', and sidles up to the old man with an outrageous fib, 'Syr I am sent unto you by the Markgrave', he begins, 'who understanding that two of his kinsemen are lately placed under your governement, hath a desire to see them, and therefore sent me to intreat you that you would gyve them

---

[126] Ibid. 51–2; Helgerson, *Elizabethan Prodigals*, 51–5.
[127] See Christopher Gaggero, 'Pleasure Unreconciled to Virtue', in *Tudor Drama before Shakespeare, 1485–1590*, ed. Lloyd Edward Kermode, Jason Scott-Warren, and Martine van Elk (London: Palgrave Macmillan, 2004), 168–93, at 181–3.

lybertie this afternoone, to the end he may common with them.'[128] Of course, the Markgrave is no kin to the elder sons, but the schoolmaster, impressed at this prestigious connection, grants the boys liberty. In the next two scenes the elder boys anticipate the pleasures of this afternoon off, and in the last scene of Act 2 we see Pandarina leading them into Lamia's lodgings. Act 3 begins with this long-awaited 'afternoon' at an end; Dick Droom, another servant in Lamia's household, comes out on-stage and begins a vivid, colloquial account of the financial success of the afternoon's seduction, only to be interrupted by the approach of the two younger brothers, who have spent the same afternoon contemplating their lessons and are now wondering about the whereabouts of their siblings. Into this gathering burst the elder brothers simulating anger at having been ill-treated at the Markgrave's house: 'This was a proper messanger in deede,' exclaims Phylautus, 'he myght have mocked others though he mocked not us.' Phylosarchus, on cue, defends the fictive messenger: 'O syr you do him wrong, for it seemeth unto me that the poore fellow is as sorie for it as we are miscontented.' They feign to have just noticed their brothers, and on being questioned, explain that the messenger must have made a mistake, for the Markgrave seemed not to know them when they arrived: 'When we came to him he knewe us not . . . but with a grim countenance turned his backe, and desyred us to goe ere we dranke: a Margrave, quoth you?'[129] This is the only instance in the whole play of a 'suppose' in the sense of a deliberate deception (though the final scenes make impressive use of 'supposes' in the sense of anxious conjectures as the fathers scan letters for news of their sons). Its development from Eccho's simple spur-of-the-moment falsehood into the boys' naturalistic and highly mimetic narration of their off-stage visit to the Markgrave (which, of course, was no more nor fictitious than their off-stage visit to Lamia, though the latter is the 'suppose' of the play as '*fabula*', and the former is the '*fallacia*' or the 'suppose' designed to fool other characters) is so impressive that, to prevent confusion, it is flagged up in the margin as 'A fine excuse'.

The full structural and moral significance of this 'suppose', however, emerges retrospectively, after the Markgrave has ordered the arrest on suspicion of Lamia, Eccho, and Pandarina. For, as we see in the elab-orate representation of a pre-trial examination in Act 5, Scene 4, the unstaged sexual secrets of the 'afternoon' between the end of Act 2 and the beginning of Act 3 emerge as the crucially missing piece of 'evidence'

---

[128] Gascoigne, *Works*, ed. Cunliffe, ii. 38.   [129] Ibid. ii. 46–7.

in the puzzle of Phylosarchus's acquaintance with Lamia. We know that on the eve of their arrest, Lamia's household was preparing a feast, provided for by Phylosarchus: in Act 4, Scene 3, Dick Droom salivates over these provisions: 'a fat brest of veale, a capon, a dosen of pigeons, a couple of rabets, and a stoupe of wine'.[130] Dick, out buying olives for sauce when the arrest takes place, escapes, but Eccho is not so lucky. News of the arrest spreads to Gnomaticus; an indignant Nuntius complains to him of the injustice of these proceedings. It is 'open wronge', he declares, that this honest gentlewoman, her kinswoman, and their fellow have all been cast into prison simply because 'they suffered an honest youngman (and Sonne to a welthy Burgher) to suppe with them yesternight'. Their imprisonment awaiting trial is against the course of justice at common law, the Nuntius goes on; they should have been granted bail, for 'they proffer good suretyes to bee always forth comming untill their behaviour be tryed'.[131] As we saw in Chapter 2, English law since the Bail and Committal acts of 1555 and 1556 required Justices of the Peace to establish the grounds for bail or imprisonment by means of a pre-trial examination. The written record of this examination was supposed to supply the judges at gaol delivery with a means of 'evaluating the justice of any bailment'.[132] Two points are crucial to grasp here. One is that just as the Marian statute constituted an early instance of concern to monitor the impartial justice of local governance, so Gascoigne's play prepares to demonstrate the impartiality and justice of the Markgrave's refusal of bail by following this indignant *vox populi* report of his rigour with a meticulous pre-trial examination. The other point, however, involves the date at which the Marian statute really began to take effect, and constitutes the relationship between drama and legal practice. For Langbein's analysis of the 1555 and 1556 statutes is throughout illustrated by references to William Lambarde's 1581 *Eirenarcha* and Michael Dalton's 1618 *Countrey Justice*; succeeding editions of both of these manuals for Justices bear witness to the expansion and increasing complexity of pre-trial examination. But before Lambarde's *Eirenarcha*, the only manual written in English for Justices of the Peace unlearned in the law was William Fleetwood's 1577 manuscript treatise, composed two years after Gascoigne's play. The opening of Fleetwood's manual gives us some idea of Justices' prevalent ignorance of legal requirements for bail or arrest in the 1570s. He imagines a Justice of the Peace dismissing the need for learning on the subject:

[130] Ibid. ii. 62.   [131] Ibid. ii. 70.
[132] John H. Langbein, *Prosecuting Crime in the Renaissance* (Cambridge, MA: Harvard University Press, 1974), 11.

'Let me alone,' the typical justice will say, 'I will do, as near as I can, the best. If any Offender come into my hands, he shall walk the Gaol, and there he shall be forth coming, until the Justices of Gaol-delivery come down.'[133] But the law was, of course, more complicated, and the Justice was required to show that he had examined the suspect so as to justify either imprisonment or bail with sureties for being 'forthcoming' (the technical legal term for awaiting trial, having been arrested[134]). It is likely that in the 1570s only a limited number of Justices put the Marian requirements into practice, since as late as 1614 'one lawyer MP commented that "few" magistrates "knew fifty" of the requisite statutes' imposing duties on them.[135] Gascoigne's play, then, designedly contributes to the reformation of local governance by representing popular ignorance and resentment of apparently summary justice, only to reveal, through the unfolding detective drama of the pre-trial examination and its sequence, the equity involved in the conjectural labour of gathering and evaluating evidence.

Gascoigne devotes a whole scene to the Markgrave's examination of Eccho. Everything turns on the question of what exactly can be proved by the festive preparations visible to the arresting officers. Was this, as the people of Antwerp were saying, the wrongful arrest of an honest woman for inviting a young man to supper? The Markgrave's problem lies in establishing any proof of professional collusion between Eccho and Lamia in securing the patronage of Phylosarchus, since Eccho's presence at the feast proves no more than a casual acquaintance. So the Markgrave sets about questioning Eccho, and we infer similar scenes of questioning Lamia and Pandarina:

SEVERUS. Come on sirha, what acquaintance have you with these Ladyes?
ECCHO. Sir I have but small acquaintance with them.
SEVERUS. No? What did you there then?
ECCHO. Sir I had wayted uppon them into the Towne that day (as I doe uppon divers others for my lyving) and they prayed me to suppe with them in part of recompence for my travaile.
SEVERUS. Mary sir you fare was good as I understand, and meete for much better personages then eyther of you. Tell me who provided it? And who paid for it?
ECCHO. I know not Sir, it was enough for me that I knew where it was, I never asked from whence it came for conscience sake.

---

[133] Fleetwood, *Office of a Justice of Peace*, sig. Abr. See above, p. 189, for the date of this treatise's composition. [134] See, e.g., *2 Henry VI*, 2. 1. 175.
[135] Hindle, *State and Social Change*, 11.

SEVERUS. Well jested fellow *Eccho*, but I must make you sing another note before you and I part. Tell me how came you acquainted with *Phylosarchus*?

ECCHO. I have knowen him long since sir, as I know divers other young gentlemen in this Towne.

SEVERUS. Yea, but how came it to passe that he should have bene there at supper that night?

ECCHO. That I cannot tell, neyther do I knowe whether he should have bin there that night or no.

SEVERUS. Yes that you can, did you never see him there before?

ECCHO. I saw him there once, in other honest company, but what is that to me? Had I any thing to do with his being there? or doth it followe of necessity that beecause he was there once before, therfore he should have been there that night also?

SEVERUS. No, but you know well enough if lyst that he should have been there, and that the banquet was prepared for him. You were best to confesse a trueth.

ECCHO. Sir I will not confesse that which I knowe not, neither for you nor for never a man on live. He might have beene there for all mee, & he might have beene away also if he list, for any thing that I know.

SEVERUS. Well, it were but lost labour to talke anie longer with you, go take him and carrie him to the mill, and there let him be whipped everie day thryse, untill he confesse the circumstances of al these matters, wee may not suffer the Sonnes of honest and welthy Burghers to bee seduced by such lewde fellowes, and they to scape skotfree.[136]

I have quoted the whole of this astonishing scene because it proves not only how closely the conjectural arguments and intrigue plots of classical and neoclassical comedy were thought to mesh with the processes of forensic enquiry, but also how far ahead of the forensic game, as it were, drama was. This scene of the examination of a *status conjecturalis* or conjectural issue, as Cicero called it, exists in print in 1575, thirteen years before Lambarde expanded his *Eirenarcha* to include a discussion of the examination of suspects and a Ciceronian table of the rhetorical causes of suspicion.[137] Moreover, this scene does not merely stand alone, as a forensic set-piece. It is thoroughly integrated into the evidential plot precipitated by Eccho's 'device' at Act 2, Scene 3; this device, along with the temporal indicators or 'reality effects' of the afternoon off and the preparations for the supper feast, have all been sequentially disposed with the evidential difficulties of their narrative reconstruction in mind. The

---

[136] Gascoigne, *Works*, ed. Cunliffe, ii. 78–9.

[137] See William Lambarde, *Eirenarcha: or of The Office of the Justices of the Peace in foure Bookes* (London: Ralph Newberry, 1592), 218–19. This table first appears in the 1588 edn., STC 15165.

problematic identification of circumstantial forensic *narratio* with moral ambiguity and deception, which derives not only from Terence's *Phormio* but from Cicero's *Pro Milone*, *Pro Roscio Amerino*, and *De inventione*, is being resolved by an emphasis on *narratio* as investigative reconstruction by a figure of exemplary moral authority.

So, of course, the drama of the Markgrave's frustrating search for evidence does not end with his prescription of whipping for such slippery customers as Eccho. Anxiety has been building in the final scenes of Act 5, as the two fathers and Gnomaticus scan the letters they receive from Douai for news of what's become of their unreliable elder sons. (Interestingly, the habits of forensic suspicion manifest themselves in these scenes, too, as tutor and fathers compare the information coming from the divergent sources of their different letters and decide that they have not been 'deceived' by them.[138]) In the midst of this, Gnomaticus takes the opportunity to thank the Markgrave for his diligence in arresting the 'lewde company' who were the reason for sending the two elder brothers away to Douai. The Markgrave confides, however, that the arrest has not been completely successful: 'I have examined them also', he says,

I can not find hitherto any proofe against them whereby they ought to be punished: and though I desire (as much as you) to see them condingly corrected, yet with out proofe of some offence I should therin commit a wrong. True it is that *Eccho* is knowen commonly in this Town for a Parasite and a flattering fellow, and the young woman also doth not seeme to be of the honestest, but yet there no body which will come in and say this or that I have seene or knowen by her. Shee confesseth that *Phylosarchus* and *Phylautus* were there one night at a banquet, and that *Phylosarchus* should have supped there the same night that they were taken, and when I ask her to what end, she answereth that he was a suter to her for mariage, and for witnesse bringeth in her Aunt as good as her selfe, in the mean time I have no proofe of evill wherwith to burthen her. And then maister *Eccho* (on the other sid) he standeth as stiffe as may be, and sayeth that he knoweth not whether *Phylosarchus* should have supped there or not, and for lack of proofe I am able to go no furder.[139]

This passage reads uncannily like one of Fleetwood's letters to Burghley on his examinations of London suspects: 'by examynations of such as we dealte withall in the forenoone, we could learne nothing'; 'He would fayne have denied his being there: but my proofe went too strong'; etc.[140] Here

---

138 Gascoigne, *Works*, ed. Cunliffe, ii. 80.   139 Ibid. ii. 82.
140 Wright (ed.), *Queen Elizabeth and her Times*, ii. 86, 159.

the Markgrave has the ingredients for suspecting that Phylosarchus and Phylautus have been deliberately ensnared by a confederate plot involving the ladies and Eccho, but he cannot prove this, since Lamia's story is one of an innocent courtship, and Eccho denies any knowledge of her relations with Phylosarchus. It is at this point that the precise significance of Gascoigne's plotting of Eccho's 'device' in Act 2, Scene 3, and the subsequent ambiguity surrounding the events of the unstaged 'afternoon' between Acts 2 and 3 finally emerges. For the father of Phylosarchus suddenly recalls Gnomaticus, telling him of Eccho: 'Yea Sir but doubtles that *Eccho* was the first cause of their acquayntaunce, for the first tyme that my Sonne was there, was one afternoone, at which tyme *Eccho* came to their School Master in your name, and craved liberty for them to come and speake wyth you.'[141] The Markgrave is, of course, astonished to learn of his own apparent part in this story. 'With me?', he asks, and Gnomaticus takes up the tale, recounting to the amazed Markgrave how he had, reputedly, behaved rudely to the two young men: 'when I gave them leave to come unto you, they returned (after two or three howers respyte) and sayde that you knew them not...and furthermore they seemed angry.'[142] This idealized Markgrave suppresses any indignation at his name being taken thus in vain, and catches gratefully at the evidential point: 'but thys is somewhat yet', he says, 'by this meanes I have good cause to punish Master *Eccho*', and the scene ends with the Markgrave preparing to hear 'what answer he is able to make unto these matters'.[143]

The not very numerous body of critics who have commented on *The Glasse of Government* are, of course, united in being aghast at the play's unremittingly harsh view of how justice—poetic and otherwise—should operate: Lamia and Pandarina end up on cucking-stools, Eccho is whipped about the town, and Phylautus and Dick Droom are executed for robbery in Germany, and Phylosarchus is whipped to death in Geneva for fornication. We can speculate as to what caused Gascoigne to produce such a severe reaction to the indulgence with which youthful sexual licence and financial deception is treated in *Supposes*, but to do so is to return to the disputed territory of debate over the sincerity of Gascoigne's 'repentance' and the nature of the 'censorship' exercised by the High Commission. I hope to have shown, rather, that what is significant about *The Glasse* is less its moral difference from *Supposes* than its formal similarity: both plays are organized around an understanding that the forensic work of

[141] Gascoigne, *Works*, ed. Cunliffe, ii. 82.   [142] Ibid.   [143] Ibid. ii. 83.

conjectural arguments contributes enormously to the sophistication of dramatic mimesis, by engaging the audience in the work of evaluating the probabilities of the inferences drawn by different characters. Gascoigne's legacy for Shakespeare, then, is of great significance. As Charles Knight put it, 'the spectator of The Comedy of Errors will very soon detect the differences of the Dromios and Antipholuses, and . . . while his curiosity is kept alive by the effort of attention which is necessary for this detection, the riddle will not only tease him, but its perpetual solution will afford him the utmost satisfaction.'[144] Shakespeare's sense that the material of New Comic intrigue might be turned into a plot of detection-without-intrigue (a plot in which characters' surmises and false inferences as to how they have been wronged seems to give us insight into their 'histories' and 'characters') clearly derives from the tragicomic potential of inference in *Supposes* (in which Philogano surmises his son to have been murdered), as well as from plays like *Glasse of Government*, which established the Egeon-like figure of the magistrate as detective, and associated the New Comic intrigue plot with criminal frauds requiring detection. Thus, while *The Glasse* was never performed, it was not as egregious or uninfluential as critics seem to have thought. Its turning of the intrigue plot into the material of a plot of evidential enquiry can be paralleled in Sidney's *Old Arcadia*, also dated to the late 1570s, and contemporary non-literary texts, such as Buchanan's *Detection of the Duinges of Mary Quene of Scottes*, shared a similar structure. Most striking of all, as we shall see in the next chapter, the play's crucial insight into the ways in which intrigue could be embedded in a plot which essentially put the work of civic justice on trial was to prove important for the innovative rewriting, in the 1590s, of genres invented in the 1580s: that is, the chronicle history play (which will be treated in Chapter 5) as well as revenge tragedy and romantic comedy (discussed in Chapter 6).

---

[144] *Pictorial Edition of . . . Shakespeare*, ed. Knight, i. 257–8.

5

Forensic Rhetoric on the Popular Stage: Shakespeare's Histories

Ginzburg's Lost Camel and Auerbach's Weary Prince: Inference and Conjecture in *2 Henry IV*

We have seen how, between 1550 and 1570, the elements of intrigue and forensic argument that drove the dramatic action of Roman New Comedy were adapted, in the learned circles of the universities and Inns of Court, to the requirements of a civic humanist plot of the magisterial detection and examination of abuses. But how were these elements and their political-didactic adaptations assimilated by the popular stage? There was, we may assume, quite a lot of continuity in terms of political-didactic interests between the Inns of Court drama of the 1560s and 1570s and the popular dramaturgy of the 1570s and 1580s. As Scott McMillin and Sally-Beth Maclean have shown, first Robert Dudley, Earl of Leicester, and then Leicester and Francis Walsingham together, were setting a reformed agenda for the most prominent companies of players in the 1570s and 1580s. In 1574 Leicester received a royal patent for Leicester's Men to play without hindrance throughout the realm; in 1583 Walsingham recruited three of Leicester's Men to form the all-star Queen's Men, who, blest with royal patronage, would popularize a Protestant and patriotic theatre, centred on the new non-allegorical genre of the 'English history play', to London and the provinces.[1] Continuity is evident here: it was Leicester who had sponsored *Gorboduc* in 1561, and Walsingham who sought Thomas Norton's advice later on matters of governance, while Sidney, who echoes Norton's writings in *Old Arcadia*, was Leicester's

[1] Scott McMillin and Sally-Beth Maclean, *The Queen's Men and their Plays* (Cambridge: Cambridge University Press, 1998), 18–32.

nephew, married Walsingham's daughter, and was godfather to the son of Richard Tarlton, the most famous actor of the Queen's Men.[2] But such continuities of reformed Protestant commitment are not matched, in the drama of Leicester's or the Queen's Men, by any interest in the forensically driven plots and arguments of texts such as *Arcadia*, or *The Glasse of Government*, or *Ane Detectioun*. Leicester's Men played drama thematically concerned with the commonwealth and the workings of justice, but not formally indebted to evidential models. One of their plays was *Cambises, King of Persia*, probably written by the Cambridge scholar Thomas Preston, and derived from Richard Taverner's humanist *Garden of Wysedom* (*c*.1538).[3] This play depicts the abuses of tyranny, but formally speaking it is an example of what David Bevington calls the 'hybrid chronicle', mingling allegorical and historical figures and effectively alternating episodes of grave matter and clownage so as to enable extensive doubling of parts. The Queen's Men in the 1580s did develop a new, non-allegorical mode of drama, and especially a new genre: the English history play. But theirs, as McMillin and Maclean show, was a dramaturgy which made effective use of the resources of visual theatre. Verbally it was less inventive, mingling rambunctious prose for clowning scenes with regular, end-stopped verse for grave matters, but not deploying the mimetic resources of forensic rhetoric, which is perfectly designed to help an audience infer and so *imagine* what they cannot see.

Shakespeare did something with the civic humanist dramatic materials favoured by previous playwrights and companies, something that pushed their political concerns in the direction of creating an illusion of inwardness, or what the eighteenth century called 'character'. *Hamlet* itself, for example, derives its plot, probably via an *Ur-Hamlet* written by Thomas Kyd, from the fifth story in the 1572 volume of François de Belleforest's *Histoires Tragiques*. In Belleforest's book, the prefatory argument of this story alludes very pointedly to tyrannous injustice in recent memory in Scotland, and a queen's conspiracy to kill her husband, and king.[4] Yet however much the *Ur-Hamlet* may have invited such typically civic humanist, anti-tyrannical and indeed topical reading, Shakespeare's version (no doubt for many reasons) has been notoriously resistant, and

[2] McMillin and Maclean, *Queen's Men*, 25.

[3] See William A. Armstrong, 'The Authorship and Political Meaning of *Cambises*', *English Studies*, 36 (1955), 289–99.

[4] François de Belleforest, *Le Cinquiesme Tome des Histoires Tragiques* (Paris: 1572), fols. 149–91.

has invited many other, less overtly political and more 'inward' kinds of interpretation. It is as if civic humanist political concerns, though present, are submerged in Shakespeare's plays by techniques of dramatic storytelling which urge us to make sense of events by exploring the perceptions and motivations of the dramatis personae themselves above all else.

What might these techniques be? McMillin and Maclean argue that the Queen's Men came upon the English history play as part of their campaign to rival what Marlowe was doing with the new poetic technology of the blank verse line in the morally ambiguous *Tamburlaine*. The Queen's Men's plays vaunted truth, plain speaking, and Christian monarchy; for their *Selinus*, written to rival Marlowe's *Tamburlaine*, the Marlovian enemy, as McMillin and Maclean put it, 'is not just Tamburlaine but the blank verse line itself'. But to see the coming dramatic revolution merely in terms of what Marlowe was doing with iambic pentameter is, as McMillin and Maclean themselves note, 'to leave Kyd out of the picture', along with Kyd's specific contribution to popular dramaturgy, the meticulously causal plotting of action.[5] For Marlowe's characters may, in Thomas Nashe's irreverent though appreciative words, be 'embowell[ing] the cloudes' with their aspiring speeches, but Marlowe's plots, for the most part, conformed to the episodic alternation of grave and comic action that Bevington has described as dominating earlier in the century.[6] When the young Shakespeare, however, appropriated and rewrote the plots of the greatest hits of the Queen's Men's repertory—the English history plays—he was not simply, as McMillin and Maclean suggest, transforming their humdrum, end-stopped verse and visual dramaturgy into the sonorous and metaphorical magic of the blank verse line.[7] When Shakespeare rewrote *The Troublesome Raigne of King John*, *The True Tragedy of Richard III*, *King Leir*, and *The Famous Victories of Henry the Fifth*, he transformed them mimetically as well as metaphorically. He adapted the forensic strategies of argument typical of classical intrigue plots into more inward dramas of inference and conjecture, prompting us, as readers or audience, to participate in the processes by which characters rhetorically invent the intentions, motivations, occasions, and

---

[5] McMillin and Maclean, *Queen's Men*, 158, 167.

[6] Thomas Nashe, *The Works of Thomas Nashe*, ed. Ronald B. McKerrow (Oxford: Basil Blackwell, 1966), iii. 311.

[7] See the excellent example given by McMillin and Maclean. To dramatize the mysterious appearance of five moons at King John's second coronation, the Queen's Men 'rigged up a display of the five moons themselves', where Shakespeare's play 'delivers this event not visually but narratively' (*Queen's Men*, 163).

histories which enable them—and us—to construe the 'facts' of their own and one another's 'cases', or causes. For this reason, I propose, the underlying civic humanist concern with the commonwealth or *respublica* is frequently, in Shakespeare's rewriting of the Queen's Men's plays of the 1580s, all but overwhelmed by the characterological effects of forensic inference or conjecture as aspects of a dazzling new departure in dramatic mimesis.

This and the next chapter will be concerned with three genres of the 1590s to which Shakespeare contributed: namely, chronicle English history play, revenge tragedy, and romantic comedy. It will be my argument that essential to Shakespeare's innovative work in each of these relatively novel genres was the adaptation of the forensic rhetoric and plot structure of classical comedy and the 'detective' Terentian plot pioneered by Gascoigne, Whetstone, and Sidney in the 1570s. Before I turn to such a survey, however, I would like to offer an exemplary analysis of Shakespeare's use of inference in the rewriting of materials from *The Famous Victories of Henry the Fifth* as *The Second Part of Henry IV*. And before I turn to this specific instance of rewriting, I will prepare the ground with some discussion of what function 'inference' has been thought to perform as an epistemological model in various kinds of learning and practice.

Carlo Ginzburg's essay on the importance of inference as an epistemological model prior to the emergence of the 'humane sciences' includes the discussion of an ancient fable celebrating the power of interpreting signs as evidence which has long been recognized to have an important place in literary history, specifically histories of the detective novel. Ginzburg paraphrases the many variants of this story of 'Serendipity and the Three Princes' thus:

An oriental fable that circulated among Kirghiz, Tartars, Jews, Turks, and others, relates the story of three brothers who meet a man who has lost a camel or, in variant versions, a horse. They describe it for him without hesitation: it is white, blinded in one eye, and carries two goat-skins on its back, one full of wine, the other of oil. They have seen it? No, they have not. So they are accused of stealing it and brought to trial. For the brothers, this is a moment of triumph: they demonstrate in a flash how, by a myriad of small clues, they could reconstruct the appearance of an animal on which they have never laid eyes.[8]

---

[8] Carlo Ginzburg, 'Clues: Roots of an Evidential Paradigm', in *Myths, Emblems and Clues*, trans. John and Anne C. Tedeschi (London: Hutchinson Radius, 1990), 96–125, at 102. See Theodore Remer (ed.), *Serendipity and the Three Princes* (Norman, OK: University of Oklahoma Press, 1965).

As Ginzburg goes on to explain, this story, translated into Italian in the mid-sixteenth century, achieved an extraordinary Europe-wide popularity in the eighteenth century, when Voltaire worked it into his novella *Zadig* (1745). From *Zadig*, as many scholars and critics have noted, direct and indirect lines of influence run to Thomas Huxley, Edgar Allen Poe, and Arthur Conan Doyle.[9] Peter Brooks has argued that the detective novel is 'the narrative of narratives', a novelistic form which exposes the 'double logic' according to which all novels are written. The detective novel, that is, uses the hermeneutic device of 'detecting' or following clues to *construct* the apparent coherence of the narrative's solution, while pretending that this coherence already existed in a set of events (the crime) anterior to its inferential reconstruction in the sequence of the narrative.[10] If this is so, then the tale of the three brothers, and that of *Zadig*, are central to the history not only of detective fiction, but of the novel itself.

Ginzburg's own interest as a historian lies in making visible the emergence of a massively influential but under-theorized epistemological model in the human sciences (a model which he calls, variously, the conjectural, presumptive, semiotic, or divinatory paradigm, and which involves the analysis or diagnosis of signs or symptoms in particular cases). At the stage of his argument in which he introduces the tale of the three brothers, he speculates suggestively on its hint that in tracking or hunting lies the origin of narrative itself:

Obviously, the three brothers are repositories of some sort of venatic lore, even if they are not necessarily hunters. This knowledge is characterized by the ability to construct from apparently insignificant experimental data a complex reality that could not be experienced directly. Also, the data is always arranged by the observer in such a way as to produce a narrative sequence, which could be expressed most simply as 'someone passed this way'. Perhaps the actual idea of narration…may have originated in a hunting society, relating the experience of deciphering tracks. This obviously undemonstrable hypothesis nevertheless seems to be reinforced by the fact that the rhetorical figures on which the language of venatic deduction still rests today—the part in relation to the whole, the effect in relation to the

---

[9] Ginzburg, 'Clues'; Alexander Welsh, *Strong Representations* (Baltimore and London: Johns Hopkins University Press, 1992), pp. ix–xi; Régis Messac, *Le 'Détective Novel' et l'influence de la pensée scientifique* (Paris: H. Champion, 1929); John Kerrigan, 'Sophocles in Baker Street', in *Revenge Tragedy* (Oxford: Clarendon Press, 1996), 59–87.

[10] Peter Brooks, *Reading for the Plot* (New York: Random House, 1984), 25. See also Laura Marcus's summing up of Brooks's view in 'Detection and Literary Fiction', in *The Cambridge Companion to Crime Fiction*, ed. Martin Priestman (Cambridge: Cambridge University Press, 2003), 245–67, at 247.

cause—are traceable to the narrative axis of metonymy, with the rigorous exclusion of metaphor.[11]

In the last part of this charming hypothesis of the hunter as the inventor of narrative, Ginzburg looks for support to Roman Jakobson's famous distinction between the paradigmatic (or substitutional) and syntagmatic (or combinative) functions of language, which relate, respectively, to the rhetorical figures of metaphor and metonymy.[12] The process of inference itself—the conjectural reconstruction of a whole camel or horse from idiosyncrasies in the traces of its having 'passed this way'—is metonymic or, more properly, synecdochic, suggests Ginzburg, and this constitutes evidence of its affinity with *narrative*, which likewise, according to Jakobson, emphasizes metonymy over metaphor. All of this, of course, concurs with those histories that relate abductive, or inferential, reasoning to the emergence of the novel and the detective novel. Important here are the questions of tense and sequence, but also the question (not discussed by Ginzburg) of how the ordering of narrative—the sequence in which the 'clues' are presented—relates to or even produces the 'truth' of the past as an anterior construction. For the notion of narrative sequence as the order in which one enumerates the signs of something having 'passed this way', while fitting Ginzburg's idea of the speculative aspect of historical reconstruction, is clearly at odds with the work of the novelistic plot of detection, which, while it 'presents itself as a repetition and rehearsal . . . of what has already happened', in fact *produces*, through the detective's work of inference, the thematic coherence that we accept as the solution to the enigma.[13]

How might such thinking about inference relate to histories of drama? These distinguish themselves from histories of the novel by being concerned less with probable accounts of 'what has passed' than with presentness, and presence, performance, enactment, spectacle. Thus, David Bevington interprets the relation of dumb shows 'described in the past tense' in printed texts of *Gorboduc* and *The Misfortunes of Arthur* as signs of an erudite tradition of literariness at odds with a popular tradition of performance.[14] Yet innovations in popular drama in the 1580s and 1590s have more to do with the effects of inference as synecdoche—allowing

[11] Ginzburg, 'Clues', 103.
[12] Roman Jakobson, 'Two Aspects of Language and Two Types of Aphasic Disturbances', in Roman Jakobson and Morris Halle, *Fundamentals of Language* (The Hague: Mouton, 1956), 69–96. [13] Brooks, *Reading for the Plot*, 25 and 29.
[14] David M. Bevington, *From Mankind to Marlowe* (Cambridge, MA: Harvard University Press, 1962), 37.

audiences and readers to infer past events from insignificant verbal details, as well as showing characters engaged in similar activities of inferring—than has generally been allowed. Katherine Maus is one of the few critics to have written of 'the theatre audience's necessary, but perilous and frustrating, reliance upon inferential reasoning'. In English Renaissance drama, she observes,

> we are presented less with a story than with the synecdoche of a story: not with pitched battles between rival armies but with 'alarums within' and short representational skirmishes...In a theatre that insists so self-consciously upon its own representational limitations, the spectator is obliged to evaluate *symptoms*, behavior the cause of which may be hidden or withheld. The art of spectatorship is an art of diagnosis. Does Hamlet behave erratically because he *is* mad or because he is pretending to be mad? What motivates Antonio's generosity to Bassanio?[15]

Maus does not develop a full-blown account of spectatorship-as-diagnosis, since her concern is primarily to develop a suggestive analogy between the position of spectator and that of the jealous husband who is so often a central figure in the drama of the late sixteenth and early seventeenth centuries. However, if we turn to the place and significance of Shakespeare in Erich Auerbach's monumental survey of the representation of reality in Western literature, *Mimesis* (first published 1946), we find, surprisingly enough, that it is Shakespeare's enabling of audiences and readers to infer complex situational histories and social surroundings for his characters that Auerbach identifies as distinguishing the genius of this dramatist and his time. To be sure, Auerbach himself, with his 'innocent', pre-structuralist use of the concept of mimesis as the representation of reality, makes no mention of inference or conjecture as rhetorical forms of argument, but characteristically approaches Shakespeare's achievement by way of a discussion of the representational roles played by high and low literary styles: Shakespeare's tragic works, he observes, abundantly represent the mixture of high and low.[16] However, when he comes to reflect on the prevailing view, in the 1940s when he was writing, of what constitutes the distinctiveness of Elizabethan tragedy, his own refinement of

---

[15] Katherine Eisaman Maus, 'Horns of Dilemma: Jealousy, Gender and Spectatorship in English Renaissance Drama', *English Literary History*, 54 (1987), 561–83, at 576.

[16] Eric Auerbach, *Mimesis*, trans. Willard R. Trask (Princeton: Princeton University Press, 1953), 312–13. My comment on the innocence of Auerbach's use of the term 'mimesis' echoes Terence Cave: 'One shudders at the difficulty of rewriting *Mimesis* now, when the concept of representation has become a battlefield on which rival factions fight openly (if at times obscurely) for an impossible victory' (*Recognitions* (Oxford: Clarendon Press, 1988), 5). For representatives of different sides in the battle, see Christopher Prendergast, *The Order of Mimesis* (Cambridge: Cambridge University Press, 1986); A. D. Nuttall, *A New Mimesis* (London: Methuen, 1983).

that view attributes to the mixture of high and low styles a power of world creation that could be described as the product of inference or conjecture from signs. The general view that Elizabethan tragedy differs from Greek tragedy in offering a new sense of the individual ('the hero's individual character plays a much greater part in shaping his destiny') is one that Auerbach wants to qualify. The subjects of antique tragedy, drawn from national mythology and history are not less individual, but require, he suggests, no special, detailed depiction. However, 'with the great variety of subject matter and the considerable freedom of Elizabethan theater', he writes,

we are in each instance given the particular atmosphere, *the situation and the prehistory of the characters*. The course of events on the stage is not rigidly restricted to the course of events of the tragic conflict but covers conversations, scenes, characters, which the action as such does not necessarily require. Thus we are given a great deal of 'supplementary information' about the principal personages; *we are enabled to form an idea of their normal lives and particular characters* apart from the complication in which they are caught at the moment.[17]

Once again, as with the discussion of A. C. Bradley in Chapter 3, we return to an appreciation of Shakespeare (and 'Elizabethan tragedy' generally, though no other author is instanced) that singles out the plays' capacity, by including detail surplus to plot requirements, to suggest that characters have 'prehistories' and 'normal lives'. Auerbach goes on to explain this phenomenon in terms of the legacy of the cosmic drama of Christianity, which assumes a sacred connection binding all levels of society, and thus gives profound meaning to the repetition of a central dramatic action at different social levels in subplots and secondary actions. But it is also possible to see the examples of Shakespeare's 'prodigally lavish' surplus of invention in terms of an economy of plot in which questions of conjecture and inference, and of what we, as well as the characters, are likely to conjecture or infer from certain actions and situations, are central to the design of the sequence of action, and are indeed calculated to produce precisely the effects of 'normal lives' and 'prehistories' that Auerbach so appreciates.

Auerbach's witty opening example of Shakespeare's mixing of styles, the example of Hal as 'The Weary Prince' in *2 Henry IV*, is a case in point. Auerbach quotes a section from the beginning of Act 2, Scene 2, of *2 Henry IV* which seems not only to fit, but to comment reflexively upon, Shakespeare's readiness to juxtapose high and low. In this scene—apparently in

---

[17] Auerbach, *Mimesis*, 319–20; my italics.

father's weeping hesitation to conjecture the meaning of the disguise and the gesture, and in a highly theatrical reversal, the son offers the dagger to his father as the instrument of filicide before they are both reconciled.[23] There is every reason to think that this scene would work well in the theatre.[24] For a reader, however, the prince's grief and repentance in *Famous Victories* seem expediently timely. What Shakespeare—whether or not with an eye to print, and whether or not trying to fill out a sequel to *1 Henry IV*—did with these materials, however, was to imagine the transitional time of a monarch's final illness as a period particularly fertile for the cultivation of conjecture, shaped for some by fears of the imminent dismantling of all judicial institutions and systems of redress, and for others stuffed with hopes that proximity to those at the centre of power will offer prosperity in the new, corrupt regime. The 'action' of Shakespeare's *2 Henry IV* is thus less action as such than a series of diagnoses, or conjectures, about the state of the commonwealth's case in the present transitional time. And as this conjectural 'state of the case' depends largely on what can be inferred to be going on the minds of those who will succeed to power, or who are plotting the regime's overthrow (Prince Hal and the Earl of Northumberland, respectively), trifling matters, gestures, and details of speech become evidential material to be examined for signs of change in these men's moods and responses to events.

This is why, of course, the play opens with an ostentatious throw-back to the representational strategies of the hybrid morality play in the figure of Rumour, who enters 'painted full of tongues', and defines himself as 'a pipe | Blown by surmises, jealousies, conjectures' (Induction, 15–16). Though it may seem as though Rumour's effects are exhausted after the first, false account of Hotspur's victory at Shrewsbury has been corrected by the sadder truth, this is not so. For inferences immediately begin to be drawn by observers of Northumberland's impassioned reaction to the news of his son's death. Morton (Umfreville in Q) probes, sceptically: 'It was your presurmise', he points out to Northumberland, 'That in the dole of blows your son might drop. | You knew he walked o'er perils, on an edge, | More likely to fall in than to get o'er' (1. 1. 168–71). With this testing of the sincerity of Northumberland's theatrical gestures (his throwing away of his crutch and invoking of murderous

---

[23] For an interesting reading of this scene, see Sally Robertson Romotsky, 'Henry of Monmouth and the Gown-of-Needles', *Intertexts*, 8, no. 2 (2004), 155–72.

[24] I am grateful to Ed Gieskes, who witnessed the recent production at the Queen's Men Conference in Toronto, September 2006, and reported to me that the scene in question did prove emotionally effective.

spirits), Morton concludes by encouraging the Earl with hearsay: the Archbishop of York, he hears, is up in arms, and the scene concludes with Northumberland excitedly counselling 'the aptest way for safety and revenge' (1. 1. 213). The next scene of consultation, in Northumberland's absence, presses more critically on the question of his state of mind. The rebels, calculates Hastings, can count on 25,000 men, but the promise of greater 'supplies live largely in the hope | Of great Northumberland, whose bosom burns | With an incensed fire of injuries' (1. 3. 12–14). Lord Bardolph puts the pertinent question: must they count on the accuracy of their conjecture of what burns in Northumberland's bosom, or may 'our present five and twenty thousand | ... hold up head without Northumberland'? 'With him we may', comes Hastings's answer, to which Lord Bardolph sternly responds, 'in a theme so bloody-fac'd as this | Conjecture, expectation and surmise | Of aids incertain should not be admitted' (1. 3. 14–24). It does no harm, protests Hastings, 'To lay down likelihoods and forms of hope' (1. 3. 35). But Northumberland's mind, swayed by Lady Percy's persuasions, is, as he says himself, like the full tide on the turn, 'That makes a still-stand, running neither way', oscillating between Scotland and York (2. 3. 62–3). By the mid-point of the play, the audience knows that the tide has at last turned and that Northumberland is bound for Scotland, so that the rebels are, accordingly, only 25,000 strong. Henry IV, however, is sleepless with worry, lacking the audience's privileged insight into Northumberland's vacillating intentions, as he stands, at the mid-point of the action (the beginning of Act 3), wondering what to do. The figure of Rumour underlies his desolately fatalistic belief that he is doomed, that Richard II prophesied his fall: 'They say the Bishop and Northumberland are fifty thousand strong', he tells Warwick. These rumoured figures, bespeaking a 'division of ... amity' between himself and Northumberland, cause him to infer the fulfilment of Richard II's prophecy of Northumberland's betrayal (3. 1. 79). It is the audience's or reader's knowledge of Northumberland's hesitating uncertainty, belying the precipitate 'forms of hope' laid down by the rebels, that enables us to recognize in Warwick's sceptical reassurance of the King the laying bare of the principle underlying the plot of the whole play. Prophecy, Warwick explains, is nothing but the conjecture of the future, *based on inferences drawn from observation of the past*:

> There is a history in all men's lives
> Figuring the natures of the times deceas'd;

> The which observ'd, a man may prophesy
> With a near aim, of the main chance of things.

(3. 1. 80–3)

As Ginzburg notes, divination, or prophecy, is simply the activity of the conjectural or diagnostic analysis of small insights, apparently trifling signs, as this art is oriented towards the future, instead (as in hunting or law) towards the reconstruction of the past. But what concerns us, thinking about forensic transformations in dramatic mimesis in the 1590s, is the way in which Shakespeare's play innovatively thus conceives the present and past as materials for observation, diagnosis, and conjectural reconstruction as 'forms of hope' or hypotheses of 'the main chance of things'. The play further distinguishes those who expediently lay down forms of hope for themselves without diagnosing more expertly and complexly for the good of the commonwealth as 'shallow', whereas another sort of diagnostician—one who looks to the common good—is more profound, has depth. So Hastings, the readiest to 'lay down forms of hope', and to prophesy the continuance of resistance to Henry IV is declared 'much too shallow | To sound the bottom of the after-times' (4. 2. 50–1) by Hal's brother, John of Lancaster, while Falstaff, though flattering himself to have taken the measure of Master Robert Shallow, Esquire, shallowly sees in him nothing but the hope of a creditor against the coming of the new king, failing utterly to diagnose the pernicious effects of his corruption of local government.

Thus, just as the rebels continue to draw hopeful, but ultimately mistaken, inferences about the nature of Northumberland's feelings in relation to his son's death, so doings in Eastcheap are determined by uncertainty about Hal's feelings in relation to the sickness of his father. The King's sickness buoys Falstaff's failing confidence in his diminishing credit, prompting him to imagine new lucrative uses for a gouty foot (excuse for a military pension) and to fire off letters to likely creditors, including Mistress Quickly and Hal himself. Not all are prepared to give credit: Master Dommelton, the tailor, refuses Bardolph's bond for satin for Falstaff's new cloak and slops, and Mistress Quickly enters an action of debt against Falstaff, bringing officers to arrest him. Given that both Bardolph and Falstaff, however, are supposed to be still under suspicion or 'in question' for the notorious robbery at Gad's Hill, and that Bardolph in particular walks free because, as Falstaff says, of the 'box of the ear that the Prince gave' to the Lord Chief Justice, it seems surprising—and very funny—that they continue to evade pre-trial examination (1. 2. 60, 194). A whole scene plays wittily on Falstaff's inattention to the Lord Chief Justice as a symptom of the King's dying illness, when in fact the latter (with all its implied presumptions of the imminence of Hal's succession, the favour Falstaff hopes to enjoy, and the perils faced by the Lord Chief Justice) underpins Falstaff's legal immunity. The Lord Chief Justice proposes to 'physic' Falstaff's 'deafness' to his summons, offering to 'punish you by the heels' to 'amend the attention of your ears' (that is, to imprison him on suspicion until the Assizes, 1. 2. 123–5), but his failure to carry out this half-humorous threat points to the effects of 'th'unquiet time' (1. 2. 150), and uncertainty about what, for the regime, lies ahead.

Falstaff's ingenious improvisations to preserve his immunity are, early in the play, deliciously funny, if touched with cynicism; but as our vision broadens out across the commonwealth, the implications of the tide which seems to be turning in his favour become more sinister. As Falstaff traverses the country and takes up musters in Gloucestershire, the effects of Hal's impending succession on the administration of local justice are spelled out in the brilliantly sketched sycophancy of Justice Shallow's hospitality. Shallow's opening enquiries as to the welfare of Justice Silence's daughter and son set the tone of concern with old school tie networking which will dominate these scenes, rising to ludicrous heights in Shallow's claims to have been Falstaff's wild fellow law student at the Inns of Court. The great man, he assures Justice Silence smugly, on Bardolph's bringing commendations from Falstaff, 'greets me well' (3. 2. 63). But in the next moment he reveals the slenderness of any actual acquaintance with Falstaff, venturing to ask 'how my lady his wife doth?' This embarrassing gaffe is met with Bardolph's scornfully pretentious reply that 'a soldier is better accommodated than with a wife' (3. 2. 64–7). Undeterred, however, Shallow cynically urges his servant, Davy, to be cloyingly attentive to the comfort of their influential guests, 'for they are arrant knaves, and will backbite' (5. 1. 31–2), while Davy, in turn, reveals a no less cynical understanding of the patronage relations of court and counties in the administration of local justice. Just as Falstaff, to whom Shallow's ends are perfectly transparent, has the manipulable Justice of the Peace 'tempering between my finger and my thumb', so the Justice's man, Davy, knows he can count on his master to support his corrupt friend, William Visor, in his case against Clement Perkes 'a'th'Hill'. 'That Visor is an arrant knave', protests Shallow, but Davy knows how the system works: 'I have serv'd your worship truly, sir, this eight years; and if I cannot once or twice in a quarter bear out a knave against an honest man, I have little credit with your worship. The knave is mine

honest friend, sir, therefore I beseech you let him be countenanc'd...'
(5. 1. 38–51)

If we return at this point to the scene which gave Auerbach his chapter title 'The Weary Prince', we find that Auerbach's suggestive use of it as exemplifying the mimetic power of Shakespeare's stylistic range does not tell the whole story. For though Hal is ribbed by Poins for the indecorum of his weariness, underlying both the teasing and the suggestion of despondency that gives rise to it lies the audience's or reader's consciousness of all the other conjectures building on the hopes of the present time. It is not just, then, that Hal's declaration of weariness suggests an inner sadness at odds with the presumption of Poins and others that he rejoices in the illness of his father. It is, rather, that presumptions about what Hal is likely to do, pervading the entire play, acquire a kind of semiotic substantiality and a predictability that enables Hal, in turn, to seem to be conjecturing the likely form of his companions' hopeful thoughts before they have given voice to them. In other words, the prevalence of presumptions about what Hal is likely to do enables us—and Hal—to anticipate and *suspect* the motives underlying his friends' apparently affectionate uses of him. We are complicit in the process that produces his friends as 'shallow', easily sounded, easily seen through. And this in turn enables the reader or audience to form some sense—though, as the play's critical history shows, not at all a comfortable one—that Hal's dissembling with his friends until the time of his father's death is less cynical than ethical, a 'deeper' dissembling for the sake of the commonwealth. For example, moments after the conversation about Poins's hosiery and linen which so intrigued Auerbach, the question of the conversation's timing is raised. Poins, inferring the lightness of Hal's mood from his readiness to revert to their usual idiom of ironic banter, gloats that not many princes would 'talk so idly...their fathers being sick as yours at this time is'. Hal, dry and non-committal, asks what Poins would think if he 'should weep?' 'I would think thee a most princely hypocrite', says Poins, and Hal promptly puts him in his place: 'thou art a blessed fellow, to think as every man thinks. Never a man's thought in the world keeps the road-way better than thine: every man would think me an hypocrite indeed' (2. 2. 57–60). Shakespeare has here reimagined Ned's confident conjecture in *Famous Victories* that any expression of 'a little sorrowing' on Hal's part would be 'to make folks believe | The death of your father greeves you, And tis nothing so' (*Famous Victories*, 738–9). The significant distinction, however, lies in what Hal does with this conjecture: he anticipates it, and makes no comment about its accuracy other than to say, deprecatingly, 'It would be every man's thought' (2. 2. 56). Like Prospero, the hero of Jonson's *Every Man In his Humour*, which was written just at this time, Shakespeare's Hal remains silent on the question of his own mood, or temper, preferring to signal how well he reads others' mistaken diagnoses of it rather than to reveal it.[25] At this point in the scene, then, Hal seems ready to leave the question of his mood thus in question when a letter arrives from Falstaff. The letter's meagre contents corroborate Hal's reading of others' conjectures about him, for once Falstaff's transparently self-interested claims to kinship with Hal have been dispensed with, all that is left of the letter is a warning: 'Be not too familiar with Poins, for he misuses thy favours so much that he swears thou art to marry his sister Nell' (2. 2. 127–9). Hal gives no immediate sign of being dismayed at this, but asks in passing, 'But do you use me thus, Ned? | Must I marry your sister?' (2. 2. 138–9). Ned denies it, but Hal makes no reassuring comment of belief in him. Once again, the significant 'action' of the scene is the implicit work of conjecture; we sense, more effectively because it is unspoken, the presence of the scepticism and suspicion that works to distance the Prince from both Falstaff's and Poins's cynically flattering attempts to observe his moods, while each backbites and informs upon the other in a fashion adumbrating the court politics of the reign which they imagine is to come.

Thus we can see that Ginzburg's 'conjectural' or 'evidential' paradigm, though most obviously bearing an affinity to the model of reading as detection, has relevance as a model for understanding something about the changes that take place in the plotting of dramatic action on the popular stage between the 1570s and the 1590s. *2 Henry IV* offers a stronger, more intense sense of mimesis—of imitating life as we experience it—than *The Famous Victories of Henry Fifth* partly because the playwright has decided to plot many unstaged events (Hal's assault on the Justice, the Justice's arrest

---

[25] On 4 Aug. 1600, Jonson's *Every Man In* was recorded in the Stationers' Register as being 'staied', along with *As You Like It*, *Henry V*, and *Much Ado about Nothing*. Shortly after, on 23 Aug. the Stationers' Register recorded the entry of '*Muche a Doo about nothinge*' and '*the second parte of the history of kinge* HENRY *the iiiith with the humours of Sir* IOHN FALSTAFF: Wrytten by master Shakespere. xij^d'. Both *Much Ado* and *2 Henry IV* were said to have been '*sundrie times publikely acted, by the right honourable, the Lord Chamberlaine his servants*'. On 14 Aug. 1601, *Every Man In* was registered 'As it hath beene sundry times publickly acted by the Honorable the Lord Chamber*laine his servants*. Written by BEN JOHNSON.' See Andrew Gurr, *The Shakespeare Company, 1594–1602* (Cambridge: Cambridge University Press, 2004), 291–2. As Robert Miola points out, Shakespeare was experimenting with the fashion set by Chapman and Jonson for 'humours' comedy in *1 Henry IV*, *2 Henry IV*, *Henry V*, and *The Merry Wives of Windsor* (Miola (ed.), *Every Man in his Humour* (Manchester: Manchester University Press, 2000), 14). I argue more fully for Shakespeare's engagement with what Jonson was doing in *Every Man In* in Ch. 7.

of Hal), along with the previous play's events (the Battle of Shrewsbury) as the material of 'historical' allusion and analysis, traces of 'something having passed this way', from which inferences can be drawn. Although the play's explicit orientation of this inference drawing towards the future is not in itself forensic, it is nevertheless, like the forensic 'conjectural state of the case', a controversy requiring the invention of arguments '*ex causa, ex persona, ex facto ipso*' ('from the cause of the action, from the character of the person involved, and from the nature of the act') in order to deliberate effectively about the future. After all, as Kathy Eden has written, 'it is forensic oratory which lends its procedures to the other two branches—deliberative and epideictic'.[26] Thus, though the signs by which we interpret Hal as a character are nothing like the footprints by which the form of the lost camel is inferred by the Princes of Serendippo, it is nevertheless by inference that his father can imagine that Hal's moods, when he is King, will be like 'a whale on ground', uncontrollable tantrums that will need time, and no doubt lots of humouring—to '[c]onfound themselves with working' (4. 4. 41). And it is as a result of unostentatious moments of resistance to this highly persuasive *doxa*, or highroad of men's thought, that Hal's reformation seems less, in Shakespeare's play, like a theatrical conversion than like the revelation of a capacity for self-government that was always potentially 'inward'.

'Commons within': Participatory Justice and Forensic Rhetoric in *The First Part of the Contention (2 Henry VI)*

Shakespeare's rewriting of *Famous Victories* in *2 Henry IV* arguably gained a sense of inwardness for the hero at the expense of retaining the vividness of the earlier play's depiction of the role of participatory justice in the politics of the commonwealth. Though Shakespeare's Henry V does, in the end, behave like a constitutional monarch in explicitly submitting his 'intents' to the 'directions' of the Lord Chief Justice (5. 2. 120–1), the play's pervasive suggestion of an analogy between Falstaff's decrepitude and the 'body of our kingdom', 'rank' with political corruption (3. 1. 38–9), has prompted many critics to see the play as the dramatization of an incarnational model of the commonwealth as mystical body, rather than seeing it as the dramatization of the deliberative work involved in conjecturing the form of a 'commonweal' as opposed to a lucrative network of

[26] Kathy Eden, *Poetic and Legal Fiction in the Aristotelian Tradition* (Princeton: Princeton University Press, 1986), 9.

power, a 'private weal' of clientage, corruption, and extortion.[27] It is no wonder, then, that the two parts of *Henry IV*, along with *Henry V*, have been at the centre of debates about the possibility of subversion in Renaissance drama, for these plays adapt a previous company's dramatic concern with 'commonwealth' themes to a new dramaturgy of inference and conjecture (or what Gascoigne would have called 'supposes') centring on a single monarch-hero. Yet it would be wrong to conclude from this that Shakespeare's use of inference and of a forensic rhetoric of plot is necessarily always as focused on the monarch. In earlier experiments in revenge tragedy and chronicle history we see Shakespeare adapting the rhetoric of classical and reformed forensic drama to the forms of English participatory justice in such a way as to suggest that the latter is a form of political agency and an instrument against oppression. We have seen how this works in *Titus Andronicus*, and I will show, here, how it is central to one of Shakespeare's earliest experiments in chronicle history, *The First Part of the Contention betwixt the two Famous Houses of York and Lancaster* (printed 1594), which we know as *2 Henry VI*.

Before we turn to *2 Henry VI*, however, it is worth pausing over the fact that although English criminal justice is participatory, the civic detective plots of the 1570s tend to ignore this fact, presenting the virtuous magistrate (Gascoigne's Markgrave, Sidney's Euarchus, Whetstone's Ulrico) as the repository of skill in the weighing of presumptions and analysing of evidence. At the same time, however, a tradition of representing 'Justice' in the abstract as a figure of pre-eminent importance in the commonwealth, and as defining the boundaries of governmental power in terms of responsibility to the people, was fairly continuous throughout the drama of the sixteenth century. J. Wilson McCutchan observed that the treatment of 'Justice' as a morality-play personification changed over the course of the fifteenth and sixteenth centuries in ways that unsurprisingly suggest an increasing civic consciousness in drama. Though indebted to the representation of Justice as a judge of souls and one of the Four Daughters of God in the mid-fifteenth century *Castle of Perseverance*, 'Justice' in Nicholas Udall's *Respublica* (1553) has acquired newly secular

---

[27] The *locus classicus* for the 'incarnational' model is, of course, Ernst H. Kantorowicz, *The King's Two Bodies* (Princeton: Princeton University Press, 1957). For accounts of discourse on the 'commonwealth' that follow the model of deliberation for the public good, see W. R. D. Jones, *The Tudor Commonwealth 1529–1559* (London: Athlone, 1970); William Sherman, 'Anatomizing the Commonwealth', in *The Project of Prose in Early Modern Europe and the New World*, ed. Elizabeth Fowler and Roland Greene (Cambridge: Cambridge University Press, 1997), 104–21; Lorna Hutson, 'Not the King's Two Bodies', in *Rhetoric and Law in Early Modern Europe*, ed. Lorna Hutson and Victoria Kahn (New Haven: Yale University Press, 2001), 166–99.

features. She commits the offenders against the commonwealth—Avarice, Insolence, and Oppression—to the 'custodie' of 'People, representing the poore Commontie', and though it is 'Nemesis' who actually oversees the trial of these suspects, a sense of the participatory justice system is evident when 'People' concludes, 'Chil lyver hym [I'll deliver him] to the Constable', until, as Nemesis says, 'tyme maie serve | texamine *and* trie their cause'.[28] Though 'Justice' is not personified as such in *Nice Wanton*, the representation in that play of the judge, Daniel, as one who did not take bribes of Iniquity but would 'tary for the verdite of the quest ere I go', is one which clearly idealizes not only judicial due process but the participatory system.[29] In the 'Tragicall Comedie' of *Apius and Virginia*, by R. B. (S. R. 1567–8), 'Justice' is the civic virtue abandoned by the lecherous Roman judge, Apius, which, along with Conscience, emerges, in one scene, from the judge's breast.[30] In *King Daryus* (printed 1565) and *Liberality and Prodigality* (printed in 1602, but believed to have been performed in some form at the Christmas revels at court in 1567–8), the figure of 'Equity' appears both as a person and in the virtue exercised by King Daryus in judging between his counsellors.[31] The 'hybrid chronicle', mixing historical and allegorical figures, likewise makes the exercise of justice, along with the judging of good counsel, the pre-eminent virtue of government. In *Cambises*, as we have seen, King Cambises' single virtuous deed consists in heeding 'Commons Complaint', 'Proof', and 'Trial' against the corrupt judge, Sisamnes, who has declared earlier to the audience his plans to 'abrogate the law as I shall find it good'.[32]

In the morality tradition, however, though 'Justice' might be civic and associated with the 'commontie', it could scarcely be represented as evidential. Conversely, in the classically influenced tradition, the evaluation of evidence (the weighing of presumptions and circumstances

[28] J. Wilson McCutchan, 'Justice and Equity in the English Morality Play', *Journal of the History of Ideas*, 19 (1958), 405–10. See Nicholas Udall, *Respublica*, ed. W. W. Greg (London: EETS, 1952), ll. 1802–4, 1910, 1918.
[29] *A Preaty Interlude called, Nice Wanton* (London: John King, 1570), sig. B3r.
[30] R. B., *A New Tragicall Comedie of Apius and Virginia* (London: William How for Richard Jones, 1575), sig. C1r.
[31] McCutchan, 'Justice and Equity', 408. *A Pretie new Enterlude both pithie and pleasaunt of the Story of Kyng Daryus* (London, 1565), sig. B4r; *A Pleasant Comedie, Shewing the Contention between Liberality and Prodigality* (London: Simon Stafford for George Vincent, 1602), sigs. F1r–F3v. On the 1567 performance of *Liberality and Prodigality*, see Bevington, *Mankind to Marlowe*, 29.
[32] *Cambyses, King of Persia*, in *Drama of the English Renaissance*, ed. Russell A. Fraser and Norman Rabkin (Upper Saddle River, NJ: Prentice-Hall, 1976), 117–18. On the learned, humanist basis of the play in Richard Taverner's *Garden of Wisdom*, and on its authorship by Thomas Preston of King's College and later Trinity Hall, Cambridge, see Armstrong, 'Authorship and Political Meaning of *Cambises*'.

and inferring of likely motives) was rarely represented as a popular, participatory activity, but rather as the sole prerogative of the judge or magistrate. Indeed, this judiciary discretion might well be represented as open to abuse. In Whetstone's *Promos and Cassandra* (1578) forensic arguments are continually being twisted and inverted by the corrupt magistrates of the city of Julio, under the governance of Promos, judicial deputy for the absent King of Bohemia and Hungary. One of Promos's officers, the pettyfogger Phallax, detains a woman 'on suspicion' of wantonness so that he may lewdly 'searche her faultes' himself, instead of gathering testimony.[33] In a similarly lewd parody of equitable judgment, the governing magistrate Promos comes to the conclusion that he must betray his promise to marry Cassandra and reprieve her brother after deflowering her: 'having well the circumstaunces wayde', he muses, 'I finde I must unsware the oathe I tooke' (p. 468). Phallax meanwhile employs promoters, or paid informers, who likewise misuse evidential concepts. In one scene, Rapax, one of the informers, accuses John Adroynes of fornication with his father's maid (a capital offence in Julio) on the 'proof' that another paid informer, Gripax, saw them kiss. 'Can not fo[l]ke kys, but they are naught by and by?', asks the terrified John Adroynes, but Phallax informs him that 'This presumption friend wyll touch thee shrowdlie', and that if he is lucky enough to escape with his life, he will be 'terribly whipped' (p. 494). It is John Adroynes who, in the end, takes satisfaction in conveying to a stranger in the woods the news that Promos himself has come up for trial in open court by King Corvinus of Bohemia, and has been condemned to death for raping a maid. The stranger is none other than Andrugio, who was condemned to death by Promos for having had premarital sex with his fiancée, Polina, but, secretly spared by the gaoler, has lived exiled in the woods ever since. John Adroynes's news thus inadvertently precipitates the final recognition, since Andrugio then feels free to return to Julio and reveal himself to his sister, a revelation which prompts the King to pardon Promos, now married to Cassandra, after all (pp. 512–13).

Though critics still sometimes write as though the 'learned' tradition was one thing, and the 'popular' quite another, it seems fairly clear that both Senecan and Terentian Inns of Court plays had an impact on episodic and morality drama in the 1580s. As Marie Axton has pointed out, *2 Seven Deadly Sins*, a play associated with some of the actors later

---

[33] Whetstone, *Promos and Cassandra* (1578), in Bullough (ed.), *Narrative and Dramatic Sources of Shakespeare* (London: Routledge & Kegan Paul, 1968), ii. 465. Further references to page numbers in this edition will be given in the text.

named in the Quarto text of *2 Henry VI* (*The First Part of the Contention*), appears to have been a production in which 'professional and coterie traditions meet'.[34] We can see from the surviving plot of the play how the allegorical and deliberative traditions are blended: as Henry VI lies asleep on-stage, Pride, Gluttony, Wrath, and Covetousness enter at one door, while Envy, Sloth, and Lechery come in at another and overcome them. When Henry awakes, Envy passes over the stage, and the poet Lydgate speaks, introducing a dumb show featuring *Gorboduc* 'wth 2 Counsailors' and his sons, Ferrex and Porrex. As Axton observes, 'Gorboduc, played by Richard Burbage, enacts Sackville and Norton's crucial addition to the chronicle story after he "hath *Consulted with his Lords* he bringeth his 2 sonnes to severall seates".'[35] A moment of Senecan deliberative drama is thus translated into the gestures of a dumb show within a mixed allegorical and chronicle-style representation of Henry VI, showing both how versatile popular dramaturgy could be and how open were the channels of influence between traditions.

In a similar way, the court morality *Liberality and Prodigality* blends a traditional allegorical 'contention' structure with a circumstantially specific fictional sequence in five acts, including a detailed verbal reminiscence of Gascoigne's *Supposes*.[36] Moreover, although the allegorical plot of *Liberality and Prodigality* means the play cannot actually accommodate forensic argument, or scenes of evidence evaluation, it nevertheless leans as far as the genre will permit in the direction of presenting such scenes. In Act 5, a crime is committed: Prodigality, accompanied by Dick Dicer and Tom Tosse, murders the curmudgeonly yeoman, Tenacity, in order to retrieve

[34] Marie Axton, *The Queen's Two Bodies* (London: Royal Historical Society, 1977), 78. On the shared acting personnel in *2 Seven Deadly Sins* and *The First Part of the Contention*, see Scott McMillin, 'Casting for Pembroke's Men', *Shakespeare Quarterly*, 23 (1972), 141–59, at 157. See also McMillin and Maclean, *Queen's Men*, 93.

[35] 'The Platt of the Secound Parte of the Seven Deadlie Sinns', in W. W. Greg (ed.), *Dramatic Documents from the Elizabethan Playhouses* (Oxford: Clarendon Press, 1913), ii: *Reproductions and Transcripts*; Axton, *Queen's Two Bodies*, 78–9.

[36] See *A Pleasant Comedie, Shewing the contention betweene Liberalitie and Prodigalitie as it was played before her Majestie* (London: Simon Stafford for George Vincent, 1602), sig. C4[r]. Here Dandeline, the Hostess of the Inn, opens Act 3 by complaining about her serving maid: 'By my truth truly, had I not come in the rather | She had laid me to the fire, the loyne of veale and Capon both together, | Not waying (like an vanity girlish mother) | That the one would ask more rosting then the other; | So that either the Veale had been left stark raw, | Or else the Capon burn, and so not worth a straw.' This is a reminiscence of Gascoigne's parasite, Pasafilo, supervising the dinner in the feigned Erostrato's house, as Philogano arrives in Ferrara: 'Marie, *Dalio* would have layd the shoulder of mutton and the Capon both to the fire at once, like a foole, he did not consider that the one would have more roasting than the other.' *Ero*. 'Alas, I would this were the greatest fault'. *Pa*. 'Why? and either the one should have bene burned before the other had bene roasted' (*Supposes*, 5. 3. 5–10, in *Hundreth Sundrie Flowres*, ed. Pigman, 49).

Money, lately gone from the former's custody to the latter's. The dastardly deed not being shown, the audience learns of it gradually, in retrospect, as the justice system goes into action. First, in Act 5, Scene 2, '*The Constables make hue and cry*', and the innkeeper calls for his scull and brown bill to join in, asking the constables, 'how stands the case?' 'Not farre from this place', one replies, a 'plaine simple man' was spoiled and robbed as he rode along. 'It was my hap to come then present by him', says a constable, 'And found him dead, with twenty wounds upon him.' The innkeeper immediately asks what became of the villains? The constable indicates where they fled, and they depart off-stage in pursuit.[37] Two scenes later, the sheriff recounts the facts of the case to Vertue and Equity:

> This gallant, I tell you, with other lewd franions,
> Such as himselfe, unthrifty companions,
> In most cruell sort, by the high way side,
> Assaulted a countrie man, as he homewards did ride,
> Robbed him, and spoiled him of all that they might,
> And lastly, bereav'd him of his life out-right.

'O horrible fact!', exclaims Vertue, and charges Equity:

> Therefore goe you, Equity, examine more diligently
> The maner of this outragious robbery:
> As the same, by examination shall appeare,
> Due justice may be done in presence here.[38]

Prodigality's arraignment follows in Scene 5 of Act 5, dramatized with the attention to procedural ritual that marks similar scenes in *Nice Wanton* and *The Famous Victories* (the crier calling the prisoner, the clerk asking him to hold up his hand, and then reading the indictment, etc.). Just as Equity's pre-trial examination is not actually represented, however, so the courtroom scene stops short of any trial, as Prodigality confesses that 'my fact falles out so apparantly' and appeals to the Prince's mercy.[39] Nevertheless, in the gradual, retrospective manner by which we learn the 'facts' of the allegorical crime—first summarily from the constable, then in more circumstantial detail from the sheriff—this late example of the morality plays shows plainly how much the genre has been affected not only by five-act classical drama's concern with causality and probability, but by a perception of the affinity between five-act drama and the culture of evidence evaluation (as in the Host's 'how stands the case?') being

---

[37] *Liberalitie and Prodigalitie*, sig. E4^{r-v}.   [38] Ibid., sig. F1^v–2^r.   [39] Ibid., sig. F3^{r-v}.

diffused through society by the demands of the participatory justice system.

A perception of the affinity of the classical intrigue plot and the popular culture of evidence evaluation is the key to the plotting of *The First Part of the Contention betwixt the two Famous Houses of York and Lancaster* (printed 1594), which we know as *2 Henry VI*.[40] In this play, as I noted in Chapter 1, there occurs a sequence of action in which an extraordinary emotional pressure is brought to bear on the discovery of a sudden death, which turns rapidly into a murder investigation. At the beginning of this sequence, which occurs about half-way through the play, the King and peers assemble, awaiting Duke Humphrey's arrival to answer charges against him. The audience watching either version of the play, Q or F, would already know that the murder has taken place; there's a tense and painful irony in the King's weak protestation that proceedings against Humphrey be conducted on 'good evidence' (F) or 'just proofe' (Q 1206). Into this sinister atmosphere the announcement that Humphrey has been found 'Dead in his bed' has cataclysmic effects (Q 1211). The King faints, and then responds with horror to the sight of the Duke of Suffolk, as if he suspects what has happened. And then, as if King and people are united in their refusal to accept this death as natural, the Earls of Warwick and Salisbury come on-stage, Warwick reporting that the commons report that 'good Duke Humphreys death' is murder, and that the Duke of Suffolk and the Cardinal are guilty (Q 1239). The command is given to 'view' the body, and, that done, Warwick swears an oath which, as Emrys Jones notes, is 'quite exceptionally heightened', swelling 'without pause for three lines', even in Q's elsewhere laconic text:

> Now by his soule that tooke our shape upon him,
> To free us from his fathers dreadful curse,
> I am resolv'd that violent hands were laid,
> Upon the life of this thrise famous Duke.

(Q 1250–3)

To support this 'dreadful' oath, Warwick then makes the speech that, as I suggested in Chapter 1, seems to be modelled on the idea of the coroner's investigation *super visum corporis*. Here is that speech again, as it appears in Q:

[40] Quotations and line numbers referring to the 1623 Folio text are taken from Charlton Hinman (ed.), *The Norton Facsimile* (New York: Norton, 1996), and are noted in the text as parenthetical F followed by line numbers. Those referring to the 1594 Quarto (Q) are taken from *The First Part of the Contention 1594*, ed. William Montgomery (Oxford: Malone Society Reprints, 1985), and appear in the text as parenthetical Q followed by line numbers.

> Oft have I seene a timely parted ghost,
> Of ashie semblance, pale and bloodlesse,
> But loe the blood is setled in his face,
> More better coloured than when he liv'd,
> His well proportioned beard made rough and sterne,
> And fingers spred abrode as one that graspt for life,
> Yet was by strength surprisde, the least of these are probable,
> It cannot chuse but he was murthered.
>
> (Q 1256–63)

And here is the speech as it appears in F:

> See how the blood is setled in his face.
> Oft have I seene a timely-parted Ghost,
> Of ashy semblance, meager, pale and bloodlesse,
> Being all descended to the labouring heart,
> Who in the Conflict that it holds with death,
> Attracts the same for aydance 'gainst the enemy,
> Which with the heart there cooles, and ne'er returneth
> To blush and beautifie the Cheeke again.
> But see, his face is blacke, and full of blood;
> His eye balles further out, than when he lived,
> Staring full ghastly, like a strangled man:
> His hayre uprear'd, his nostrils stretcht with strugling:
> His hands abroad display'd, as one that graspt
> And tugg'd for Life, and was by strength subdude.
> Look on the sheets his haire (you see) is sticking,
> His well proportion'd Beard, made rough and rugged,
> Like to the Summers Corn by Tempest lodged:
> It cannot be but he was murdred here.
> The least of all these signes were probable.
>
> (F 1864–82)

This later version of this speech, though amplified, clearly builds upon a conception which is essentially present in Q.[41] What the dramatist is

---

[41] To argue thus is necessarily to take up a position within the debate about authorship and attribution that is inseparable from any critical account of the *Henry VI* plays. While Heminge and Condell ensured the attribution of the *Henry VI* plays to Shakespeare by inclusion of them in the 1623 Folio, the charges of plagiarism levelled against 'Shakes-scene' by the *Groatsworth of witte* (1592) caused Edmund Malone to propose Greene and Peele to be authors of plays which Shakespeare had rewritten; this theory held until the revolution caused by the work of A. W. Pollard and W. W. Greg distinguishing 'good' from 'bad' Quartos and identifying the latter as the playing company's 'memorial reconstruction' of the play for performance. Despite Laurie Maguire's excellently sceptical account of the basis on which readings were identified as evincing signs

presenting here is the rhetorical invention of the suspicion, or conjecture, that Humphrey's death was not, as Suffolk implicitly claimed, of natural causes. Again, this conception, though present in Q, is amplified and made more explicit in F, where the King prays to God, the eternal Judge, that he be forgiven his suspicion if it prove false: 'O thou that judgest all things, stay my thoghts: | My thoughts, that labour to perswade my soule | Some violent hands were laid on Humfries life: | If my suspect be false, forgive me God' (F 1838–41). Although Warwick's speech genre may, in both texts, appear anachronistic in being recognizable to us as the reasoning associated with forensic pathology and the hermeneutics of the detective novel, the scene's effect, needless to say, is nothing like that of crime fiction, not only because there is no mystery to us about Suffolk's guilt, but also because Duke Humphrey, unlike the corpses that litter most detective fiction, has been, for us, a public-spirited yet passionate, astute, and, above all, *vital* presence for the first half of the play. Emrys Jones has suggested that the 'effect of wildly exaggerated clamour' of F's treatment of Humphrey's death may derive from the modelling of Humphrey's persecution and death on Christ's Passion in the mystery cycles, since there seems to be something

of faulty memorial reconstruction rather than signs of various kinds of intelligent rewriting, Roger Warren's 2003 edition of *2 Henry VI* for the Oxford Shakespeare still identifies *The First Part of the Contention* as a reported text, essentially endorsing the conclusions of Peter Alexander and Madeleine Doran in the 1920s, who, working independently, had argued that the Quarto versions of *2* and *3 Henry VI* are memorial reconstructions of the corresponding Folio texts. Though Warren's edition prefers occasional Quarto readings, such as the greater 'dramatic logic' of Q's stage direction for the opening scene, he dismisses Steven Urkowitz's argument that Q and F each have validity as Shakespearean alternatives. See Roger Warren, 'The Quarto and Folio Texts of *2 Henry VI*', *Review of English Studies*, n.s. 51 (2000), 194–207, and Stephen Urkowitz, '"If I Mistake in Those Foundations Which I Build Upon"', *English Literary Renaissance*, 18 (1988), 230–55. It is not part of the purpose of this book to make a supporting case for Urkowitz's argument by means of detailed discussion of textual variants. However, I feel as sceptical as Scott McMillin about the consequences of the Alexander–Doran hypothesis, which allowed critics to imagine Shakespeare as 'the venturesome young author who as early as 1590–1 designed a serious and realistic group of plays on the Wars of the Roses, in a form close to F' ('Casting for Pembroke's Men', 141). Whether *1 Contention* is a reported text or, as now seems more plausible to me, a Shakespearean alternative reflecting an earlier conception of the play that became *2 Henry VI*, it repays analysis as an example of how a dramatist or dramatists might, prior to 1594, have made innovative use of a perceived affinity between the forms of English participatory justice and the forensic rhetoric of Plautine and Terentian comedy to produce a new kind of genre—the inferentially plotted chronicle history, thematically concerned with justice in the commonwealth, and formally concerned with causality and probability. For this reason, and because the Folio text of *2 Henry VI* rhetorically amplifies suggestions of forensic emplotment already present in *1 Contention*, I take the latter as an example of the state of the art in the adaptation of forensic argument to the chronicle history play of the early 1590s.

hyperbolic about the death of a good man—'even such a good man as Duke Humphrey', occasioning such emotional stress.[42] My suggestion, however, would be that it is not simply the death of Humphrey the man, but the loss of 'Justice'—both in Humphrey's death and in the suspicion of his unjust murder—that releases such feeling here. The spiritual charge to the scene's arousal of emotion seems inseparable from the passion for justice and for the administration of justice in the *respublica* that Humphrey himself embodied, and it is this passion that the commons, in refusing to accept the peers' report of his death, and demanding what amounts to an inquest, momentarily revive over his corpse, before the sight of it vanishes for good in the brutally vengeful class war that ensues.

What Shakespeare appears to be doing, in terms of plot, with Warwick's forensic speech over the body of Duke Humphrey is, then, of considerable significance (both dramatic and political) in a play which models its scenes of the popular uprising, quite unhistorically, on an earlier popular movement (the Peasants' Revolt of 1381) in which the people aimed their rage specifically at the institutions of the common law.[43] Arguments that Shakespeare conflated the two popular movements without any purpose will not hold up: apart from Dick the Butcher's famous suggestion, 'let's kill all the Lawyers' (F 2394), and Cade's command that men go 'to th'Innes of Court, downe with them all' (F 2634), it is clear that the entire rebellion has, as Craig Bernthal argues, been conceived as a 'legal carnival', a series of mock-trials which invert the judicial abuses of the play's first half, visiting horrible revenge on the hapless representatives of law and literacy.[44] But Bernthal's view that Cade's legal carnival thereby functions 'as an unmasking of the Tudor (and all other) judicial systems: a demonstration that judicial decision-making is really just the exercise of raw power cloaked in the rhetoric of equitable language', while true in the absolute sense that the Tudor judicial system was indeed oppressive and frequently corrupt, does not sit comfortably with the play's invocation of something like a 'judicial system' at work in Warwick's coroner-like address to King and commons on the signs of foul play on the corpse

---

[42] Emrys Jones, *The Origins of Shakespeare* (Oxford: Clarendon Press, 1977), 46.

[43] See, e.g., the excerpt from the third volume of Holinshed's Chronicles (1587 edn.) in Bullough (ed.), *Narrative and Dramatic Sources of Shakespeare*, iii. 131, where the 'commons also in the counties of Sussex, Hertford, Cambridge, Suffolke, and Norfolke, and other shires about...began to shew proofe of those things which they had before conceived in their minds, beheading all such men of law, justices, and jurors as they might catch'.

[44] See Craig A. Bernthal, 'Jack Cade's Legal Carnival', *Studies in English Literature, 1500–1900*, 42, no. 2 (Spring 2002), 259–74, esp. 264–70.

of Duke Humphrey.[45] That is to say that Warwick's positioning of the commons as a kind of jury, which, via Salisbury, delivers up to the King the verdict that condemns Suffolk ('They say by him the good Duke Humphrey died' (Q)) feels profoundly, if temporarily, cathartic precisely because it seems to break through an increasingly stifling sense of judicial procedure as the plaything of those in power in the regime, returning us for a moment, by way of a popular forensic investigation, to an emotional understanding of the ideal sense in which justice is conceived of as at once a spiritual and a civic virtue.

As my metaphor of 'breaking through' something which 'stifles' would suggest, I see the first half of the play's action, in both the Folio and the Quarto texts, as plotted more or less in the form of a continuous intrigue, a mode of action which is often likened to a web closing round its victims. To argue thus is to oppose in this instance the more common view that chronicle history—as a new genre in the 1580s and 1590s—was not causally plotted. Paul Dean, for example, has endorsed Geoffrey Bullough's description of chronicle history plays as wave-like, successively introducing figures who dominate the action for a time, then yield to others, so that 'the episodes ... are not related causally but spatially'.[46] Within this essentially episodic action, Dean argues for the derivation of certain scenes in *2 Henry VI*—Eleanor Cobham's practising of necromancy (1. 2, 4), the Simpcox episode (2. 1), and the Cade scenes (4. 2, 6–8, 10)—from 'romance' histories, such as Greene's *James IV* or *Friar Bacon and Friar Bungay*. But a case can equally well be made for seeing the action of both *1 Contention* and *2 Henry VI* up until the death of Cade as adapting, after the manner of the Inns of Court dramatists of the 1570s, the forensic intrigue of Roman New Comedy to forms of civic tragedy and tragicomedy which depict the consequences of the abuse of justice. Such a reading would point out that Eleanor Cobham's necromancy, far from being merely an 'episode', is part of what York in F calls a 'pretty Plot, well chosen to build upon' (F 686), that is, a ground on which to build the case against Duke Humphrey, thus bringing him within the compass of suspicion of treason. The Simpcox episode likewise contributes circumstantially to the plausibility of the (otherwise trumped-up) charges later brought against Humphrey at the Parliament of Bury, amongst which it was alleged that he 'did devise | Strange Tortures for Offendors' (F 1421–2). The Jack Cade scenes, as I have mentioned, are

[45] Ibid. 271.

[46] Paul Dean, 'Shakespeare's Henry VI Trilogy and Elizabethan "Romance" Histories', *Shakespeare Quarterly*, 33, no. 1 (1982), 34–48, at 36–7.

not merely episodic, but have been clearly structured as parodies of the corrupt forensic strategies of legal procedure in the first half of the play, proceeding as they do as a series of trials in which Jack Cade pronounces sentence on the hapless representatives of the common law: the Clerk of Chatham (F 2402–27), Lord Saye (2658–2750), and, in Q (1839–52), on the Serjeant-at-law. The mock-trials of all of these are brutally carnivalesque. Cade says he must 'examine' the Clerk of Chatham and, having done so, sentences him to be hanged with pen and inkhorn about his neck. Lord Say is beheaded 'for pleading so well for his life' (F 2739–40). The serjeant complains to Cade that his wife has been raped, but Dicke Butcher defends his action as a legal one; because the serjeant was going to arrest him, 'I went and entred my Action in his wife's paper house' (Q 1845); the hapless officer of the law is sentenced to have his tongue cut out.[47]

In earlier chapters I noted how another early Shakespeare play, *Titus Andronicus*, generates a civic revenge plot by transforming the forensic tactics of Roman New Comedy's amorous youths and wily slaves into the criminal methods of Aaron and Tamora, playing on the transformation by way of jokes on the spatial and rhetorical senses of 'plot' as preparation against legal detection. *1 Contention* likewise shows Shakespeare thinking about how to connect historical episodes and generate intelligible dramatic action by the forensic and inferential means evident in Latin comic drama. The opening scene establishes, with admirable economy and intelligibility, the alignments and grudges of various parties, as they react to each other's reactions to the unfavourable terms of the marriage treatise negotiated by the Earl of Suffolk with King René, father of Margaret of Anjou, who becomes Henry VI's wife and Queen of England. In the following conjugal scene between Duke Humphrey, Protector of the Realm, and his wife, Dame Eleanor Cobham, we learn by way of her dream of her potentially treasonous ambitions, but it is the advent of a messenger from the King, with an invitation to join the newly married couple hawking at St Albans the next day, that introduces that note of temporal and spatial specificity so characteristic of intrigue plots (a similar hunting invitation likewise adumbrates a 'plot' in *Titus Andronicus*) and establishes a recognizable *occasio* or opportunity for Eleanor's scheme to confer with witches and conjurers. Moments after she has secretly arranged with Sir John Hum to use the time of the King's absence thus, her accomplice reveals himself to be part of a larger plot which, through the entrapment of Dame Eleanor, will slowly bring Duke Humphrey into

---

[47] *First Part of the Contention*, 52–3; Bernthal, 'Jack Cade's Legal Carnival', 266–7.

compass of suspicion of treason, enabling his indictment. Entrapment, of course, is a common feature of the forensic plot of New Comedy: it occurs in *Poenulus* and *Miles Gloriosus* and, most famously, in *Andria*.[48] *1 Contention* thus, far from being episodic, seamlessly and economically weaves the entrapment of Eleanor Cobham into a larger web of suspicion being woven to justify charges against Duke Humphrey.

Intrigue plots, of course, need to introduce apparent contingency to enable the illusion of improvisation; it must seem as though, as Sidney's Pyrocles says of his amorous intrigue, 'time itself discover[s] new secret helps', or, in the words of Iago, as if 'wit depends on dilatory time' (*Othello*, 2. 3. 373).[49] So in the scene after the larger plot to entrap Eleanor Cobham has been revealed, an apparently contingent case of mistaken identity offers Suffolk what he recognizes as an opportunity to further suspicion against his enemies. In a scene reminiscent of *Promos and Cassandra*, where the just deputy, Ulrico, hears citizens' complaints against the corrupt Phallax, Suffolk and Margaret are mistaken for Duke Humphrey and his wife, and are pestered with citizens proffering complaints against abusers of law, including, ironically, 'A complaint against the Duke of *Suffolke* for enclosing the commons of long Melford' (Q 333). But as well as economically thus dramatizing both Humphrey's probity and Suffolk's tyrannous rapacity, the scene demonstrates Suffolk as a brilliant forensic opportunist, a criminal Phormio. In the complaint of the apprentice, Peter Thump, that his master treasonously supported the Duke of York's claim to the throne, Suffolk sees a way, unclear to the audience as yet, to throw suspicion on York.

In the next scene, Suffolk's strategy reveals itself. This scene, a dispute between York and Somerset over who should be regent of France, has been one of the cruxes for regarding *1 Contention* as a memorial reconstruction: Humphrey has an unmotivated exit, evidence to some critics, such as Roger Warren, that Q's scene is 'a confused report' of the scene as it occurs in F or in another source (though Scott McMillin plausibly argues for Humphrey's exit as a solution to casting problems, enabling doubling).[50] However, regarding the scene in *1 Contention* as a part of a continuous intrigue reveals that it has an underlying forensic logic that would be no less intelligible on-stage than the version we find in F. In

[48] Adele C. Scafuro, *The Forensic Stage* (Cambridge: Cambridge University Press, 1997), 358–9.
[49] Philip Sidney, *The Old Arcadia*, ed. Katherine Duncan-Jones (Oxford: Oxford University Press, 1985), 17.
[50] Warren, 'Quarto and Folio Texts of *2 Henry VI*', 199; McMillin, 'Casting for Pembroke's Men', 147–9.

F, the dispute over the regentship leads into an attack on Humphrey, as Margaret challenges the necessity of Humphrey remaining as the King's Protector, and Humphrey's exit at the barrage of charges against him is retrospectively inferred to be as a result of his 'Choller' at being challenged (F 547). In Q, however, Suffolk's initiating of charges against Humphrey, concluding in an affirmation of Somerset's worthiness over York is not simply, as Warren claims, 'abruptly switch[ing] back to the question of the Regentship', but the introduction of a new forensic strategy against Humphrey and York together, via the 'evidence' that Suffolk has opportunely gathered in the previous scene from Peter Thump's charges of treason against his master.[51] Though the motive for Humphrey's exit is not as sharply defined to a reader as it would be if attacks on his governorship and private life had continued to escalate, as they do in F, it would be clear enough to an audience of Q that Suffolk's opportune bringing on of the apprentice against his master constitutes a triumph of forensic strategy for his party, and in some ways this version of the scene promotes a greater sense of the connection between the trial by battle of Thump against Horner and the defeat of Gloucester. For in Q Humphrey's and Warwick's support for York has clearly been defeated with an impeccable show of law, and the irony is that Humphrey himself must uphold the propriety of the defeat: 'For that these words the Armourer should speake, | Doth breed suspition on the part of *Yorke*, | Let *Somerset* be regent over the French, | Till trials made and *Yorke* may cleare himselfe' (Q 463–7).

Hall's *Chronicle* is Shakespeare's authority for the conception of Suffolk as 'the very organ, engine and diviser of the destruccion of Humfrey the good duke of Gloucester'; but it was the dramatist's own decision to draw on legal anecdotes extraneous to Hall's treatment of Humphrey's demise in order to plot that destruction as a malevolent intrigue comedy, a series of forensic strategies giving it 'Colour . . . by course of Law' (F 1538–9).[52] An aspect of Humphrey's vulnerability to his enemies' machinations is his very confidence both in judicial procedure and in his own exercise of judicial discretion. For example, there is no suggestion, in either Hall or Holinshed, that the apprentice's triumph over his master in the trial by battle (an incident unrelated, of course, to Humphrey's fall) actually gave divine proof of his master's treason. Both authors express a somewhat patrician disgust that a master 'beyng . . . overladed with hot drynkes' might be beaten by his servant, and I think it unlikely, *pace* Dominique

[51] Warren, 'Quarto and Folio Texts', 198.
[52] See the extracts from Hall in Bullough (ed.), *Narrative and Dramatic Sources of Shakespeare*, iii. 112.

Goy-Blanquet, that the outcome of this trial by battle, engineered as it was as part of Suffolk's larger plot, was intended to prove the immanence of God in human affairs.[53] It would seem rather, from a legal point of view, that the choice of trial by battle—a form of proof which, far from being the foundation of medieval folklaw, was consistently discouraged as doubtful and dangerous—implicates Humphrey's use of his judicial discretion here, since he appoints it as an appropriate mode of proof precisely because he judges the armourer's case more probable. In both texts the armourer pleads that he has 'good witness' of his servant's vow to be even with him for a past punishment, and in F Humphrey explicitly chooses trial by battle because the armourer 'hath witnesse of his servants malice' (F 606); yet in actual practice, as Richard Firth Green has demonstrated, judicial duels tended not to be allowed 'where unimpeachable witnesses could be marshalled against a plaintiff', but were a 'last resort', when no other means of proof or ground of compromise could be found.[54]

It is easy to see that the so-called Simpcox episode is likewise plotted to adumbrate and lend plausibility to the charges that his enemies will bring against Humphrey. Moreover, its emplotment as such is clearest in Q, where the scene's legal features stand out more prominently and almost pedantically. In this scene, which derives from anecdotes told by Thomas More and John Foxe, Duke Humphrey incisively exposes a fraudulent miracle involving a man who claimed to have been born blind and pretended that a visit to the shrine of St Alban had cured him. Shakespeare's use of this scene fits with the suggestion made by Edward Hall (who was, of course, a common lawyer as well as a chronicler) that the reason why Duke Humphrey became vulnerable to his enemies' charges that he had violated common law in his punishment of criminal offenders was because of his use of the civil law's methods, which allowed the judge more discretion in investigating the facts of an individual case: 'for surely the duke, being very well learned in the lawe civill, detestyng malefactors, and punishyng their offences, gat great malice and hatred of such as feared to have condigne reward for their ungracious actes and mischevous doynges'.[55] The civil law contours of Humphrey's examination of Simpcox

---

[53] See Hall, ibid. 105; Dominique Goy-Blanquet, *Shakespeare's Early History Plays* (Oxford: Oxford University Press, 2003), 91–3. Bernthal discusses the class biases of the chroniclers—Holinshed, Stow, and Hall—as evinced by their recording of this incident, in 'Treason in the Family', *Shakespeare Quarterly*, 42, no. 1 (1991), 44–54, esp. 52–3.

[54] Richard Firth Green, *A Crisis of Truth* (Philadelphia: University of Pennsylvania Press, 2002), 90. Green gives a persuasive account of trial by battle as a judicial last resort, hedged about by regulations 'intended to make [it]...seem as unattractive as possible' (78–92).

[55] Hall in Bullough (ed.), *Narrative and Dramatic Sources of Shakespeare*, iii. 107.

are evident in both texts, but are, interestingly, much more pronounced in *1 Contention* than in the Folio text (a difference that does not seem explicable in terms of any theory of memorial reconstruction, since the earlier text simply has a different, though equally deliberate, conception of the scene). It is as if more mature reflection on the scene's dramatic function revealed that it was possible to sketch in its civilian features more impressionistically. In *1 Contention* there is no mistaking the dramatist's desire to reproduce the civilian form of judicial examination. Whereas in F Humphrey only participates in contributing a few especially sceptical and revealing questions to Simpcox, who claims to have been cured of blindness by St Alban, Q has Humphrey conduct the entire interrogation on his own, asking the miracle claimant no fewer than seventeen sharp and witty circumstance-probing questions. In both texts, too, Shakespeare departs from his sources in presenting a more severe, not to say sadistic, wit in Humphrey's discretionary sentencing of the fraudulent pair, as the whips brought on to prove Simpcox far from lame suggest to Humphrey the horrifically cruel sentence that Simpcox and his wife should be 'whipt through every Market Towne | Till they come to Barwick' (F 909–10).

The first half of the play (or in F the opening two acts) may be seen, then, as a sequence of cynical manipulations of judicial procedure which exploit a certain vulnerable naivety in Humphrey's and Henry's readiness to enforce and accept, rather than instrumentally to exploit, the course of law. In the turning point of the play's action—the scenes of Humphrey's aborted trial, his secret murder, and the unleashing of popular anger in the aftermath of that murder—we have the coroner's inquest speech made by Warwick, with which I began.

Here at last we begin to see why Warwick's speech is so important and so charged with emotion. Critics have misunderstood its use of merely probable, uncertain signs; one writes that in terms of modern forensic pathology,

all the signs triumphantly listed by Warwick happen to be *non-specific*, that is, they do not point unequivocally to a violent death ... the red or blackened face, as well as the protruding eyes, are consistent with physical changes which occur because of such factors as lapse of time and temperature and position of the body ... He intimates signs of struggle: dishevelled hair and rumpled beard, nostrils stretched, hands clutching ... these, too, could have occurred *after* natural death ... [56]

It's certainly true that England, with its amateur-based criminal justice system, was lamentably belated in developing any standards of medical

---

[56] David Thatcher, 'Cover-up', *Shakespeare Newsletter*, 50, no. 4 (2000–1), 105–18, at 114.

evidence by comparison with its civil law Continental counterparts.[57] Even the few pages devoted in the mid-seventeenth century by Thomas Brugis in his *Vade Mecum or, a Companion for a Chyrugion* (1651) to 'the manner of making Reports to a Magistrate, or Coroner's Inquest' is, as the author acknowledges, merely a précis of Ambroise Paré's notes for surgeons performing autopsies in French civilian cases.[58] However, the reasons why the signs Warwick adduces are uncertain are not, in fact, to do with the incompetence of English medical forensics in this period, but are, rather, tied up with the importance of this dramatic moment as the only glimpse the play affords of participatory justice as popular political agency. Just as Brugis, unlike his author, Paré, orients his instructions in the diagnosis of signs of violent death to a 'Coroner's Inquest', a body of ordinary people rather than a professional judge, so Warwick, formulating his evidence in response to the commons' demands, performs an act of *probable forensic reasoning* which impressionistically attributes the power of fact finding, of evidence evaluation, to such ordinary people, the 'commons' who define 'the commonwealth'.

As such, Warwick's speech, and Salisbury's subsequent reporting back of the commons' 'verdict', transforms what in Hall's *Chronicle* is nothing but the uncertainty of rumours that Humphrey had been murdered into popular forensic activity, the people's initiation of judicial investigation. The speech, and its subsequent development in Warwick's confrontation with Humphrey's murderers, draws upon the very same classical discussions of forensic rhetoric as did the pre-trial examinations taken by Justices of the Peace. In 1588 Justice William Lambarde enlarged his *Eirenarcha, or the Office of Justices of the Peace* to include the adaptation of instructions, taken from the discussion, in Cicero's forensic rhetoric, the *De Inventione*, of how to argue the case in a conjectural issue (Fig. 5).[59] Lambarde equates the Justice's examination and taking of informations from witnesses with

---

[57] J. D. J. Havard, *The Detection of Secret Homicide* (London: Macmillan, 1960), 1–5.

[58] Thomas Brugis, *Vade Mecum or, a Companion for a Chyrugion*, 6th edn. (London, 1679), 288–95; see Jenny Ward, 'Brugis, Thomas (*b.* in or before 1620, *d.* in or after 1651)', in *Oxford Dictionary of National Biography* (Oxford: Oxford University Press, 2004).

[59] William Lambarde, *Eirenarcha: or of The office of the Justices of the Peace, in foure Bookes* (London: Ralph Newberry, 1592), 209–11. Prefacing the diagram, Lambarde writes: 'Touching the points that may ingender Suspition, I need not to say much, knowing that I speake to men of discretion and wisdome, to whom *omnium mendacium est pellucidum* ['every lie is transparent'] And yet seeing that *initia debent ab arte proficisci, quamquam caetera facile comparabit exercitatio* ['beginnings must proceed by art, though practice will easily provide the rest']: I take it not unserviceable to insert here, such a Briefe (or minute) thereof as I haue collected out of Cicero, and others, whereunto all the rest (which all the wit of man may inuent) will easily be referred.' See also Barbara Shapiro, 'Classical Rhetoric and the English Law of Evidence', in *Rhetoric and Law in Early Modern Europe*, ed. Victoria Kahn and

251

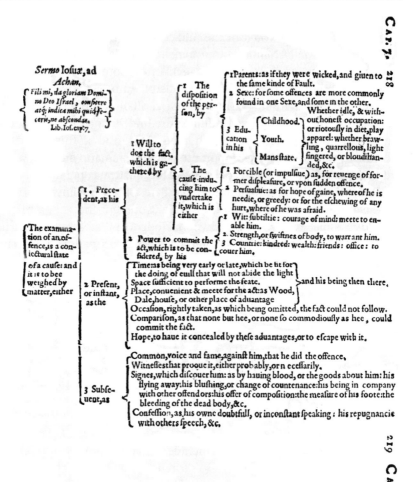

Figure 5. 'Briefe (or minute)...collected out of Cicero' of 'what things be material to induce Suspicion', William Lambarde, *Eirenarcha* (1592), pp. 218–9. Reproduced with permission from British Library, 883b4(1).

the Ciceronian issue of fact: 'The examination of an offence, is a conjectural state of a cause', he writes. He then arranges Cicero's classification of arguments of 'suspicion' into a table, dividing the material for proving the case into matter 'Precedent', 'Present', and 'Subsequent'.

Lorna Hutson (New Haven: Yale University Press, 2001), 64–6; Cicero, *De inventione*, trans. H. M. Hubbell (Cambridge, MA: Harvard University Press, 1949), 2. 14–51.

Precedent includes motive, or 'cause'; 'Subsequent' includes rumour and witnesses, as well as bodily signs, and traces at the scene of the crime such as the hair sticking (in F) on Gloucester's sheets.[60] Shakespeare draws on this early modern conjunction of classical forensic rhetoric and vernacular legal culture. Warwick begins with Lambarde's 'subsequent matter', and argues from signs on the dead body that Gloucester was murdered. In Q and F the Queen and Suffolk reply respectively, maintaining that Humphrey could not have been murdered, being in Suffolk's and the Cardinal's protection, unless Warwick is accusing them. But Warwick replies incisively with the category of motive: 'But Both of you were vowed D. Humfries foes' (F 1886). Margaret retaliates: 'Than you belike suspect these Noblemen ...[?]' (F 1890), and Warwick again eschews the chivalric invitation to personal confrontation, delivering instead a speech playing on the notion of the *eikota*, or probable sign, typical rhetorical instances of which were blood-stained clothes, a blood-stained weapon, or the placing of the body:

> Who finds the Heyfer dead, and bleeding fresh,
> And sees fast-by, a Butcher with an Axe,
> But will suspect, 'twas he that made the slaughter? ...
> Even so suspitious is this Tragedie.
>
> (F 1892–98)[61]

The images in this speech—the bleeding body, the proximity of an enemy with a weapon—were textbook examples of proofs which almost seem to come under the category of the 'entechnic' or 'inartificial' because they come with case, like witnesses and rumour.[62] But they are nevertheless technical or artificial proofs precisely because they are uncertain, and may be argued either way: they are signs, indications or traces from which something else is inferred.[63] In the exemplary case that Cicero gives (from which Lambarde has abstracted his table) the blood-stained sword has been planted on the suspect, vividly demonstrating that it is not an irrefutable proof.[64] So it is not that Warwick's earlier 'viewing' speech establishes demonstrably that Humphrey has been violently done to death, but that it performs discursively, as does the rest of the scene, Warwick's probable invention of the people's suspicion.

[60] Lambarde, *Eirenarcha*, 218–19.
[61] Quintilian, *Institutio oratoria*, books 3–5, trans. Donald A. Russell (Cambridge, MA: Harvard University Press, 2001), 5. 9; Cicero, *De inv.* 2. 14 ff.   [62] Quintilian, *Inst.* 5. 9. 1.
[63] Ibid. 5. 9. 9.
[64] Cicero, *De inv.*, 2. 43: '*Post rem ... quod cruentum gladium habuerit*' ('Pertinent events after the deed are ... that the accused had a blood-stained sword').

Although, as Emrys Jones notes, 'Salisbury and Warwick are soon to ally themselves with ambitious York and so forget their care for the commonwealth', their function in this scene is clearly to invoke an evanescent civic ideal of Justice as the collaboration between ordinary people and voluntary representatives of law, both speaking and responding to a language of probable investigation and moral accountability.[65] The concept of such a collaboration—present, as we saw, in the late morality *Liberality and Prodigality*—accords with what historians examining the records of informations and examinations taken by Justices of the Peace have found for this period. The work of Cynthia Herrup and Malcolm Gaskill, for example, shows that the interactions between ordinary people and the formal representatives of the law—constables, coroners, and magistrates—cannot simply be understood in class-confrontational terms.[66] Herrup offers countless examples of neighbours doing the detective work and bringing evidence to the justice.[67] Gaskill likewise documents the late sixteenth to late seventeenth century in England as a transitional period in terms of lay participation in the work of detection and bringing suspects before the law. By about 1800, he writes, the professionalization of medical forensics meant that popular testimony and detective work 'no longer carried as much weight either when JPs and coroners first heard it at pretrial stage, or most especially when they forwarded it as evidence in a court of law'.[68] But for the period he documents, he offers a wealth of instances in which ordinary people—neighbours, kin, and friends of victims—actively engaged in what he calls 'popular forensic techniques' in order to gather evidence and present it as convincingly as possible before the coroner or Justice. Gaskill, like Herrup, gives us examples of men and women exhuming bodies or noticing suspicious marks on bodies they were preparing for burial, measuring footprints and skeletons, and reporting the evidence of rumour, of dreams, and of apparitions. This is clearly not an inquisitorial model; nor does it bear any resemblance to the 'conditioned passivity' with which we, nowadays, allow professional authorities to step in and take over when murder enters our lives. Rather, it seems, the ordinary parishioners of the sixteenth and seventeenth centuries made use, to the extent that they could, of the scope for redress afforded by official

---

[65] Jones, *Origins of Shakespeare*, 163.

[66] This is Malcolm Gaskill's phrase, *Crimes and Mentalities in Early Modern England* (Cambridge: Cambridge University Press, 2000), 239.

[67] Cynthia B. Herrup, *The Common Peace* (Cambridge: Cambridge University Press, 1987), 67–92.   [68] Gaskill, *Crimes and Mentalities*, 279.

procedures, deploying their own forensic strategies within the available boundaries.[69]

Yet the point to stress here is not only that this scene represents a civic ideal, but that it imbues that ideal with a spiritual intensity. Emrys Jones, as we saw, remarked on the almost indecorous intensity of the emotion surrounding the suspicious circumstances of Humphrey's death. 'It hovers uncertainly', he says of the sequence, between seeming to give 'appropriate tragic expression to what was indeed a cataclysmic event, a turning point in England's history', and 'an effect of wildly exaggerate clamour, as if heightened by the lurid colours of melodrama'.[70] Jones accounts for this uncertain effect by suggesting that the sequence leading to Humphrey's death is patterned after the sequence of plays in which Christ is tried by Caiaphas, Herod, and finally Pilate, before being sentenced and crucified. If this model was in Shakespeare's mind, he may be said to have done something very remarkable with it. The trial plays in the York cycle (which Jones used as his example) present various kinds of legal procedure—ecclesiastical law in Caiaphas's and Annas's trial, Chancery procedure presided over by Pilate—as being eminently open to manipulation. 'As law-givers, Annas and Caiaphas, Pilate and Herod all demonstrate intentions not connected with the common good', observes Pamela King, 'but with immediate political expediency.'[71] When Jesus is, in a final hearing, brought to the bar to be tried for felony, a hiatus of fifty lines in the manuscript makes it unclear what the jury decided (presumably, the release of Barabbas).[72] Nevertheless, if Shakespeare remembered the form of the York plays, or a similar sequence, when he conceived the sequence of accusations made against Humphrey in *1 Contention*, it is clear that the effect he achieved was not so much to make Humphrey Christ-like, or to have Humphrey embody, as did Christ, the divine Justice that reveals the diabolic expediency of his own earthly trial. Rather, having Warwick respond to the commons' desire to know the order of Humphrey's death, Shakespeare locates the ideal of Justice not in Humphrey himself, but in the transformation of the commons' sorrow and anger into an evanescent expression of faith in the possibility that they themselves might, by their verdict, bring about the Justice for which he stood.

From this we may conclude that Shakespeare's idea of representing the political effectiveness of the commons off-stage by having them

---

[69] Ibid. 253–63.   [70] Jones, *Origins of Shakespeare*, 46.
[71] Pamela M. King, 'Contemporans Cultural Models for the Trial Plays in the York Cycle', in *Drama and Community*, ed. Alan Hindley (Belgium: Brepols, 1999), 200–16.
[72] Ibid. 211.

demand, through Warwick, to hear 'the order' of Humphrey's death, is not 'traditional' but innovatory: it draws implicitly on a discourse of the voice of the people as the agents of the disclosure of God's justice, but that discourse itself, incompatible with the theological doctrine of secret penance for secret sins and with the seal of the confessional, had not always existed. In *1 Contention* and later *2 Henry VI*, Shakespeare has adapted Gascoigne's idea of representing Plautine or Terentian forensic intrigue as a process in which the villains are engaged. But where Gascoigne simply turns the errors of comic intrigue into deceptions visible to and punishable by a 'good governor', Shakespeare presents his good governors—Henry VI and Humphrey, Duke of Gloucester—as exhibiting far too simple a faith in the transparency of evidential processes and in the inability of justice to be arbitrarily manipulated. By Act 3, so many corrupt or dubious trials and judgments have passed for truth and justice, that Henry's continuing faith in the immanence of God in judicial process appears naïve in the extreme; the law appears indeed to be nothing but aristocratic power cloaked in procedure. Our sense that this is so reaches its climax in F after the murder of Duke Humphrey, with the guilty Queen Margaret's attempt to deflect suspicion in an extraordinarily long and passionate speech, in which she remonstrates with her husband for showing more concern for the dead Duke than for her (F 1773–1821). 'Was I for this', she exclaims to Henry, 'nigh wrack'd upon the Sea',

> And twice by aukward winds from Englands banke
> Drove back againe unto my Native Clime ...
> Yet Æolus would not be a murtherer,
> But left that hatefull office unto thee.
> The petty vaulting Sea refus'd to drowne me,
> Knowing that thou wouldst have me drown'd on shore
> With tears as salt as Sea through thy unkindnesse.

> (F 1782–8)

This speech continues to play in this baroque manner with the personification of the sea as eschewing the murder that her husband will not stick to commit. In its elaborately tasteless ingenuity, it is clearly modelled (though no editor has remarked on this) on the most famous and most imitated epistle of Ovid's *Heroides*, *Dido to Aeneas*. Ovid's *Heroides* was the most obvious model for representing a kind of female speech that gave the effect of being both impassioned and forensically or legally manipulative.[73] Here the Ovidian subtext—self-incriminatingly explicit in Margaret's references to Suffolke as 'Ascanius' seducing Dido with tales of his father—signals that the Queen is attempting to arrogate to herself the position of plaintiff, of the victim of romantic deception and breach of marital promise (F 1816). This speech, then, is a last-ditch attempt to continue the corrupt uses of legal procedure that have characterized Humphrey's enemies through the preceding two acts. Margaret's excruciatingly hypocritical performance forms a climax of this kind of fraudulent legality: with astonishing bad taste, she claims that her husband, who lies prostrate with grief at the death of the man she helped kill, is her 'murderer', as Aeneas was Dido's. It is at the end of Margaret's speech, when hypocritical manipulations of the law can apparently go no further, that we have, in F, the crucial stage direction: *Noyse within. Enter Warwicke, and many Commons.*[74] And Warwick speaks:

> It is reported, mighty Soveraigne,
> That good Duke Humfrey Traiterously is murdred
> By Suffolk and the Cardinal *Beaufords* meanes.
> The Commons like an angry Hive of Bees
> That want their Leader, scatter up and downe,
> And care not who they sting in his revenge.
> Myself have calm'd their spleenful mutinie,
> Until they heare the order of his death.

(F 1824–31)

Warwick's passive voice, 'It is reported' subtly reconfigures, and gives forensic weight to, what in his source (Hall's *Chronicle*) has the claustrophobic, Tacitean feel of rumour in a world of power politics that dare not speak out. Hall reports how Duke Humphrey was found dead in his bed the night after his imprisonment at the Parliament of Bury in 1447. His body, says Hall, was

shewed the lordes and commons, as though he had died of a palsy or empostome: but all indifferent persons well knewe, that he died of no natural death but of some violent force: some judged him to be strangled: some affirm that a hote spitte was put in at his foundament: other write, that he was stiffeled or smoldered between two feather beds. [75]

---

[73] See Lorna Hutson, 'The "Double Voice" of Renaissance Equity and the Literary Voices of Women', in *"This Double Voice"*, ed. Danielle Clarke and Elizabeth Clarke (London: Macmillan, 2000), 142–63.   [74] The Quarto omits to mention the commons at this point.
[75] *Hall's Chronicles*, quoted from Bullough (ed.), *Narrative and Dramatic Sources of Shakespeare*, iii. 107–8.

In Hall's account, the 'viewing' of the body is part of the cover-up, and rumour is, as a result, the only possible mode of political discourse. But in Shakespeare's play, the same uncertainty as to exactly what violence was used on Humphrey—smothering or strangulation—takes a new form, *performing*, in Warwick's speech, the very act of offering the probabilities as such—as evidence, as indeterminate or conjectural signs arousing suspicion—to the commons, in response to their request to 'hear the order of his death'. Warwick's speech cuts so powerfully through Margaret's specious forensic rhetoric because it creates, by its mode of address, the commons as an audience capable of judging the probability of the facts. It turns rumour—the angry humming of the commons—into a forensic scenario, and in using the word 'forensic' in this context, it seems relevant to recall its etymological connection with the Roman forum, the place of public and political accountability.

6

Forensic Rhetoric in Early Revenge Tragedy and Early Romantic Comedy: Kyd, Lyly, and Shakespeare

Popular Forensic Techniques and Dramatic Narrative

In the ninth scene of the anonymous play *Arden of Faversham* (printed 1592), a curious reality effect is suddenly introduced in the form of an unfinished story, which Arden, after an interruption from his servant, Michael, asks his friend Franklin to resume. 'Come Master Franklin,' says Arden, 'onwards with your tale.' 'Do you remember where my tale did leave?', asks Franklin. 'Aye', says Arden, 'where the gentleman did check his wife.' And Master Franklin takes up the story:

FRANKLIN. She being reprehended for the fact,
        Witness produced that took her with the deed,
        Her glove brought in which there she left behind,
        And many other assurèd arguments,
        Her husband asked her whether it were not so.
ARDEN.   Her answer then? I wonder how she looked,
        Having forsworn it with such vehement oaths,
        And at that instant so approved upon her.[1]

What the dramatist was after, clearly, was a heightening of tension by means of the ironic relation of this inset narrative to the danger the two men are in—Arden's servant has just left on a slight pretext so as to facilitate yet another attempt on Arden's life by the incompetent villains Shakebag and Black Will. Franklin, suddenly overcome with an

---

[1] *The Tragedy of Master Arden of Faversham*, ed. M. L. Wine (London: Methuen and Co., 1973), Sc. 9, ll. 74–81.

emotion that we must read as intuitive apprehension, cannot complete the description Arden desires of 'how she looked', this unnamed female suspect, when answering what seems to have been a judicial enquiry set up by her husband. The obvious thematic resonances with the 'fact' yet to occur and be proved against Alice, however, are of less interest here than the passage's easy allusion to a popular culture of forensic evaluation, of the reading of 'tokens' and weighing of evidence. Against this fictitious woman's having 'forsworn' the easily guessable fact, the prosecution brings in witnesses, an abandoned glove, and 'many other assured arguments', to prove a different narrative. Like the Host's 'how stands the case?' in the late morality *Liberality and Prodigality*, this inset story alludes easily to a popular diffusion of forensic techniques and a culture of evidence evaluation such as clearly affected the dramatic shaping of tragic narratives of violent death and the quest for justice or retribution.

Subha Mukherji has written persuasively of the connection between what she calls a 'providential evidentiary practice' which involved rituals such as cruentation, or the bier-rite (the practice of having a suspect touch the victim's body, to see if it will bleed afresh as proof of guilt), and the plot making of domestic tragedy, in which '[t]okens in the drama of divine judgement become aids to judicial discovery'.[2] Analysing *A Warning for Fair Women*, the Chamberlain's Men's play that told the story of the murder of the merchant George Saunders by his wife's lover in 1573, Mukherji shows how the play strives to heighten the sense of miraculous disclosure when it comes to dramatizing the judicial processes by which suspicion of George Browne, Saunders's murderer, conclude in conviction. An incidental victim of the murderer was reported by Arthur Golding—who wrote up the case in one of the earliest of such printed accounts of true life crime in English—to have remained alive, in spite of fatal wounds, only long enough to identify the suspect. In *Warning*, this figure becomes the pathetic John Beane, the miraculous strangeness of whose survival is emphasized, and whose testimony, as well as acquiring the unimpeachable force of 'last dying words', is characterized, as Mukherji persuasively explains, as a kind of cruentation: 'I gave him fifteene wounds', trembles Browne, 'Which now be fifteene mouthes that doe accuse me.'[3]

[2] Subha Mukherji, *Law and Representation in Early Modern Drama* (Cambridge: Cambridge University Press, 2006), 112. See also Robert P. Britain, 'Cruentation in Legal Medicine and Literature', *Medical History*, 9 (1965), 82–8.
[3] *A Warning for Fair Women*, Sc. 14, ll. 1995–6, ed. Charles Dale Cannon (The Hague: Mouton, 1975), 155. See also Arthur Golding, *A briefe discourse of the late murther of master George Saunders* (London: Henry Bynneman, 1573), sig. A4[r].

Mukherji's observations are illuminating, opening up for modern appreciation and criticism a play which up until now we have not been well equipped to understand. Yet even within so strongly providentialist a representational scheme as that plotted in *A Warning for Fair Women*, there are moments when the dramatic depiction of collaborative forensic activity inevitably and quite unintentionally adumbrates the sense of epistemological contingency, of the possibility of there being competing explanations for any set of evidential signs, that Carol Clover has identified as a hallmark of modern Anglo-American expectations of narrative.[4] Thus, for example, the play depicts George Browne moments after having committed the murder, drinking at the buttery at court in Woolwich with a certain Master James. Master James notices that Browne's hose are all bloody; 'It seemes but newly done', comments a yeoman of the buttery. Browne, thinking quickly, comes up with a plausibly circumstantial narrative about having come across the fields from Eltham, and killed a hare by the way, and the moment apparently passes. A few scenes later at court, however, we see three lords come on with Master James, reading letters informing of the murder. A fourth lord enters with a waterman, and he asks the latter to tell his tale again before the lords. The fourth lord explains:

> Tis noysd at London, that a marchants slain,
> One maister *Saunders* dwelling neere Tames streete,
> And that *George Browne*, a man whom we al know
> Is vehemently suspected for the fact,
> And fled upon't and this same water man
> That brought me downe saies he row'd him up.
> And that his hose were bloody, which he hid
> Stil with his hat sitting bare head in the boate
> And sigh'd and star'd as one that was afraide.[5]

The lord asks the waterman to confirm this, and then asks him to describe George Browne's doublet, breeches, and hose. A second lord asks Master James whether this description agrees with the clothes Browne had on when he drank with him in the buttery? And was his hose, he asks further, all bloody? At Master James's corroboration, the third lord instructs them to take the reports to John Beane: 'Conferre the markes the wounded fellow telles with these reports.' In this rather exhaustive rehearsal of the procedures of corroborating testimony, we have a fleeting

---

[4] Carol J. Clover, *The People's Plot* (Princeton: Princeton University Press, forthcoming).
[5] *Warning*, Sc. 12, ll. 1693–1701.

sense of the possibility of doubt and evidential conflict, because the processes themselves are designed to introduce it: at every moment we expect someone to introduce a fact which does not quite fit, for the sense of an alternative explanation shadows the very processes of pre-trial examination and open trial. Even John Beane here features as an empirical witness whose task is to tell what he saw, rather than as miraculous agent of providential disclosure.

In drama of the kind represented by *Arden of Faversham* and *A Warning for Fair Women*, however, such experiences of hermeneutic uncertainty (and of the consequent sense of reality they afford by introducing an expansive horizon of interpretative contingency) are minimal and evanescent. In *Arden of Faversham*, indeed, the action unfolds with a claustrophobic inevitability, as every time a character is called for, or a scheme of action is suggested, that character or action follows immediately. At the same time, however, varieties of popular drama which were clearly influenced by the forensic rhetoric of Roman New Comedy were being written and performed, offering audiences quite a different hermeneutic experience. This neoclassically influenced drama, which was led in the field of tragedy by Kyd, and in that of comedy by Lyly, adapts the forensic rhetoric of New Comedy to elements of English legal culture in innovative, and in Kyd's case, powerfully mimetic ways.

The Revenge Tragedy Debate

Chapter 2 has already made an argument for the relevance of the evidential transformation of popular legal culture for the understanding of the form of a specific revenge tragedy—Shakespeare's *Titus Andronicus*—and yet the question of the relation of legal culture to the emergence of the genre as a whole has so far been avoided. The critical debate surrounding the cultural significance of revenge tragedy has repeatedly turned on the question of the opposition of justice to revenge, defining 'revenge' as the private citizen's appropriation of a penal violence that was, as critics such as Eleanor Prosser assumed, 'the prerogative of the State'.[6] Ronald

---

[6] Eleanor Prosser, *Hamlet and Revenge*, 2nd edn. (Stanford, CA: Stanford University Press, 1971), 5. For the origins of the term 'revenge tragedy', see A. H. Thorndike, 'The Relation of *Hamlet* to the Contemporary Revenge Play', *PMLA* 17 (1902), 125–220. See also Lily B. Campbell, 'Theories of Revenge in Renaissance England', *Modern Philology*, 28, no. 3 (1931), 281–96; Fredson Bowers, *Elizabethan Revenge Tragedy* (Princeton: Princeton University Press, 1940).

Broude pointed out a few years after Prosser that public and private were not so easily distinguished in a participatory legal system which placed responsibility on victims and witnesses to pursue malefactors.[7] Yet, even with this knowledge it remained unclear how, if at all, to relate this popular judicial culture to the emergence of such plays as *Hamlet* and *The Spanish Tragedy*. Foucauldian interpretations, such as James Shapiro's influential reading of Kyd's play, ignored the complicating factor of participation in English criminal justice and assumed a competitive relationship between the two kinds of scaffold performance, drama, and state execution.[8] Even more recently, however, the most influential interpretations of Shakespeare's and Kyd's plays have preferred, for different reasons, to focus not on the ethical/legal questions of violence and retribution, but on psychoanalytically influenced models of thinking about memory, trauma, and loss.

In an article on revenge tragedy in the late seventeenth century, John Kerrigan looks back to John Pykerynge's highly political interlude *Horestes* (1567) as the origin of the English genre, and observes, quoting Lily B. Campbell, that it is now 'almost a truism' that the genre was encouraged by post-Reformation providentialism.[9] His justly acclaimed book *Revenge Tragedy*, however, eschews political and legal contexts for making sense of the dramaturgy of *The Spanish Tragedy* and *Hamlet*, developing, rather, a comparison between the public uses of memory to stir revenge in Aeschylus's *Oresteia* and the more private forms taken by 'Elizabethan remembrance'.[10] Kerrigan's decision to abandon legal-epistemological contexts in this chapter seems surprising in view of the excellent earlier chapters which make use of such contexts for Greek drama and medieval romance. For example, the previous chapter in his book, which discusses medieval vengeance, deftly and brilliantly traces the fortunes of classical revenge through its transformations first by the blood feud and the *judicium Dei*, and then by the Christianization of the latter in the jurisdiction of penitence and confession and

---

[7] Ronald Broude, 'Revenge and Revenge Tragedy in Renaissance England', *Renaissance Quarterly*, 28, no. 1 (Spring 1975), 38–58.

[8] James Shapiro, ' "Tragedies naturally performed" ', in *Staging the Renaissance*, ed. David Scott Kastan and Peter Stallybrass (New York and London: Routledge, 1991), 99–113.

[9] John Kerrigan, 'Revenge Tragedy Revisited', *The Seventeenth Century*, 12, no. 2 (1997), 207–29, at 209. 'John Pikerynge', author of *Horestes*, may be Sir John Puckering, late Lord Keeper of England; *Horestes* is a politically topical play, likening Mary, Queen of Scots to Clytemnestra and Darnley to Agamemnon. See Marie Axton, *The Queen's Two Bodies* (London: Royal Historical Society, 1977), 58–60; *Three Tudor Classical Interludes*, ed. Marie Axton (Cambridge: Boydell and Brewer, 1982), 29–33.

[10] John Kerrigan, *Revenge Tragedy* (Oxford: Clarendon Press, 1996), 170–92.

263

their literary counterparts, the romance landscape of knights who go on *aventures*.[11] Why, then, should shifts in legal ways of knowing—integral to changes in medieval literary forms—become irrelevant in the sixteenth century?

In the following chapter, entitled 'Remember Me!: Horests, Hieronimo and Hamlet', Kerrigan argues for closer connections than have been previously assumed to exist between Elizabethan revenge tragedy and Greek tragedy. He notes that in the latter remembrance of the past both stirs thoughts of revenge and retards the progress of the revenger: 'Identifying a paradox which recurs in revenge tragedy, Aeschylus shows the past inciting violence but notices how retrospection can offer its own satisfactions and draw an avenger back from his task.'[12] He then goes on to 'demonstrate how this ambiguity can operate to dramatic effect at high levels of structural and psychological *detail*' in Elizabethan drama.[13] It is surely right that remembrance of the dead has this profoundly ambiguous effect on the would-be avenger of the death. Indeed, Stephen Greenblatt's account of Purgatory as a cult of remembrance for the dead enables a reading of *Hamlet* in which the imperative to remember completely eclipses, and makes strangely anomalous, the very suggestion that Hamlet should be engaged in the pursuit of revenge. 'The trouble is', as Greenblatt writes, 'that Purgatory, along with theological language of communion (houseling), deathbed confession (appointment), and anointing (aneling), while compatible with a Christian (and, specifically, a Catholic) call for remembrance, is utterly incompatible with a Senecan call for vengeance.'[14]

While bearing in mind both Kerrigan's idea of a more private, less Greek idea of remembrance that exists in strong tension with the call to revenge, as well as Greenblatt's sense of the incompatibility of a form of familial remembering linked to Purgatorial intercession and one that demands vengeful action for one's kin, I would like to suggest, however, that neither of these readings can account for the oddity of the rise of revenge tragedy, or the tragedy of intrigue, as a *genre* in this period. Greenblatt's reading of *Hamlet* cannot really be applicable to revenge tragedy in any wider sense, since other revenge plays do not draw back in horror, as *Hamlet* does, from the pursuit of retributive justice; they do not, as Greenblatt says, enact a shift 'from vengeance to remembrance'.[15] Yet they, too, are surely products of the loss of penitential theology's relation to the *judicium Dei*:

---

[11] Kerrigan, *Revenge Tragedy*, 145–69.   [12] Ibid. 171.   [13] Ibid.
[14] Stephen Greenblatt, *Hamlet in Purgatory* (Princeton: Princeton University Press, 2001), 237.   [15] Ibid. 207.

products, that is, of the loss of the romance landscape of penance and purification that Kerrigan describes in his previous chapter on 'Orestes and Medieval Vengeance', as well as products of the loss of Purgatory as the post-mortem guarantor of the working of penitential theology.

Part of the problem here seems to be the ascription of too much explanatory power to the idea of 'remembrance'. Purgatory was not merely a cult of memorialization, and retarding qualities are, *pace* Kerrigan, common to revenge plays whether or not they are concerned with the intractability of memory as incitement to vengeance. In *Titus Andronicus*, as we have seen, the sequence of action is explicable in terms of a private, evidential enquiry necessitated by the suppression of the space of trial, followed by maddened attempts to 'publish' the evidence (Titus's petitioning of Pluto for 'justice' and shooting arrows to the gods 'to send down Justice' (*Titus Andronicus*, 4. 3. 13–15, 52)), culminating in an ingenious, bloody finale, at which the question raised is how, afterward, the 'facts' leading up to the carnage will be related to a wider public: so Marcus, holding Aaron's and Tamora's child, will explain who was 'chief architect and plotter of these woes' (5. 3. 121). In Kyd's *Spanish Tragedy*, of course, explication of the meaning of the murderers' deaths is exactly what Hieronimo denies his stupefied, royal audience, but the reading of this bloodbath as 'justice' is reasserted in the by now familiar appropriation of the *topos* of catabasis, or descent into the underworld: Andrea takes on himself the role of 'judge', dealing out the appropriate dooms: 'Let loose poor Tityrus from the vulture's gripe, | And let Don Cyprian supply his room; | Place Don Lorenzo on Ixion's wheel' (*Spanish Tragedy*, 4. 5. 30–3).

Kerrigan's privileging of memory and Greenblatt's interpretation of Purgatory as almost exclusively a cult of remembering the dead combine to produce ways of reading early examples of revenge tragedy that necessarily exclude or render meaningless these plays' attempts to deal with the ethical problems raised by the very idea of the pursuit of justice in a Christian world without a post-mortem place of trial or purgation, where the mistakes, omissions, and material contingencies of this life can be squared with the idea of a final reckoning by God. Human judgements are uncertain, and in any case, the processes of justice in this world can be prevented, as revenge tragedies show, by all sorts of political contingencies. An intermediate time and space, a time and space of trial and penitential purgation, helps to make thinkable and bearable not only the daily horror of human injustice, but also the profound, metaphysical terror of the idea of God as Judge.

As we saw in Chapter 1, the implication of fifteenth-century drama in the sacrament of penance produced a way of recognizing collective culpability before God, while ensuring that within the deferred time-space of reckoning that constitutes a call to penance, Justice was always trumped by Mercy as a possibility, as the deferral of finality. Though God says, at the very end of *The Castle of Perseverance*, that those who have not performed the seven deeds of mercy 'schul to helle lake | In byttyr balys to be brent: my jugement it is', the fate of Humanum Genus is actually mercifully suspended by virtue of the penitential form taken by the play.[16] Justitia has pleaded to God that Humanum Genus, or Mankind, made his confession too late, was not profoundly contrite, and failed to do penance: 'Ouyrlate he callyd Confescion; | Ourlyt was hys contricioun; | he made nevere satisfaccioun.' Misericordia, or Mercy, however, argues that Christ has made satisfaction for Man, and that Mankind is accordingly their kin. God judges the cause in Mercy's favour, and asks Mankind to sit at his right hand, but gives Justice her due by recalling the reckoning to come when 'Myhel his horn bloweth at my dred dom | the count of here conscience schal putten hem in pres | And yeld a reknynge | Of here space whou they han spent | And of here true talent'.[17] Thus, we can see that the inevitable dramatic victory of Mercy over Justice is made possible by the penitential theology in which the play participates (as part of an encouragement to the audience to make their shrift) and by the idea of Purgatory itself as a space between, in which the contingent possibilities of an unjust judicial reckoning—the possibility that one might die, for example, without having performed sufficient penance to purge one's sin—might be brought into the equation. As Thomas More argued through his Purgatorial ghosts, it is Purgatory that 'hyghly declareth [God's] greate mercy and goodnes'. This is because 'payne ys allway due to synne | and is not allwaye clene forgeuen wythout conuenyent penaunce done or other recompence made', but 'payne is not allwey done | nor eny recompense made in the mannes lyfe', yet confession and absolution having ensured that, 'the man dyscharged of hell by hys conuersyon: all ye payn y^t remayneth muste nedys be sustayned here wyth vs in purgatory'.[18]

---

[16] *The Castle of Perseverance* (1420–5), in *The Macro Plays*, ed. Mark Eccles (Oxford: EETS, 1969), ll. 3639–40. [17] Ibid. 3427–9, 3619–22.

[18] Thomas, More, *The Supplycacyon of Soulys* (1529), in *The Yale Edition of the Complete Works of St. Thomas More*, vii, ed. Frank Manley, Germain Marc'hadour, Richard Marius, and Clarence H. Miller (New Haven and London: Yale University Press, 1990), 111–228, at 176.

266

If we compare the ending of *The Castle of Perseverance* in God's reminder that unrepentant sinners 'schule to helle lake | in byttyr balys to be brent' with that of Kyd's *Spanish Tragedy*, figuring Revenge haling Horatio's murderers 'down to deepest hell' and Don Andrea assigning their individual dooms to specific torments, we need to acknowledge, I think, an iconographic similarity, however superficial in effect. This similarity surely arises from the fact that, as Le Goff tentatively but persuasively proposed, conceptions of an afterlife are necessarily meditations on the problems of justice in this life. 'The ideas', he wrote, 'that living human beings formed about the other world were inspired, I think, more by a need for justice than by a yearning for salvation, except perhaps in brief periods of eschatological fervour.'[19] Le Goff links the development of Platonic and Orphic conceptions of an afterlife featuring a scale of punishments—or punishments somehow deemed appropriate to crimes done in a lifetime—both to the Athenian system of justice and to belief in metempsychosis.[20] Greenblatt, however, astutely pointed out that while medieval Christian scenes of Hell borrow this iconography of distinctive punishment for distinctive types of sin—'thieves hung over flames; the envious plunged first into vats of ice and then into boiling water; the angry stoned by raging demons; the proud stretched on rotating wheels, and so forth'—the main difficulty for Christian visual artists was 'not to distinguish among various forms of hideous torment in Purgatory, but to distinguish between any of these and the identical torments of Hell'.[21] The solution was to indicate the temporary quality of Purgatorial punishment: the fact that it would have an end. Of one such image—a fifteenth-century French manuscript showing three souls suffering in a vat filled with red flames—Greenblatt asks, 'How do we know that the vat is Purgatory and not Hell? Because above the vat an angel is lifting up a fortunate soul who *has completed the term of suffering* while below a demon thrusts his pronged fork at the burning figures crowded into a Hell-mouth'.[22] As Le Goff has brilliantly explained, the distinction between Purgatory and Hell lies in no other feature than this, Purgatory's intermediateness. Purgatory mediates the impossible finality of binary judicial thinking, the finality of the distinction between guilt and innocence, between eternal bliss and eternal damnation. As a third place, located unlike the other two places *in time*, Purgatory enabled

[19] Jacques Le Goff, *The Birth of Purgatory*, trans. Arthur Goldhammer (Aldershot: Scolar Press, 1990), 210.   [20] Ibid. 21–2.

[21] Greenblatt, *Hamlet in Purgatory*, 53–4.

[22] Ibid. 54–5; my italics (the image is shown at p. 55).

the development of complex discriminations in the way in which '[t]he other world was supposed to correct the inequalities and injustices of this one', allowing, for example, for the development of changing attitudes towards certain kinds of sin—usury, unintentional homicide, and so forth.[23] Without Purgatory, the idea of separating *culpa* from *poena*, and discriminating between the intentional component in sin and the residue of sin for which satisfaction must always (according to the conception of justice as a reckoning) be made, could not have evolved, nor with it the priest's borrowing of the forensic topics of circumstantial invention—*quis, quid, ubi, quando*, etc.—to weigh degrees of intentional guilt, and assign penance. For, as William Lyndwood prescribed in the early fifteenth century,

> The priest ought dylygently to note and marke the circumstances of the cryme, the qualyte of the persone, the kynde of the synne, tyme and place cause and continuaunce in the synne the devout mynd of the penitent. And these thynges consydered and dylygently weyed and dyscretely, let hym injoyne the penytent the greater or lesse penaunce.[24]

The loss of Purgatory meant more, then, than the loss of connection with dead kin, though clearly that itself involved a psychic transformation of incalculable consequence. The loss of Purgatory also meant the displacement into this world of the psychological burden of thinking how earthly contingencies and the uncertainties of human judgement relate to the finality of there being only a 'reckoning' after death, leading to one of two alternatives: eternal torment or eternal bliss. Casuistry takes up some of the burden of this thinking, as does, in a different way, the doctrine of predestination; but among the various imaginative discourses that are informed by it must surely be included the forensically driven plots of revenge tragedy. As we saw in Chapter 1, the idea of Divine Justice as a doomsday reckoning of sin tends to be figured as diabolic (for example, Tutivillus and the other demons in the 'Iudicium' play of the Towneley plays, consulting their briefs of sin and casting 'hasardars and dysars, | fals dedys forgars | Slanderars, bakbytars, | All unto hell'[25]). This sense of the contamination of guilt by association with the process of damning to hell is opposed to the promise of mercy held out

---

[23] See, e.g., Jacques Le Goff, *Your Money or Your Life*, trans. Patricia Ranum (New York: Zone Books, 1988).

[24] William Lyndwood, *Constitutions prouincialles and of Otho and Octhobone Translated in to Englyshe* (London: Robert Redman, 1534), fol. 95ᵛ.

[25] *The Towneley Plays*, ed. Alfred W. Pollard, EETS, extra series, no. 71 (Oxford, 1897), 378.

by the Christian tradition of the priest's merciful examination, which takes intention and circumstances into account, and which is enabled by the deferral of judgement known as the purifying ritual of penance in this life, or of Purgatory in the next. In revenge tragedy, the task of taking circumstances in to account likewise works, though precariously and uncertainly, to decontaminate the revenger from the guilt inherent in his desire for justice, his desire to see not only death but eternal torment overtake the murderers of his kin. Thus, the revenger's 'delay' tends to be less the product of a rhythm of propulsion and retardation by the ambiguous processes of memory, than a series of processes of enquiry into the circumstances of the wrong, seeking evidence of the murderer's identity, and corroboration of that evidence, while being all the time aware of being under scrutiny and in profound danger himself, both in the political state and in the state of his soul.

Readings of *The Spanish Tragedy* and of *Hamlet* from the point of view of these plays' concern with 'remembrance' can be illuminating, but they risk losing sight of the plays' concern with laying bare, by the political denial of due process, the painful, ethical question of what it means, in a Protestant world, to pursue justice, to risk being mistaken in one's own judgement that someone else's guilt was deserving of death. A pre-Reformation Hamlet is impossible to conceive, not only because the Senecan call to avenge would not, prior to the Reformation, be permitted to complicate the son's intercession for his father's soul, unhouseled in death, but also because a pre-Reformation counterpart would not show such a concern as Shakespeare's Hamlet does to ensure a properly circumstantial reconstruction of his own intentions, being responsible (as he is) for a good many deaths (including those of Polonius, Rosencrantz and Guildenstern, and finally, that of the King) in the pursuit of his father's cause. Greenblatt offers a powerful analysis of Hamlet's complicated sense of the contamination of all humanity—including his beloved father—by its own gross fleshliness, which is another manifestation of the play's sense of the incompatibility of imagining justice as the purification—purgation—of sins, and imagining it as a judicial sentence.[26] However, his focus on the importance of remembrance as an act of personal witness to the beloved father perhaps slightly obscures the undeniable importance of Hamlet's final concern not so much with the afterlife as with an evidential reconstruction of his own actions and intentions *in this world*. Pondering the way in which the ghost of the father vanishes, finally, not only from view, but almost

---

[26] Greenblatt, *Hamlet in Purgatory*, 237–44.

from speech, Greenblatt turns to the play's close and notes that when Hamlet 'finishes off' Claudius, 'he thinks not of his father's spirit in the afterlife but of his mother's'. He perceives, however, an important qualification to this 'climactic oblivion' in Hamlet's request to Horatio that he live long enough 'To tell my story'. 'Through Horatio', Greenblatt continues,

> Hamlet's story will live on, and insofar as that story involves the remembrance of his father, so, too, the memory of the Ghost will survive in narrative. But Horatio, of course, never heard the ghost speak, and even if we imagine that Hamlet has related what he was told, the friend's narrative cannot and will not be an intimate, personal act of remembering the beloved father.[27]

It seems to me that there was never any question of Hamlet's desire that Horatio should bear personal witness to Old Hamlet, and, indeed, the terminology of 'bearing witness' being invoked here, with its suggestion of the attrition, over the generations, of the authenticity of memory, seems to derive, powerfully, from Marianne Hirsh's conception of the second-generation memory, or 'postmemory', of the children of Holocaust survivors.[28] What Hamlet begs Horatio to do, however, is to *justify* his actions to those who would condemn them: 'Report me and my cause aright | To the unsatisfied', he says (5. 2. 344–5). It is, as Othello says, the 'cause'—Hamlet's legal 'case'—that he wants Horatio to narrate to his would-be judges after his death. Hamlet repeatedly anticipates both his own condemnation in a retrospective narrative and his exoneration by circumstances, and to Horatio, it seems, he has communicated everything that has happened since they saw the ghost: 'You do remember all the circumstance?', 'Remember it, my lord!', Horatio replies, fervently (5. 2. 2–3). Hamlet's concern with gathering evidence in anticipation of post-mortem charges of regicide and murder could be said to be a marker of the extent to which Purgatory's mediation of degrees of guilt and of the material contingencies that intervene to prevent satisfaction for sin had been conceptually transformed into the moral probabilities afforded by a circumstantially rich dramatic narrative of personal response to horrific injustice: such a morally complex and morally uncertain narrative as we refer to when we name 'revenge tragedy'.

---

[27] Greenblatt, *Hamlet in Purgatory*, 227–8.
[28] Marianne Hirsch, 'Past Lives', *Poetics Today*, 17, no. 4 (Winter 1996), 659–86. I owe this insight to Christine Hong.

The Cry and Revenge of Blood: Providence and Due Process

In the light of this, let us reconsider the definition of 'post-Reformation providentialism' and its relation to the habits of evidence evaluation encouraged by the demise of mandatory confession and the increase of processes of governance involving participatory justice in the late sixteenth century. Lily B. Campbell, whom John Kerrigan cites on this topic, points out that the verse from St Paul to the Romans that underwrote the tragic providentialism of both the Middle Ages and the Renaissance, 'Vengeance is mine, I will repay, saith the Lord', constituted both a threat—against private vengeance—and a promise, 'I will repay'.[29] The texts she refers to in support—Thomas Beard's *Theatre of Gods Judgements* (1579, 1612), John Reynolds's *Triumph of Gods Revenge against the crying and execrable Sinne of Murder* (1621), and Thomas Cooper's *The Cry and Revenge of Blood* (1620) exemplify what, as we have noted, Subha Mukherji calls a 'providentialist evidentiary practice', in which the reading of uncertain signs to discover who has committed a secret crime—murder or adultery—is at once rhetorical, pragmatic, and what we would call superstitious.[30] Malcolm Gaskill analyses these printed texts in conjunction with manuscript records of informations taken by justices, and finds that they alike record habits of popular evidential thinking. In both manuscript informations and printed accounts of trials, people are recorded as acting and speaking and reporting the action and speech of others with *the evidential significance of their words and deeds in mind*. Murder victims in both manuscript and printed accounts tend to announce their own impending deaths, to cry out 'Murder' or 'I am slain', or to insist that they did not strike the first blow. But the apparent non-naturalism of these utterances may be explained by awareness, whether in the victim or in the witness reporting events, of the evidential status of 'last dying words'. The words themselves are forensically oriented to enlist the help of a Justice in bringing about a trial.[31] Gaskill's findings expose the positivistic bias of imagining an opposition between 'irrational' and 'providentialist' practices and a forensic outlook which includes a capacity to evaluate probability and coherence in narratives of the facts. In fact, as Gaskill shows, awareness of the forensic or evidential significance of words and deeds is popularly pervasive, and the awareness itself

---

[29] Campbell, 'Theories of Revenge', 281–3.
[30] Mukherji, *Law and Representation*, 95–134, at 115.
[31] Malcolm Gaskill, *Crimes and Mentalities in Early Modern England* (Cambridge: Cambridge University Press, 2000), 235–7.

conditions behaviour. The work of both Gaskill and of Herrup enables us to see that the rhetoric of providential disclosure, of the community as merely an agent of divine justice, along with frequent recourse to so-called irrational proofs such as cruentation or the bier-rite, are not in any way incompatible with the development of 'forensic' or 'detective' habits of mind among ordinary people. Gaskill gives numerous examples of manuscript informations and printed accounts in which the bleeding of the corpse is one among many proofs alleged against a suspect; it tends to confirm other causes of suspicion, rather than acting as a divine proof all on its own.

In one printed account of a murder which took place in 1656, of which records also exist in manuscript, we can see clearly how the rhetoric of providential disclosure does not simply describe a faith in the working out of God's purpose in this world, but rather enables and justifies human agency—popular detective work—of the kind that takes place in revenge tragedy. The case in question was that of the murder of John Neill, a clockmaker, stationer, and merchant of Glasgow, who was found by the road between Waltham and Theobalds by labouring men going to work at about six in the morning of the 26 February 1656.[32] The body 'was brought under the examination of a Coroners Jury', but they could not give a verdict, 'wanting evidence in the case'.[33] However, Mr Neil's London friends, who had been expecting him to arrive presently in London, were concerned at his non-appearance and, hearing that there had been a body found near Waltham, went there and, to their distress, found that the stabbed and lifeless body was indeed their friend's. About the same time, the innkeeper who had given Mr Neil lodging the night before his death also heard and came to see whether the man killed and the man he had lodged were one and the same. His intention was to inform a Justice of the Peace if it were the case. But before he could see the corpse or meet with a Justice, Mr Neil's friends

met with him, (whom indeed they thought as yet they had reason to suspect) and caused him to go along with them to see the dead body, which he did, and said he knew him well: then they caused him to touch it, (as is usual in cases of suspicion) but there appeared no Symptom of guilt in him: and for further proof of his innocence, he became the key (in the hand of God) wherewith the whole truth

---

[32] *A true and faithful relation of that Horrible Murder committed on the body of Mr. JOHN NEIL, Late Stationer and Merchant of Glasgow in Scotland* (London: James Cottrel, 1656). For the identification of Roger Hill (d. 1667) as the examining Justice in this case, see J. S. Cockburn, 'Introduction', in *Calendar of Assize Records* (London: Her Majesty's Stationery Office, 1985), 98–9.   [33] *A true and faithful relation*, 3.

was opened: for going with Mr *Neils* friends to the Justice, he gave such a lively description of the party that lay with Mr *Neil* at his house, that one of them had a sudden persuasion wrought at his heart, that he knew the man, such a one being lately come to *London* from *Scotland*, having store of money, and good clothes: which persuasion of his, he immediately imparted to some of the rest.[34]

Here we see both the recourse to the 'irrational' proof of the bier-rite—the innkeeper is required by Mr Neil's friends to prove his innocence by touching the body—and the deployment of a rhetoric of providential consequence. But neither the bier-rite nor the providential emplotment obviates the salient fact that Mr Neil's friends themselves engage in the sceptical enquiry, the detective work that will uncover Neil's murderer. Once the innkeeper has described Mr Neil's travelling companion, and one of Neil's friends recalls him and where he lives in London, the rest 'procured a warrant, and a Constable to execute it', and searched the Westminster lodgings of the suspected party, where they found 'divers papers belonging to Mr. Neil', which they 'sealed up for the present, and carried him to the *Gatehouse*, till…they might examine him before a Justice of the Peace'. The Justice of the Peace in this case was Roger Hill (d. 1667), whose examination notes are preserved in the British Library. Hill itemized each piece of evidence, following each item with the word 'testi' or 'witness' and the name of the witness who could vouch for the item's authenticity and explain its significance. Thus, for example, Neil's notebooks were found on Dick's person when he was apprehended, and the Justice has Mr Thomas Underwood, stationer of London, testify to his knowledge of these notebooks, which he identified as books of Neil's riding expenses on his commercial trips to London.[35] Although the author of the printed pamphlet affirmed the innkeeper to be the key to the truth 'in the hand of God', the hands of Mr Neil's London friends might equally be said to be the agents of disclosure, especially in the dexterity with which they made use of the procedures of the constable's warrant and the deliberation with which they shaped and prepared the evidence before they took it to the Justice.

Thomas Cooper's *Cry and Revenge of Blood* works similarly. The text is not, as one might imagine from encountering references to it in literary-critical debates over revenge tragedy, a theoretical disquisition on Protestant providentialism, but a printed account of a real murder investigation in Halesworth, Suffolk, which came to the Bury Assizes in 1620. Three carcasses were discovered when a farmer of Halesworth

---

[34] Ibid. 4. [35] BL Add. MS 46, 500, fol. 90.

decided to dredge his pond. Cooper describes how the farmer went to the local Justice of the Peace, who saw to it that the carcasses were taken 'charily' out of the mud, and 'using the helpe of Chyrugeon', each was laid out, so as to make 'a speciall search into each carcase, concerning fractures, or any such defect, that might give any light for the particular knowledge of them...To this end the inhabitants were called unto this spectacle, and so inquiry made amongst them concerning such parties, as were missing within compasse of remembrance.'[36] A mother volunteered that 'it had formerly been related to her' that two of her children were 'gone for Ireland' and a third was 'in the Lowe countries', speeches that now seemed suspicious, especially since the last was made by one Worlich, in whose company her son was before he went missing. Yet how to test whether these unrecognizable bodies were her children's? Her son, John Leeson, was six feet tall, but he also 'had two teeth broken out of an upper jaw by a former accident'. Not only did one of the skulls, 'being searched', prove thus, but this evidence helped to discover a suspect, for a weaver named Land, one of the men seen drinking and gaming with Worlich and John Leeson before the latter went missing, took the skull away 'to a barbar to plucke out more teethe'.[37] The barber, of course, turned witness against Land, and ultimately, on the basis of these and many other conjectures of suspicion, Land and Worlich were indicted for the murder.

Using a language of likelihood and probability, Cooper mixes what we would call superstition happily with what we would call forensic evidence. The arrest on suspicion of Land for going to a barber to have more teeth knocked out of the skull might seem to come out of Agatha Christie. But then Cooper goes on to argue that the carcasses are likely to be those of siblings not only because all three of these siblings went missing, but because 'they lay in one grave together, and therefore were like to lie in one belly'.[38] For our purposes, though, what is most important about his account is not only Cooper's identification of popular detective work as providentially directed, but his explanation for the temporality of providential discovery—God's deferral or delay in revenging—in terms of a satisfying of *this-worldly evidential standards in processes of justice*. Prior to the Reformation a homicide—even one who killed 'for covetise of good'—might be assigned secret penance, if his slaying was not public,

---

[36] Thomas Cooper, *The Cry and Revenge of Blood expressing the nature and haynousness of wilful murther exhibited in a most Lamentable History thereof, committed at Halsworth in High Suffolk* (London, 1620), sigs. G1^v–G2^r. [37] Ibid. sig. G2^v.
[38] Ibid. sig. G2^r.

'not openly knowe[n]', other than to the parish priest to whom he made confession.[39] As we have seen, the twelfth-century conceptual division of *culpa* and *poena* stipulated that, while *culpa* vanished with absolution, *poena* required penance, either in this world or in the extension of time and space known as Purgatory, and conceived of as a trial or purification to satisfy eternal justice. So, as the author of the fifteenth-century *Speculum Sacerdotale* advised parish priests, their flock must be 'agastid' by warnings to make confession and do penance betimes in Lent, because

thei that ben noght purgid in the world be penaunce whiche we calle a-boue satisfaccion, he schal be purged yf so be that he shall be sauyd in the tother world, *scilicet*, in the moste spitous fire of purgatorie. And for-thy it is beste to man to be clensid bi satisfaccion here in this world that he mowe passe hens sikirlye after his dethe.[40]

The loss in England of Purgatory as that combination of punitive, purifying, and probative trial by ordeal, or what Le Goff calls 'the projection into the afterlife of a highly sophisticated legal and penal system', put new imaginative pressure on the need for such trials to be performed by collaboration with secular judicial authorities in this world.[41] Instead of the sinner performing secret penance in satisfaction to eternal justice for his *poena*, God's providence would, through the gradual agency of forensic investigation, work to satisfy the community—God's people—that justice had been done, that they, working to discover who was the murderer, had not rashly condemned the wrong man. So, at any rate, goes Thomas Cooper's reasoning. Why, he imagines the reader asking, 'seeing that murder is so crying a sinne that it calls for speedy and continuall vengeance

---

[39] The influential pseudo-Augustinian *De vera et falso poenitentia* which forms ch. 22, 'Of Penance', in *Speculum Sacerdotale*, ed. E. H. Weatherly, EETS, o.s., no. 200 (London, 1936), 79–80, instructs the priest thus: 'yif ther be eny man that hath trespasid in manslaughter for covetise of good or for envye, yif that it be open and i-knowe, let hym do openly penaunce...in this maner...In the firste be enioyned to hym the faste of xl days so that he faste yche Wednesday and Friday brede and water and in the to[th]er days with lenten mete. After the fastyng of these xl dayes let hym haue penaunce of vii yere in this maner. Let him in the firste, ii, and iii yere stonde without the chirche, and in yche of tho yeres make thre Quadragesimes and in yche wele faste iii daye...And ouer this let hym be besie in prayers and do large almes dedes yif that he may through fedynge of pore men and brynge of the thrall oute of the prison, helpyng and makyng of churches, brigges, wayes and siche other. And ouer this let hym kepe the faste of Friday in alle the dayes of his lyue. And yif eny man haue done manslaughter the whiche is not openly knowe, then let hym do preuy penaunce and stonde noght withoute the churche.' We must imagine, then, that parishioners knew and accepted that an open murderer might do penance thus, and so satisfy justice, and that a 'privy' murderer might do privy penance. Though 'manslaughter' is specified here, the author assumes the killing is deliberate, since he imagines the killing happening 'for covetise of good', as indeed was the motive in the murders Cooper describes in 1620.

[40] Ibid. 74.   [41] Le Goff, *Birth of Purgatory*, 5.

in the eares of the Lord' comes it to pass that 'the Lord differs [defers] the discovery and recompense thereof[?]. The answer he gives is as follows:

> There must be first a Discovery of the Crime, before it be convicted, and it must be convicted, before it be censured. For as Conscience without Knowledge is blind, and erroneous, so the will and affections without conscience, are perverse and exorbitant: Even so the condition of sinne, before it be discovered, produceth erroneous Iudgement, and *sentencing of sinne before it be convicted, is no better then to pervert Iustice, and condemn the innocent* ... so we may observe, that the wise Lord in al ordinary trials, hath kept this ordinary course: As first to discover, though not so much for his own information (unto whom all things past are present, nothing so hid as is not knowne before it be done, much more after) *as for our satisfaction*: so also in the second place, to convince sinne being discovered, and then to execute upon the same.[42]

God defers or delays vengeance for murder because there must first be a judicial discovery of the sin, or crime—not for God's information, but for *our satisfaction*—for otherwise the condition of our sin produces erroneous judgement in conscience and an unjust revenge instead of a just judgement. Cooper's logic may be flawed, but his reasoning perfectly describes the increasingly evidential turn taken both by the Protestant discourse of conscience and by English common law, and helps us to understand that the passion for revenge expressed in late sixteenth-century drama is not different in kind from a passion for justice.[43] English revenge tragedy seems expressive, then, not of a residual blood feud in conflict with the state's monopoly of penal violence, but of a passion for detection that is the satisfaction of conscience *in this world* that occulted blood-guilt has been, however violently or ambiguously, proved and discovered by those who have suffered most anguish and wrong.

Cooper dedicated his *Cry and Revenge* to Sir Henry Montague (1564–1642), Lord Chief Justice of the King's Bench and later Earl of Manchester, who was also dedicatee of Michael Dalton's *The Countrey Justice* (first published in 1618). He included, too, a prefatory epistle to Sir Henry North, High Sheriff of Suffolk, and to all the Suffolk Justices of the Peace. He was moved to write, he tells North, after hearing of murder at the Assizes, 'the Detection whereof, together with the most fayre and honourable carriage of the business, did so affect me: that I could not think my time better spent, then in taking notes of such special Passages

---

[42] Cooper, *Cry and Revenge of Blood*, sig. F3ᵛ; my italics.

[43] For William Perkins's likening of conscience to judge who 'holdeth the assize', see Barbara Shapiro, *'Beyond Reasonable Doubt' and 'Probable Cause'* (Berkeley: University of California Press, 1991), 14–16.

as fell out therein'. Cooper's emotions were aroused by the collaborative, inferential process of detection itself, by 'the wisdom of the Justice' (because 'this ... is not easily to be compassed of a private brain') who, with 'the helpe of a Chyrurgeon', saw to it that 'the carcases were searched and measured', and called 'the inhabitants unto this spectacle' to hear their 'remembrance' as to who from the locality might have gone missing. Describing the trial, he insists that 'the manner of these Trials by witnesses to prove the fact, and Jurors to find the same' is 'a course ... warrantable, by the practice of God himselfe'. As well as confessions of the accused, there were, he says admiringly, 'no lesse then 28 Evidences ... taken by the worthy Justice, all of great moment, by way of circumstance and consequence to prove the same', though 'no more then 18' were produced at the bar, where time is precious.[44]

Hieronimo, Justice and Dramatist

Of course, all twenty-eight of the evidences might have been erroneous, and the Justice's conjectures might have been false; Worlich, referring to the 'Lowe Countries', might not, as the Justice expounded it, have sinisterly meant 'the bottom of the pond'.[45] But it was in Latin dramatic writing, not in vernacular legal practice, that there could be a developing awareness of the tragic, as well as comic, uses of false inference, the 'supposes' and 'surmises' that are mimetically and emotionally effective in theatre and fiction. *The Spanish Tragedy* was probably written and first performed between 1585 and 1590. By 1585 its author, Thomas Kyd, was writing for the Queen's Men, the most privileged and successful of the theatre companies at that time.[46] The favoured genre of the Queen's Men's pre-eminent writer, Robert Wilson, was, as McMillin and Maclean explain, the 'medley', which featured a predominantly visual style of performance, expounding action by means of costumes, shields, tableaux, and eloquent gestures. 'The unmistakeable sign', write McMillin and Maclean, 'is crucial to this system—the gesture no eye can misread, the accent no ear can misunderstand.'[47] Kyd learned how to use this kind of theatre well: in the second scene of *The Spanish Tragedy*, the Spanish army

---

[44] Cooper, *Cry and Revenge of Blood*, sigs. A3^r, G1^v–G2^r, G4^r. Cooper does not tell his readers who the Justice was.   [45] Ibid., sig. G3^v.

[46] See Thomas Kyd, *The Spanish Tragedy*, ed. J. R. Mulryne (London: A & C Black, 1989), pp. xi, xiii–xiv. References to act, scene, and line of this edition are henceforth given in the text.

[47] Scott McMillin and Sally-Beth Maclean, *The Queen's Men and their Plays* (Cambridge: Cambridge University Press, 1998), 127.

has to *'enter and pass by'* as a visual demonstration of having returned victorious and undiminished by battle with the Portuguese (1. 2. 110). But Kyd was also ambitious to do something new: he married the visual, emblematic theatre of the Queen's Men with a newly intricate dramaturgy of suspicion and probable conjecture, a dramaturgy of the *mistakable* rather than unmistakable sign. This innovation of Kyd's was long ago identified by Alfred Harbage as the adaptation to tragic situations of the plot techniques of Roman intrigue comedy, and Lukas Erne has more recently claimed Kyd as the first dramatist to represent human causality skilfully on-stage.[48]

There is, nevertheless, a strange laboriousness in Kyd's concern to demonstrate causality in the movement of action from Hieronimo's first discovery of the murder of his son, through his slow corroboration of evidence as to who were the killers, to his final, meticulous enactment of revenge as the following of a scripted plot. As T. S. Eliot noted, Kyd's interest in plot does not come from Seneca: ' "Plot" in the sense in which we find plot in the *Spanish Tragedy* does not exist for Seneca at all ... *The Spanish Tragedy*, like the series of Hamlet plays, including Shakespeare's, has an affinity to our detective drama.'[49] What seems particularly intriguing, though, is the strangely obtrusive way in which a topography of justice—a vision of the other world as a series of emblematically distinct torments, each fitting a particular crime—is slowly, as the play goes on, transposed into the concept of a movement across this worldly space—a 'journey' or 'middle way', involving a series of crossroads—which becomes, in turn, a metaphor for the weighing of alternatives, for reasoning probably, for decision making, and for plotting a course of action. This last concept materializes, of course, in the book of Hieronimo's play, which he distributes 'in several abstracts drawn' (4. 1. 141), determining the parts—and several dooms—allotted to Horatio's murderers, brilliantly insisting as he does so that the King, as bewildered spectator, should make an effort to follow it: 'Here comes Lorenzo; look upon the plot, | And tell me, brother, what part plays he?' (4. 4. 33–4).

---

[48] Alfred Harbage, 'Intrigue in Elizabethan Tragedy', in *Essays On Shakespeare and Elizabethan Drama in Honour of Hardin Craig*, ed. Richard Hosely (London: Routledge & Kegan Paul Ltd., 1963), 37–44; Lukas Erne, *Beyond the Spanish Tragedy* (Manchester: Manchester University Press, 2001), 4. Erne omits any consideration of Gascoigne and Whetstone, understandably in view of the fact that *Supposes* is a translation, and *The Glasse of Government* and *Promos and Cassandra* are unlikely to have been staged, though Gascoigne's grasp of dramatic causality is superior to Kyd's.

[49] T. S. Eliot, 'Introduction', in *Seneca His Tenne Tragedies translated into English* [1581] ed. Thomas Newton (London: Constable and Co. Ltd., 1927), p. xxiii.

The problem with an interpretation of the play that focuses exclusively on the simultaneously inciting and retarding effects of remembrance of the dead is that it smoothes over the weirdness of Kyd's insistent metaphorical transposition of a hellish topography of justly distributed torments into the almost ploddingly slow process of judicial decision making on the basis of probable conjecture. This aspect of the play, though less immediately appealing than its representation of Hieronimo's passionate moments of remembrance, is nevertheless crucial, for it is the public-spirited care that Hieronimo takes in his role as an investigator of the 'causes' of others that likewise distinguishes his deliberations at the crossroads of decision making about how best to pursue justice for his beloved son, and these moments, in turn, powerfully enlist our sympathy for him, and ensure a kind of satisfaction in the appalling end.

Kerrigan observes that when Hieronimo first apprehends the sickening horror of the sight in his arbour where his son hangs lifeless, he takes from his son's body a memento, and makes a vow: 'See'st thou this handkercher besmeared with blood? | It shall not from me till I take revenge' (2. 5. 51–2). While his wife speaks the rhetoric of providential disclosure: 'The heavens are just, murder cannot be hid', Hieronimo himself implicitly assumes that heavenly agency (2. 5. 57). Two short scenes later, however, he is completely at a standstill, the murder remains 'unrevealed' by the sacred heavens, and fiends that should be tormenting the murderers are inhabiting not hell, but Hieronimo's night thoughts, 'sally[ing] forth' and framing his 'steps to unfrequented paths', driving him on 'to seek the murderer' (3. 2. 5–21). He has, though, no idea where to begin when, providentially or diabolically, '*A letter falleth*', addressed to him. Kerrigan notes the visual resemblance of this letter, written in blood ('*red ink*'), to the 'bloody handkercher', and concludes that it is 'another memento, inciting revenge'.[50]

Such a reading of the bloody letter, however, produces the play's action as repetitive series rather than causal sequence. The letter is not a memento at all, but evidence—though highly suspect evidence, at first—of the identity of Horatio's killers. Hieronimo keeps it not to remind him of his son, and to stir thoughts of vengeance, but in order that he might continue to 'try' or test its assertions by corroborating what it says with other forms of evidence. From the moment he reads it, he subjects its contents to sceptical scrutiny: 'My son slain by Lorenzo and the prince!

---

[50] Kerrigan, *Revenge Tragedy*, 176.

| What cause had they Horatio to malign?' (3. 2. 33–4). Equally, though, he wonders what motive Bel-imperia could have for accusing her own brother: 'Or what might move thee, Bel-imperia, | To accuse thy brother, had he been the mean?' (3. 2. 35–6). It is all too fishy: just as Hieronimo's first thought on encountering a body in his arbour was to suspect a plan 'to lay the guilt on me' (2. 5. 11), so, now, he suspects that he is betrayed, 'And to entrap thy life this train is laid' (3. 2. 38).

The letter fulfils Hieronimo's wish for 'some mean' to turn nightmare into direction—the word, as Kerrigan excellently glosses it, offers the sense of 'both "opportunity" and "middle course"', thus recalling 'the path along which Minos sent Andrea to Revenge'.[51] Andrea's path lay between a field on the right, where lay lovers and martialists, and a steep descent on the left, which

> Was ready downfall to the deepest hell,
> Where bloody Furies shake their whips of steel,
> And poor Ixion turns an endless wheel;
> Where usurers are choked with melting gold,
> And wantons are embraced with ugly snakes,
> And murderers groan with never-killing wounds,
> And perjured wights scalded in boiling lead,
> And all foul sins with torments overwhelmed.
>
> (1. 1. 64–71)

''Twixt these two ways', says Andrea, 'I trod the middle path' (1. 1. 72). This third *way*—Kyd's invention, for in book 6 of the *Aeneid* there are only two ways, the right to Elysium, the left to Tartarus—corresponds to the notion of Purgatory as a third *place*, the locus of torment not as damnation but as trial and purification. It is suggestive, then, that Kyd should transpose this idea of a 'middle way' back, via Andrea's watching of the play, into the probable 'means' or opportunities by which the action progresses, as Hieronimo proceeds to try 'by circumstances' the testimony of the letter (3. 2. 47). It is indeed as if Kyd, like Thomas Cooper, has metamorphosed the purifying idea of a Purgatorial 'satisfaction' for sin after death into the probative idea of God's working through the people and the officers of justice to discover evidence 'for our satisfaction', ensuring that we do not 'pervert Iustice, and condemn the innocent'.[52]

It is important, then, to realize that the scene intervening between Hieronimo's discovery of his son's body and the opportune falling of the

[51] Kerrigan, *Revenge Tragedy*, 176.   [52] Cooper, *Cry and Revenge of Blood*, sig. F3ᵛ.

letter in his path is not so much indicative of time passing as admonitory of the consequences of failure to examine evidence. Act 3, Scene 1, brings the ambassador from Spain to Portugal, to inform the Viceroy of his son's welfare in Spain, and to begin negotiations for an alliance between Spain and Portugal by marrying the Viceroy's son to Castille's daughter. The Viceroy, of course, had, at the ambassador's entrance, just been giving one of his nobles, Alexandro, his passport to the 'lake' of hell, as a 'homicide', for killing his son. The audience is fully aware of how the Viceroy got his evidence for conviction: in Act 1, Scene 3, he lay prostrate with fears for his son's fate in the wars against Spain. Alexandro intervened with a reasoned likelihood: 'No doubt, my liege, but still the prince survives' (1. 3. 43). This nobleman developed the probability of his comforting supposition in successive stichomythic responses to the Viceroy's conviction of the contrary:

VICEROY   Survives! ay where?
ALEXANDRO In Spain, a prisoner of mischance of war.
VICEROY   Then have they slain him for his father's fault.
ALEXANDRO That were a breach of common law of arms.
VICEROY   They reck no laws that meditate revenge.
ALEXANDRO His ransom's worth will stay from foul revenge.
VICEROY   No, if he lived the news would soon be here.
ALEXANDRO Nay, evil news fly faster still than good.

(1. 3. 43–50)

Alexandro's conjectures are supported not by what he purports to have seen or heard, but their probability is inherent as they develop arguments from law (the death of Balthazar would be a breach of the law of arms), from commonplaces (bad news travels quickly), and from political experience (why kill a prince, whose ransom will be valuable?) to build up a convincing case. His enemy, Viluppo, by contrast, pours into his sovereign's ear a forged tale, backed by repeated assertions of personal witness: 'Then hear the truth which these mine eyes have seen', he begins, and proceeds to describe how Alexandro apparently discharged a pistol in the Prince's back. The Viceroy asks what became of his son's corpse? 'I saw them', Viluppo embellishes confidently, 'drag it to the Spanish tents' (1. 3. 59–75).

What Hieronimo decides to do, then, with the 'mean' or way afforded by the fallen letter is crucially, if somewhat laboriously, defined against the Viceroy's precipitate condemnation of Alexandro on the strength of Viluppo's evidence. At the end of his invention of arguments of suspicion concerning the letter, Hieronimo decides on a course of action: to 'Close, if I can with Bel-imperia | To listen more, but nothing to bewray' (3. 2. 51–2). In case Bel-imperia is part of the trap, he plans to reveal nothing of what he knows, and to gather what he can from her demeanour. With the almost over-neat irony characteristic of Kyd, however, Hieronimo's very caution provokes suspicion on the part of Lorenzo, and precipitates a false inference: Lorenzo, hearing from Pedringano, Bel-imperia's man, that Hieronimo has enquired of the whereabouts of his mistress, falsely supposes that Serberine, Balthazar's servant, has betrayed them. Even though Pedringano points out the unlikelihood of this, Lorenzo proposes to have Pedringano murder Serberine, for 'This sly enquiry of Hieronimo | For Bel-imperia breeds suspicion | And this suspicion bodes a further ill' (3. 2. 108–10). To Balthazar he seems about to reveal the whole plot, 'For I suspect', he begins, 'and the presumption's great, | That by those base confederates in our fault, | ... We are betrayed' (3. 4. 9–11). Interrupted by the news of Pedringano's slaughter of Serberine, Lorenzo knows that everything now rests on the former being condemned to death, and silenced forever: 'now or never ends Lorenzo's doubts', he says, as he departs to arrange things with Pedringano's executioner (3. 5. 79).

The ironies, however, compound, as Hieronimo is appointed judge in Pedringano's case. Of course this puts Hieronimo in remembrance: 'This makes me to remember thee, my son', he says, as Pedringano mounts the scaffold (3. 6. 98). But the emotional effects of remembering cannot be separated from the ironies of discovery, as Hieronimo, though lamenting that he must 'toil in other men's extremes' without providing for his own 'redress' (4. 6. 1–4), nevertheless finds himself in receipt of more corroborating evidence as a result of his judicial efforts. Pedringano's letter to Lorenzo, brought to Hieronimo by a terrified hangman, dispels all his doubts as to the veracity of Bel-imperia's letter:

> Now see I what I durst not then suspect,
> That Bel-imperia's letter was not feigned...
> Now may I make compare, twixt hers and this,
> Of every accident; I ne'er could find
> Till now, and now I feelingly perceive,
> They did what heaven unpunished would not leave.

> (3. 7. 49–56)

Though Hieronimo's journey to revenge may be punctuated by painful remembrance, its sequence and progress are determined by this cautious investigatory process and the retaliation it duly provokes. Once he has corroborated Bel-imperia's letter, he has his evidence, but the problem has now become how he is to turn this private knowledge into public accusation. 'I will', he proclaims, in words remembered and imitated by Shakespeare in *Titus Andronicus*, 'go plain me to my lord the king | And cry aloud for justice in the court, | Wearing the flints with these my withered feet' (3. 7. 69–71).

Once again, sequence is rendered into space, and investigation or deliberation into a choice of paths to worlds other than this, or to the traversing of a place where judgment is enacted as pain and torment. So in Act 3, Scene 11, when Hieronimo meets two 'Portingales', who are asking for directions to Lorenzo's house, he tells them 'List to me, and I'll resolve your doubt'.

> There is a path upon your left-hand side,
> That leadeth from a guilty conscience
> Unto a forest of distrust and fear,
> A darksome place, and dangerous to pass:
> There shall you meet with melancholy thoughts,
> Whose baleful humours if you but uphold,
> It will conduct you to despair and death;
> Whose rocky cliffs when you have once beheld
> Within a hugy dale of lasting night,
> That, kindled with the world's iniquities,
> Doth cast up filthy and detested fumes,
> Not far from thence, where murderers have built
> A habitation for their cursed souls,
> There, in a brazen cauldron, fixed by Jove
> In his fell wrath upon a sulphur flame,
> Yourselves shall find Lorenzo bathing him
> In boiling lead and blood of innocents.

(3. 11. 12–29)

In one way, of course, we understand that Hieronimo is here trying to convey to these Portuguese strangers that he knows that the Duke of Castille's son—soon to be their prince's brother-in-law—is guilty of murder. The knowledge means nothing to them, of course; 'Doubtless this man is passing lunatic', says one (3. 11. 32). In another way, however, this lurid topography of guilt, pain, and punishment is Hieronimo's imaginative projection of the hopes he has of bringing Lorenzo to justice. By this time, however, it is the very invocation of these landscapes of everlasting torment itself that is beginning to cancel out the feeling, in the play, that reliance on divine justice might be an option. In the next scene, indeed, Hieronimo comes on with props that emblematically signify his need to decide between two 'paths' to justice. One, which involves suicide, is figured as 'trudging' to appeal to the judge of the underworld. The other involves appealing to the King of Spain, who is about to pass over the stage. He speaks hypothetically of pursuing this second route: 'perhaps I come to see the king, | The king sees me and fain would hear my suit' (3. 12. 1–2). But then he anticipates being struck 'mute' by standers by, and opts for the alternative: not justice at the King's hands, but suicide, to stand before the Eternal Judge. 'Away, Hieronimo, to him be gone: | He'll do thee justice for Horatio's death. | Turn down this path' (3. 12. 12–14). Yet post-mortem justice seems a contradiction. It is not that Hieronimo dreads everlasting punishment for suicide, but that he cannot imagine justice without his collaboration, justice as taking place after death: 'For if I hang or kill myself, let's know | Who will revenge Horatio's murder then?' (3. 12. 17–18). So, flinging away the instruments of suicide, 'This way I'll take', he says. The 'way' is not a wild or violent one; it is the path of judicial due process: Hieronimo, a judge and plaintiff with a good deal of evidence for his case, pleads for justice with his King.

Once again, with heavy but powerful irony, one 'mean' or opportunity works against another, and Hieronimo's maddened attempt to reveal his evidence by digging in the earth to 'bring my son and show his deadly wounds' only confirms the King's suspicions of his madness, which Lorenzo is very happy to corroborate (3. 12. 73). Kyd skilfully and plausibly hints that political considerations—the impending alliance of Spain and Portugal planned in the marriage of Balthazar to Bel-imperia—render Hieronimo inaudible at court, and prevent awareness of anything so inconvenient as an arraignment of the Prince of Portugal for murder, now that a peace treaty has been signed.

Hieronimo has evidence and the ear of the King, but cannot get justice. At the next deliberative crossroads, the famous '*Vindicta mihi*' speech, he pits God's injunction to patience in Romans 12: 19 against Seneca's advice that the criminal's only guarantee of safety is through further crimes, and decides on a stance of patience, a clandestine alertness to opportunities for revenge. Citizens come to him seeking justice—he is renowned for his 'pursuit of equity', which was a term coming to be used quite generally for the circumstantial consideration of evidence at common law: Thomas Cooper praises 'the Equity and solemnity of that honourable trial' at which those who murdered the Leesons were found guilty by the jury.[53] Hieronimo's conscientiousness as a public servant, however, does him no good. The devastatingly heedless destruction of good local governance by global political ambition is painfully and effectively expressed in Kyd's skilful juxtaposition of Hieronimo's wild destruction of his plaintiffs' evidences with the smug unwareness of a court rapt in the thought of the imperial consequences of diplomatic triumph: an imminent alliance between Spain and Portugal via the marriage of Castille's princess, Bel-imperia, and the concealed murderer, Prince Balthazar. How perfect, then, that Hieronimo's skill as a dramatic writer of intrigue should enable him to seize this new 'mean' or opportunity that his forensic skill as a reader of evidence was forced to miss. Hieronimo's earlier work as a dramatist at the Spanish court demonstrated his skill in the representational strategies of the 'medley', when he entertained the Portuguese ambassador with a playlet featuring three knights with scutcheons capturing three kings with crowns. His dramatic *pièce de résistance*, however, is an intricately plotted intrigue, already extant as a text in a book, which both requires audience attention to cause and effect and confounds that attention by being performed in sundry languages. And where the medley style was perfected by improvisation, Hieronimo's carefully scripted intrigue dictates a causally plotted course of action which his actors—the murderous noblemen—are *bound to follow, even to their deaths*. This fantasy of classical dramatic plotting as retribution for class injustice is brilliantly conceived, as Hieronimo turns aside Prince Balthazar's repeated expressions of nervous hesitation by appealing to the snob value of tragedy. 'What, would you have us play a tragedy?', exclaims Balthazar, and Hieronimo ripostes with the example of Nero, and 'kings and emperors' delighting in plays (4. 1. 86–8). Having related the argument and cast the play, Hieronimo replies again to Balthazar's reservations, 'Hieronimo, methinks a comedy were better.' 'Fie', says Hieronimo, with delicious irony, 'Comedies are fit for common wits: | But to present a kingly troop withal, | Give me a stately-written tragedy, | *Tragedia cothurnata*, fitting kings, | Containing matter, and not common things' (4. 1. 155–61). The Kings, princes, and aristocrats that were so unaware, or so wilfully despising of such 'common things' as Horatio's death, Hieronimo's cause, or the love of Bel-imperia for a commoner like Andrea, are so beguiled by their faith in tragedy's aristocratic credentials that they enact upon one another the just punishment for murder that it was once Hieronimo's task, as Spain's Knight Marshall, to

---

[53] See Cooper, *Cry and Revenge of Blood*, sig. G4ʳ.

dispense as part of every citizen's legal right. How fitting, indeed: it is little wonder that, as Ben Jonson tells us, there were some who would still 'swear, *Jeronimo*, or *Andronicus* are the best plays' as many as thirty years later.

Supposing Paternity: Romantic Comedy

The innovation of the 1570s, the civic detective plot, transforms intrigue comedy, and that transformation in turn informs the rewriting of episodic and medley styles of drama as causally plotted histories and tragedies in which characters suspect, conjecture, and draw inferences. What, however, happened to comedy itself? It will hardly come as a surprise at this stage in my argument if I suggest that the same legal and civic concerns that determined the form taken by the vernacularization of classical and neoclassical comedy in the 1570s leave discernible traces on the development of romantic comedy in the 1590s, and may even contribute to the 'inward' or psychological turn thought to be characteristic of plots of disguise and deception in that period.

Before going further, it is worth noting the extent to which, by the late 1590s, Roman intrigue comedy had been assimilated to an English legal landscape and attuned to the increasingly explicit evidential language of English criminal justice. This we can see by a quick glance at the choice of vocabulary used by Richard Bernard in his 1598 facing-page translation of Terence's plays for schoolboys learning Latin. For example, Terence's play *Adelphoe*, or *The Brothers*, opens with Mitio, Aeschines' adopted father, defending a rather indulgent upbringing of his son on the grounds that an authoritarian regime doesn't teach boys self-discipline: 'a person who acts under threat of punishment watches his step only as long as he believes he'll be found out', as the most recent translator puts it. Bernard translates this as 'hee will take heed whilst he supposeth that which hee doth, shall be brought in examination, and come under coram'. To be 'brought in examination' alludes to the pre-trial examination of suspects by Justices of the Peace, while to be 'brought under coram' means to be brought before a legal tribunal.[54] Other phrases are likewise translated into English legal terms: the friends whom a man consults about a legal problem are his

[54] Richard Bernard, *Terence in English* (London: John Legatt, 1629), 250. For a modern Latin text and English translation, see *Terence, Adelphoe*, 70–1, trans. John Barsby (Cambridge, MA: Harvard University Press, 2001), ii. 258–9. For 'coram', see B. J. Sokol and Mary Sokol, *Shakespeare's Legal Language* (London: Continuum, 2000), 72–3.

'advocates'; an allegedly criminal deed is a 'fact'; a trial before the *'iudices'* (judges) is said to have 'come to the issue'; *'refrixerit res'* ('the thing will be cold') becomes 'I shall have a cold suit of it'; *'potius quam litis sequar'* ('rather than I pursue the case') is translated as 'rather then I should sue him'.[55] Terence's approximation of the written indictment of Greek comedy, *'dicam scribere'* ('to write out a summons') is translated as 'enter an action', while Latin legal summonses, such as *'ambula in ius'*, *'in ius te voco'*, and *'eamus in ius'* ('go to court', 'I summon you to court', 'let's go to court') are translated variously according to the appropriate English legal court involved.[56] Moreover, the plays' concern with the related forensic and mimetic qualities of probability and verisimilitude are clearly caught in Bernard's translation and related to the English legal terminology of 'suspicion'. In *Adelphoe*, Act 4, Scene 4, Aeschines worries, justifiably, that his beloved will believe that he has abandoned her because he has, for his brother Ctesipho's sake, rescued the music-girl Bacchis from the hands of a pimp: 'but this it is that I feare, that they should beleeue their suspition of mee to bee true: there are so many probabilities concurring together. I my selfe tooke her from him, I my selfe paied the money, and shee is brought home to mee.'[57] While variants on the word *suspicio* appear elsewhere in Terence's Latin in this scene, Aeschines here speaks neither of *'suspicio'* nor of *'probabilitas'*: these are Bernard's English terms.

Bernard's translations indicate just how steeped, conceptually, in the English legal culture of local, participatory governance these exemplary Latin comedies had become by the end of the sixteenth century. And the same legal culture helped shape the way in which they were imitated in the vernacular. It is well known that the English imitation of Roman New Comedy, as well as being extremely belated by comparison with that of Italy, did not take an explicitly exuberant Italian delight in erotic deceptions. In the 1590s there are no great celebrations of successful sexual

---

[55] See Bernard, *Terence in English*, 365, 247, 276, 373, 261. Compare Barsby's more neutral translations of the same phrases, *Terence*, ii. 11, 255, 25, 277.

[56] For Roman forms of legal summons, see Adele C. Scafuro, *The Forensic Stage* (Cambridge: Cambridge University Press, 1997), 87–95. Scafuro explains that 'There is no equivalent in Roman procedure for a written indictment or complaint such as would be presented...to a magistrate in mid-fourth century Athens. Plautus and Terence refer to written complaints with variants on the phrase *dicam scribere*...on six occasions...forms of *dicam scribere* suggest that the Roman playwrights...may have had in mind *diken graphesthai* (literally, "to have a suit written down", i.e. "to sue")' (pp. 95–6). See Bernard, *Terence in English*, 373, 374, 423, 424, and compare Barsby, *Terence*, ii. 25, 121, 127.

[57] Bernard, *Terence in English*, 286. Terence's Latin (*Adelphoe*, 4. 4. 627–8) does not contain the words *'suspicio'* or *'probabilitas'*: *'ipsum id metuo ut credant. tot concurrunt veri similia'*. Barsby translates: 'I'm afraid they won't believe it anyway, so many clues point in one direction' (*Terence*, ii. 322–3).

intrigue in English to compare with Machiavelli's *Mandragola*. The particularly sexual aspect of the *'inganni'* (deceptions) of Gl'Intronati di Siena's *Gl'Ingannati* was precisely what Shakespeare omitted in his imitation of the play in *Twelfth Night*.[58] When Aretino's outrageous *Il Marescalco*—which ends with the woman-hating stablemaster being permitted to 'marry' his young boyfriend—inspired Jonson to write *Epicoene*, the resulting English play offered a much more legalistic and less explicit triumph of the queer over the heterosexual. In Jonson's play, Dauphine and his page-boy succeed in diverting Morose's wealth away from his perfectly legitimate plan to marry and get heirs, and we must assume that they do so to ensure the prosperous continuance of their own queer *ménage*. However, the legalistic means by which they trick Morose temporarily turns the theatre, in Katherine Maus's words, into 'the ecclesiastical judge's revelatory courtroom'.[59] The complicated, legalistic response of English writers to Continental plots of erotic deception can be traced back, as we have seen, to the reception of the earliest English imitations of Italian intrigue comedy in the 1560s and 1570s. While Jeffare's *Bugbeares*, taken from Grazzini's *La Spiritata* (1561), seems to have been a success—it was never printed—the revised text of Gascoigne's *Supposes* (1575) was followed by *The Glasse of Government* (1575) and by Whetstone's *Promos and Cassandra* (1578), which told the story of a young woman's chastity despoiled by a corrupt magistrate.[60] Shakespeare's rewriting of *Supposes* as the subplot of *The Taming of the Shrew*, and of *Promos and Cassandra* as *Measure for Measure*, shows that he was far from indifferent to his predecessors' concern with how to adapt the licentious supposes and evidential substitutions of Roman New Comedy and *commedia erudita* to the English stage. In *The Taming of the Shrew*, the indulgence with which Ariosto and Gascoigne regard Polynesta's affair with the disguised Erostrato translates into the disturbing implication that Bianca, wooed similarly by Lucentio, will prove adulterously inclined as a wife. We are all married, Petruchio tells Lucentio at the end of the play, but 'you are sped'; that is, you have been brought to the destiny of cuckoldry (5. 2. 185).[61] In *Measure for Measure* certain representational risks with evidential uncertainty simply

[58] On the way in which Shakespeare chastened *Gl'Ingannati*, particularly in depicting the relationship between Olivia and Sebastian as unconsummated, see Lorna Hutson, 'On not being Deceived', *Texas Studies in Literature and Language*, 38, no. 2 (Spring 1996), 140–74.

[59] Katherine Eisaman Maus, *Inwardness and Theater in the English Renaissance* (Chicago: University of Chicago Press, 1995), 145.

[60] On Jeffare as the author of *Bugbeares*, see *Early Plays from the Italian*, ed. R. Warwick Bond (Oxford: Clarendon Press, 1911), 81–3.

[61] Compare Christopher Marlowe, *Doctor Faustus*, 4. 2. 123, in *Drama of the Renaissance: The Tudor Period*, ed. Russell A. Fraser and Norman Rabkin (Upper Saddle River, NJ: Prentice-Hall,

are not taken: where Whetstone's Cassandra yields to the magistrate and then complains for justice to a King who must decide, *without knowing the facts*, whether or not she is telling the truth and whether or not Promos is guilty, Shakespeare's Duke Vincentio stage-manages not only the chastity-preserving bed-trick, but the feigned evidential uncertainties of the whole trial.

Shakespeare's early comedies show him acutely aware of the problems posed by a drama in which the supposes that make a comic recognition probable cannot be distinguished from the supposes that enable the frauds and betrayals of con men and whores. But, as we saw from his adaptation of reformed detective drama in *Comedy of Errors*, he also saw its profound mimetic possibilities: Philogano's horrified surmise of a worse suppose than the substitution of Dulippo for Erostrato suggested to Shakespeare (as well as to Jonson) that human anxieties, desires, and the pretentious fantasies that Jonson called 'humours'—which actively generate conjectures of suspicion—may be exploited as emotional resources without the dramatist needing to plot criminal activity or sexual misdemeanour to support them. Thus the jealous supposes that enable Adriana and Antipholus to compose plausible cases of adultery and madness against one another make them seem real to us, not in spite of, but *because* we know their evidence is false. And in *A Midsummer Night's Dream*, a play which alludes explicitly to the same 'sharp Athenian law' of paternal power over marriage that always threatens lovers in the fictitious 'Athens' of Roman New Comedy, the imaginative power of Puck as the popular name given to supposes generated by anxiety or fear ('in the dark, imagining some fear, how easy is a bush suppos'd a bear' (5. 1. 21–2)) easily triumphs over the courtly lip-service paid to the insipid magic of 'love' as a means of overcoming patriarchal opposition and bringing about the desired comic dénouement. Helena's readiness to anticipate being mocked by Demetrius and Lysander is so active, so suspiciously creative, that she situates herself as inadvertently starring in a show contrived by the others, in which they 'counterfeit sad looks' and 'Make mouths' upon her when her back is turned and 'Wink at each other, hold the sweet jest up': all this, in spite of their tear-stained *sincerity*, their protestations to the contrary (3. 2. 237–9). Of course we infer a psychic history of increasing insecurity about her beauty as the cause of this extraordinarily powerful surmise: 'Through Athens I am thought as fair as she, | But what of that? Demetrius thinks

1976), 315. Faustus conjures up horns upon the heads of the courtiers of the German Emperor, Charles, and one of them observes, 'we are all sped'.

not so' (1. 1. 227–8), and 'No, no, I am as ugly as a bear . . . ' (2. 2. 94), and Helena inevitably seems to us the most real and individual of all the lovers.

We need, then, to complicate the popular account of Shakespearean romantic comedy as a form that rejects a neoclassical, Jonsonian conception of theatrical probability. It is true that Shakespeare flouted Jonson's strict neoclassicism, suggesting that cross-wooings, disguises, magicians, Bohemian sea-coasts, and providential tempests need not seem to be, as Fabian says in *Twelfth Night*, part of 'an improbable fiction'.[62] Yet discussions of the debate over dramatic poetics played out in Jonson's allusions to 'York and Lancaster's long jars' or 'tales, tempests and such-like drolleries' sometimes miss the point that Shakespearean romantic comedy is itself a highly 'probable' genre, and that its probability derives from its extraordinarily sophisticated adaptation of the forensic strategies of emplotment and disclosure found in Roman New Comedy.[63] We need, in other words, to make a distinction between the 'romance' conventions of native English comedies in a play such as the Queen's Men's *Clyomon and Clamydes* (printed 1599, probably performed in the 1580s) and the 'romance' motif which forms the *anagnorisis* of New Comedy, in which the contours of kinship and identity—and their attendant legal ramifications—are suddenly radically altered by an unexpected revelation.[64]

This distinction involves the extent to which the poet or dramatist exploits a revelation—a change in the contours of knowledge—to produce a sense of the contingencies of knowing, a sense informed by watching characters act upon conjectures which often turn out to have been based on false premises or false inferences. *Clyomon and Clamydes* might seem at first glance to be a play interested in exploiting such ironic effects: in it mistakes of identity are endemic, as knights appear to be indistinguishable once in possession of one another's shields, and the Vice, whose name is really 'Subtle Shift', passes himself off to one knight after another as 'Knowledge'.[65] There is, however, almost never any sense of 'knowledge' as other than belief dictated by unambiguous signs: though the knights and princesses are persistently mistaken, knowledge is not, for them, an epistemological problem. Clyomon, son of the King of Denmark, has

[62] Hendrik Gras, '*Twelfth Night, Every Man out of his Humour* and the Middle Temple Revels of 1597–98', *Modern Language Review*, 84, no. 3 (1989), 545–64, at 548.

[63] See Ben Jonson, *Every Man in his Humour*, in *Ben Jonson: Five Plays*, ed. G. A. Wilkes (Oxford: Oxford University Press, 1988), Prologue, 11.

[64] On the question of the dating of *Clyomon and Clamydes*, see McMillin and Maclean, *Queen's Men*, 94–5.

[65] *Clyomon and Clamydes* (1599), ed. W. W. Greg (Oxford: Malone Society, 1913). Line references to this edition are given in the text.

made a vow to be known by no other name than 'the knight of the golden shield' while seeking knighthood. In the course of his errantry, he casually incurs the enmity of Clamydes, who, courting Juliana, daughter of the King of Denmark, has received from her a white shield, and accepted a challenge to slay the virgin-devouring serpent that terrorizes her father's land. So it is that while Clamydes is mainly preoccupied with finding and slaying the serpent, the two knights also spend a great deal of the play attempting rather unnecessarily to keep an appointment with each other to have a duel to the death. When they finally appear before Alexander the Great, ready to fight one another, however, the Macedonian King tricks Clyomon into revealing his identity by asking, not his name (which he has vowed never to reveal), but his country and parentage. Clyomon is unable to do other than disclose that he is the son of Denmark's King, and this information prompts Clamydes to respond with fraternal enthusiasm: 'And are you son to *Denmarke* king? Then do embrace your frend, | Within whose heart here towards you, all malice makes an end: | Who with your sister linked is, in love with loyal heart' (l. 1849). The fight is off, and there almost seems, in a rudimentary way, something 'forensic' about this revelation, for Clamydes himself is about to need Clyomon's help in establishing his own identity at the Danish court. This is because the cowardly knight Brian Sans Foy has earlier stolen not only Clamydes' white shield, but the head of the serpent he had slain, which he was bringing back as proof, so that he could claim the hand of Juliana, Princess of Denmark. At the Danish court, Juliana naturally rejects Clamydes' claim to be himself: 'Avant dissembling wretch, what credit canst thou yeeld? | Wher's the serpent's head thou brought, where is my glittering Sheeld? . . . The want of these bewraies you quite, and shewes you are not he' (ll. 2030–1). But it is neither Clyomon's credible witnessing nor Clamydes' narrative of the treachery of Brian Sans Foy that proves the truth of Clamydes' case: nothing can do that but the threat of armed combat in which Brian's trademark cowardice definitively manifests itself. Sans Foy confesses his own identity, and Juliana is immediately without further doubt persuaded: 'Is this *Clamydes*? ah worthy Knight, then do forgive thy deere' (l. 2110).

None of these revelations of identity seems to affect the characters' sense of the past or future, since none of the characters is ever seen to be using inferences drawn from what they think they know about each other to conjecture a past or plan a future. Juliana gives no reason for disbelieving Clamydes' perfectly plausible (and, indeed, true within the play) narrative of how Brian Sans Foy enchanted him and stole the serpent's head, so her reaction to the revelation that Brian Sans Foy is not in fact Clamydes cannot include any sense of her view of this past—a past which includes most of what has happened to Clamydes during the play—as something affecting her at all. Hence time and space seem foreshortened in the play. As McMillin and Maclean observe, 'Although the play ranges over the lands known to Alexander the Great', everyone is always 'in the vicinity'.[66] Because no one is thinking in terms of likelihood, or reasoning from signs, there can be no sense of the mental and emotional journey involved in putting the facts together, in changing the story, and altering the case. Leaving no scope for conjecture or for the drawing of inferences—with the entailed risks, of course, of false inference, or paralogism—*Clyomon and Clamydes* can offer no sense of spatial contingency or distance, but neither can it suggest the presence of the *past*, or a sense of the characters' histories. For, as we have seen, fiction gives a far more powerful sense of there being a past—of something 'having passed this way'—when that sense is the product of signs or traces from which characters draw inferences and conjecture a future. So it is not that the coincidences and cross-wooings of Elizabethan dramatic romance are inherently improbable, but that for them to be made probable, to include a sense of the spatial and temporal contingency that we experience in our lives, their agents and participants must invent arguments of conjecture and suspicion just as readily as they do in revenge tragedy, or in the Jonsonian dramatic satires which are more 'neere and familiarly allied to the time'.[67]

In classical comedy and its imitations, as we saw in Chapter 4, there's something scandalous about the way in which the signs which give evidence of what happened anterior to the plot—in the play's remote 'past'—are indistinguishable in kind from the falsified evidence used by the intriguers to promote their deceptions. So in *Phormio* the character called 'Stilpho' turns out to be the secret history of Chremes's identity in Lemnos, and not a mere plausible fiction produced in a lawcourt by Phormio. So Dulippo, far from being merely the impostor who fooled all Ferrara about his gentlemanly status and identity, is apparently, as Cleander probably infers from the evidence, the son and heir he lost at Otranto. In such 'romantic' solutions to the spiralling dangers of false evidence and faked proof, of course, the past must seem to have been hidden, to have been a secret involving sex, substitution, and (usually) money or inheritance: children, as Ariosto said, '*per l'adietro sieno stati suppositi, e sieno*

---

[66] McMillin and Maclean, *Queen's Men*, 150–1.
[67] Jonson, *Every Man Out*, 3. 6. 201, quoted by Gras, '*Twelfth Night*', 547.

qualche volte oggidi' ('have been substituted for one another in the past, and sometimes are today'). Thus, in addition to the scandal of the 'truth's' emergence as merely another set of uncertain evidential signs—moles, birthmarks, names, and narratives—there is often the suggestion of sexual clandestinity, of illegitimacy.

For English writers the potential sexual and financial disorder entailed by the recognition plot compounded the ever-present scandal of its dependence on paralogism, or false inference, for identifying a child's paternity on the basis of unreliable signs and tokens might be tantamount to insinuating cuckoldry. The potential moral difficulty for English dramatists here might be best illustrated by a dramatist who simply ignored it. In Ben Jonson's early essay in romantic comedy of this kind, tellingly entitled *The Case is Altered*, a supposed beggar but actual rich miser, Jacques de Prie, turns out, in the good case-altering style of neoclassical romantic recognition, to be one Melun, former steward to Lord Chamount of France. Jacques confides to the audience that years ago, when Lord Chamount had gone to fight in Italy, he stole both his Lord's gold and his Lord's daughter, Isabel, renaming the latter 'Rachel'. As Jacques tells the audience part of this story, he explains, somewhat ambiguously, that the daughter went with him voluntarily, because she held him in such affection:

> ...it lov'd me so, that it would leave
> The nurse her selfe, to come into mine armes...
> And since her Lady mother that did dye
> In child-bed of her, lov'd me passing well,
> It may be nature fashion'd this affection,
> Both in the child and her: but hees ill bred,
> That ransackes tombes, and doth deface the dead.
> I'le therefore say no more: *suppose* the rest.[68]

Jonson draws our attention to the inferential epistemology of this kind of plot in the most scandalous way: we are asked to 'suppose' the nature of the affection that Lord Chamount's wife bore to her steward. Rather surprisingly—and in a way we cannot imagine happening in Shakespeare—the licentious implications of this suppose do not unsettle the play's dénouement. At the end of the play Jacques's supposed daughter, Rachel, is discovered to be Isabel, Lord Chamount's daughter, and nothing is said that would cast doubt on the legitimacy of her origins, or make her seem less than socially and morally worthy of the faithful love

---

[68] Ben Jonson, *The Case is Altered*, 2. 1. 38–47, in *Complete Works*, ed. C. H. Herford and Percy Simpson, iii (Oxford: Clarendon Press, 1927), 126; my italics.

shown to her all along by Lord Paulo Ferneze. It is impossible to think of
Shakespeare introducing such a doubt early on, and not either dispelling
it or turning it to tragedy. Indeed, we might want to read the characteristic
Shakespearean reflex of anxiety over the proof of paternity ('I think this
is your daughter'; 'Her mother hath many times told me so' (*Much Ado*,
1. 1. 104–5)) as part of an attempt to contain the speculative licence
that accompanies an evidential dramaturgy, a dramaturgy of probable
inference.

John Lyly's *Mother Bombie* (printed 1594) reveals in a different way the
moral difficulties that English dramatists had in adapting the combination
of fraudulent probable rhetoric and romantic *anagnorisis* that formed the
staple of Roman New Comedy. In Lyly's play, no fewer than four witty and
wily servants plot an equal number of comic substitutions to fool their
four masters, each of whom wants, for a variety of reasons, to have his
daughter or son married to another's son or daughter in a way that seems
to them auspicious, but that is actually mercenary and deceitful. Priscius
and Sperantus, fathers of Livia and Candius—who are in love with each
other—want to marry them more advantageously, as they think. Priscius
wants Livia to marry Memphio's son, Accius, whom he does not realize
to be a fool, and Sperantus wants to match Candius to Stellio's Silena,
being equally unaware of her mental deficiency. The fathers of the fools
ask their servants to help them plot a way to get their children married
to Livia and Candius without their folly being discerned, and this pretext
for deception enables the servants to plot a more complicated scheme
enabling Livia and Candius to deceive their fathers and marry one another. By the first scene of Act 4 this has been safely done, but new problems
have arisen: a couple who are brother and sister, Maestius and Serena, are
experiencing troubling feelings of sexual love for one another, while the
simpleton Accius and the no less foolish Silena now begin haphazardly to
woo one another in Candius's and Livia's clothes (these disguises having
been part of the earlier plot to conceal their simplicity). Naturally the
fathers of Accius and Silena discover, at this point, that all is not well
and are very angry. The dénouement, however, comes about not by an
evidential reconstruction, or by a 'recognition', but by a confession. Just
as the foolish pair are about to wed one another, a woman comes in to
forbid the banns. She is Vicina (meaning 'neighbour'), who has come to
Mother Bombie, the wise woman of Rochester, because she aches with
remorse of conscience for a substitution she performed eighteen years
ago. Accius and Silena, she explains to the wise woman, are hers: she
substituted them in infancy for Maestius and Serena, who are not in fact

brother and sister. The latter pair are accordingly freed by this disclosure to fulfil their desires legitimately, and marry after all, thus satisfying their new-found fathers, Memphius and Stellio, who now have no need for elaborate subterfuges to conceal the folly of their children. Lyly's decision to have the plot's solution discovered by a wise woman to whom people bring their worries and dreams, rather than as the result of an evidential process set in motion by a judicial magistrate (Gascoigne's Markgrave, Shakespeare's Egeon, Jonson's Justice Clement) is clearly motivated by a desire to distance the processes of substitution, disguise, and forgery that generate probability and suspicion (Vicina's counterfeiting of birth-marks and moles, the servants' plots to disguise the amorous couples, and the fathers' collusion in plots to fool one another) from the processes by which the truth is revealed and legitimacy asserted. When people come to Mother Bombie for detective work, she does not draw infer-ences from signs and weigh probabilities; she *knows* everything already, revealing her knowledge obliquely in riddling, prophetic speeches. These riddling speeches prompt confessional responses, acknowledgements of secret guilt, on the part of those who come to her for help. They thus draw a firm moral line between the unreliable but probable signs that facilitate deception and the utterly reliable (because confessional) means by which deception is discovered. So, for example, when the servants Rix-ula and Halfepenie, both participating in the plot to deceive the fathers, decide to seek help from Mother Bombie in Act 3, Scene 4, their quests for knowledge reveal not, as they hope, the guilt of others or prospects for the success of their own deceptions, but consciousness of their own transgressions. A silver spoon has been stolen, which Rixula's master will make her pay for unless she can recover it; Halfepenie wants to know what will become of their 'devices' or plots to deceive their masters. Rixula asks Mother Bombie: 'Nay, Gammer, I pray you tell me who stole my spoone out of the butterie?'[69] But Mother Bombie's riddling response transforms Rixula's suspicion of theft into a guilty memory of sexual assignation:

BOM. Thy spoone is not stolne but mislaide;
　　　 Thou art an ill huswife, though a good maid;
　　　 Looke for thy spoon where thou hast like to be no maide.
RIX. Bodie of me, let me fetch the spoone! I remember the place!

(3. 4. 1289–92)

---

[69] John Lyly, *Mother Bombie*, in *Four Tudor Comedies*, ed. William Tydeman (Harmondsworth: Penguin, 1984), ll. 1287–8. Line references to the play in this edition are given in the text.

Halfepenie's dream of 'prunes in velvet caps and prest satten gowns like judges' and 'a whole handfull of currants to be araigned of a riot', for whom 'twelve raisons of the sunne were impannelled in a Jewry', until 'judge, jurors, rebels and bailiefe [bay leaf]' were 'swept . . . into a porredge pot', is interpreted by Mother Bombie as a token of his babyishness (dreaming of milk and fruit) and of impending punishment ('wantons must have rods' (3. 4. 1284)) for his part in plots of cozening and deception over marriages. The play is full of the usual references to legal deceptions: the servants manage to cozen a hackneyman out of arresting Dromio for mistreating his horse by making the arresting serjeant drunk and then signing a fake bond and taking an acquittance. 'Sir, I have his aquittaunce', says Dromio triumphantly, at the end; 'lette him sue his bonde' (5. 3. 2234). But while these evidential forgeries are treated as mere peccadilloes in the wake of Mother Bombie's revelations—'We wil paie the hire of the horse' (5. 3. 2243–4), Memphio tells the angry hackneyman—we can only be struck by how differently the proofs of the children's paternal origins have been treated. Vicina tells an astonished assembly that Memphio's son had a mole under his ear, and she framed one under Accius' ear 'by arte', but 'you shall see it taken away with the juyce of mandrage' (ll. 2153–4); but it is her earlier confession to Mother Bombie, not this proposed empirical 'triall', that marks this story about Accius and Silena not as a mere 'probable fiction', but as the play's hidden truth.

Shakespeare, of course, found a variety of much more sophisticated solutions to the problem Lyly confronted in *Mother Bombie*. *Love's Labour's Lost*, for example, is never taken to be a romance plot, but it wittily refers to the scandal of so many romance dénouements (the recognition of a child's legitimacy and paternity by probable signs, which in turn removes all obstacles against love) by concluding with the obstacles against love still in place, and an unborn child whose paternity remains 'putative', concealed even from the critics.[70] Moreover, the play may be said to recruit forensic rhetoric or artificial proof against itself, for it concludes by vindicating the power of conscience and the value of marital good faith over an endlessly generative and deceptive rhetoric of probability. We can see in it, too, how a play's capacity to create a sense of the past

[70] See Michael Dalton, *The Countrey Justice* (London: John More, 1635) on bastardy, 37: 'Every Justice of peace, upon his discretion, may binde to the good behavior, him that is charged, or suspected, to have begotten a Bastard child, to the end that he may be forth comming when the child shall be borne, otherwise there will be no *Putative* father, when the two Justices (after the birth of the child) shall come to take order according to the Statute of 18. El.c.3.'

is itself the product of evidential plotting. *Love's Labour's Lost* opens by generating evidential uncertainty about two kinds of transgression alleged to have taken place before the play's action begins. One of these alleged transgressions appears to be sexual: Costard is arrested by the constable for an offence that *seems* unambiguous—he's been 'taken with the manner' (i.e., 'caught in the act') with Jacquenetta—but the precise manner in which he has offended nevertheless remains hilariously elusive, not least because of the dense thickets of forensic rhetoric by means of which Armado, striving to render Costard's guilt transparent (or *evidentissima*, as Quintilian would say) manages instead to plunge it into 'obscene and preposterous' obscurity. Patricia Parker has noted that Armado's otiose and redundant questions, 'The time when? About the sixth hour... the ground which... the place where...' 'recall the "circumstances most commonly requisite in presentments before Justices of peace" '.[71] But the real joke is that these 'pointes that may ingender Suspicion', as Lambarde called them in 1592, seem completely beside the point in Costard's case, since he enthusiastically pre-empts suspicion, jumping in to 'find' (or 'invent') himself and his fact: 'The manner of it is, sir, I was taken with the manner', he insists, anticipating the evidence against him. To be taken with the 'manner' or 'mainour' in English common law meant being taken with the loot in one's hand; the phrase could almost be said to distinguish between arrests of evidently guilty thieves and arrests on suspicion.[72] So even as Armado's letter labours about the circumstances of the offence—'consorted, contrary to thy established proclaimed edict and continent canon, wherewith? O with—but with this I passion to say wherewith—' (1. 1. 260–1)—Costard makes the proofs against him as manifest as possible: 'with a wench', and, in response to the King's examination, even pleads guilty: 'Sir, I confess the wench' (1. 1. 283). It's not on the issue of fact, then, but on that of law that Costard brilliantly proceeds to quibble. 'It was proclaim'd a year's imprisonment to be *taken with a wench*', the King declares (1. 1. 287–8, my italics). Costard replies that he was *taken with a damsel*, but the alternative 'damsel' was apparently anticipated in the legal drawing up of the proclamation. Costard tries 'virgin', but that term was also foreseen in the proclamation, so Costard promptly denies Jaquenetta's virginity and calls her a 'maid', bringing the

---

[71] Patricia Parker, *Shakespeare from the Margins* (Chicago: University of Chicago Press, 1996), 230 and 354. See also John Hoskyns, *Directions for Speech and Style* [1599], ed. Hoyt T. Hudson (Princeton: Princeton University Press, 1935), 28.

[72] See J. G. Bellamy, *Criminal Trial in Later Medieval England* (Stroud: Sutton Publishing, 1988), 44, 105; Sokol and Sokol, *Shakespeare's Legal Language*, 366; J. H. Baker, *Manual of Law French* (Trowbridge: Avebury Publishing, 1979), 136.

legal altercation to a bawdy conclusion: 'This maid will not serve your turn, sir', intones the King. 'This maid will serve my turn, sir', asserts Costard, thus outrageously breaking the letter of the law once again (1. 1. 298–9).

The reason for all the immensely enjoyable fuss about what precisely Armado saw Costard doing emerges gradually and obliquely in relation to the following scene's encounter between Navarre and the Princess of France, which opens up another case of alleged wrongdoing as Navarre accuses the Princess's father of having failed to repay the loan of 100,000 crowns for which Aquitaine is security, while the Princess responds that Navarre does 'the King my father too much wrong... in so unseeming to confess receipt | Of that which hath so faithfully been paid' (2. 1. 153–6). Boyet, instructed to go and fetch the acquittances which would be common law proof of the debt's repayment, replies that these have not yet arrived, and only 'tomorrow' will it be possible to 'have a sight of them' (2. 1. 163). Deliberately deferring the sight of the acquittance, Shakespeare transforms the dispute into the archetypal case of 'conscience' which defined the limits of the common law with relation to Chancery. The King's courts of common law offered no remedy for the debtor who, bound in a written obligation, paid off his debt and failed to take, or lost, the written receipt or acquittance of his payment; such a debtor would have to seek his or her remedy in Chancery, where the Chancellor was empowered to examine the facts of the case and discover who was behaving unconscionably according to procedures more like those of civil or canon law.[73] The dramatic point of this is to unsettle our sense of the motives at work in the subsequently rapid transition of Navarre and his men from oath-bound celibates into impassioned wooers. It is not possible simply to think in terms of Navarre and his men 'falling in love' in ways libidinally unconnected with their consideration of matrimonial prospects, for the language of love in this play is bound up at every turn with the terminology of *good faith* and of *making bargains*.[74] Histories of

---

[73] See J. H. Baker (ed.), *The Reports of Sir John Spelman* (London: Selden Society, 1977), ii. 37–9; W. T. Barbour, *The History of Contract in Early English Equity*, ed. Paul Vinogradoff (Oxford: Clarendon Press, 1914), 25–40. For procedures of examination in the Elizabethan Court of Chancery, see W. L. Jones, *The Elizabethan Court of Chancery* (Oxford: Clarendon Press, 1967), 236–63.

[74] Though the language of faith in making and keeping bargains is used in serious contexts, such as that of the Aquitaine dispute and of the Queen's final repudiation of Navarre's offer to marry her, jokes about bargaining made by Costard also expose the gynophobic treatment of women as fleshly prizes that is the disavowed effect of the courtiers' competitive, epideictic rhetoric. When Moth tricks Armado into turning a '*l'envoie*'—the gracious parting words of a courtly lyric poem—into a 'goose' (French *l'oie*, 'goose'), Costard appreciates the trick by

contract that divorce its commercial and legal emergence from contexts of conscience, good faith, and promises to love and marry introduce a division that simply did not exist in the early modern period.[75] As Barbara Kreps has written, the legal historians' debate over

> whether the common law's insistence on 'consideration' developed independently or was derived from the canon law's *causa* . . . is a strong indication that as the common law courts and Courts of Equity developed the principles of contractual actions, these courts shared with canon law the need to define conditions of commercial exchange *that begin with the ethical understandings presumed to inhere in promises*.[76]

What one editor of the play calls 'the rather tiresome business of Aquitaine' works subtly to introduce uncertainty as to the good faith and the speculative motives of both the men and the women in the wooing and mockery that ensues.[77] Immediately after the interview of the Princess and Navarre, Boyet triumphantly if cynically describes Navarre as a bargain ready to be had on the cheap, an easy way of recovering Aquitaine for the crown of France: 'Methought all his senses were lock'd in his eye, | As jewels in crystal for some prince to buy | . . . | I'll give you Aquitaine and all that is his | And you give him for my sake but one loving kiss' (2. 1. 242–3, 248–9). But even as the Princess and Navarre conclude their interview, the audience is made privy to negotiations no less bargain-driven in Dumaine's enquiry after Katherine's 'name' (heartily satisfied by Boyet's reply that she is 'heir of Alençon') and Longueville's seeking the same information about Maria, which Boyet mischievously frustrates by identifying her merely as 'a woman' and 'her mother's' daughter, until Longueville's anger forces him to confess: 'She is an heir of Falconbridge' (2. 1. 205).

---

saying, 'the boy has sold him a bargain, a goose, that's flat' (3. 1. 101). When Armado offers him a 'remuneration' for taking a letter to Jacquenetta, he asks Berowne how much 'carnation ribbon' a remuneration would buy (3. 1. 145–6). Both the goose and the carnation ribbon connote femininity, since a goose could mean a prostitute, and 'carnation' meant flesh-coloured: both jokes fleetingly expose the investment of epideictic rhetoric at Navarre's court in the very fleshly market of indiscriminate concupiscence that it so fastidiously repudiates.

[75] St German famously gave marriage as an example of a *quid pro quo* that would give an action for a promise at common law: 'yf a man saye to another mary my doughter and I wyll guye the .xx.li. Uppon thys promyse an accyon lyeth if he mary hys doughter | and in this case he can not dyscharge the promyse thoughe he thought not to be bounde therby | for yt ys a good contracte | and he may have quid pro quo | that is to saye | the preferment of hys doughter for hys money' (*Doctor and Student*, ed. T. F. T. Plucknett and J. L. Barton (London: Selden Society, 1974), 231).

[76] Barbara Kreps, 'Contract and Property Law in *The Devil is an Ass*', *Ben Jonson Journal*, 8 (2001), 85–122; my italics.

[77] Shakespeare, *Love's Labour's Lost*, ed. G. R. Hibbard (Oxford: Oxford University Press, 1994), 60.

In the same scene, Rosaline's paternity and hereditary expectations are not mentioned, but she herself repudiates the implication that she is, therefore, sexually available 'pasture' for any casual suitor: 'My lips are no common', she says, 'though several they be', alluding to distinctions in land law between communally and privately owned property (2. 1. 223).[78]

This language of negotiation destabilizes further the already rather overdetermined and scarcely referential range of epithets connoting 'beauty' (which are practically reduced, in the course of the play, to the schematic polarity of 'fair' and 'black'). Though the princess herself denies Boyet's suggestion that her beauty (or what she calls her 'dear grace', slyly suggesting both 'expense' (in 'dear') and fleshliness (in 'grace/grease')) is a rhetoric with which she can be 'prodigal' in 'parley' with Navarre as the play's chief 'inheritor', the play's subsequent language of female beauty, parodying the inflationary and cheapening effects of courtly hyperbole, ranks each of the Princess and her ladies as only 'fair' to the extent that her position in a patrilineal system of legitimacy and inheritance attracts the epithet from a bargain-hunting suitor. Hence the Princess is able to joke with the forester, who fails to cash in on an opportunity to praise her in identifying a 'fair' vantage-point or prospect from which to *aim* at something: 'A stand where you may make the fairest shoot'. 'I thank my beauty', says the Princess, wickedly; 'I am fair that shoot, | And thereupon thou speak'st the fairest shoot' (4. 1. 10–12). There's an implicit joke here on the Princess's 'fair' as the effect of her occupying the position of the 'white' or bull's eye in archery, but it is to the forester's credit, as she well knows, that he failed to enter into the obligatory courtly position of competitive negotiation, and neglected this facile opportunity for bargain-hunting praise. (We can tell that the Princess is not supposed to transcend her ladies in any exceptional degree of physical beauty, since Costard hilariously identifies her as 'the thickest and the tallest' among them (4. 1. 48).) By contrast, it is no coincidence that it is Rosaline, the only one of the ladies whose patrilineal expectations (and consequently, her position as a matrimonial prospect) have not been identified who is repeatedly referred to in terms expressive of profound gynophobia, as the antithesis of 'fair' (connoting 'value-laden', and suggesting orderly and legitimate succession), and as the essence of 'black' (suggesting the precarious dependence of this patrilineal order on

---

[78] This speech is given to Katherine in the Riverside Edition, but it makes sense to reverse the speech tags for Katherine and Rosaline in 2. 1, as John Kerrigan has argued. See John Kerrigan, 'Shakespeare at Work: The Katherine–Rosaline Tangle in *Love's Labour's Lost*', *Review of English Studies*, 33, no. 130 (1982), 129–36.

the proverbially capacious and indiscriminate female genitalia).[79] In the climax of Berowne's exercise in the paradox of proving Rosaline 'fair' by proving 'No face is fair that is not full so black', he attempts to degrade male vision—the play's mark of judgement in negotiation—as a means of praising his beloved (4. 3. 249); but the attempt produces a grotesque *mise-en-abyme* of the implicit aims of his paradoxical effort to elevate feminine looked-at-ness above masculine looking. 'O, if the streets were paved with thine eyes', he says to Longueville, 'Her feet were much too dainty for such tread!'; but Dumaine caps this with: 'O vile! then as she goes what upward lies | The street should see as she walk'd overhead' (4. 3. 274–6).

To 'confess the wench', as Costard did upon his arrest, might seem to be what Navarre and his men resolve to do, as they one by one betray to one another and to the King their breaking of their oaths and transgressing of the statute against consorting with women. After Berowne's letter to Rosaline has been delivered to the King as 'treason' by Costard, that conscientious 'member of the commonwealth' (4. 3. 188; 4. 1. 41), Navarre and his men turn with relief to their companion in guilt to provide them with rhetorical—that is, with 'artificial'—*proofs* to find them innocent of breach of faith. They need some 'salve for perjury', as Dumaine calls it (4. 3. 285). But just as the gynophobia revealed by Berowne's attempt to prove black fair would suggest, this apparent oath breaking for 'love' lacks an essential ingredient: that of willingness to contract faith with the beloved. A competitive rhetoric of probability that allocates beauty in accordance with position in a patrilineal system of inheritance is bound to be undone at every turn by the recognition that a child's paternity is never susceptible to ocular proof, and that no amount of surveillance will prove that dark prospect fair, unless mutual good faith—the love that should underwrite what the Princess calls 'a world-without-end bargain'—renders further proof unnecessary. Such a willingness to dispense with the 'sight' of proofs (such as the acquittance Navarre demanded at the outset) requires the acknowledgement that though women, as well as men, will 'do the deed', they are not therefore, as Rosaline points out, necessarily

---

[79] There is, of course, a discourse of racial difference discernible in these relentless antitheses and hyperbolic comparisons, most marked when Dumaine imagines Jove swearing Juno to be 'but an Ethiop' in comparison with Katharine (4. 3. 117). But this discourse of racial difference is an effect, not a cause, of the polarizing of beauty as visibility/value (fair) and invisibility/not-value (not-fair/black). While this is not to say that its effects are not pernicious, it is to say that analysing the racist effects of these antitheses is not relevant to the more limited argument I am making here about the play's mockery of the strategies of artificial proof in epideictic rhetoric, and their undermining of 'good faith'.

'common' (2. 1. 223), but, as 'several' or autonomous moral agents, are capable of keeping faith no less than breaking it.

So, finally, we can see why Shakespeare anticipated the dispute over what had 'faithfully been paid' in the matter of Aquitaine by Costard's arrest on the suspicions rhetorically invented by Armado and acted upon by Constable Dull (constables were authorized to arrest 'suspected persons...which haunt any house, where is suspition of baudrie', as Lambarde wrote in 1582).[80] The indeterminacy of the proof against Costard and the precise nature and duration of his relationship with Jaquenetta are brilliantly exploited by the former in his extremely public discomfiting of Don Armado by accusing him in front of the King and nobles. 'Faith, unless you play the honest Troyan', he confronts Armado, 'the poor wench is cast away. She's quick; the child brags in her belly already. 'Tis yours' (5. 2. 675–7). Critical disagreement over whether the child actually 'is' Costard's or Armado's underscores Shakespeare's brilliant inversion of the conventional use, in the classic catastrophe or dénouement of learned comedy, of a 'romantic' discovery of the truth of paternity.[81] Normally, as we have seen in *Phormio* and *Supposes* (though the formula is common to Roman New Comedy), the discovery of paternity serves to legitimize the probable forgeries on which amorous intrigue has thrived, and to prove that all is well, and no one has been acting in bad faith. In *Love's Labour's Lost*, by contrast, the play's witty refusal to reveal who is the father of Jaquenetta's baby works to insist on preserving a distinction between the forensic rhetoric that makes a fiction—and a play—seem probable and the risky extension of *faith* without which no one would 'make a world-without-end bargain' to marry and love another.

---

[80] William Lambarde, *The Duties of Constables, Borsholders, Tythingmen...* (London: Thomas Wright, 1602), 11.

[81] See Dorothea Kehler, 'Jaquenetta's Baby's Father: Recovering Paternity in *Love's Labour's Lost*', *Renaissance Papers*, 1999, 45–54.

7

Jonson's Justices and Shakespeare's Constables: Sexual Suspicion in the Evidential Plot

Judgement and Conversation in the 1590s

A pamphlet of 1597 exposing the frauds of 'knights of the post' (men who could be hired to swear oaths to bail suspects out of prison) opens with a vignette which jokes tellingly on the skills associated with judicial examination. The narrator, a Justice of the Peace, tells us that he was travelling on foot across Hounslow Heath (notorious for highway robberies) when he overtook another traveller on foot and gave him good day. The stranger, evidently a bit of a joker, demurred about the goodness of the day, explaining that he was hungry and penniless, though he also confessed that only the previous day he had been in possession of 'as much money as would fill a quart potte, if my wisdome had been so good to keepe it'. The narrator, shocked, replies that such a rapid wasting of so much money deserves the punishment of hunger: 'he that would spend so prodigally, and so much in one day, without any regard, in my opinion is worthy to fast the next day without pitty.' But the stranger pounces on the narrator's unwarranted inference: 'So, sir, I have your judgement already (quoth he:) it is pitty you should be made a Justice of peace, that can examine a cause no better.' It appears, at length, that it was not a quart pot stuffed with coins that the stranger had managed to spend the previous day, but 'as much money as filde a quart': that is, no more than a single penny, the price of the quart of ale he'd spent it on, the day before, at Colebrook.[1]

---

[1] E. S., *The Discoverie of the Knights of the Poste* (London, 1597), sig. A2^v–A3^r.

Shakespeareans have taken interest in this pamphlet because of Shakespeare's evident familiarity with it, and his allusions to it in *1 Henry IV* (1. 2. 80–1). Slight as it is, however, the opening anecdote I have quoted suggests a more general relevance, for it throws light on perceptions of the relationship between popularly diffused forensic skills (the skills exhibited by Justices in 'examining causes') and the witty exchanges that were, by 1597, fast becoming the staple of romantic comedy and a new kind of drama known as 'humours' comedy. The thriftless Falstaffian stranger instructs the narrator-Justice solemnly in the rudiments of pre-trial judicial examination: 'If you had asked me how I had spent so much money in so short a time and how much the sum had beene, you showen some wit,' he remonstrates, 'but to pronounce me prodigall at the first dash, for so trifling a cause, argues in deede a man of small discretion.'[2] Thus it would seem that the once somewhat esoteric skills of rhetorical invention pertaining to the office of Justice of the Peace—the invention of probable conjectures of suspicion from various narratives of the facts—have already become indistinguishable from the 'wit' and 'judgement' exercised in more informal contexts by the variety of fictional social types (ne'er-do-wells, rogues, gallants, gentlemen, gentlewomen, clowns, maids) coming to prominence in satirical representations of urban fashionable life and low life both in print and on the stage.

About the time of this pamphlet's publication, the word 'judgement' was being used more and more in contexts suggestive of the refinement of an individual's eloquence and social skills through the interactions of what was now being called, in certain handbooks on the art, 'conversation'.[3] When the stranger in the pamphlet challenges the narrator, 'So, sir, I have your *judgement*', he intends the word's judicial sense, since the narrator is a Justice of the Peace, but also suggests those broader contexts of socially refining interlocution in which we are called upon to grasp allusions, interpret witticisms, and make assessments of each other's moral worth and social status. The dramatization of encounters like these was, for the very first time, becoming the staple of a new kind of comedy. In 1598, Shakespeare's company, the Chamberlain's Men, performed in a new play

---

[2] E. S., *Discoverie of the Knights*, sig. A3ᵛ.

[3] Dominant among the meanings of 'conversation' in the sixteenth century was that of consorting or having dealings with others, often with a sense of being judged by the nature of that consorting, so including 'manner of conducting oneself', 'behaviour'. The meaning of 'familiar discourse' did not come to prominence until late in the sixteenth century; the *OED* records the word in this meaning first in 1580. Thereafter, this meaning quickly began to dominate. See Anna Bryson, *From Courtesy to Civility* (Oxford: Oxford University Press, 1998); Lorna Hutson, 'Civility and Virility in Ben Jonson', *Representations*, 78 (2002), 1–27.

by Ben Jonson in which a fashionable braggart asks his listener to 'observe me *judicially*' (my italics), as he affectedly describes his escapades in battle and expresses disdain for a plain-speaking man by claiming that he lacks such powers of judicial observation: 'why he has no more judgement than a malt horse', he complains to his poet-friend, but then quickly declares the poet lacking in this faculty, too: 'your dearth of judgement makes you seem tedious.'[4] Though the braggart, Bobadilla, abuses the words 'judgement' and 'observation', however, they are also the skills for which the play's two heroes and friends value one another. One of the heroes, Lorenzo, brings his absurd cousin, Stephano, over to meet his friend, Prospero, in the city, and Prospero asks Lorenzo to describe the cousin's 'humour' so as to relish it better. 'Nay', replies Lorenzo, 'I'll neither do thy judgement, nor his folly that wrong, as to prepare thy apprehension': Lorenzo assumes that Prospero's 'judgement' will be capable of discerning and drawing out the most choicely ridiculous qualities of Stephano's humour by merely conversing with him (*EMI, Q,* 2. 3. 62–3).

The advent of this so-called humours comedy in the late 1590s may be seen as a response to the currency of arts of sociable self-improvement, such as those set out in Stefano Guazzo's *Civile Conversatione* (translated into English by George Pettie and Bartholomew Young in 1586).[5] Human-ist education had encouraged a rhetorical versatility or opportunism based on reading; Erasmus had advised schoolboys to 'read through every type of writer' in order to gather materials for *copia* of thought, and have them 'in ready money' to fit the cause and occasion of speaking, or compo-sition.[6] Guazzo reoriented the Erasmian programme in the direction of adaptability to levels of style (acquired by exposing oneself to the different 'humours' of a range of social, racial, and religious types) and attuning one's manners and speech to what is both locally and currently esteemed, what is *fashionable*.[7] But in keeping with its primary sense of 'frequenting'

---

[4] Ben Jonson, *Every Man in his Humour* (1601 Quarto) ed. Robert S. Miola, The Revels Plays (Manchester: Manchester University Press, 2000), 2. 3. 130; 1. 3. 165, 218–19. Further references to this edition are given in the text as '*EMI, Q*' followed by act, scene, and line number.

[5] Stephano Guazzo, *The Civile Conversation of M. Stephano Guazzo*, G. Pettie and B. Young (London: Thomas East, 1586).

[6] Desiderius Erasmus of Rotterdam, *On Copia of Words and Ideas*, trans. Donald B. King and H. David Rix (Milwaukee, WI: Marquette University Press, 1999), 87.

[7] In the first book of Guazzo's *Civile Conversatione*, Anniball explains to his friend, William, that frequenting company requires the work of fitting oneself to others' humours. He describes a journey from Padua to Venice, where he had to keep company with people of diverse nations and religions, but 'seeing that I had so well framed my selfe to y[e] humours of others, and that I had got my selfe honestly away being very well thought of by the companie when I was gone: so likewise, when you shal be acquainted with the course of the world, & when by

or 'having dealings with', the word 'conversation' carried with it a sense, which Guazzo developed, of being judged in the very act of frequenting company, or of the frequenting of company as coextensive with judging and being judged. He stressed that 'the judgement wee have to knowe our selves, is not ours, but wee borrow it of others', and he went on to define 'conversation' as a process of self-correction, of submitting oneself to the judgements, expressed by subtle hints and signs, of those whose company one frequents:

for so much as when we are by divers persons advertised, blamed, reproved or by signes made more advised for some fault, which wee commit either in word or deed, at the length we are content to submit our selves to the common opinion of al men, and come to acknowledge in our selves some imperfection, which wee indevour to correct by other mens judgement.[8]

Moreover, those of 'good judgement', Guazzo explained, don't tarry to be openly reproved, but internalize and anticipate the processes of criticism by observing others. They 'are mooved of their owne proper will, to wayghe diligently the sayings, the dooinges, the behaviour of others'.[9]

In the context of this book's study of the contribution of forensic rhetoric and participatory justice to the emergence of an inferential dramaturgy, two points need to be made about the representation of similar sociable arts in the kind of comedy initiated and developed by Jonson in the 1590s and 1600s. One is that Guazzo's imagining of sociable mingling as a scene in which every saying is tacitly or implicitly weighed or judged by critical interlocutors perfectly describes the action of Jonsonian comedy, where the close-ups of small talk, moments in the 'judicial observation' of what people are saying to one another, suddenly take centre-stage. Related to this is a new kind of reflexivity: we become aware that the dramatis personae are themselves products of their playgoing and reading experience (including the reading of Roman New Comedy and English imitations, with the pervasive forensic rhetoric of each). In *Every Man In*, for example, Matheo exclaims over the 'fine speeches' of Act 3 of *The Spanish Tragedy*, as Hieronimo, suspecting, seeks a means to discover his son's murder ('Is't not simply the best that ever you heard?', Matteo asks Bobadilla (*EMI, Q*, 1. 3. 139–40)). Also in *Every Man In*, Thorello, the jealous husband, quotes Terence's *Eunuch*, imagining his servant '*rimarum plenus*', full of leaks, and so to be suspected

long use, you shall be brought to abide the companie of such people, you shall perceive that if it be not good for your health, yet at least it shall not be hurtful' (sig. A5ᵛ).

[8] Guazzo, *Civile Conversation*, 115.   [9] Ibid.

(*EMI, Q,* 3. 1. 54). In the Folio version of the play, Thorello—now called Kitely—confesses that he learned a verse about 'suspicious eyes' and 'credulous breath' from reading or watching 'a jealous man's part in a play'.[10]

This focus on the dramatic revelation of the self as the product of reading and conversing, however, also requires that the audience experience the sequence of events, the dramatic action, in a new way. In order for a character to reveal his capacity and discretion in weighing the doings, sayings, and behaviour of others, one common way of thinking of plot—as the intrigue-based action that would suffer the case to be altered by evidence which cast new light on anterior events (a letter falling, a confession of child substitution, a witness to rape or murder brought forward, someone thought dead brought from hiding)—would have to be dispensed with. So Jonson abandoned the evidential revelations of past actions that characterized his *The Case is Altered* and embraced, instead, a sequence in which no immediate dilemma is set out, and no history emerges to resolve it. In Jonsonian comedy, the play's opening tends to signal that the day's unfolding will itself produce opportunity and material, whether that day is leisurely or (as in *The Alchemist*) a day of frantic business. The more leisured plays allow witty and competent conversers to observe, and occasionally take advantage of, those more in thrall to subjective delusions than themselves. The 'play' in these cases becomes more or less coextensive with the day's unfolding of the follies of these deluded but aspirant men of fashion, and every encounter becomes another opportunity for the more clear-eyed men to savour and prosper from the exquisite absurdity of these others. Thus, in *Bartholomew Fair*, Quarlous and Winwife go to the fair only in order to see what 'sport' may be 'engendered' by following a fly like Bartholomew Cokes, whom they have targeted as worth watching precisely because of his promising imbecility, revealed in abject conversational failure (1. 3. 125–6). 'What a rogue in apprehension is this!', Quarlous comments, on noting Cokes reply to his betrothed with a non-sequitur, 'To understand her language no better'. It is this comment that prompts Winwife's proposal that they follow Cokes for the day (1. 3. 122–3). But their pursuit of Cokes shapes apparent contingency as a whole play in itself, though its audience misses some choice moments: 'We had wonderful ill luck, to miss this prologue o' the purse', laments Quarlous, on arriving too late to see the first

---

[10] *Every Man in his Humour*, 5. 5. 74, in *Ben Jonson: Five Plays*, ed. G. A. Wilkes (Oxford: Oxford University Press, 1988). Subsequent references to *Every Man In* (Folio text), *The Alchemist*, and *Bartholomew Fair* (*BF*) will be taken from this edition.

pickpocketing of their hero, 'but the best is, we shall have five acts of him ere night: he'll be spectacle enough!' (3. 2. 1–3).

The second point that needs to be made, however, concerns the relationship of this new dramatic focus on the observation of conversational exchanges to the forensic invention of circumstantial proof as *enargeia*, or vividly evidential narrative. Such invention has, as we have seen, played a significant part in English generic modifications and adaptations (including romantic comedy, revenge tragedy, and chronicle history) of the Latin comic plot. I have already argued at some length that the rhetorical topics of Roman forensic rhetoric—cause, place, occasion, instrument, time, mode, and so on—had become, along with other techniques of artificial proof, staple compositional elements in humanist rhetorical education. Erasmus makes these topics the basis of his eleventh method of rhetorical amplification, 'taken from circumstances', which results 'in the whole speech being sown and fortified everywhere with close and frequent arguments'.[11] John Hoskyns likewise recommends that 'you inquire in every controversy for the circumstances', which are these, 'the persons who and to whom, the matter, the intent, the time, the place, the manner, the consequences'.[12] In previous chapters I have suggested that the rhetorical invention of circumstances is a feature of forensic *narratio* that, deployed in various ways, produces the mimetic effects we associate with both early and later Shakespearean drama. At this point, however, it is time to take account of the hitherto ignored fact that Shakespeare's mature tragedies tend to associate the mimetic power of these very forensic techniques with the forces of evil. It was for this reason that Alexander Welsh, for example, mistakenly assumed that Shakespeare was not interested in the power of forensic rhetoric to conjure up evidence of 'things not seen'. Welsh wrote that 'the dramas of Shakespeare obviously assumed quite a different stance towards circumstantial evidence from that which prevailed in the eighteenth and nineteenth centuries. For Shakespeare, reliance on evidence for conviction seems to have been either a poor joke or a vicious game: Polonius, not Hamlet, is his master detective and maker of representations: and his evil genius of circumstances was Iago.'[13] Welsh argues that while trials require circumstantial evidence when there are no eyewitnesses, 'theater need not expressly develop any evidence of things not seen'.[14]

---

[11] Erasmus, *on Copia*, 57.

[12] John Hoskyns, *Directions for Speech and Style*, ed. Hoyt T. Hudson (Princeton: Princeton University Press, 1935), 28.

[13] Alexander Welsh, *Strong Representations* (Baltimore and London: Johns Hopkins University Press, 1992), 133–4.   [14] Ibid. 102.

This book, of course, has consistently argued the contrary; indeed, it has argued that Shakespeare's innovation was to develop an inferential dramaturgy, a dramaturgy that deployed the rhetorical topics of circumstance in order that audiences should infer the details of times, places, motives, and intentions with a more vivid and spacious imaginative power than direct representation could ever master. Yet Welsh is right to note that *Hamlet* and *Othello* (not to mention *Lear*) demonize precisely these mimetic techniques. As we saw in Chapter 3, Hamlet's speeches have proved so irresistible to character criticism precisely because they reflexively anticipate and set up an inviting resistance to the 'mimetic prejudice' that character criticism shares with the forensic rhetoric deployed by Polonius and the others who invent, from Hamlet's words, evidence of the Hamlet that 'passes show'. One of Hamlet's defining features is his consciousness of being about to be construed evidentially. 'How all occasions do inform against me', Hamlet's famous self-rebuke at 4. 4. 32, is one which oddly constitutes the self in anticipated retrospect as part of a judicial narrative of time, place, occasion, circumstance, and motive. Noting the demonization of such forensic techniques in Shakespeare's mature tragedies, Patricia Parker has argued that '[t]he preoccupation with spying and informing in *Hamlet* and *Othello* raises the crucial question of the reliability of *evidence*, including substitutes for ocular proof'. She links this 'recognition of opacity—of what could not, even on stage, be brought to light or forth to show—is part of what has been described as the "crisis of representation" in this period, a crisis of which the theater functioned, paradoxically, as a revelatory instrument'.[15] What escapes Parker's formulation, I think, is the fact that forensic rhetoric was seen by Shakespeare primarily as an instrument of mimesis, and only secondarily as a morally threatening distortion of the truth behind the evidence—or, to put it another way, the concept of 'evidence' was still too strongly associated with the rhetorical invention of arguments for the latter to seem to be primarily a 'distortion' of or 'substitute' for the former's anterior or empirical 'reality'. It is not, then, that forensic techniques and information gathering as represented in *Othello* and *Hamlet* raise questions about reliability of evidential rhetoric in relation to something that would otherwise be visible and demonstrable, but that the evidential and mimetic techniques which Shakespeare in earlier plays used to create the effects which Auerbach celebrated as enabling us to 'form an idea of

---

[15] Patricia Parker, *Shakespeare from the Margins* (Chicago: University of Chicago Press, 1996), 259.

[characters'] normal lives', have now (though not abandoned as mimetic techniques) become decisively associated, within the probable fiction of the play itself, with malevolence and with the imagination's credulous susceptibility.[16]

Why should this be? In Chapter 3, I noted in passing that Harold Jenkins persuasively linked Polonius in *Hamlet* to Ben Jonson's jealous merchant, Thorello, in *Every Man in his Humour*. The forensically disposed Polonius found Hamlet's wild response to the suggestion that he walk out of the air 'into his grave' full of meaning, 'How pregnant sometimes his replies are!' (*Hamlet*, 2. 2. 206–9), just as the suspicious Thorello could find in his wife's naïve 'good truth it is this new disease;...come in out of the air' suggestive of cunning and secrecy: 'How simple and how subtle are her answers!' (1. 4. 198–201). The same passage in Jonson has been seen, by generations of critics, as a source for *Othello*. Thorello, oppressed with weighing the circumstantial likelihood of his wife's adultery with one of Prospero's lascivious mates, feels suddenly unwell: 'Troth my head aches extremely on a sudden' (*EMI*, Q, 1. 4. 193), just as Othello feels 'a pain upon my forehead' after Iago's first teasing hints of the probabilities of Desdemona's infidelity (*Othello*, 3. 3. 283).[17] It will be the argument of this chapter that we should see Shakespeare's increasing interest in dramatizing the abuse of *evidentia*, or of the circumstantial *enargeia* of forensic rhetoric, by villains like Iago, Polonius, and Edmund in *Lear*, as a response to the implications of Jonson's innovative dramaturgy. For Jonson's invention of a new, hyper-mimetic style of social comedy, focusing on moments of minutely observable social and linguistic exchange, was one that took the forensic invention of probabilities in a new direction. We have already seen how generally diffused were the skills of inventing and interrogating circumstantial probabilities, whether in rhetorical or judicial contexts. Richard Bernard's *Guide to Grand Jury Men*, though not published until 1627, exemplifies this trend, as the author advises that grand jurors investigating reports of people falling into fits as a result of witchcraft should, like

judicious Spectators...weigh seriously the occasion, of entring into the fits, with all circumstances, before whom, at what time, in what place, who those be which are about him or her, what both the party and they doe before, in the time of

---

[16] Eric Auerbach, *Mimesis*, trans. Willard R. Trask (Princeton: Princeton University Press, 1953), 319. See Ch. 5, p. 224.

[17] Arthur Murphy noted the parallel in 1757: 'It is observable that Kitely and Othello complain of an Head-ach, when first their Wives come to them, amidst their Suspicions.' See *Ben Jonson: The Critical Heritage: 1599–1798*, ed. D. H. Craig (London: Routledge, 1990), 481.

the fit, and after; and withall, to observe the manner how the partie entreth, continueth, and endeth the fits ... [18]

Jonson's drama anticipates such sceptical, circumstantial observation being used by 'judicious spectators' in all sorts of contexts, not merely forensic ones. In his plays we see the transformation of the mimetic uses of rhetorical probability into the mimetic uses of that kind of probability associated with the development of calculation, prediction, and risk.

Thus in Jonson's drama the focus on scenes of social observation shades into a focus on intelligence gathering and inventing probabilities for opportunity and advantage. This was not without its corollary in the prescriptive literature of 'conversation'—the author of one such manual warned his readers to beware of conversationalists who try to exact information, and who 'thinke they may easily (as by observing the manner of his reply, by noting the private and subtile motions of his countenance, and the fashions of his behaviour) collect some probability of their surmises: which done, they ... cease not their pursuit, till they be maisters of the game'.[19] In Jonson, however, fools, knaves, and wits alike display something of this forensic disposition. Yet it is only the last whose creativity is such that it is aligned with that of the playwright and rewarded with success in the dénouement. Thus *Every Man In* shows how the layering of forensic habits of reasoning in character after character produces social interaction as a series of calculably contingent opportunities, to be harnessed and directed by those who reveal least about their own circumstances and desires. Prospero and Lorenzo, observing Thorello's readiness to invent suspicious interpretations of his wife's behaviour, easily secure his absence at a juncture crucial to the success of their own plot, but this does not mean that they are the play's villains: quite the contrary. They are the play's exemplars of virility, its 'real men'.

Social and legal historians have emphasized the growth of popular legalism (litigation as well as participation in criminal process) in precisely this period as an index of the extent to which 'the subjects of the crown might draw upon its institutions as a resource to serve their own interests'.[20] My earlier chapters have interpreted the complexities of

[18] Richard Bernard, *A Guide to Grand Jury Men, Divided into Two Bookes* (London: Felix Kingston for Ed. Blackmore, 1627), 43.
[19] Daniel Tuvil, *The Dove and the Serpent in which is conteined a large description of all such points and principles, as tend either to Conversation or Negotiation* (London, 1614), 13.
[20] Steve Hindle, *The State and Social Change in Early Modern England, c.1550–1640* (Basingstoke: Macmillan, 2000), 13.

the vernacular adaptation of classical forensic plots to representations of English participatory justice largely in civic and characterological terms. These chapters have thus offered an interpretation of theatre's relation to the institutions of judicial power which runs counter to the still dominant critical account of Renaissance theatre as spectacular counterpart (whether subversive or containing) to the spectacularly upheld judicial power of the Crown. But if the popular, rhetorically informed law-mindedness represented in Shakespeare's plays has a civic dimension, that dimension depends on the moral limitation of our sense of what forensic rhetoric can prove. In *2 Henry VI*, Warwick's coroner-like invention of causes of suspicion about Humphrey's death responds to popular demand for such probable reasoning; but in *Love's Labour's Lost* the use of similar probable reasoning as a 'salve for perjury' is rejected when the Queen of France refuses Navarre's suit on the very grounds that his rhetorical promiscuity has undermined his oathworthiness: 'your oath I will not trust' (4. 3. 286; 5. 2. 782). In Jonson, the hermeneutic uncertainty that Shakespeare grounded in the idea of good faith becomes grounded, instead, in the idea of discretionary calculation. It becomes impossible to make the kind of moral distinction between 'trustworthy' and 'untrustworthy' that is germane to Shakespeare's drama. In *Every Man In*, Prospero/Wellbred and Lorenzo/Knowell may trust one another, but their conduct depends on a sense of discretion so uncompromising that it amounts to deceit and distrust of everybody else. The same could be said about Dauphine and Clerimont in *Epicoene*, and about Winwife and Quarlous in *Bartholomew Fair*, not to mention Lovewit and Jeremy (who are more blatantly deceptive in their uses of law) in *The Alchemist*. So, for example, in *Epicoene*, Clerimont laughs to think how Sir John Daw and Sir Amorous La Foole are both so ambitious of a reputation for sexual prowess that each claims to have slept with Mistress Epicoene herself (neither knowing, as the audience still does not, that 'she' is a boy). 'And for the bride', Clerimont tells Dauphine, 'they have made their *affadavit* against her.' 'What', Dauphine replies, shocked, 'that they have lien with her?'[21] Not only that, Clerimont affirms, but they make their claim in good forensic rhetorical form, telling 'times and circumstances, with the cause why, and the place where' (*Epicoene*, 5. 2. 72–3). The joke here relies on understanding the play's alignment of moral superiority not with 'troth' or trustworthiness, but with the capacity to be sexually discreet;

---

[21] Ben Jonson, *Epicoene or the Silent Woman*, ed. Roger Holdsworth (London: A & C Black, 1990; first published by Ernest Benn, 1979), 5. 2. 71. Further references to this edition will be given in the text.

moments before, in the same scene, Clerimont reads what purports to be a 'riddle' from one of the learned ladies, Mavis, which is addressed to Dauphine. The 'riddle' turns out to be a straightforward sexual assignation: 'Call you this a riddle?', exclaims Clerimont, 'What's their plain dealing, trow?' (*Epicoene*, 5. 2. 60–1). Discretion in matters sexual is not, in itself, a virtue; the evident intellectual superiority in Jonson's play of those who are most discreet, however, has the effect of suggesting that sexual regulation of a traditional sort, applied to these gentlemen, would amount to a prurience as gross as the lasciviousness attributed to the collegiates.

Thus, the pervasive law-mindedness and forensic awareness of Jonson's comedies works to obliterate traditional moral distinctions as it educates the audience in making new kinds of discrimination between forms of everyday conduct. In such a dramatic world, there can be no a priori distinction between the official figure of authority—the Justice of the Peace—and the witty gallant who has absorbed skill in judging causes as a mundane matter of what Daniel Tuvil calls 'conversation or negotiation'.[22] In *Every Man In* the wit of the gallants is clearly paralleled with that of the Justice in examining causes, for though Justice Clement's examination unambiguously reveals the guilt of Prospero and Lorenzo as liars and circulators of sexual slander, the outcome involves no punishment, but congratulation and approval of the secret marriage between Lorenzo and Hesperida that was their ostensible motive. Likewise in *Bartholomew Fair*, although Justice Overdo declares it a 'special day for detection' (2. 1. 38–9), he mistakes the likelihoods of the situation he is observing, and in attempting to protect the person he takes to be a deserving young man in peril, he affords the same proficient thief a perfect opportunity to pick a purse. Just as he misconstrues what he affects to spy out, however, the educated gallants who treat the fair as a spectator sport observe everything perfectly: 'Will you see sport?', asks Winwife, as both watch the cutpurse, Edgeworth, tickle the ear of his victim, Cokes, to draw his hand opportunely out of his pocket. As Edgeworth passes the stolen purse to Nightingale, audaciously engaged in singing a ballad against cutpurses, the gallants practically applaud: 'fore God he is a brave fellow', approves Winwife, 'pity he should be detected' (3. 5. 149–50). They are, to some

---

[22] Tuvil's *The Dove and the Serpent* discusses '*all such points and principles, as tend either to* Conversation *or* Negotiation' (title-page). Conversation becomes synonymous with negotiation: ch. 5 teaches 'How to converse in Court' and how to 'purchase favour', while ch. 9 treats 'Of Negotiation in general', and ch. 11 instructs in framing styles appropriate to different kinds of negotiation.

extent, our surrogates: we, too, are encouraged by Jonsonian drama to observe closely, *judicially*, and to relish the ironies of making judgement. But important ethical questions—evident in the baffled discomfort of the audience which is sometimes apparent in modern productions of Jonson—are raised when the plays seem to encourage and reward gentlemanly collusion with *deceptio visus*, with the kind of evidence manipulation that Iago performs on Othello.[23] To call the plays 'satires' does not entirely deal with the issues raised here, since the gentlemen—Lorenzo Junior or Young Knowell in *Every Man In*, Eugene Dauphine in *Epicoene*, Lovewit in *The Alchemist*, Quarlous in *Bartholomew Fair*, end up, as Jonathan Haynes put it of the last instance, 'holding all the cards'.[24] Though critics persist in identifying each of these more ambiguous kinds of ending as 'unique' within Jonson's *œuvre*, which is otherwise to be understood as moral and satirical, it would seem, by contrast, that the harshly moral ending of *Volpone* is actually the egregious one.[25] What is needed, perhaps, is some account of the developing relationships and contrasts between the dramaturgy of Jonson and Shakespeare as both develop the forensic uses of false inference, surmise, and suspicion in the later 1590s and 1600s.

Mimesis in Jonson and Shakespeare

Shakespeare, as we saw, transformed the dominant dramaturgical modes in place at his arrival on the theatrical scene precisely by exploiting the uses of false inference to make us aware of the contingency of fictional characters' access to knowledge about one another, which in turn invited the audience to infer, in a quasi-forensic manner, motives for their false surmises, and so build up a sense of their histories and inner lives. While this doesn't exactly mean that Shakespeare is 'imitating life' according

[23] This discomfort was very evident in Nicholas Hytner's 2006 production of *The Alchemist* at the National Theatre, when Simon Russell Beale's Face transformed himself into Jeremy and proceeded to betray the venture tripartite. His appeal to the audience to be his 'jury' (Hytner's substitution for Jonson's reference to trial by 'country') was met with unease and bewilderment.

[24] Jonathan Haynes, *The Social Relations of Jonson's Theater* (Cambridge: Cambridge University Press, 1992), 128.

[25] For example, Andrew Gurr suggests that the ending of *The Alchemist* is unique: 'In the long series of Jonson plays which normally allow neither the wits nor the virtuous to win very much at the end, Lovewit gets away with material gains strikingly better than any other character', 'Who is Lovewit? What is He?', in *Ben Jonson and Theatre*, ed. Richard Cave, Elizabeth Shafer and Brian Wolland (London: Routledge, 1999) 5. Haynes, on the other hand, finds the end of *Bartholomew Fair* unique: 'The twist by which boy gets girl but his friend gets her money is highly unusual, if not unique' (*Social Relations of Jonson's Theater*, 128).

314

to the Platonic metaphor of the mirror (discussed in Chapter 3), it does mean that his use of forensic rhetoric tends to enhance our sense of the circumstantial reality of the world which we infer from the speeches of characters. Jonson's mimetic technique, however, has often seemed to critics to be unequivocally ambitious to simulate the world outside the theatre in some exact sense. Pauline Kiernan, for example, bases her contrast between Shakespeare and Jonson on these grounds. Taking 'mimesis' implicitly in a Platonic sense (she defines it as 'a skilled imitation of nature that is so life-like we are deceived into thinking the imitated subject is the real thing'), Kiernan argues that Shakespeare rejected this 'mimesis concept of art', but that Jonson embraced it. Jonson, in her terms, holds a 'theory of drama as mimesis, in which the poet stands outside nature, holding up a mirror'.[26] But Kiernan never engages critically with Jonson's drama, which seems rather, as Sean McEvoy has written, 'to assert that on-stage action is in some sense *continuous* with the "off-stage" world'.[27] McEvoy quotes suggestively from an account of a performance of *Every Man in His Humour* at Joan Littlewood's Theatre Royal Stratford East in 1960: 'I couldn't believe', wrote Philip Hedley, describing the performance, 'this was by the author I had found so difficult to read at university. Indeed, I couldn't believe it hadn't been written yesterday. I had never seen English actors like these... *They seemed to be improvising*, but they weren't. They really talked to us.'[28]

They seemed to be improvising—this is, indeed, precisely the achievement of Jonson's greatest drama, the impression we have that speech and events are so freshly spontaneous, so contingent, that the action turns and changes with men's quick-thinking responses to the new opportunities everywhere created by conversation, negotiation, and confrontation. In Jonson's plays, opportunities feel genuinely opportune, to the extent that one can sense an opportunity missed, as it were, as if there really were other directions the action might have taken, given the possibility of a character responding differently. In *Every Man In*, for example, the foolish Stephano, or Stephen, discovers that a sword sold to him by the disguised Musco (Brainworm in the Folio) was not a fine Toledo, as Musco had claimed, but a cheap imitation. Stephano confronts Musco: 'You sold me a rapier, did you not?'... 'You said it was a Toledo, ha?'... 'But it is none.' As Musco confesses each of these facts, including the lie about the Toledo,

[26] Pauline Kiernan, *Shakespeare's Theory of Drama* (Cambridge: Cambridge University Press, 1996), 8, 68.
[27] Sean McEvoy, 'Hieronimo's Old Cloak', *Ben Jonson Journal*, 11 (2004), 67–87, at 68.
[28] Ibid. 67; my italics.

however, Stephano quickly and foolishly retreats from the opportunity he himself has created: 'Gentlemen bear witness, he has confessed it. By God's lid, an you had not confessed it—' (EMI, Q, 2. 3. 178–85). It quickly emerges that, in spite of Stephano's unconvincing swagger, there will be no violent or legal confrontation, and the brilliant comedy of Stephano's cowardly backtracking will be obvious to anyone. Nevertheless, for a moment some sort of clash had seemed imminent. Thus does Jonson's best drama, by plotting near misses and directions not taken, produce a sense of the potential latent in each encounter, and of the continually developing possibility of unexpected outcomes.

There is, moreover, an ethical dimension to this carefully achieved illusion of contingency. In *Bartholomew Fair*, for example, Quarlous catches sight of Dame Purecraft, the rich widow being pursued by his friend, Winwife, as she approaches Ursula's booth in anticipation of eating roast pig. Quarlous suggests that this festive present is the perfect convergence of time and location, the perfect opportunity to court her: 'thou'lt never be master of a better season or place' (3. 2. 117–18). But Winwife holds back: 'I love not enterprises of that suddenness, though', he demurs. Quarlous is revealingly impatient: 'you are a modest undertaker, by circumstances, and degrees; come, 'tis disease in thee, not judgement' (3. 2. 125–7). The opportunity for courtship passes unseized, and it will be Quarlous, of course, who wins the rich widow, for he, as Haynes notes, 'understands the uses of disruption', and, unlike Winwife, understands how an unexpected turn of events creates 'opportunity for the man with a quick wit and a quick hand'.[29]

If, as earlier in Chapter 3, we turn from a Platonic understanding of mimesis as mirror to the quasi-equivalence, apparent in Aristotle's *Poetics*, of mimesis and *muthos*, or plot, we begin to make out exactly how innovative Jonson's departure from the modified neoclassicism of Shakespeare's early 1590s drama must have seemed.[30] For, in the words of Ricoeur's extrapolation from Aristotle, 'to make up a plot is already to make the intelligible spring from the accidental, the universal from the singular, the necessary or probable from the episodic'.[31] Shakespeare, as we have seen, learned from the Aristotelian plot structure of Roman New Comedy

---

[29] Haynes, *Social Relations of Jonson's Theater*, 128.

[30] Jonson was a close reader of Daniel Heinsius's *De Tragoediae Constitutione Liber* (1611), which commented on Aristotle's use of 'muthos' (translated as 'fabula') to mean both the material of tragedy and its organization as dramatic action. See Ch. 3, p. 115. Jonson translated Heinsius in his *Discoveries* (1641).

[31] Paul Ricoeur, *Time and Narrative*, trans. Kathleen McLaughlin and David Pellauer, i. (Chicago and London: University of Chicago Press, 1984), 41.

to produce a heightened sense of cause and effect, of an *intelligible* from an apparently *natural* sequence, by indicating the passage of time impressionistically, combining a sense of rapidity and proleptic anticipation with references to longer, repetitive sequences of habitual time, suggesting an anterior temporal space, as it were, 'behind the scenes'. Jonson, by contrast, invented a form of plot which strove to make the accidents making up the present moment seem precisely *accidental*, so that what the audience follows and discriminates between as these moments accumulate are the processes by which a range of characters (mostly men) attempt to shape these accidents into something intelligible and prosperous. Just as Shakespeare's plots engage forensic rhetoric to create the impression of a natural sequence sown with proofs of time, place, instrument, and so forth, so Jonson's plots engage similar rhetorical techniques with different effect, to show how what seems to have happened may be the product of a forensic shaping of the anticipatory desires and fears of those involved into something quite illusory, if highly effective for certain men's purposes. What is different, however, is that whereas Shakespeare's drama refuses to endorse deliberately contrived illusion-mongering, or evidence manipulation on the part of characters, it frequently maintains this ethical stance, this distinction between truth and falsehood, by an illusionistic management of the *evidentia* afforded by the plot's narrative sequence, which prevents the audience from reconstructing exactly what it thinks it has seen. Jonson's dramaturgy works the opposite way: the illusions and evidential manipulations managed by characters are endorsed at the end of the play by the distribution of wealthy marriages and alliances thus brought about, but the audience *has seen everything*, and, as Dryden noted of *Epicoene*, everyone in the audience is 'a proper judge of what he sees' because 'all faults lie open to discovery'.[32] It is to the audience's attentiveness that Jonson appeals for judgement on the decorum of the dénouement, particularly its disruption of generic expectations. Thus, as Sean McEvoy says, Jonson's drama asserts the continuity of the dramatic representation with the off-stage world in these moments of appeal to the audience's ethical and aesthetic judgement.

To exemplify the distinction just drawn, we may first observe how commonly both dramatists make use of a dénouement, a last act, that involves some sort of evidential reconstruction, or trial, of the suspicions

---

[32] John Dryden, 'Of Dramatic Poesy' (1668), in *John Dryden: Selected Criticism*, ed. James Kinsley and George Parfitt (Oxford: Clarendon Press, 1970), 60.

invented in the first three acts. Thus, as we saw, Shakespeare's 1594 *Comedy of Errors* has the Ephesian community rehearse the various perjuries and breaches of faith to which its citizens have borne witness, only to find these explicable in the belief-beggaring but emotionally powerful recognition of a double set of twins. In *Every Man in his Humour*, the suspicions that draw various characters to Cob's house to detect and bring before the law the illicit sexual activities of their loved ones are revealed by the Justice's examination of the witnesses to be the product of deliberate deception, of a playing on jealous susceptibilities and fears. In both instances, jealous imaginations produce the illusion of having been wronged, but Shakespeare's delightfully preposterous plot contrives it that no one need deliberately deceive, whereas Jonson's requires Prospero and Lorenzo, or Wellbred and Knowell, to orchestrate suspicion so as to produce the 'prosperous' climax of confusion and error.

A more revealing contrast, however, can be made between later plays by Shakespeare and Jonson. Shakespeare wrote *Othello* for the King's Men at the Globe in 1604, and Jonson wrote *The Alchemist* in 1610 for Shakespeare's company at their new playhouse, the Blackfriars, where *Othello* was also subsequently performed.[33] Both plays are concerned, in quite different ways, with the capacity of a rhetorical theatre, or of a certain rhetorical manipulation of desire, to produce the illusion of having seen things impossible to view. In a powerful and suggestive study of the rhetorical dramaturgy of *Othello*, Joel Altman argued that we should see a connection between Iago's characteristic reliance upon the master trope of improbability—'hysteron proteron', or the figure of preposterous reversal—and the cunning temporal distortions and reversals in the unfolding of the dramatic narrative that, paradoxically, contribute to our mesmerized sense of the play's probability and reality as an imaginative experience. Altman analyses Act 1, Scene 3, of *Othello* as Shakespeare's demonstration of the inherently passionate nature of composing evidence into a probable conjectural narrative. In this scene the Venetian Senate attempts to make sense of conflicting information as to the numbers and purpose of a Turkish fleet in the Mediterranean. The moment of inference in this and other, similar instances in the play is, as Altman says,

passionately grounded in some relational notion of identity' ('I hate the Moor'; 'A maiden never bold'; 'We must not think the Turk'), and upon this literally

---

[33] Gurr, 'Who is Lovewit?', 11; *idem, Shakespearean Company*, 294.

empirical foundation it layers successive bits of evidence in inductive fashion, which will either confirm the thesis already postulated ('Whether I am in any just term affin'd | To love the Moor') or lead to an inference that is, at it were, a natural extension of the original thesis ('judgment . . . must be driven | To find out practices of cunning hell'; 'Nay, in all confidence, he's not for Rhodes'). In none of these situations, it should be noted, do we find a process of logical implication. It is not syllogism that is at work, but invention, induction, and intuition—that power which 'sees into' evidence, uncovers relationships, and infers conclusions.[34]

Altman appeals to humanist dialectic, and to its uses of scholastic terminology, to explain the cognitive psychology behind both Iago's consummate art of leading both Roderigo and Othello to draw inferences preposterously and the art of Shakespeare's play in making Othello's plight tragically plausible. Yet the rhetorical ways of knowing and representing described here by Altman might equally be thought to derive from the pervasiveness of forensic rhetoric as the basis of instruction in *copia*, in elementary narrative composition, in Roman New Comedy, and, increasingly, in popular legal culture. The alert schoolboy who read the *narratio* from Cicero's *Pro Milone* in his Aphthonius might (as we saw in Chapter 3) have noticed a similar preposterousness at work in Cicero's composition of that narrative into a coherent, motivated whole.[35] Be that as it may, the profound significance of Altman's analysis lies in the analogy it draws between Iago's vicious use of *hysteron proteron* as a means of leading others to infer the likelihood—the palpability to thinking—of quite fantastic scenarios and Shakespeare's own brilliantly preposterous invention, in *Othello*, of 'double time'. For Altman takes the mid-nineteenth-century analysis of double time in *Othello* by John Wilson (*alias* Christopher North) quite seriously: the blending of different illusions of time passing satisfy 'the need for two kinds of probability: long time is needed to convince the audience that what Othello imagines has taken place could have taken place: short time is needed to make Othello's gullibility credible'.[36] Altman shows that from the moment the play opens and all through Act 2, temporal distortions affect the processes by which we learn about events supposed to be happening, so that our

[34] Joel Altman, 'Preposterous Conclusions', *Representations*, 18 (1987), 129–57, at 137.
[35] Cicero, starting from the problematic fact of Clodius and his men having been brutally murdered by Milo's heavily armed and numerous guard, nevertheless led his readers to infer Milo's lack of malicious intention by suggesting that the very numerousness of Milo's retinue be read as the sign of a leisured, encumbered departure, proof that, as preposterously as any in *Othello*, supports a premiss passionately grounded in a relational identity. For Cicero, as everyone knew, hated Clodius. See Cicero, *Defence Speeches*, trans. D. H. Berry (Oxford: Oxford University Press, 2000), 191–3.
[36] Altman, 'Preposterous Conclusions', 145. See Ch. 3, p. 118.

sense of the urgency and presence of these events is an illusion contrived by rhetorical reversals of antecedent and consequence, of effect and cause. The opening moments of the play give the sense of taking place at the very moment at which Othello and Desdemona are being married, but this illusion is partly the effect of Brabantio's circumstantial questions on discovering that Desdemona is, indeed, missing: 'Now Roderigo, | Where didst thou see her? ... With the Moor, say'st thou?—Who would be a father!— | How didst thou know 'twas she?—O, she deceives me | Past thought!—What said she to you? ... Are they married, think you?' (*Othello*, 1. 1. 162–7). A few lines later, the next scene opens with Iago urging Othello to anticipate Brabantio's legal challenge: 'But I pray you, sir, | Are you fast married?' (1. 2. 10). The marriage's dramatic reality is thus entirely the product of Brabantio's first challenging of the evidence for it, and Iago's then asking Othello to pre-empt such a challenge by being legally married: both are *forensic* constructions which bring a situation into verbal being by defensively anticipating the need to gather evidence. Altman associates other such reversals with the rhetorical figure of *metalepsis*, a variant of metonymy, in which causal or consequential relations between a term and its substitute may be reversed, and the stages between them suppressed.[37] These alternations and reversals of tense and sequence disorient the audience, making it incapable of distinguishing the probable from the improbable. Indeed, Altman demonstrates conclusively that Iago's own collapses and reversals of tense and mood are the grammatical counterpart of the plot's conflation of times and actions: the extraordinary mimetic achievement of 'double time', then, is Shakespeare's Iago-like triumph over the audience, his transformation of all of us into Othello.

Thus it is that when, in Act 5, Othello acknowledges that his killing of Desdemona is 'pitiful', but just, for 'Iago knows, | That she with Cassio the act of shame | A thousand times committed' (5. 2. 211–13), the audience is not, Thomas Rhymer-like, scornful of Othello's ludicrous arithmetic, but feels anguish that he could imagine such things. Yet though the scene concludes with even Othello acknowledging the increasingly apparent probability of a counter-narrative, as Emilia exclaims that her husband begged her to steal the handkerchief, and the dying Roderigo yields both a letter and a speech ('after long-seeming dead') accusing Iago, the audience is no more in a position to reconstruct this evidence

---

[37] Altman, 146–7. On metalepsis, see ibid. 153 n. 12, which refers the reader to Victoria Kahn, *Rhetoric, Prudence and Skepticism in the Renaissance* (Ithaca, NY: Cornell University Press, 1985), 143–9.

with a retrospective look at the previous five acts than is Othello himself, as John Wilson's exhaustive attempt to do just that conclusively demonstrates.[38]

Here, then, is where we can draw an instructive contrast with Jonson's use of forensic rhetoric in the interests of an ethical dramatic mimesis. In Jonson's *Alchemist*, Face, like Iago in *Othello*, might be thought to stand for the play's own rhetorical capacity to deceive the eyes. Face exhibits skills roughly analogous to those deployed by Iago in cultivating various plausibly honest aspects that enable him to refute even eyewitness evidence by the power of this deceptive *ethos*. Though Lovewit's neighbours corroborate one another's testimony as to the invasion of the house in his absence, their evidential assurance falters when confronted with Face's sheer face. These visitors 'did pass through the doors, then', he bristles, 'Or walls, I assure their eyesights, and their spectacles' (*Alchemist*, 5. 2. 25–6). This is one of many instances of Face's capacity to endow deception with a truth-like clarity, but any comparison here or elsewhere with Iago's capacity to lead his hearers 'to the door of truth' 'by imputation and strong circumstances' (*Othello*, 3. 3. 406–7) must acknowledge a distinction in the two plays' positioning of the audience as judges of what they have heard and seen. Whereas Shakespeare's play disables the audience's ability to judge, in Emilia's words, 'what place? what time? what form? what likelihood?' (*Othello*, 4. 2. 138), Jonson's invites and rewards the audience's minute observation and recollection of precisely such circumstantial detail. So, for example, when Dol first comes in and tells Face and Subtle (who are busy arguing over which of them will have the widow Pliant) that Face's master has unexpectedly returned, Subtle confronts Face: 'You said he would not come, | While there died one a week, within the liberties' (*Alchemist*, 4. 7. 115–16). Face immediately counters this charge: 'No: 'twas within the walls' (4. 7. 117). A careful auditor might recall that neither is precisely correct. Way back in the opening sequence, as Subtle started at the sound of the door and prayed that the interruption be not Face's master back from the country, Face replied, airily, 'Oh, fear not him. While there dies one a week | O' the plague, he's safe from thinking towards London' (1. 1. 182–3). So—Jonson gives us all the evidence, but that evidence is far from conclusive. What are we to infer, if Face did not, originally, specify whether his master was counting the death toll within the city or without, from the fact that he now distorts the account, and

---

[38] John Wilson ['Christopher North'], 'Dies Boreales, no. 6', *Blackwood's Edinburgh Magazine*, 67 (Apr. 1850), 481–512.

claims to have specified 'within the walls'? Subtle seems sceptical, too: 'Was't so? Cry you mercy: | I thought the liberties' (4. 7. 118–19).

When Jonson wrote *The Alchemist*, Londoners and their correspondents were just beginning to get accustomed to consulting the weekly Bills of Mortality for data about the rates of death and the inferences that might be drawn from them. J. C. Robertson has traced the basic format of the *Bills* to the 1560s, noting that their layout was recast in 1570, when the Privy Council, expressing 'suspicion . . . [of] the weeklie certificates delivered to [them] of such as dye within this Cittie . . . of the plague' commanded greater rigour of the searchers of the dead before they returned their certificate to the parish clerks. From the 1610s the weekly returns of the Company of Parish Clerks were printed as Bills of Mortality, with a set of summary totals at the foot of the sheet, showing which parishes were clear and which weren't. These parishes were divided into 'Within the Walls' and 'Within the Liberties'.[39] In London, as Robertson comments, 'death rates became a commodity that was quoted in parochial units'.[40]

As several critics have noted, *The Alchemist* mischievously explores the nature of theatre and theatricality by securing a particularly precise correspondence between Blackfriars Theatre, situated within the walls, and Lovewit's house, occupied by Face, Subtle, and Doll for the duration of the plague.[41] R. L. Smallwood suggests that hearing Face's first remark that his master will not return, 'While there dies one a week, | O' the plague', the audience will 'remain subconsciously apprehensive that the activities we are watching with such pleasure may be brought to an immediate halt at any time'.[42] Face's 'While', however, does not just indicate a sense of the imminence of his master's arrival—it's not quite that he 'may arrive at any time'. 'While' rather suggests a return that is—in the theatrical illusion, at least—a *calculable* probability.

The translation of the senses of the word 'probability' from a primarily rhetorical to a primarily calculable set of associations was, of course, very gradual, and rhetorical senses of the word persisted into the eighteenth century. However, one of the seventeenth-century spheres of activity that

[39] J. C. Robertson, 'Reckoning with London', *Urban History*, 23, no. 3 (1996), 325–50, at 328–31. I owe this reference, and much else in this discussion of the references to mortality bills in *The Alchemist*, to a very generous readiness to share scholarship and insights on the part of Professors Peter Holland and William Sherman, editors of the forthcoming edition of *The Alchemist* as part of the Cambridge *Complete Works*, and of Dr Mark Jenner in the History Deparment at York.   [40] Ibid. 328.

[41] See, e.g., R. L. Smallwood, 'Here, in the Friars'; Peter Womack, *Rereading Literature* (Oxford: Basil Blackwell, 1987), 117–18; McEvoy, 'Hieronimo's Old Cloak', 70–1.

[42] R. L. Smallwood, ' "Here, in the Friars" ', *The Review of English Studies*, n.s. 32, no. 126 (1981), 142–60, at 150.

has been taken as adumbrating a new way of thinking about probability was the analysis of these very Bills of Mortality.[43] In choosing to hint, from the outset, at the determining of the play's action by this variable yet calculable limit, Jonson suggests a relationship between generic expectation, based on rhetorical probability, and the brilliance of adjusting generic expectation and the rhetorical commonplaces that govern it to a moment by moment *calculation* of possible outcomes, likely returns on a risk. For the activities of both Face and Lovewit, from the moment of Face's confession to the latter until the moment that both turn to the audience and apologize for having 'outstripped' the 'canon' of dramatic probability, are actually shocking departures from moral and rhetorical norms or expectations. If Iago manages, preposterously, to make it seem probable in Othello's eyes that Desdemona was 'that cunning whore of Venice, that married with Othello', then it is only a little, if at all, less preposterous that Face should so easily slip from con man to faithful servant and Lovewit change from returning *senex* into Spaniard impersonator, roaring boy and bridegroom, and all this not before the eyes of a gullible Drugger or Dapper, but before the audience itself. As Smallwood notes, Face's announcement to Subtle and Doll that it was he who arranged Lovewit's return ('I sent for him, indeed' (*Alchemist*, 5. 4. 129)), 'has a curious plausibility, even for the audience'.[44] But this 'curious plausibility' is one which, as Face himself acknowledges in his last speech, comes at the expense of a certain outrage to moral and generic expectations: 'My part fell a little in this last scene.' Lovewit's apology to the audience for the implausibility of all this, like Face's retrospective claim to have sent for Lovewit, preposterously reverses cause and effect: 'If I have outstripped | An old man's gravity, or strict canon, think | What a young wife and a good brain may do' (5. 5. 153–5). In both cases, it is precisely because the audience is not being deceived by the theatrical illusion that its acceptance of the probability of Lovewit's and Face's triumph feels like the acceptance of a new moral code, a legitimizing of the creative triumph of calculation and opportunism—'think what a ... good brain may do', indeed. Moreover, this appeal to the audience to tolerate deviations from dramatic decorum shades insensibly into a demand that their acquittal should make a new moral law: 'I put myself | On you, that are my country', concludes Face (5. 5. 162–3). This disturbing effect, though more pronounced in *The Alchemist* than elsewhere, is quite typical of Jonson's

---

[43] Ian Hacking, *The Emergence of Probability* (Cambridge: Cambridge University Press, 1975), 11.　　　　　　　　　　　　　　　[44] Smallwood, 'Here, in the Friars', 153.

comedy, and it is, I suggest, something to which Shakespeare's post-1597 drama was responding.

Justice Clement and Justice Leonato: Jonson and Shakespeare on Evidence

To argue that Shakespeare's drama was, from about 1597 on, responsive to Jonson's, and vice versa, is not in itself to say anything new. Andrew Gurr, among others, has traced interactions between Shakespeare and Jonson throughout their playwriting, from the parody of *Romeo and Juliet* in *Poetaster*, through links between *Lear* and *Volpone*, both written for the Globe company in 1605, to the two magician plays, *The Alchemist* and *The Tempest*, both written for the Blackfriars in 1609–10. It is, as Gurr puts it, 'inconceivable that each of them did not know a fair amount about what the other was doing'.[45] Yet, in practice, evidence for this interaction and its effects is generally more likely to be sought in Jonson's writings than in Shakespeare's, as if the influence could work only one way. Moreover, interpretations of the importance of the interaction tend to reinforce rather than interrogate commonplaces about Shakespeare's and Jonson's dramaturgical differences: Shakespeare's defiance of the neoclassical unities and Jonson's adherence to them are repeatedly illustrated, as I mentioned in the previous chapter, with reference to the prologue from the revised version of *Every Man in his Humour* and the remarks, in the Induction to *Bartholomew Fair*, about servant-monsters and making 'Nature afraid ... like those that beget Tales, Tempests, and such like drolleries' (Ind. 112–14). It should be possible, however, to argue that the playwrights involved were aware of the moral and political stakes of the choices they made with regard to the extent of their neoclassicism, and I think this is precisely what becomes clear if we look at the prologue to the 1615 edition of *Every Man In* more closely.

Jonson's 1615 prologue retrospectively presents his 1598 play as a radical innovation in its own time, and does so by defining its achievement against the impressionistic temporal probability of the previous decade's major generic innovation: the chronicle English history play. This was the genre that thriftily managed 'with three rusty swords, | And help of some few foot-and-half-foot words' to 'Fight over York and Lancaster's long jars | And in the tiring house bring wounds to scars' (*EMI*, *F*, Prol.

---

[45] Gurr, 'Who is Lovewit?', 11.

9–12). But Jonson's innovation is not simply characterized, by contrast, as the substitution of a familiar, conversational style for iambic bombast, and realistic for impressionistic time. These technical innovations are related to an ethical project in which, typically, the affectionate regard of one man for another is linked to one man's admiration for another's judgement of how to use the occasions offered by conversation—whether to use restraint and discretion, for example, or bold opportunism. Jonson's prologue concludes with the hope that the substitution of a focus on a habitual, conversational style of speech and conduct ('deeds, and language, such as men do use') will enable the audience to discriminate, laughingly, between the 'popular errors' that have characterized the bombastic 'monsters' of an earlier drama and the true 'men' revealed by this new way of unfolding dramatic time on-stage.

The troubled figure of Thorello constitutes an intermediate category between the 'monsters' of uncomprehending admiration for linguistic excess (Matteo, Bobabilla, and Stephano) and the 'men' who command a truly conversational and intelligently allusive plain style (Prospero and Lorenzo). Thorello is the condensation into a stock social type—the bourgeois, calculating, possessively uxorious merchant—of the forensic habits of thought associated with Roman New Comedy. He exceeds his dramatic role (Garrick's eighteenth-century adaptation of the play made him into its anguished hero, and played down the charisma of the gallants) partly because he expresses consciousness of his own position as a stock figure (anticipating, for example, that if he were to rebuke Prospero's lascivious friends, they would 'Contrive some slander that should dwell with me', saying, 'That I were jealous' (*EMI, Q,* 1. 4. 92–6)), but mainly because this very self-consciousness exemplifies, in exaggerated form, the forensic tendency to prolepsis that makes his imagination crucially generative of the action of this play (by affording its opportunities), and inspirational of the way in which action might be generated via such busy imaginations (Polonius/Hamlet, Iago/Othello) in later tragedies. That Shakespeare acted in *Every Man in his Humour* in 1598 is well known, and critics have largely accepted J. W. Lever's proposal that Shakespeare had Jonson's 'Thorello' in mind when he named his hero 'Othello'.[46] My concern, however, is less with resemblances between 'Thorello' and 'Othello' as isolated dramatis personae than with the former imagined as a kind of figure for the demands increasingly being made upon the audience

---

[46] J. W. Lever, 'Introduction,' in *Every Man in his Humour* (Lincoln, NE: University of Nebraska Press, 1971), pp. xxiv–vi.

to project future developments in the dramatic action from details that might be construed as causes, or clues.

In what follows I am going to argue that Jonson's *Every Man in his Humour* and Shakespeare's *Much Ado about Nothing* may be read as plays in dialogue with one another over the ethics of inventing 'probable' but false scenarios of sexual suspicion concerning women. Shakespeare had dramatized such a situation once before, in *The Comedy of Errors*, where, of course, Antipholus of Ephesus is naturally incensed at having the doors of his house barred to him and his dinner guest, the merchant Balthazar. The latter, however, urges him not to break down the door. First, he offers in forensic terms the reasons why the evidence should as yet be weighed in favour of Adriana's fidelity to him:

> Have patience, sir. O, let it not be so!
> Herein you war against your reputation,
> And draw within the compass of suspect
> Th'unviolated honour of your wife.
> Once this—your long experience of her wisdom,
> Her sober virtue, years and modesty
> *Plead on her part some cause to you unknown.*
>
> (3. 1. 86–92; my italics)

How Antipholus might judge Adriana, however, from his 'long experience' of her wisdom and virtue, needs to be distinguished from what people will say, knowing little or nothing of either of them. So Balthazar persuades Antipholus that forcing the door will, in effect, provoke such rumours of sexual scandal, that the slander, an intruder whom it is impossible to expel, will share his habitation even after death:

> If by strong hand you offer to break in
> Now in the stirring passage of the day,
> A vulgar comment will be made of it,
> And that supposed by the common rout
> Against your ungalled estimation,
> That may with foul intrusion enter in,
> And dwell upon your grave when you are dead.
>
> (3. 1. 99–105)

Later, of course, the tormented Antipholus does not hesitate to air in public his suspicions of Adriana, whom he calls a 'dissembling harlot' (4. 4. 102). Once the errors are discovered, and Adriana is vindicated in the revelation that Antipholus has a twin, however, these slanderous accusations against her have no further power. From Balthazar's cautionary words, and from the records of the church courts in London in the late sixteenth and early seventeenth centuries, however, it seems that this was not always so in practice. Suits alleging sexual slander became, in this period, the most popular type of litigation engaged in by women, and by the end of the sixteenth and beginning of the seventeenth centuries, women brought cases up to five times more often than men did. Laura Gowing writes that by 1633 defamation suits had come to account for the largest part of the consistory courts' business, as much as 70 per cent, with 85 per cent of cases being brought by women.[47] Since it was expensive and time-consuming to sue to restore a reputation damaged by sexual slander, we must assume that the stakes were high for the women who went to law. Gowing acknowledges that the battles fought out in the courts were as much about slandered neighbourliness as about sexual reputation; nevertheless, the very focus of litigation on this issue indicates the vulnerability of women to moral structures that in practice made household honour depend on female rather than male sexual reputation. As Gowing writes, 'While the homilies, sermons and law of the church stress the culpability of both men and women for illicit sex, the idiom of slander holds women entirely responsible for it, for it contains no words to condemn male sexual misconduct.'[48]

Before Jonson wrote *Every Man in his Humour*, Shakespeare had written no play in which he showed concern about the ease with which sexual misconduct might be proved against women, no play in which he dealt with the legally embroiled tragic or tragicomic consequences of such slander. In the wake of *Every Man In*, however, he wrote a number of such plays: *Much Ado About Nothing*, *Othello*, *The Winter's Tale*, and *Cymbeline*, while his rewriting of *Promos and Cassandra* as *Measure for Measure* strikingly alters the earlier play's readiness to allow the heroine's case to be judged by a judge who has not, like Duke Vincentio, been eavesdropping on and influencing proceedings all along, but who simply listens to Cassandra's evidence. I will argue that this new interest of Shakespeare's in developing what Terence Cave has described as 'a plot of the psyche...the plot of mistaken jealousy', characterized by 'suspicion and anxiety', and attempting to pre-empt our sexual suspicion (in the case of a character like Cassandra/Isabella) is, in part at least,

[47] Laura Gowing, 'Language, Power and the Law', in *Feminism and Renaissance Studies*, ed. Lorna Hutson (Oxford: Oxford University Press, 1999), 428–49.   [48] Ibid. 430.

327

a response to the general direction in which Jonson was taking the evidential plot.[49]

For as Jonson transformed popular law-mindedness and the increasingly popular and pervasive forensic rhetorical disposition into calculable 'humours', susceptibilities which might be exploited by the most observant and opportunistic characters in the play, his plays showed little interest in the social and legal consequences that might follow upon the opportunistic unleashing of what Altman calls 'the erotic and improbable energies of the imagination'.[50] Throughout *Every Man In*, Prospero deliberately and calculatingly exacerbates Thorello's fears that his wife may have committed adultery, leading him to the point of imagining he has caught her in the act, 'Close', as he puts it, 'at your villany', at what he imagines is a bawdy house run by Cob's wife, Tib (*EMI, Q*, 5. 1. 48). Legal action follows: 'I'll have you every one before the Doctor', says Thorello, and marches the assembled company off to Doctor Clement (Justice Clement in the Folio), who efficiently tries the evidence and finds that Thorello has been gulled by Prospero. Thorello, however, can't quite discard the image of the assignation he had so vividly imagined; 'say, i'faith', he says, many lines later, to his wife, 'was it not a match appointed 'twixt this old gentleman and you?' (*EMI, Q*, 5. 3. 425–6). What Shakespeare dramatizes in *Much Ado* is the ease with which an invention of sexual suspicion such as Prospero brilliantly contrives may overwhelm more probable counter-narratives and accumulate its own irrefutability, so that, for example, Don Pedro can assert, with outrageous improbability, that Hero's suspected sexual partner has 'Confess'd the vile encounters they have had, | A thousand times in secret' (*Much Ado*, 4. 1. 88).

It has been commonly assumed that in *Every Man In* Jonson exchanged the old idea of a sequential comic plot of 'cross-wooing'—that is, a thwarted and finally successful romantic courtship—for what Jonathan Haynes has called the 'satirically observed part[y]', in which we as audience join observers on-stage who have gathered together certain eccentric types in order to note or comment upon their eccentricities.[51] The apparent plotlessness of Jonson's play has accordingly been stressed, and Anne Barton's appreciative words quoted: 'Unity of time becomes...a way of evoking, in detail, the life of a great mercantile Renaissance city as it moves through its day.'[52] Yet although the action's apparent lack of

[49] Terence Cave, *Recognitions* (Oxford: Clarendon Press, 1988), 282–3.
[50] Altman, 'Preposterous Conclusions', 151.
[51] Haynes, *Social Relations of Jonson's Theater*, 27, 48.
[52] Anne Barton, *Ben Jonson* (Cambridge: Cambridge University Press, 1984), 46.

directedness seems thus explicable in terms of satiric realism, or Dutch realist painting, Jonson's dramatic motive for producing this impression of leisured opportunity is, as I have been trying to suggest, rather to enable the audience to appreciate the judgement of men who *use the opportunities* thus afforded. The Italian names of the Quarto help us see this more clearly: the plan which enables Lorenzo to attain 'Hesperida' was conceived and carried out by the timely-happy dramatist of daily life, 'Prospero'.

This is why Jonson sets up no immediate legal or romantic dilemma. Rather, as so many Restoration comedies would later do, this play starts in the morning, with an apparently empty day to fill with leisured amusement. Lorenzo is invited by Prospero to spend the day in the city, observing the mannerisms of Bobadilla and Matheo, two aspirant gentlemen who have evidently, in the manner recommended by Guazzo, 'diligently give[n] ear to the woordes of others' to improve their social standing.[53] The central scenes of the play have been assumed to be constructed as amorphously plotless conversations merely to enable us to relish the delicious pretensions of Bobadilla, Matheo, and Lorenzo's rustic cousin, Stephano. But these leisurely middle scenes of the play crucially furnish an opportunity for Lorenzo to meet and elope with Prospero's sister, Hesperida, whose status as virginal treasure is clearly signalled by her name. While appearing to invite Lorenzo along with other gallants to Thorello's house purely for a morning's conversational entertainment, Prospero proves to have been clandestinely concerned throughout the latter part of the play with his project of becoming his best friend's brother-in-law, and with permanently allying Thorello's family to the family of Pazzi (Lorenzo's surname, which means 'crazy'), all without either the knowledge or permission of either paterfamilias. The party in Thorello's warehouse which we observe in scenes 3. 2, 3. 4, and 4. 2 is not only the occasion for our laughter at the pretensions of the gulls; it is also the means by which a distracting smokescreen of unnecessary suspicion and anxiety is *deliberately* blown across the minds of the very group that would certainly have opposed Prospero's plans: that is, Lorenzo's father, Lorenzo Senior, Prospero's brother, Thorello, Cob, the water-bearer, and Giuliano, Prospero's half-brother. These all, for various reasons, perceive or imagine the gallants to be behaving in ways which threaten the honour of their own households and kinsfolk, especially kinswomen, and they all feel impelled, at one point or another, to appeal to the local Justice,

---

[53] Guazzo, *Civile Conversation*, 136–7.

Doctor Clement, for warrants to keep the peace and for his examination of the suspicions they have conceived. What is radically new about Jonson's play, then, is the way in which the heroes—Prospero and Lorenzo, better known by their Folio names as Wellbred and Knowell—anticipate and exploit popular participation in the legal enforcement of sexual morality as a means of facilitating their own dubiously clandestine matrimonial project.

From his first appearance on-stage in Act 3, Prospero not only withholds information about himself (we only realize in retrospect the extent to which he orchestrates the match between Hesperida and young Lorenzo), but permits and even, we must infer, calculatingly encourages the circulation of the most scandalous misreadings of both his epistolary style and his 'conversation' (in the period's sense of the company he keeps) so as to ensure that Lorenzo Senior, Thorello, Thorello's wife Bianca, Cob, and the others all *suspect the worst*, first about the immoral conduct taking place at Thorello's house, and latterly about a series of imagined sexual assignations involving, among others, Lorenzo Junior and an imagined merchant's wife, rumoured to have been appointed at Cob's house. In other words, Prospero—helped not a little by Musco, the wily slave of Roman comedy revived—not only deliberately invites his interlocutors to invent plausible conjectures of sexual suspicion about one another, but even seems to bank on their prevalent law-mindedness, their conviction—surely the legacy of the reformation of manners and increase of governance since the 1570s—that the law and its officers are the appropriate means by which each can obtain redress for his or her imagined injuries, his or her sexual suspicions of a husband, wife, or errant son.

Jonson's innovative audacity here really cannot be overemphasized. If Quarlous, in Haynes's memorable formulation, is the epitome of the man who 'understands the uses of disruption', Prospero-Wellbred is the man who 'understands the uses of suspicion'.[54] To say that Prospero understands the uses of suspicion is not simply to say that imaginations like Thorello's are vulnerable to his audacity. It is to say that Prospero knows how to exploit a popularly pervasive law-mindedness with regard to offences of all kinds, including sexual immorality. As a technical, legal term, 'suspicion' was applicable not only to felony, but covered peoples' imaginings of all kinds of potentially anti-social behaviour. Constables were empowered to 'take (or arrest) suspected

---

[54] Haynes, *Social Relations of Jonson's Theater*, 128.

persons, which walke in the night, or sleep in the day: or which haunt any house, where is suspition of baudrie: and they may carrie them before a Justice of Peace, to find suerties of their good behaviour'. Neighbours were 'compellable to helpe and assist him', should he meet any resistance.[55] Those duped by Prospero, Musco, and Lorenzo in *Every Man In* are all enthusiastic participants in this culture of popular law enforcement. Old Knowell of the Folio text, to take just one example, is an escapee from the moral world of the 1570s and Gascoigne's *Glasse of Government*, and believes his son is headed for depravity and ruin by 'conversing' with those of Wellbred's suspected morals (*EMI*, F, 2. 5.65), though Justice Clement does his best to reassure him: 'your son is old enough to govern himself', he says (*EMI*, Q, 3. 7. 73–4), reflecting, perhaps, a newer generation's attitudes to the moral policing of the liberally educated.[56]

Two kinds of 'humour' linked with suspicion and law-mindedness enable the enterprising gallants to propel the action forward towards the climactic scene outside Cob's house in Act 5, Scene 1. The first of these is, of course, Thorello's jealousy. In two longish speeches, this humour expresses itself forensically, in Thorello's adumbration of the likelihoods or probabilities of his wife committing adultery with one of Prospero's crew during his absence. To Giuliano he complains,

> Why't cannot be, when there is such resort
> Of wanton gallants, and young revellers,
> That any woman should be honest long.
> Is't like that factious beauty will preserve
> The sovereign state of chastity unscarred,
> When such strong motives muster and make head
> Against her single peace? No, no: beware
> When mutual pleasure sways the appetite,
> And spirits of one kind and quality
> Do meet to parley in the pride of blood.
> Well (to be plain) if I but thought, the time
> Had answered their affections, all the world
> Should not perswad me, but I were a cuckold:
> Marry, I hope they have not got that start.
> For opportunity hath balked them yet,

[55] William Lambarde, *The Duties of Constables, Borsholders, Tythingmen . . .* (London: Thomas Wight, 1602), 11.

[56] See, e.g., Joan Kent, 'Attitudes of Members of the House of Commons to the Regulation of "Personal Conduct" in Late Elizabethan and Early Stuart England', *Bulletin of the Institute of Historical Research*, 46 (1973), 41–71.

> And shall do still, while I have eyes and ears...
> My presence shall be as an iron bar
> Twixt the conspiring motions of desire...
>
> *(EMI, Q, 1. 4. 164–81)*

The whole speech answers the question of likelihood ('Is't like?') by detailing the proofs that come under the topic of motive (the appetite whetted by the thought of mutual pleasure, the wanton, youthful company, their resort to his house, the beauty of his wife), and then settling, with relief, on the two topics that make his cuckoldry seem, as yet, unproved or improbable: time and opportunity. By Act 3, Scene 1, an appointment with another merchant prompts him to reconsider his position with regard to the probabilities of time and opportunity:

> Stay, let me see: an hour to go and come,
> That will be the least; and then 'twill be
> An hour, before I can dispatch with him,
> Or very near: well, I will say two hours.
> Two hours? Ha? Things never dreamt of yet
> May be contrived, ay, and effected too,
> In two hours' absence. Well, I will not go.
> Two hours! No, fleering Opportunity,
> I will not give your treachery that scope.
> Who will not judge him worthy to be robbed,
> That sets his doors wide open to a thief,
> And shows the felon where the treasure lies?
> Again, what earthy spirit but will attempt
> To taste the fruit of Beauty's golden tree,
> When leaden sleep seels up the dragons eyes?
> Oh, Beauty is a project of some power,
> Chiefly when Opportunity attends her:
> She will infuse true motion in a stone,...
> Pour rich device into an empty brain,
> Bring youth to Folly's gate, there train him in,
> And after all, extenuate his sin.
> Well, I will not go, I am resolved for that.
>
> *(EMI, Q, 3. 1. 6–29)*

By now, Thorello sees time and opportunity as themselves sufficiently generative of transgression: the felon and the adulterer are no longer the products of premeditation, motive, and habitual resort: unguarded, beauty and treasure are likely to occasion crimes and furnish the criminals with means (motion, rich device) they would otherwise lack.

Aristotle's division of rhetoric into deliberative, forensic, and epideictic distinguishes the first two by tense: deliberative rhetoric relates to the future, forensic to the past. Here, however, we can see how insistent Jonson is on the orientation of Thorello's forensic disposition towards the future (and, incidentally, how the characteristic metalepses of *Othello* were suggested to Shakespeare). Thorello's readiness to consider rhetorical probabilities is beginning to push the concept of 'probability' into the future-oriented sense that it would acquire at the end of the seventeenth century. What this means for the play is that Thorello's anticipatory reckoning of the likelihoods of his wife's infidelity become the very opportunity he dreads—although the 'project of some power' involves marriage with his sister, Hesperida, not an assignation with his wife, Bianca.

The other humour or disposition exploited by the witty gallants is the pervasive law-mindedness of all the characters, from Cob to Giuliano, Bobadilla to Stephano, Thorello to Old Lorenzo. Jonson had already in *The Case is Altered*, suggested a readiness to go to law for every slight offence as a pretentious habit: when Count Ferneze sees his servants wearing finery bought with gold they have stolen, he asks, 'What, are my hinds turnd gentlemen?', and one of them, Onion, replies, 'Hinds, sir? Sbloud and that word will bear action, it shall cost us a thousand pound a peece, but weele be revenged' (5. 13. 10–13). In *Every Man In*, the readiness of almost everyone to settle their quarrels with one another via the law proves most opportune for Musco, who, disguised first as the Justice's clerk and then as an arresting serjeant, makes warrants and arrests with aplomb, finally ensuring the convergence of all upon the house of the Justice, Doctor Clement.

Jonson combines Thorello's jealousy with the law-mindedness of other characters to create just that potent mix of mutual, legally actionable suspicion that Prospero's plot needs. We see this in the incident of Cob's visit to the Justice of the Peace, where, encountering Thorello, he ignites the latter's worst fears and sends him tearing back to the warehouse to anticipate and prevent the debauchery he imagines taking place. In Act 3, Scene 2, Thorello has finally left his residence, and Prospero, Lorenzo, and Musco, along with the three gulls, Bobadilla, Matheo, and Stephano, have the place to themselves. Cob, wandering in, expresses disgust at their taking of tobacco, and is promptly cudgelled by Bobadilla in an uncharacteristic burst of physical violence. As the gallants settle down after this disruption to be regaled by some of Matheo's limply derivative poetry, Cob takes himself off to get his revenge on Bobadilla by craving

333

the peace of the local Justice, Doctor Clement.[57] Craving the peace, or asking a Justice to bind another person to the peace, was one of those practices interestingly poised between private litigation and communal law enforcement which was, apparently, on the rise in the period. Necessarily prompted by fear of a neighbour's or family member's unexpected physical assault, this increasingly popular legal recourse encapsulates, as Steve Hindle writes, the 'complementary relationship between violence and litigation'.[58] It is also a practice which indicates the hermeneutic complexity of the division between acceptable and non-acceptable behaviour in early modern society, and Jonson's use of it as such is characteristically rich, implicating Bobadilla in charges of cowardly expediency in submitting to the warrant, while at the same time suggesting that requesting it was an act of resourcefulness on Cob's part. In agreeing to bind a party to the peace at another's request, a Justice of the Peace was required to take an oath from the party requesting it to the effect 'that he standeth in feare of his life, or some bodily hurt to be done to himselfe', so that craving the peace did not become a means of simply conducting a feud or being 'at variance' with a neighbour.[59] Accordingly, when Cob craves that Doctor Clement will grant a warrant to bind someone to the peace, Lorenzo Senior asks him, 'Why, dost thou go in danger of thy life for him?' (*EMI*, Q, 3. 3. 79–80). 'No, sir', replies Cob, 'but I go in danger of my death every hour by his means; an I die within a twelve-month and a day, I may swear by the laws of the land that he killed me' (*EMI*, Q, 3. 3. 81–3). This last joke alludes to the common law limitation of a year and a day as the period within which an injury could be said to have been the felonious cause of another's death, but it is also a brilliant parody of the way in which popular forensic strategies, no less than learned uses of forensic rhetoric, tend to anticipate the evidential reconstruction of events before the events themselves have even taken place.[60] Clement, after expressing a patrician disgust with the thought of the likes of Cob giving opinions on tobacco, finally does grant the water-bearer his warrant, and it is apparently served on Bobadilla, a fact which gives him a convenient though shameful excuse not to respond to Giuliano's later challenge to a duel: 'Well, gentlemen, bear witness

[57] That the Quarto's Florentine setting was meant to be recognized as a contemporary English setting is suggested by the fact that in the Quarto Cob comes 'to crave the peace of your worship', even though he is visiting an Italian civil lawyer (3. 3. 69–70).

[58] Hindle, *State and Social Change in Early Modern England*, 105.

[59] Michael Dalton, *The Countrey Justice* (London: John More, 1635), 159.

[60] See, e.g., Sir John Baker, *The Oxford History of the Laws of England*, vi: *1483–1558* (Oxford: Oxford University Press, 2003), 555.

I was bound to the peace, by Jesu', he insists, pathetically (*EMI, Q,* 4. 2. 122–3).

Jonson brilliantly parallels Cob's proleptic law-mindedness with the erotic prolepses generated by Thorello's excitably forensic habits of reasoning. Cob's visit to the Justice inflames Thorello with the thought that he might learn from Cob what is going on at his warehouse. Everything Cob says refutes Thorello's suspicions, but Jonson, with delightful precision, ensures that Thorello derives from each denial further material for conjecture. He expresses his certainty that his sister and wife would welcome the gallants. 'Like enough', Cob concedes, in a general way, 'yet I heard not a word of welcome' (*EMI, Q,* 3. 3. 26). Thorello supplies an inference as fantastic as it is swooningly erotic: 'No, their lips were sealed with kisses', and then asks, desperately, 'Cob, which of them was't that first kissed my wife? | My sister, I should say. My wife, alas, | I fear not her. Ha? Who was it, say'st thou?' (*EMI, Q,* 3. 3. 30–2). Cob's professions of ignorance are in vain. Thorello arrives back at his house for the aftermath of a nearly violent confrontation. Giuliano had drawn his sword in outrage at the sight of Matheo's attempt to court Hesperida, egged on by Prospero's lewdly mischievous suggestion that Bianca get herself 'a servant that can rhyme and do tricks too' (*EMI, Q,* 3. 4. 114–15). (The word 'tricks', which provokes a horrified response from Giuliano, might indeed have been considered actionable under certain conditions in a slander suit against Prospero, since its sexual meaning, deriving from Latin, *meretrix*, or whore, was familiar.[61]) In the general melée that ensues, Hesperida's and Bianca's praise of Lorenzo as a civil young gentleman, 'of very excellent good partes', only makes matters worse by arousing further suspicions: 'Good parts? How should she know his parts?', frets Thorello (*EMI, Q,* 3. 4. 196). In the meantime, Prospero and Lorenzo, riding the tide of misdirected suspicion and general confusion, are plotting the 'conveyance' (*EMI, Q,* 5. 2. 189) of Hesperida; Musco is dispatched, disguised as the soldier whom Lorenzo Senior had taken into service that day, to

---

[61] Jonson's revels editor, Robert Miola, notes the sexual innuendo at *EMI,* 3. 4. 114 ff. If, say, Hesperida had been able to prove that Prospero's insinuation of her sexual familiarity with Matheo, implied in the word 'tricks', had damaged a specific proposal of marriage from another suitor, she might even have had a case in common law. See, e.g., the case of a woman who successfully brought an action for slander in the King's Bench in 1606 against a man who declared that another man had had 'the use of her body', thus leading to her suitor's withdrawal of his marriage proposal. See John March, *Actions for Slander, or a Methodicall Collection under Certain Grounds and Heads of what words are actionable in LAW, what not?* (London, 1647), 31. The point of having Prospero run the risk of defaming and so devaluing Hesperida as a marriageable prospect is, surely, to emphasize his intimacy with and authority over Lorenzo, who, trusting him, will want Hesperida anyway.

encounter the old man again, and stir up his fears for his son. He offers Lorenzo Senior a richly circumstantial description of a feast attended by citizens' wives at which his son, Lorenzo, has arranged to meet one of these women 'at one Cob's house, a waterbearer's, that dwells by the wall' (*EMI, Q,* 4. 1. 42–3). He then, dressed as the Justice's clerk, entices Thorello out of his house with a false message from the Justice so that Lorenzo and Hesperida can elope. Back at Thorello's residence, however, we see Prospero improvising a way to get both Thorello and Bianca to converge on Cob's house, imagining each other guilty of a sexual assignation there. Prospero is receiving a dressing down for having disturbed the peace and provoked Giuliano to draw his sword. He dryly responds that no harm came of it, and Bianca asks what harm might have come it? 'Might?', replies Prospero, 'so might the good warm clothes your husband wears be poisoned, for anything he knows, or the wholesome wine he drunk even now' (*EMI, Q,* 4. 3. 16–18). Thorello immediately recalls that his wife served him wine, and 'bade me wear this cursed suit today'. His mind races ahead to indict and convict her: 'See, if God suffer murder undiscovered?' (*EMI, Q,* 4. 3. 20–2). Though nothing more comes of this moment, it furnishes Prospero, perceiving Thorello's imaginative suggestibility, with his next cue: as Thorello moments later looks for his wife, Prospero confides in him 'whither I suspect she's gone . . . To Cob's house I believe; but, keep my counsel' (*EMI, Q,* 4. 3. 137–9). Playing Thorello's game of forensic conjecture, of inventing suspicions, Prospero easily manipulates man and wife, and gets them out of the way: Bianca herself hurries off because Prospero hints broadly at the sexual attractions of Cob's house: 'Cob's wife is an excellent baud, indeed, and oftentimes your husband haunts her house—marry, to what end I cannot altogether accuse him. Imagine what you think convenient' (*EMI, Q,* 4. 3. 92–5). Thus, by the end of Act 4, Scene 3, Prospero has successfully caused all the potential opponents of Lorenzo's and Hesperida's elopement to converge on Cob's house, and has, moreover, exposed the inherent ambiguity of the ubiquitous legal phrase, 'a suspected house'. For Cob's house has now, indeed, become a 'suspected house', but only by Prospero's deliberate invention of suspicion about it.

In the brilliant sequence of Act 5, Jonson dramatizes, first, the community's readiness to subject itself to law, and then—after Justice Clement's revelation of how they have all been duped—enacts a critique of the very law-mindedness that would make domestic sexual conduct a public matter for the constables and other officers of justice, rather than a private matter for the liberal gentleman and his household. In Act 4, Scene 10,

suspicions go on reinforcing one another. As Lorenzo Senior knocks on
Cob's door, Cob's wife, Tib, asks, 'you are no constable I hope?' 'Oh,
fear you the constable?', retorts Lorenzo Senior, immediately suspicious
(*EMI, Q*, 5. 1. 4–5). Indeed, Lorenzo Senior is ready to fetch the constable,
but for the entrance of Bianca, whom he now suspects to be his son's
appointed lover. Thorello joins them, luxuriantly triumphant to have
caught his wife, and ready to believe that all are her accomplices: 'I'll
ha you every one before a Justice', he declares in the 1616 text (*EMI, F*,
4. 10. 58)—in the 1601 Quarto, this appears as 'I'll have you every one
before the Doctor' (*Q*, 5. 1. 74). Lorenzo Senior then advises Cob not
to beat his wife, but 'if she have done wrong in this, let her answere
it afore the magistrate' (*EMI, Q*, 5. 1. 90–1). When it comes to showing the cause before the Justice, however, the case, as Justice Clement
puts it, is altered (*EMI, Q*, 5. 1. 28). By dint of asking each person by
whom they were directed to Cob's, and at what time, Clement easily
discovers at least some of the facts: 'Why this is a mere trick, a device;
you are gulled in this', he exclaims (*EMI, Q*, 5. 3. 34–5), without yet
knowing why. But already, at this stage, Clement repudiates the ideology of the Justices' handbooks, which imply that responsibility for the
surveillance of sexual mores lies with the parish and its officers. Justices of
the Peace were responsible, under the statute of 18 Eliz.c.3, for bastards,
and were empowered, on their discretion to bind to good behaviour any
man suspected of having begotten a bastard.[62] 'Suspected houses', as we
have seen, could be searched by constables and Justices of the Peace.
But Clement unexpectedly distinguishes between the Justices' jurisdiction
and the question of personal conduct. Bianca tells Clement, 'And please
you sir . . . my brother Prospero told me that Cob's house was a suspected
place . . . And that my husband used thither daily.' 'No matter', replies
Clement, '*so he use himself well*' (*EMI, Q*, 5. 3. 17–21; my italics). The
question of whether a brothel-haunter did or did not 'use himself well' is
beyond the competence of an officer of justice to discover, and Jonson's
Clement seems to be suggesting that it should be so. In excluding Matheo
and Bobadilla for their failures in poetry and physical courage and in
admiring the wit Musco's appropriations of his own legal authority, and
(finally) in endorsing the secret marriage, and the £3,000 dowry illicit-
ly thereby conveyed to Lorenzo, Clement makes the virile, liberal uses
of gentlemanly wit the new governor of manners, the new partner of
the law.

[62] Dalton, *Countrey Justice*, 37–8.

In *Much Ado About Nothing*, Shakespeare dramatizes the hazard that the plot of *Every Man In* suppresses: the risk, that is, that the invention of a suspicious scenario such as that orchestrated by Prospero, Musco, and Lorenzo, would acquire its own delusional reality, its own lurid probability, overwhelming attempts at evidential reconstruction, and requiring, finally, ritual rather than legal means of resolution. If we recall that *Every Man In* was originally set in Florence, we can see that the Messina of *Much Ado* attempts to reproduce something like the atmosphere of the new urban 'humours' comedy: its gallants and gentlewomen are all (with the exception of Don John) equally determined to make social capital out of wittily observing and 'break[ing] comparisons on' one another's oddities of speech, dress, and behaviour (*Much Ado*, 2. 1. 146). 'Apprehension', a keyword in Jonson's *Every Man In*, is likewise prominent in *Much Ado*: Beatrice is said to 'apprehend passing shrewdly' (*Much Ado*, 2. 1. 81). Later, Beatrice asks Margaret, who has suddenly taken to innuendo, how long she has 'profess'd apprehension?' (3. 4. 67). Although the scenes of noting and observing are less elaborate, and there is no parading of pretentious eccentrics after the fashion of Chapman or Jonson, something like the Jonsonian fashion for character drawing is suggested by the fact that wit frequently takes the form of ridiculing the habits and demeanours of others: Beatrice's mockery of Don John during his absence from dinner, for example: 'How tartly that gentleman looks! I never can see him but I am heart-burn'd an hour after' (2. 1. 3–4), followed rapidly by the company's taking up the grotesque notion of a man composed of Don John and Benedick: 'half Signor Benedick's tongue in Count John's mouth', etc. (2. 1. 11–12). As in *Every Man In*, too, the inflation of oaths suggests a pervasive moral bankruptcy, a general lack of trust among the gallants—'By my troth', swears Don Pedro, 'By my faith', ripostes Claudio, and 'by my two faiths and troths', mocks Benedick; but what Claudio had originally said betrayed a suspicious reflex, a lack of trust in his interlocutors' motives, worthy of Guazzian conversation manuals. 'You speak this to fetch me in, my lord', he had said, nervously (1. 1. 222–7). In both plays, too, one man agrees to make a clandestine conveyance of a woman to his friend, though in Jonson the discreet carriage of this plot is merely another proof of the heroes' moral integrity as friends, expressing their mutual affection in the understated efficiency of Prospero's device. 'Why, what shall I swear by? Thou shalt have her, by my soul', protests Prospero, after Lorenzo has already told him not to swear. Lorenzo replies, 'I pray thee, have patience, I am satisfied. Prospero, omit no offered occasion, that may make my desires complete, I beseech thee' (*EMI, Q*, 3. 6. 31–5). In *Much Ado*, however, the friends' similarly dismissive attitude towards oaths and alertness to the offered occasions of conversation and negotiation provoke misunderstanding and distrust: 'Let every eye negotiate for itself', Claudio concludes bitterly, sourly misconstruing Don Pedro's courtship of Hero on his behalf (*Much Ado*, 2. 1. 178).

The crisis of *Much Ado*—Claudio's accusations against Hero in the church in Act 4, Scene 1—can be seen as the logical consequence of Jonson's plot, with its transformation of the 'countenance' of law from the support of traditional moral codes to the applause of gentlemanly wit. In Jonson's play, as we have seen, the Justice's examination of the order of time elegantly discovers that there has been some 'device'. But Shakespeare—and this is the key contrast—refuses to allow that the examination of *evidence* might be a solution to Hero's plight. Critics, of course, have found it frustrating and incomprehensible that Hero says nothing in her own defence. Lewis Carroll, writing to Ellen Terry, recalled that Borachio had said: ' "I will so fashion the matter that Hero shall be absent." ' He went on,

Well, granting that Hero slept in some other room that night, why didn't she say so? When Claudio asked her,

> What man was he talk'd with you yesternight
> Out at your window betwixt twelve and one?

why didn't she reply

> I talk'd with no man at that hour, my lord
> Nor was I in my chamber yesternight,
> But in another, far from it remote?

And this she could prove by the evidence of the housemaids, who must have known that she occupied another room that night.[63]

The play, however, anticipates Carroll's criticism, but deliberately, in the bungling of the constables' evidential reconstruction, disables it. In order to understand precisely why, we have to look once again at the full achievement of the dénouement of Jonson's play.

Act 5 of the Quarto of *Every Man in his Humour* slowly and inexorably subordinates the authority of law to the devices of wit and the defence of poetry. In doing so, however, it effectively renders the reputation

---

[63] Lewis Carroll, Letter to Ellen Terry, quoted in A. R. Humphreys, 'Introduction', in *Much Ado About Nothing* (London: Arden Shakespeare, 1981), 66.

of a young bride vulnerable to the readiness of judicial authority to countenance whatever, among the gallants, passes for wit and poetry. For it is not simply that Clement's judicial examination discovers Prospero's fraud: the whole scene works towards the fulfilment of the prologue's later promise that 'men' will be distinguished from 'monsters' by bringing on, in successive entrances, first Bobadilla and Matheo, with their case prepared against Giuliano, and then the latter, with Stephano, both in the custody of Musco, who is disguised as an arresting serjeant. Clement is by turns horrified by Bobadilla's ostentatiously unmanly cowardice and regaled by Musco, who proceeds to 'uncase' and take the risk of regaling the Justice with the narrative of his many disguises and frauds, including his theft of Clement's clerk's garments, in which he 'carried a message to signor Thorello in your name. Which message was merely devised but to procure his absence, while Signor Prospero might make a conveyance of Hesperida to my master' (*EMI*, *Q*, 5. 3. 186–90).

Like a credit card fraudster selling his story to the broadsheets, Musco triumphs in Clement's unadulterated admiration: his work, Clement marvels, is an epic, a newly discovered *Iliad*. The newlyweds, with the man who masterminded this 'conveyance', then make their appearance. The young couple say nothing at all, their anxiety registered by Clement, while Prospero teasingly likens Lorenzo to the prodigal son, and lewdly jokes that Hesperida still, if she's unhappy with her new husband, has 'a cloak for the rain' in her old lover, Matheo (*EMI*, *Q*, 5. 3. 252). No one contradicts this singularly inappropriate sexual banter, while Clement goes about the final business of the scene: the humiliation of Bobadilla and Matheo. As the latter's plagiarized verses are ridiculed, Lorenzo Senior says something disparaging about poetry, prompting from his son a passionate set-piece speech in poetry's defence. This oration, corresponding to Musco's earlier triumphant narrative, finally fully legitimizes Lorenzo's and Hesperida's marriage, and in so doing, identifies the gallants' uses of sexual suspicion as legitimate and uncompromising to them.

In *Much Ado*, the precise equivalent to Justice Clement in office and station is Signor Leonato. For, just as Jonson's play set in Florence had characters binding one another over to the peace in the fashion of English common law, so Shakespeare's Messina features constables, a watch, and a Justice of the Peace. We know that Leonato is the Justice, though nowhere is he addressed as such (indeed, neither is Clement in the 1600 Quarto of *Every Man In*), because in Act 3, Scene 5, the constables, Dogberry, and the headborough, Verges, explain to him—eventually—that they have 'comprehended two aspicious persons, and we would have them this morning examined before your worship' (*Much Ado*, 3. 5. 45–6). Although Dogberry must sadly have missed the pleasure of reading of the considerable responsibilities of his office in Lambarde's *Duties of Constables*, he and Verges were following that book's advice. On a report of suspicious behaviour, a constable 'may arrest the suspected person', wrote Lambarde, 'and he shall doe well to carrie him to a Justice of Peace together with him that doth suspect him, to that end they may both bee examined as appertaineth'.[64]

What Shakespeare has done, in effect, is to imagine Clement's reaction were he, like Leonato, a guardian and a kinsman of a woman at the centre of a scenario of sexual suspicion such as Prospero and Lorenzo have masterminded. Clement's approval of the wits closes off the possibility that those less well positioned to manipulate suspicion—the older men and the women—might have a case. Leonato is both a Clement and a Lorenzo Senior or Thorello, both the Justice smitten with wit and social status and the father or uncle helplessly implicated in the probability of the case advanced by those wits against his kinswoman. Of course, his implication is partly his own fault. As a Justice, he should have taken the examination of those 'aspicious persons', as Dogberry requested, that very morning ('we would have them this morning examined before your worship', asserts Dogberry (*Much Ado*, 3. 5. 44–5)). Leonato's unseemly haste to ally himself with the protégé of Don Pedro (he even asks the friar to 'be brief' in the wedding ceremony (4. 1. 1)), coupled with Dogberry's unfortunate conviction of the unparalleled point and substance of his own eloquence, results in a fatal deviation from administrative procedure as stipulated in the handbooks. 'Take their examination yourself, and bring it me', instructs the impatient father of the bride; 'I am now in great haste, as it may appear unto you' (3. 5. 49–50). Nowhere in the literature of Justices or constables is it laid down that constables may take examinations of suspects.

Leonato's great haste produces his humiliation, a haste that signals his Jonsonian or Clement-like appreciation of fashionable wit over his sense that justicing involves responsibility to a wider community. When the examination is finally taken, the abortive wedding ceremony and the devastatingly humiliating public bewhoring of his daughter have already

---

[64] Lambarde, *Duties of Constables*, 17. If the watch should find 'cause of suspicion', Michael Dalton wrote, 'they shall forthwith deliver the said persons to the Sherife, who shall keepe them in prison untill they bee duly delivered; or else the watchmen may deliver such persons to the Constable, and so convey them to the Justice of peace, by him to be examined and to be bound over, or committed, until the offenders be acquitted' (*Countrey Justice*, 140).

taken place. 'Prince John', as the Sexton tells the suspects, 'is this morning secretly stol'n away: Hero was in this manner accus'd, in this very manner refus'd, and upon the grief of this suddenly died' (4. 2. 560–3). *Hysteron proteron*, however, operates not only at the temporal level of the play's action. Dogberry's methods of examination reveal a sense of order completely at odds with any sort of probable coherence—whether chronological or by inference of cause, or motive—that might define a narrative. Indeed, Dogberry's obsession with the priorities of hierarchy—which take precedence over grammar—initially prevent the examination getting anywhere near the composition of an intelligible narrative of the facts. 'Write down that they hope they serve God', he instructs the Sexton, 'and write God first, for God defend but God should go before such villains!' (4. 2. 18–20). But a more telling reversal takes place between thought—mere suspicion—and proof: 'Masters,' he goes on, 'it is prov'd already that you are little better than false knaves, and it will go near to be thought so shortly' (*Much Ado*, 4. 2. 20–2).

In this latter reversal, Dogberry articulates the inherently preposterous working of suspicion itself, as it had been absorbed into the 'apprehension' and 'judgement' of humours comedy. Dogberry's metaleptic reversal and suppression of the stages between cause and effect, between being 'thought' or suspected to be false and then, evidentially, 'proved' so, expresses precisely what happens in the scenes of stylistic apprehension and judgement in *Every Man In*. In these scenes the stylistic excesses classified by Jonson in *Discoveries* as preposterously 'effeminate'—such as an affected terseness and roughness, or a too-fluent facility—are enacted in Bobadilla's soldierly profession to 'love few words', and Matheo's boast of penning 'your half-score or your dozen' of sonnets 'at a sitting' (*EMI*, Q, 2. 3. 77, 84).[65] Audience laughter at Bobadilla and Matheo endorses the judgement silently passed by Lorenzo and Prospero, with the effect of extending the authority of their judgement beyond matters of decorum in language to those in *mores*, or manners. We're disabled, by these scenes, from distinguishing between the consensus represented by Prospero and Lorenzo and a wider community's sense of what might be taken as appropriate or inappropriate language or conduct. We can no longer differentiate those forms of deception, mockery, or insult which might be legally actionable or painful from those at which one should merely shrug. Glossing this effect, as it were, Shakespeare frustrates our desire

---

[65] For the relation of this scene to Jonson's classification of styles in *Discoveries*, see Lorna Hutson, 'Liking Men', *English Literary History*, 71 (2004), 1065–96, at 1078.

to understand exactly how the proofs against Hero were made so convincing (Borachio himself acknowledges, 'I tell this tale vildly' (*Much Ado*, 3. 3. 148)), and ensures that, when Hero is accused, there is a disturbing sense of uncertainty about the order and coherence of the proofs against her. Claudio begins by reinterpreting what is conventionally taken—and what will, indeed, be so taken by the friar—as proof of innocence: 'Comes not that blood as modest evidence | To witness simple virtue? Would you not swear, | All you that see her, that she were a maid | By these exterior shows?' (4. 1. 37–40). Don Pedro then, upon his honour, gives testimony against Hero's maidenhead, and Leonato, under the spell of the desire that made him so impatient for this preferment of his daughter, utterly fails to take the examination, fails to question, as Clement had, the motive underlying Don John's invitation to them to witness this scene of sexual encounter.[66]

Leonato does not examine the case because of his complicity in the structures of anticipation and tacit consensus set up by the apprehensive 'noting' of faults within the elite community of Messina. As in the scenes of apprehension and judgement in *Every Man In*, or in the literature of civil conversation, in which no one tells faults openly, but they are tacitly anticipated and corrected, or indirectly mocked by the company, so in Messina until this crisis of sexual suspicion, the space of open confrontation, of proof, has been closed off by the habit of indirect apprehension and self-correction. So Beatrice and Benedick, the most accomplished and apprehensive civil conversationalists of the company, succumb with exemplary ease to the process of self-correction in a parallel drama of 'noting' which makes us aware just how entirely in Messina (as in the Jonsonian Florence of *Every Man In*) the conceptual space in which a community might exercise moral judgement and protect itself from malevolent suspicion cast on its women has been disabled by the upwardly mobile habit of apprehending, indirectly, the critical disapproval of the conversational experts. Everyone has thus become, as it were, their own 'watch', endeavouring 'to correct by other mens judgement' faults that are, to adopt a Dogberryism, *proved* even before they actually 'go near to be thought' by others.[67]

---

[66] Of course, were this a real case of disputed matrimony, it would have been tried in the church courts; nevertheless, as we have seen, Justices of the Peace were often involved in issues of suspected sexual misconduct, since these might involve bastardy.

[67] This, incidentally, is why Jonson's humours comedies are so unamenable to critical appreciation, for the scenes in which gulls like Bobadilla, Stephano, or Matheo are 'drawn out' to express their arrogance and ignorant pretentiousness in all its grotesque fullness cannot effectively be commented on without a sense of redundancy, of stating the obvious, since the

Shakespeare's *Much Ado*, I suggest, exposes the radicalism of Jonson's play's conclusion as preposterous. In his main source, the twenty-second story in the first part of Bandello's *novelle*, Timbreo, the equivalent of Claudio, is alone when exposed to the falsified evidence of his fiancée's infidelity (he sees a man climb in at her window). The revelation that this was, indeed, a prearranged trick to deceive him comes not from the detective work of the local Italian constabulary, equivalent to Dogberry and Verges, but from the remorseful confession of his rival in love, who contrived it all. Shakespeare makes two main changes: first, he transforms Timbreo into Claudio and Don Pedro, an inseparable witty duo, à la Prospero and Lorenzo. Second, he brilliantly reimagines a villain's confession as Dogberry's unsurpassable skill in mangling a narrative of the facts. The latter change takes the form of a kind of resistance to the claims to evidential mastery implied by the former.[68] We experience the effect of the relationship most powerfully when, in Act 5, Claudio and Pedro resume their old habits of civilized mockery to make light of the challenges offered to them by Antonio and Leonato. 'We had lik'd to have had our two noses snapped off with two old men without teeth', Claudio airily informs Benedick (*Much Ado*, 5. 1. 115–16). Benedick, of course, resists being drawn into the mood of self-conscious, apprehensive mockery. Instead, to Claudio's amazement, he plays a part which we must recognize as that of the unsophisticated but dignified Giuliano in *Every Man In*. Just as Giuliano draws his sword on Prospero, enraged at his performing 'ruffian tricks' fit for a 'tavern', among Thorello's kinswomen (*EMI*, Q, 3. 4. 133–4), so Benedick challenges Claudio to fight in defence of Beatrice's kinswoman. It becomes apparent in this moment of extreme epistemological disjuncture, exacerbated by Pedro's playing the accompaniment to Claudio's foppish attempts to tease Benedick out of his earnestness, why it was that no judicial examination of the evidence could ever have taken place at the moment of Claudio's accusation of Hero. For Benedick's challenge is an uncompromising act of love for Beatrice, an act of faith in her belief in her cousin's innocence. Like the oath or the act of compurgation in medieval

scenes themselves carry, in our sense of critical consciousness of Lorenzo and Prospero, an internalized, unspoken critical commentary.

[68] For Bandello's novella, see Geoffrey Bullough (ed.), *Narrative and Dramatic Sources of Shakespeare* (London: Routledge & Kegan Paul, 1960), iii. 112–34. Claire McEachern, in her edition of *Much Ado*, attributes Shakespeare's introduction of the watch to the pressures of time in drama; to wait a year or even a week for the villain's remorse and confession would take too long (*Much Ado About Nothing*, ed. Claire McEachern (London: Arden, 2006), 23). But sudden remorse is common in the theatre, and the need to represent 'long time' has not, as we have noted, presented an obstacle to Shakespeare in other plays.

folklaw, it has no narrative dimension, no concern with reconstructing facts; rather, it 'consolidate[s] testimony into a single moment of truth, because the oath and the testimony it guarantees are coextensive'.[69] As such, it resists what we might call the Jonsonian triumph of forensic virility.

To put it another way: Shakespeare's rejection, in *Much Ado*, of the strategies of judicial *narratio* and artificial proof as means by which to arouse and dispel false inferences or conjectures of suspicion are a response to Jonson's definitive identification of these strategies with an ideal of masculinity in art and in life. For Jonson (for whom Quintilian was a favourite author) responded to Quintilian's own identification of artificial proofs (or what Donald Russell in his new translation calls 'technical' proofs) with an ideally masculine oratory. Opening his important discussion of artificial proof, Quintilian announces that this topic has been neglected by those who fail to see that arguments and artificial proofs are the masculine 'sinews' (*nervis*) of judicial oratory.[70] When Jonson, in his theoretical prose, distinguishes a 'manly' style from various extremes of effeminacy—whether these be the affection of ruggedness or a pleasing but vapid fluency—his key objection is that these other styles lack what he calls 'composition'. Some 'in composition are nothing, but what is rough and broken'; others 'have no composition at all', but, posterity will remember the poet and dramatist whom they can commend for

his subtlety in arguing; with what strength he doth inspire his readers; with what sweetness he strokes them; in inveighing, what sharpness; in jest, what urbanity he uses. How he doth reign in men's affections; how invade, and break in upon them; and makes their minds like the thing he writes. Then in his elocution to behold what word is proper, which hath ornament, which height, what is beautifully translated, where figures are fit, which gentle, which strong *to show the composition manly*.[71]

Passages like this have too long been thought to be the 'official' or 'monologic' side of Jonson speaking, while the plays express a heteroglossic cacophony, in which the spoken word is dialogic, 'permeated by the parodying consciousness of the author', as Peter Womack puts it in his

[69] These are the words of Andrea Frisch on the folklaw concept of 'ethical witnessing' (*The Invention of the Eyewitness* (Chapel Hill, NC: University of North Carolina Press, 2004), 91. See also the study of Helen A. Borrello, 'Rhetoric, the Oath and Shakespearean Representations of Legal Proof' (Ph.D. dissertation, New York University, 2003).

[70] Quintilian, *Inst.* 5. 8. 1.

[71] *Discoveries* (spelling and punctuation modernized), in Ben Jonson, *Complete Works*, ed. C. H. Herford and Percy Simpson (Oxford: Clarendon Press, 1952), viii. 587–8, ll. 788–97; my italics.

excellent discussion.[72] But if Jonson—as we can easily see in the snippets of Matthew's poetry and Bobadil's descants on the pleasures of fencing and tobacco in *Every Man In*—offers us in framed images the speech of another, we can also see that, at every compositional level of speech, of scene, of dramatic narrative, Jonson offers an intricately complicated exposure of the act of composition, or composure. That is to say, he invites us at all times to see how the diverse, 'other' consciousnesses implied by these heteroglossic utterances are constantly being recruited into the formation of plausible but illusory scenarios which play on the imaginative susceptibilities they betray. Jonson, that is to say, would never grant such compositional skill, as Shakespeare does, to a Iago (just as he would never employ techniques of probability to produce double time), because for him the optical illusions of probability produced by his wits and con men are morally aligned with their own exposure as perfectly plausible frauds, just as the optical illusion of dramatic probability that he produces is geared to the production of moments of metatheatrical awareness. Dryden astutely acknowledged Jonson's audacious acts of liter-ary appropriation and his theatrical plots as both having this same virtue of being 'open' about their radical extensions of the boundaries of legit-imacy. Of Jonson's practice of imitation, he famously said that 'he has done his robberies so openly, that one may see he fears not to be taxed by any law', while of the plot of *Epicoene* he marvelled that 'everyone is a proper judge of all he sees; nothing is represented but that with which he daily converses: so that by consequence all faults lie open to discovery'.[73] To 'show the composition manly', in other words, is always for Jonson to show—to those manly enough to see—exactly how it has been composed.

[72] Womack, *Rereading Literature*, 7.

[73] Dryden, 'Of Dramatic Poesy', in *Selected Criticism*, ed. James Kinsley and George Parfitt (Oxford: Clarendon Press, 1970), 58, 61.

Bibliography

Manuscripts

BL Add. MS 46, 500
Bodleian MS Eng. Misc. e. 479
Bodleian MS Rawl. C. 642 (37)
Folger MS V. a. 485
Folger MS V. b. 9
PRO ASSI 45/15
PRO ASSI 45/16
PRO PL 27/1

Primary Sources

Aeschylus, *Oresteia*, trans. Hugh Lloyd-Jones. London: Duckworth, 1982.

Anselm of Canterbury, *Cur Deus Homo? (Why Did God become Man?)*, trans. Camilla McNab. In *Anselm of Canterbury: The Major Works*, ed. Brian Davies and G. R. Evans. Oxford: World's Classics, 1998.

Aphthonii Sophistae Progymnasmata . . . cum . . . scholijs Reinhardi Lorichi Hadamari. London: Thomas Marsh, 1583.

Aquinas, St Thomas, *The Treatise on Law (Being Summa Theologica, I-11, 90 through 97)*, ed. and trans. R. J. Heale, SJ. Notre Dame, IN: University of Notre Dame Press, 1993.

Ariosto, Ludovico, *Le Comedie*, ed. Angela Casella, Gabriella Ronchi, and Elena Varasi. Vol. iv of *Tutte le Opere Di Ludovico Ariosto*. Milan: Mondadori, 1974.

—— *The Comedies of Ariosto*, trans. and ed. Edmond M. Beame and Leonard G. Sbrocchi. Chicago: University of Chicago Press, 1975.

Aristotle, *The Poetics of Aristotle: Translation and Commentary*, by Stephen Halliwell. London: Duckworth, 1987.

—— *The Poetics*. In *Aristotle in Twenty-Three Volumes*, xxiii, trans. W. Hamilton Fyfe. Cambridge, MA: Harvard University Press, 1927.

—— *The 'Art' of Rhetoric*. In *Aristotle in Twenty-Three Volumes,* xxii, trans. J. H. Freese. Cambridge, MA: Harvard University Press, 1926.

Augustine, St, *Letters*, iii, trans. Sr Wilfred Parsons. New York: Fathers of the Church, 1953.

B., R., *A new Tragicall Comedie of Apius and Virginia*. London: William How for Richard Jones, 1575.

Babington, Zachary, *Advice to Grand Jurors in Cases of Blood: Asserting from law and reason that at the King's Suit in all cases (where a person by law is to be indicted of killing another person) that the indictment ought to be drawn for murther*. London, 1677.

Bacon, Sir Nathaniel, *The Official Papers of Sir Nathaniel Bacon of Stiffkey, Norfolk as Justice of the Peace 1580–1620*, ed. H. W. Saunders, M.A. Royal Historical Society, Camden 3rd Series, xxvi. London, 1915.

Belleforest, Francois de, *Le Cinquiesme Tome des Histoires Tragiques*. Paris, 1572.

Bernard, Richard, *A Guide to Grand Jury Men, Divided into Two Bookes*. London: Felix Kingston for Ed. Blackmore, 1627.

____ *Terence in English: Fabulae Comici Facetissimi et Elegantissimi Poetae Terentii Omnes Anglicae factae*. London: John Legatt, 1629.

____ *The Isle of Man: Legall Proceeding in Man-shire against SIN, Wherein, by way of a continued allegory, the chief Malefactors disturbing both Church & Commonwealth, are Detected and Attached; with their Arraignment and Judicial Trial, according to the Laws of England*. London, 1659.

Blount, Thomas, ed., *Nomo-Lexicon, a Law Dictionary*. London, 1670.

Boccaccio, Giovanni, *Decameron*, ed. Antonio Quaglio, 2 vols. Milan: Garzanti, 1974.

____ *The Decameron*, trans. G. H. McWilliam. Harmondsworth: Penguin, 1972.

Bowyer, Robert, *The Parliamentary Diary of Robert Bowyer, 1606–1607*, ed. David Harris Wilson. Minneapolis: University of Minnesota Press, 1931.

Bray, Gerald, ed., *Tudor Church Reform: The Henrician Canons of 1535 and the Reformatio Legum Ecclesiasticarum*. London: Church of England Record Society and The Boydell Press, 2000.

Brugis, Thomas, *Vade Mecum or, a Companion for a Chyrugion*, 6th edn. London, 1679.

Buchanan, George (attrib.), *Ane Detectioun of the duinges of Marie Quene of Scottes, touchand the murder of hir husband*. London: John Day, 1571.

The Bugbeares, in *Early Plays from the Italian*, ed. R. Warwick Bond, 86–157. Oxford: Clarendon Press, 1911.

Cardwell, Edward, ed., *The Reformation of the Ecclesiastical Laws as attempted in the reigns of King Henry VIII, King Edward VI, and Queen Elizabeth*. Oxford: Oxford University Press, 1850.

The Castle of Perseverance, in *The Macro Plays*, ed. Mark Eccles, 1–111. Oxford: EETS 262, 1969.

Cicero, *De inventione*, trans. H. M. Hubbell. Cambridge, MA: Harvard University Press, 1949.

____ *Defence Speeches*, trans. D. H. Berry. Oxford: Oxford University Press, 2000.

____ 'In Defense of Sextus Roscius of Ameria'. In *Murder Trials*, trans. Michael Grant, 23–110. Harmondsworth: Penguin, 1975.

___*In omnes M. Tullij Ciceronis orationes doctissimorum virorum lucubrationes...adiectis Q. Asconij Pediani commentarijs*. Venice, 1547.

___*Pro Roscio Amerino*. In *Cicero*, vi, trans. John Henry Freese, 122–263. Cambridge, MA: Harvard University Press, 1934.

___*Rhetorica ad Herennium*, trans. Harry Caplan. Cambridge, MA: Harvard University Press, 1954, repr. 2004.

___*The Speeches with an English Translation*, trans. N. H. Watts. Cambridge, MA: Harvard University Press, 1931; repr. 1958.

Clyomon and Clamydes (1599), ed. W. W. Greg. Oxford: Malone Society, 1913.

Coke, Sir Edward, *The Reports of Sir Edward Coke, Knt*, 6 vols. London: Butterworth, 1826.

___*The Third Part of the Institutes*. London, 1669.

A Complete Collection of State Trials, and Proceedings for High Treason, and Certain Other Misdemeanours; commencing with the Eleventh year of the reign of King Richard II and ending with the Sixteenth Year of the Reign of King George III. To which is prefixed a new preface by Francis Hargrave, esq., 5th edn., i. Dublin, 1793.

Conset, Henry, *The Practice of the Spiritual or Ecclesiastical Courts*. London: T. Basset, 1685.

Cooper, Thomas, *The Cry and Revenge of Blood expressing the nature and haynousness of wilful murther exhibited in a most Lamentable History thereof, committed at Halsworth in High Suffolk*. London, 1620.

Cosin, Richard, An Apologie for Svndry Proceedings *by Iurisdiction Ecclesiasticall, of late times by some chalenged, and also diversely by them impugned*. London: Christopher Barker, 1593.

Dalton, Michael, *The Countrey Justice*. London: John More, 1635.

de la Tour Landry, Geoffrey, *Der Ritter vom Turn von den Exempeln der gotsforcht un erberkeit*. Augsburg, 1495.

Depositions from the Castle of York Relating to Offences Committed in the Northern Counties in the Seventeenth Century, ed. James Raine, Jr. Surtees Society, 40. London and Edinburgh, 1861.

Dramatic Documents from the Elizabethan Playhouses, ii: *Reproductions and Transcripts*, ed. W. W. Greg. Oxford: Clarendon Press, 1913.

Dryden, John, *Selected Criticism*, ed. James Kinsley and George Parfitt. Oxford: Oxford University Press, 1970.

Elyot, Sir Thomas, *The Boke named the Gouernour* [1531], introduced by Foster Watson. London: J. M. Dent, 1907.

Erasmus of Rotterdam, Desiderius, *On Copia of Words and Ideas*, trans. Donald B. King and H. David Rix. Milwaukee, WI: Marquette University Press, 1999.

The Famous Victories of Henry the Fifth: Containing the Honourable Battell of Agin-Court. As it was plaied by the Queenes Majesties Players. [London: Thomas Creede, 1598]. Repr. in *Narrative and Dramatic Sources of Shakespeare*, iv. 299–343. London; Routledge & Kegan Paul, 1962.

Fenton, Geoffrey, *Certain Tragicall Discourses written out of French and Latine*. London: Thomas Marshe, 1567.

Fish, Simon, *A Supplication for the Beggers* [1529]. In *Yale Edition of the Complete Works of St. Thomas More*, vii, eds. Frank Manley, Germain Marc'hadour, Richard Marius, and Clarence H. Miller, Appendix B, pp. 409–22. New Haven and London: Yale University Press, 1990.

Fitzherbert, Sir Anthony, and Crompton, Richard, *L'office et aucthoritie de justices de peace*. [London: Richard Tottell, 1584.], ed. P. R. Glazebrook. London: Professional Books Ltd., 1972.

Fleetwood, William, *The Office of a Justice of Peace together with instructions, How and in what manner Statutes shall be expounded*. London, 1657.

Four Revenge Tragedies, ed. Katherine Eisaman Maus. Oxford: Oxford University Press, 1995.

Four Tudor Comedies, ed. William Tydeman. Harmondsworth: Penguin, 1984.

Foxe, John, *Two Latin Comedies by John Foxe the Martyrologist*, ed. John Hazel Smith. Ithaca, NY: Cornell University Press, 1978.

Frith, John, *A Disputation of Purgatory* [1533]. In *The Works of the English Reformers: William Tyndale and John Frith*, 3 vols., ed. Thomas Russell. London, 1831.

Fulbecke, William, *A Parallel or Conference of the Civil Law, the Canon Law, and the Common Law of this Realme of England. Wherein the agreement and disagreement of these three Lawes, and the causes and reasons of the said agreement and disagreement, are opened and discussed. Digested in sundry Dialogues*. London: For the Company of Stationers, 1618.

A Full and True Relation of the Examination and Confession of W. Barwick and E. Mangall. London, 1690.

Garnier, Robert, *Théatre et Poesies de Robert Garnier*, 2 vols.: i, avec notices et notes par Lucien Pinvert. Paris: Garnier, 1923.

Garter, Thomas, *The Commody of the moste vertuous and Godlye Susanna, never before this tyme Printed*. London, 1578.

Gascoigne, George. *The Complete Works*, ed. John W. Cunliffe, 2 vols. Cambridge: Cambridge University Press, 1910.

——*A Hundreth Sundrie Flowres*, ed. G. W. Pigman III. Oxford: Clarendon Press, 2000.

——*The Posies of George Gascoigne Esquire. Corrected, Perfected and augmented by the Authour*. London: Richard Smith, 1575. Bodleian Malone 792: contains marginal annotations by Gabriel Harvey.

Gilbert, Geoffrey, *The Law of Evidence*, 4 vols. London, 1791.

Golding, Arthur, *A briefe discourse of the late murther of master George Saunders*. London: Henry Bynneman, 1573.

Guazzo, Stephano, *The Civile Conversation of M. Stephano Guazzo, written first in Italian, diuided into foure bookes, the first three translated out of French by G. Pettie*. London: Thomas East, 1586.

Hake, Edward, *Epieikeia: A Dialogue on Equity in Three Parts*, ed. D. C. Yale. New Haven: Yale University Press, 1953.

Hale, Sir Matthew, *The History of the Common Law of England*, ed. Charles M. Gray. Chicago and London: University of Chicago Press, 1971.

Hale, William, *A series of precedents and proceedings in criminal causes, extending from the year 1475 to 1640 extracted from Act-books of ecclesiastical courts in the diocese of London*. London: Francis & John Rivington, 1847.

____*A Series of Precedents and Proceedings in Criminal Causes*, ed. R. W. Dunning. Edinburgh: Bratton Publishing, 1973.

Hawles, John, *The Englishman's Right: A Dialogue between a Barrister at Law and a Juryman; plainly setting forth I. The Antiquity, II. The Excellent Designed Use, III. The OFFICE and Just PRIVILEGES of JURIES* by the Law of England. London: A. Shuckburgh, 1764.

Heinsius, Daniel, *De Tragoediae Constitutione Liber* (1611). New York and Hildesheim: Georg Olms Verlag, 1976.

____*On Plot in Tragedy*, trans. Paul R. Sellin and John McManmon, with introduction and notes by Paul Sellin. Northridge, CA: San Fernando Valley State College, 1971.

Here begynneth a lytle boke, that speaketh of Purgatorye. London: Robert Wyer, ?1531.

Heywood, Jasper, *Thyestes*, ed. Joost Dalder. London: Ernest Benn, 1982.

Heywood, John, *The Complete Works of John Heywood*, ed. Richard Axton and Peter Happé. Cambridge: D. S. Brewer, 1991.

Hobbes, Thomas, *A Dialogue between a Philosopher and a Student, of the Common Laws of England* [1681], ed. Joseph Cropsey. Chicago and London: University of Chicago Press, 1971.

Hooker, Richard, *On the Lawes of Ecclesiastical Politie*. London, 1593.

The Horrible Murther of a young boy of three years of age, whose Sister had her tongue cut out: and how it pleased God to reveale the offendors, by giving speech to the tongueless Childe. Which Offendors were executed at Hartford the 4. of August. 1606. London: Ed Allde, 1606.

Hoskyns, John, *Directions for Speech and Style*, ed. Hoyt T. Hudson. Princeton: Princeton University Press, 1935.

Hunt R. D., ed., 'Henry Townsend's "Notes of the office of a Justice of the Peace", 1661–3', *Worcestershire Historical Society Miscellany*, n. s., 5 (1967), 68–137.

Impacient Poverty: A Newe Interlude of Impacyente Pouerte, from the quarto of 1560 ed. R. B. McKerrow. Louvain: A. Uystpruyst, 1911.

Jacob's Well, An Englisht Treatise on the Cleansing of Man's Conscience [c.1440], ed. Arthur Brandeis. EETS, o.s., no. 23. London, 1900.

Jonson, Ben, *Ben Jonson: Five Plays*, ed. G. A. Wilkes. Oxford: Oxford University Press, 1988.

____*Complete Works*, ed. C. H. Herford and Percy Simpson. Oxford: Clarendon Press, 1925–52.

Jonson, Ben, *Epicoene or the Silent Woman*, ed. Roger Holdsworth. London: A & C Black, 1990; first published by Ernest Benn, 1979.

———*Every Man in his Humour*, ed. Robert Miola. Manchester: Manchester University Press, 2000.

Kyd, Thomas, *The Spanish Tragedy*, ed. J. R. Mulryne. London: A & C Black, 1989.

———*The Spanish Tragedy*. In *Four Revenge Tragedies*, ed. Katharine Eisaman Maus. Oxford: Oxford University Press, 1995.

———*The Works of Thomas Kyd*, ed. F. S. Boas. Oxford: Clarendon Press, 1901.

Kyng Daryus: A Pretie new Enterlude both pithie and pleasaunt of the Story of kyng Daryus. London, 1565.

Lambarde, William, *The Duties of Constables, Borsholders, Tythingmen, and such other lowe and Lay Ministers of the Peace, whereunto be adjoined, the severall offices of Church Ministers and Churchwardens, and Overseers of the Poore*. London: Thomas Wight, 1602.

———*Eirenarcha or the Office of Justices of the Peace* [1581/2], ed. P. R. Glazebrook. London: Professional Books Ltd., 1972.

———*Eirenarcha: or of The office of the Justices of the Peace, in foure Bookes*. London: Ralph Newberry, 1592.

Latimer, Hugh, *Sermons of Hugh Latimer, sometime Bishop of Worcester*, ed. George Elwes Corrie. Cambridge: Cambridge University Press for the Parker Society, 1844.

Leveson-Gower, esq., Granville, ed., 'Note Book of a Surrey Justice', Surrey Archaeological Collections, ix. 161–232. London: Surrey Archaeological Society, 1888.

Liberality and Prodigality: A Pleasant Comedie, Shewing the Contention between Liberality and Prodigality. London: Simon Stafford for George Vincent, 1602.

Lyndwood, William. *Constitutiones Angliae prouinciales*. London: Thomas Marshe, 1557.

———*Constitutions prouincialles and of Otho and Octhobone Translated in to Englyshe*. London: Robert Redman, 1534.

———*Provinciale, seu Constitutiones Angliae*. Oxford, 1679.

Male, George Edward, M.D., *An Epitome of Juridical or Forensic Medicine for the uses of medical men, coroners and barristers*. London, 1816.

Mankind. In *The Macro Plays*, ed. Mark Eccles. London: EETS, o.s., no. 262. London, 1969.

Mannyng (of Brunne), Robert, *Robert Mannyng of Brunne's "Handlyng Synne"* [1303], ed. Frederick J. Furnivall. EETS, o.s., parts 2, no. 123. London, 1901, 1903.

March, John, *Actions for Slander, or a Methodicall Collection under Certain Grounds and Heads of what words are actionable in LAW, and what not?* London, 1647.

McNeill, John T., and Helena M. Gamer, *Medieval Handbooks of Penance: A translation of the principal libri poenitentiales and selections from related documents*. New York: Columbia University Press, 1938.

Medwall, Henry, *Nature*. In *The Plays of Henry Medwall*, ed. Alan H. Nelson. Woodbridge, Suffolk: D. S. Brewer, 1980.

Moralité des Sept Pechés Mortels et des Sept Vertus: Nativités et Moralités Liégioses du Moyen Age, ed. Gustave Cohen. Brussels: Académie Royale de Belgique, 1953.

More, Thomas, *The apologye of syr Thomas More knight*. In *The Yale Edition of the Complete Works of St. Thomas More*, ix, ed. J. B. Trapp. New Haven and London: Yale University Press, 1979.

____ *The Debellation of Salem and Bizance*. In *The Yale Edition of the Complete Works of St Thomas More*, x, ed. John Guy, Ralph Keen, Clarence H. Miller, and Ruth McGugan. New Haven and London: Yale University Press, 1987.

____ *The Supplycacyon of Soulys*. In *The Yale Edition of the Complete Works of St. Thomas More*, vii, ed. Frank Manley, Germain Marc'hadour, Richard Marius, and Clarence H. Miller. New Haven and London: Yale University Press, 1990.

Morrice, James, *A briefe treatise of Oathes exacted by Ordinaries and Ecclesiasticall Judges, to answere generallie to all such Articles or Interrogatories, as pleaseth them to propound. And of their forced and constrained Oathes ex officio, wherein is proved that the same are unlawful*. Middleberg: Richard Schilders, 1590.

Murder will Out: An Impartial Narrative of the Notorious Wicked Life of Capt Harrison, who was Arraign'd, Try'd and Convicted . . . for the late Barbarous, Cruel and unheard-of Murder of Doctor Clench. London, 1692.

The Myroure of oure Ladye containing a devotional treatise of divine service . . . [1530], ed. John Henry Blunt. EETS, extra series 19, London, 1873.

Le Mystère de la vie et histoire de mon seigneur sainct Martin lequel fût Archevêque de Tours. In *Collection de Poesies, Romans, Chroniques publieé d'auprès d'anciens Manuscrits et d'après des Editions des xve et xvie siècles*, ed. Doublet de Boisthibault. Paris, 1841.

Nashe, Thomas, *The Unfortunate Traveller*. In *The Works of Thomas Nashe*, ed. Ronald B. McKerrow [repr. from the original edition with supplementary notes by F. P. Wilson], 5 vols. Oxford: Basil Blackwell, 1966.

Nice Wanton: A Preaty Interlude Called, Nice Wanton. London: John King, 1560. In *Specimens of Pre-Shakespearean Drama*, ed. John Matthews Manly, 2 vols. Boston, 1897.

Norton, Thomas, *Instructions to the Lord Mayor of London, 1574–5: Whereby he is to govern himself and the City. Together with a Letter from him to Sir Francis Walsingham, respecting the dealings of promoters*. In *Illustrations of Old English Literature*, ed. J. Payne Collier, 3 vols., iii. 1–23. London: Privately Printed, 1866.

Painter, William, *The Palace of Pleasure*, ed. Joseph Jacobs, 3 vols. New York: Dover Publications, 1966.

Patterson, Annabel, ed., *The Trial of Nicholas Throckmorton*. Toronto: Centre for Reformation and Renaissance Studies, 1998.

Pickering, John, *Justice's Note-Book of Captain John Pickering, 1656–60*, ed. G. D. Lumb. In *Publications of the Thoresby Society*, xi: *Miscellanea*, 69–100. Leeds, (1904).

Pikerynge, John, *Horestes* [1567]. In *Three Tudor Classical Interludes*, ed. Marie Axton, 94–155. Cambridge: D. S. Brewer, 1982.

Placita Corone, or La Corone Pledee devant Justices, ed. J. M. Kaye. Selden Society, Supplementary Series, 4, 1966.

Plautus, *M. Accius Plautus ex fide, atque auctoritate complurium librorum manuscriptorum opera Dionys. Lambini . . . emendatus*. Lutetiae: apud Ioannem Macaeum, 1577.

――― *Works*, trans. Paul Nixon, 5 vols. London: William Heinemann Ltd., 1916–38.

Plowden, Edmund, *Les Commentaries ou Reports de Edmund Plowden*. London: Richard Totell, 1571.

――― *Les Commentaries ou Reports de Edmund Plowden*, 2 parts. London: Richard Totell, 1578, 1584.

――― *The Commentaries or Reports of Edmund Plowden of the Middle Temple esq. . . . in two parts*. London: S. Brooke, 1816.

Preston, Thomas, *A Lamentable Tragedie, mixed full of pleasant mirth, containing the life of Cambises, king of Percia*. London: John Allde, n.d. (?1575).

――― *Cambyses, King of Persia*. In *Drama of the English Renaissance: The Tudor Period*, ed. Russell A. Fraser and Norman Rabkin, 61–80. Upper Saddle River, NJ: Prentice-Hall, 1976.

The Proceedings at the Assizes in Southwark for the County of Surry Begun on Thursday the 21th, of March, and not ended till Tuesday the 26 of the same month, 1678. London, 1678.

Proceedings in the Parliaments of Elizabeth I, ed. T. E. Hartley. Leicester: Leicester University Press, 1981.

Pulton, Ferdinando, *De Pace Regis et Regni viz. A Treatise declaring which be the great and generall Offences of the Realme, and the chiefe impediments of the peace of the King and the Kingdome*. London, 1609.

Quintilian, *Institutio oratoria*, books 3–5, ed. and trans. Donald A. Russell. Cambridge, MA: Harvard University Press, 2001.

Rastell, John, *A New Boke of Purgatory* [1530]. In *The Pastyme of the People and A New Boke of Purgatory: A Critical Edition*, ed. Albert J. Geritz. New York and London: Garland, 1985.

Read, Conyers, ed., *William Lambarde and Local Government: His 'Ephemeris' and Twenty-nine Charges to Juries and Commissions*. Ithaca, NY: Cornell University Press, 1962.

Readings and Moots at the Inns of Court in the Fifteenth Century, ii: *Moots and Readers' Cases*, ed. Samuel E. Thorne and J. H. Baker. London: Selden Society, 1990.

Records of the Court of the Stationers' Company 1576 to 1602 from Register B, ed. W. W. Greg and E. Boswell. London: The Bibliographical Society, 1930.

Reformatio Legum Ecclesiasticarum: The Reformation of the Ecclesiastical Laws of England, 1552, trans. James C. Spalding and gen. ed. Charles G. Nauert, Jr. Sixteenth Century Essays and Studies, 19. Kirkville, MO: Sixteenth Century Journal Publishers, Inc., 1992.

Remains of Old Latin, ii, ed. and trans. E. H. Warmington. Cambridge, MA: Harvard University Press, 1936.

Remer, Theodore G., ed., *Serendipity and the Three Princes: From the Peregrinaggio of 1557*. Norman, OK: University of Oklahoma Press, 1965.

Roper, William, 'Life of Sir Thomas More'. In *Two Early Tudor Lives*, ed. Richard Sylvester and Davis P. Harding, 197–254. New Haven: Yale University Press, 1962.

S., E., *The Discoverie of the Knights of the Poste: Or the Knights of post, or common baylers newly Discried*. London, 1597.

Select cases from the ecclesiastical courts of the Province of Canterbury, c.1200–1301, ed. Norma Adams and Charles Donahue, Jr. London: Selden Society, 1981.

Seneca, *Thyestes*, trans. Jasper Heywood. In *Seneca His Tenne Tragedies translated into English* [1581], ed. Thomas Newton, i. 53–85. London: Constable and Co. Ltd., 1927.

____ *Troas*, trans. Jasper Heywood. In *Seneca His Tenne Tragedies translated into English* [1581], ed. Thomas Newton, ii. London: Constable and Co. Ltd., 1927.

Shakespeare, William, *The Comedy of Errors*, ed. Charles Whitworth. Oxford: Oxford University Press, 2002.

____ *The First Part of the Contention* (1594), ed. William Montgomery. Malone Society Reprints. Oxford: Oxford University Press, 1985.

____ *Hamlet*, ed. Harold Jenkins. London: Methuen, 1982.

____ *Henry VI, part 2*, ed. Roger Warren. The Oxford Shakespeare. Oxford: Oxford University Press, 2002.

____ *Love's Labour's Lost*, ed. G. R. Hibbard. Oxford: Oxford University Press, 1994.

____ *Much Ado About Nothing*, ed. Claire McEachern. London: Arden Shakespeare, 2006.

____ *Much Ado About Nothing* ed. A. R. Humphreys. London: Arden Shakespeare, 1981.

____ *The Norton Facsimile of the First Folio of Shakespeare*, ed. Charles Hinman, intro. Peter Blayney. New York: W. W. Norton, 1996.

____ *The Pictorial Edition of the Works of Shakespeare*, ed. Charles Knight, 7 vols. London: Charles Knight and Co., 1842.

____ *A Pleasant Conceited Comedie called, Loves Labors Lost. As it was presented before her Highnes this last Christmas. Newly corrected and augmented by W. Shakespere*. London: 1598.

____ *The Riverside Shakespeare*, ed. G. Blakemore Evans *et al*. Boston: Houghton Mifflin Company, 1997.

____ *The Second Part of King Henry VI*, ed. Andrew S. Cairncross. The Arden Shakespeare. London: Methuen, 1957.

____ *Titus Andronicus*, ed. Jonathan Bate. The Arden Shakespeare. London: 1995.

Shakespeare, William, *Titus Andronicus*, ed. John Dover Wilson. Cambridge: Cambridge University Press, 1948.

____ *Tragicall Historie of Hamlet Prince of Denmarke*, ed. Graham Holderness and Brian Loughry. Hemel Hempstead: Harvester Wheatsheaf, 1992.

Sidney, Philip, *A Defence of Poetry*, ed. Jan Van Dorsten. Oxford: Oxford University Press, 1966.

——— *The Old Arcadia*, ed. Katherine Duncan Jones. Oxford: Oxford University Press, 1985.

Smith, Sir Thomas, *De Republica Anglorum*, ed. Mary Dewar. Cambridge: Cambridge University Press, 1982.

——— *A Discourse of the Commonweal of This Realm of England*, ed. Mary Dewar. Charlottesville, VA: University Press of Virginia, 1969.

Speculum Sacerdotale, ed. Edward H. Weatherly. EETS, o.s., no. 200. London, 1936.

Staundforde, Sir William, *Les Plees del Coron, divisees in plusors titles & common lieux*. London: Richard Tottell, 1583.

St German, Christopher, *An Answer to a Letter*. London: 1535.

——— *Salem and Bizance* [1533]. In *The Yale Edition of the Complete Works of St. Thomas More*, x, ed. John Guy, Ralph Keen, Clarence H. Miller, and Ruth McGugan, 325–92. New Haven and London: Yale University Press, 1987.

——— *St. German's Doctor and Student,* ed. T. F. T. Plucknett and J. L. Barton. London: Selden Society, 1974.

——— *A treatise co[n]cernynge diuers of the constitucyons prouynciall and legantines*. London: Thomas Godfray, [1535?].

——— *A treatise concernynge the division betwene the spirytualtie and temporaltie*. In *The Yale Edition of the Complete Works of Thomas More*, ix, ed. J. B. Trapp (New Haven and London: Yale University Press, 1979), 177–212.

Stuart Royal Proclamations, ed. James F. Larkin and P. L. Hughes, 3 vols. Oxford: Clarendon Press, 1973.

Terence, ed. and trans. John Barsby, 2 vols. Cambridge, MA: Harvard University Press, 2001.

Tourner, Cyril, *The Atheist's Tragedy*. In *Four Revenge Tragedies*, ed. Katharine Eisaman Maus. Oxford: Oxford University Press, 1995.

The Towneley Plays, ed. Alfred W. Pollard. EETS, extra series, 71. Oxford, 1897.

The Tragedy of Master Arden of Faversham, ed. M. L. Wine. London: Methuen and Co., 1973.

Treason and Murther Discovered. Being a True and Perfect Relation of the Tryal and Condemnation of James Alsop the Father, and William Alsop his son for Treason and Murther. London, 1674.

Treason and Murther: Or, The Bloody Father-in-Law, Being a True and Perfect Relation of a Horrible Murther, committed at HAM, near Stratford in Essex, on the Wife of James Alsop by her Husbands Father and Brother. London: E. Miles, 1673.

A true and faithful Relation of that Horrrible Murder committed upon the Body of Mr. JOHN NEILL ... Late Stationer and Merchant of Glasgow in Scotland, on 26 Feb. 1656. London: James Cottrel, 1656.

A True report of the horrible Murther, which was committed in the house of Sir Ierome Bowes, Knight, on the 20. day of February, Anno Dom. 1606. London, 1607.

The Tudor Interludes 'Nice Wanton' and 'Impatient Poverty', ed. Leonard Tennenhouse. In *The Renaissance Imagination*, x. New York and London: Garland Publishing, 1984.

Tuvil, Daniel, *The Dove and the Serpent in which is conteined a large description of all such points and principles, as tend either to Conversation, or Negotiation.* London, 1614.

Udall, Nicholas, *Respublica: An Interlude for Christmas 1553*, ed. W. W. Greg. London: EETS, 1952.

Vives, Juan Luis, *Opera in duos distinctos tomos.* Basel, 1555.

Walwyn, William, 'Juries Justified; or, a Word of Correction to Mr. Henry Robinson'. In *The Writings of William Walwyn*, ed. Jack R. McMichael and Barbara Taft, 433–45. Athens: University of Georgia Press, 1989.

A Warning for Fair Women, ed. Charles Dale Cannon. The Hague: Mouton, 1975.

Whetstone, George. *Promos and Cassandra* [1578] in *Narrative and Dramatic Sources of Shakespeare*, ed. Geoffrey Bullough. London: Routledge & Kegan Paul, 1968, ii. 442–514.

Whithed, Sir Henry, *Sir Henry Whithed's Letter Book*, i: *1601–1614.* Hampshire Record Series, 1. Hampshire County Council, 1976.

Wilbraham, Roger, 'The Journal of Sir Roger Wilbraham, Solicitor-General in Ireland and Master of Requests for the Years 1593–1616', ed. H. S. Scott, *The Camden Miscellany*, 10. London: Royal Historical Society, 1902.

Wilson, Thomas. *The Arte of Rhetorique* [1553], ed. G. H. Mair. Oxford: Clarendon Press, 1909.

Wright, Thomas, ed., *Queen Elizabeth and her Times, A Series of Original Letters Selected from the Inedited Private Correspondence of the Lord Treasurer Burghley, the Earl of Leicester, the Secretaries Walsingham and Smith, Sir Christopher Hatton*, 2 vols. London, 1838.

York Mystery Plays, ed. Lucy Toulmin Smith. Oxford: Clarendon Press, 1885.

Secondary Sources

Alford, John A., ' "My name is Worship": Masquerading Vice in Medwall's *Nature'*. In *From Page to Performance: Essays in Early English Drama*, ed. John Alford, 151–77. East Lansing, MI: Michigan State University Press, 1995.

Allen, Christopher, *The Law of Evidence in Victorian England.* Cambridge: Cambridge University Press, 1997).

Altman Joel B., ' "Preposterous Conclusions": Eros, *Enargeia*, and the Composition of *Othello'*, *Representations*, 18 (1987), 129–157.

_____ *The Tudor Play of Mind: Rhetorical Inquiry and the Development of Elizabethan Drama.* Berkeley: University of California Press, 1978.

Anderson, M. D., *Drama and Imagery in Medieval Churches.* Cambridge: Cambridge University Press, 1963.

Armstrong, William A., 'The Authorship and Political Meaning of *Cambises*', *English Studies*, 36 (1955), 289–99.

Ashley, Kathleen M., 'Titivillus and the Battle of Words in *Mankind*', *Annuale Mediaevale*, 16 (1975), 128–50.

Auerbach, Erich, *Mimesis: The Representation of Reality in Western Literature*, trans. Willard R. Trask. Princeton: Princeton University Press, 1953.

Austen, Gillian, 'The Literary Career of George Gascoigne: Studies in Self-Presentation' (D.Phil., Oxon, 1997).

Axton, Marie, *The Queen's Two Bodies: Drama and the Elizabethan Succession*. London: Royal Historical Society, 1977.

Baker, J. H., 'Criminal Courts and Procedure at Common Law, 1550–1800'. In *Crime in England 1550–1800*, ed. J. S. Cockburn, 49–71. Princeton: Princeton University Press, 1977.

—— 'Criminal Justice at Newgate 1610–1627: Some Manuscript Reports in the Harvard Law School', *Irish Jurist*, 8 (1973), 307–22.

—— 'English Law and the Renaissance'. In *The Legal Profession and the Common Law*, 461–76. London: Hambledon, 1988.

—— *An Introduction to English Legal History*, 2nd edn. London: Butterworths, 1979.

—— (ed.), *The Reports of Sir John Spelman*, 2 vols. London: Selden Society, 1977, 1978.

—— *Manual of Law French*. Trowbridge: Avebury Publishing, 1979.

—— *The Oxford History of the Laws of England*, vi: *1483–1558*. Oxford: Oxford University Press, 2003.

Baldwin, John, 'The Intellectual Preparation of 1215 against Ordeals'. *Speculum*, 36, no. 4 (Oct. 1961), 613–36.

Baldwin, T. W., *Shakespeare's Five-Act Structure*. Urbana, IL: University of Illinois Press, 1947.

Baltrusaitis, Jurgis, *Le Miroir: Essaie sur une légende scientifique*. Paris: Le Seuil, 1978.

Barbour, W. T., *The History of Contract in Early English Equity*. Oxford Studies in Social and Legal History, ed. Paul Vinogradoff. Oxford: Clarendon Press, 1914.

Barker, Francis, *The Culture of Violence: Tragedy and History*. Chicago: University of Chicago Press, 1993.

Barrell, John, 'Masters of Suspense: Syntax and Gender in Milton's Sonnets'. In *Poetry, Language and Politics*, 44–78. Manchester: Manchester University Press, 1988.

Barthes, Roland, 'The Reality Effect'. In *The Rustle of Language*, trans. Richard Howard, 143–4. Oxford: Blackwell, 1986.

—— *S/Z: An Essay*, trans. Richard Miller. New York: Hill and Wang, 1974.

Bartlett, Robert, *Trial by Fire and Water: The Medieval Judicial Ordeal*. Oxford: Clarendon Press, 1986.

Barton, Anne, *Ben Jonson: Dramatist*. Cambridge: Cambridge University Press, 1984.

—— *Shakespeare and the Idea of the Play*. London: Chatto & Windus, 1962.

Beckwith, Sarah, *Signifying God: Social Relation and Symbolic Act in the York Corpus Christi Plays*. Chicago: University of Chicago Press, 2001.

Bellamy, J. G., *The Criminal Trial in Later Medieval England: Felony before the Courts from Edward I to the Sixteenth Century*. Stroud: Sutton Publishing, 1988.

Belsey, Catherine, *The Subject of Tragedy: Identity and Difference in Renaissance Drama*. London: Methuen, 1985.

Bennett, Josephine Waters, 'The Medieval Loveday', *Speculum*, 33, no. 3 (1958), 351–70.

Bernthal, Craig A., 'Jack Cade's Legal Carnival', *Studies in English Literature, 1500–1900*, 42, no. 2 (Spring 2002), 259–74.

____ 'Treason in the Family: The Trial of Thumpe v. Horner', *Shakespeare Quarterly*, 42, no. 1 (1991), 44–54.

Bevington, David, 'The Comedy of Errors in the Context of the Late 1580s and Early 1590s' (1997). In *The Comedy of Errors: Critical Essays*, ed. Robert S. Miola, 335–53. New York: Routledge, 1997.

____ *From Mankind to Marlowe: Growth of Structure in the Popular Drama of Tudor England*. Cambridge, MA: Harvard University Press, 1962.

Biller, Peter, and A. J. Minnis (eds.), *Handling Sin: Confession in the Middle Ages* (York: York Medieval Press, 1998).

Borello, Helen H., 'Rhetoric, the Oath and Shakespearean Representations of Legal Proof' (Ph.D. dissertation, New York University, 2003).

Bossy, John, 'The Social History of Confession in the Age of the Reformation', *Transactions of the Royal Historical Society*, 5th ser., 25 (1975), 21–38.

Bowers, Fredson, *Elizabethan Revenge Tragedy*. Princeton: Princeton University Press, 1940.

Bradley, A. C., *Shakespearean Tragedy* [1904], with a foreword by John Bayley. Harmondsworth: Penguin, 1991.

Brigden, Susan, *London and the Reformation*. Oxford: Clarendon Press, 1989.

Britain, Robert P., 'Cruentation in Legal Medicine and Literature', *Medical History*, 9 (1965), 82–8.

Brooks, Christopher W., 'Fleetwood, William (*c*.1525–1594)'. In *Oxford Dictionary of National Biography*, ed. H. C. G. Matthew and Brian Harrison. Oxford: Oxford University Press, 2004.

____ *Pettyfoggers and Vipers of the Commonwealth: The 'Lower Branch' of the Legal Profession in Early Modern England*. Cambridge: Cambridge University Press, 1986.

Brooks, Peter, *Reading for the Plot: Design and Intention in Narrative*. New York: Random House, 1984.

____ *Troubling Confessions: Speaking Guilt in Law and Literature*. Chicago and London: University of Chicago Press, 2000.

Broude, Ronald, 'Revenge and Revenge Tragedy in Renaissance England', *Renaissance Quarterly*, 28, no. 1 (Spring 1975), 38–58.

Bryson, Anna, *From Courtesy to Civility: Changing Codes of Conduct in Early Modern England*. Oxford: Oxford University Press, 1998.

Bullough, Geoffrey, ed., *Narrative and Dramatic Sources of Shakespeare*, 8 vols. London: Routledge & Kegan Paul, 1957–75.

Burgess, Clive, '"A fond thing vainly invented": An Essay on Purgatory and Pious Motive in Late Medieval England'. In *Parish, Church and People: Local Studies in Lay Religion 1350–1750*, ed. S. J. Wright, 56–84. London: Hutchinson, 1988.

Campbell, Lily B., 'Theories of Revenge in Renaissance England', *Modern Philology*, 28, no. 3 (1931), 281–96.

Carruthers, Leo M., 'The Liturgical Setting of *Jacob's Well*', *English Language Notes*, 24, no. 4 (June 1987), 11–24.

Cave, Terence, 'The Mimesis of Reading in the Renaissance'. In *Mimesis: From Mirror to Method, Augustine to Descartes*, ed. John D. Lyons and Stephen G. Nichols, 149–65. Hanover, NH: University Press of New England, 1982.

——*Recognitions: A Study in Poetics*. Oxford: Clarendon Press, 1988.

Cawsey, Kathy, 'Tutivillus and the "Kyrkchaterars": Strategies of Control in the Middle Ages', *Studies in Philology*, 102, no. 4 (2005), 434–51.

Chalifour, Clark L., 'Sir Philip Sidney's *Old Arcadia* as Terentian Comedy', *Studies in English Literature*, 16 (1976), 51–63.

Champion, Larry S., '"What Prerogatives Meanes": Perspective and Political Ideology in "The Famous Victories of Henry V"', *South Atlantic Review*, 53, no. 4 (1988), 1–19.

Clancy, Michael T., *From Memory to Written Record: England 1066–1307*. London: Edward Arnold, 1979.

Clegg, Cyndia, *Press Censorship in Elizabethan England*. Cambridge: Cambridge University Press, 1997.

Clover, Carol J., 'God Bless Juries!' In *Refiguring American Film Genres*, ed. Nick Browne, 255–77. Berkeley: University of California Press, 1998.

——'Law and the Order of Popular Culture'. In *Law in the Domains of Culture*, ed. Austin Sarat and Thomas R. Kearns, 97–119. Ann Arbor: University of Michigan Press, 1998.

——*The People's Plot: Film, Narrative and the Adversarial Imagination*. Princeton: Princeton University Press, forthcoming.

Cockburn, J. S., 'Early Modern Assize Records as Historical Evidence', *Journal of the Society of Archivists*, 5 (1975), 215–31.

——'Trial by the Book? Fact and Theory in Criminal Process'. In *Legal Records and the Historian*, ed. J. H. Baker, 60–70. London: Royal Historical Society, 1978.

——'Twelve Silly Men? The Trial Jury at Assizes, 1560–1670'. In *Twelve Good Men and True: The Criminal Jury in England, 1200–1800*, ed. J. S. Cockburn and Thomas A. Green, 158–81. Princeton: Princeton University Press, 1988.

——(ed.), *Calendar of Assize Records: Home Circuit Indictments Elizabeth I and James I: Introduction*. London: Her Majesty's Stationery Office, 1985.

Coleridge, Samuel Taylor, *Lectures and Notes on Shakspere and Other English Poets*, ed. T. Ashe. London: George Bell and Sons, 1904.

——*S. T. Coleridge's Treatise on Method*, ed. Alice D. Snyder. London: Constable and Co. Ltd., 1934.

Collinson, Patrick, '*De Republica Anglorum*: or, History with the Politics Put Back'. In *Elizabethans*, 1–29. London: Hambledon, 2003.

——— *Elizabethan Essays*. London: Hambledon Press, 1994.

——— 'The Monarchical Republic of Queen Elizabeth I'. In *Elizabethans*, 31–57. London: Hambledon, 2003.

Constable, Marianne, *The Law of the Other: The Mixed Jury and Changing Conceptions of Citizenship, Law and Knowledge*. Chicago: University of Chicago Press, 1991.

Coogan, Sister Mary Philippa, *An Interpretation of the Moral Play, Mankind*. Washington: Catholic University of America Press, 1947.

Cormack, Bradin, *A Power to Do Justice: Jurisdiction, English Literature and the Rise of Common Law, 1509–1625*. Chicago: University of Chicago Press, 2008.

——— and Carla Mazzio, *Book Use, Book Theory, 1500–1700*. Chicago: University of Chicago Library, 2005.

Corner, G. R., *Observations on Four Illuminations representing the Courts of Chancery, King's Bench, Common Pleas, and Exchequer, temp. Hen. VI*. Repr. from *Archaeologia*, 39, for the Masters of the Bench, Inner Temple, 1909.

Costola, Sergio, 'Ludovico Ariosto's Theatrical Machine: Tactics of Subversion in the 1509 performance of *I Suppositi*' (Ph.D. dissertation, University of California at Los Angeles, 2002).

Cowden Clarke, Charles and Mary, *The Shakespeare Key: Unlocking the Secrets of his Style*. London: 1879.

Cox, John D., *The Devil and the Sacred in English Drama, 1350–1642*. Cambridge: Cambridge University Press, 2000.

Craig, D. H., ed., *Ben Jonson: The Critical Heritage: 1599–1798*. London: Routledge, 1990.

Cunningham, Karen, 'Renaissance Execution and Marlovian Elocution: The Drama of Death', *PMLA*, 105 (1990), 209–22.

——— ' "Scars Can Witness": Trials by Ordeal and Lavinia's Body in *Titus Andronicus*'. In *Shakespeare's Early Tragedies: A Collection of Critical Essays*, ed. Mark Rose, 65–78. Englewood Cliffs, NJ: Prentice-Hall, 1995.

Daston, Lorraine, *Classical Probability in the Enlightenment*. Princeton: Princeton University Press, 1988.

Davidson, Clifford, 'An Interpretation of Wakefield *Judicium*', *Annuale Medievale*, 10 (1969), 104–19.

——— *Visualising the Moral Life: Medieval Iconography and the Medieval Morality Plays*. New York: AMS Press, 1989.

Davis, E. Jeffries, 'The Authorities for the Case of Richard Hunne (1514–15)', *English History Review*, 30 (1915), 477–88.

Dawson, Anthony, 'Performance and Participation'. In *The Culture of Playgoing in Shakespeare's England*, ed. Anthony Dawson and Paul Yachnin, 11–37. Cambridge: Cambridge University Press, 2001.

Dawson, John P., 'The Privy Council and Private Law in the Tudor and Stuart Periods: I', *Michigan Law Review*, 48, no. 4 (1950), 393–428.

Dean, Paul, 'Shakespeare's Henry VI Trilogy and Elizabethan "Romance" Histories: The Origins of a Genre', *Shakespeare Quarterly*, 33, no. 1 (1982), 34–48.

De Grazia, Margreta, *Shakespeare Verbatim*. Oxford: Clarendon Press, 1991.

___'When did *Hamlet* Become Modern?', *Textual Practice*, 17, no. 3 (2003), 485–503.

Dessen, Alan C., 'Robert Greene and the Theatrical Vocabulary of the Early 1590s', in *Writing Robert Greene: New Essays on England's First Notorious Professional Writer*, ed. Edward Gieskes and Kirk Melnikoff (Aldershot: Ashgate, forthcoming).

___*Shakespeare and the Late Moral Plays*. Lincoln, NE: University of Nebraska Press, 1986.

Devereux, E. J., 'John Rastell's Press in the English Reformation', *Moreana*, 13 (1976), 29–47.

Doe, Norman, *Fundamental Authority in Late Medieval Law*. Cambridge: Cambridge University Press, 1990.

Donahue, Charles. Jr., 'Proof by Witnesses in the Church Courts of Medieval England: An Imperfect Reception of the Learned Law'. In *On the Laws and Customs of England: Essays in Honor of Samuel E. Thorne*, ed. Morris S. Arnold, Thomas A. Green, Sally A. Scully, and Stephen D. White, 127–58. Chapel Hill, NC: University of North Carolina Press, 1981.

Doran, Madeleine, *Endeavours of Art: A Study of Form in Elizabethan Drama*. Madison: University of Wisconsin Press, 1954.

Duffy, Eamon, *The Stripping of the Altars: Traditional Religion in England c.1400–1580*. New Haven and London: Yale University Press, 1992.

Duncan-Jones, Katherine, *Sir Philip Sidney: Courtier Poet*. London: Hamish Hamilton, 1991.

Eco, Umberto, *A Theory of Semiotics*. Bloomington, IN: Indiana University Press, 1976.

Eden, Kathy, *Poetic and Legal Fiction in the Aristotelian Tradition*. Princeton: Princeton University Press, 1986.

Elam, Keir, *The Semiotics of Theatre and Drama*, New Accents Series. London and New York: Routledge, 1980.

Eland, Cynthia Graham, 'The Rhetoric of Revenge: The Use of Forensic Rhetoric in *The Spanish Tragedy*, *Titus Andronicus* and *The Jew of Malta*' (Unpublished Ph.D. thesis, MacMaster University, 1984).

Eliot, T. S., 'Introduction'. In *Seneca His Tenne Tragedies translated into English* [1581], ed. Thomas Newton. London: Constable and Co. Ltd., 1927.

Elton, G. R., *Reform and Renewal: Thomas Cromwell and the Commonweal*. Cambridge: Cambridge University Press, 1973.

Erne, Lukas, *Beyond the Spanish Tragedy: A Study of the Works of Thomas Kyd*. Manchester and New York: Manchester University Press, 2001.

___*Shakespeare as Literary Dramatist*. Cambridge: Cambridge University Press, 2003.

Esmein, Adhémar, *Histoire de la Procédure Criminelle en France*. Paris: L. Larose et Forcel, 1882.

Fisher, George, 'The Jury's Rise as Lie Detector', *Yale Law Journal*, 107 (1997), 575–713.

Fletcher, Anthony, *Reform in the Provinces: The Government of Stuart England*. New Haven: Yale University Press, 1986.

Forster, G. C. F., *The East Riding Justices of the Peace in the Seventeenth Century*. York: East Yorkshire Local History Society, 1973.

Foucault, Michel, 'About the Beginnings of the Hermeneutics of the Self: Two Lectures at Dartmouth', *Political Theory*, 21, no. 2 (May 1993), 198–227.

——— *Discipline and Punish: The Birth of the Prison*, trans. Alan Sheridan. Harmondsworth: Penguin, 1977.

——— *The Order of Things: An Archaeology of the Human Sciences*, trans. anon. London: Tavistock Publications, 1970.

Fowler, Alistair, *Renaissance Realism: Narrative Images in Literature and Art*. Oxford: Oxford University Press, 2003.

Fowler, Elizabeth, *Literary Character: The Human Figure in Early English Writing*. Ithaca, NY: Cornell University Press, 2003.

Fox, Alistair, and John Guy, *Reassessing the Henrician Age: Humanism, Politics and Reform 1500–1550*. Oxford: Basil Blackwell, 1986.

Frank, Lawrence, *Victorian Detective Fiction and the Nature of Evidence: The Scientific Investigations of Poe, Dickens and Doyle*. New York: Palgrave Macmillan, 2003.

Frisch, Andrea, 'French Tragedy and the Civil Wars', *Modern Language Quarterly*, 67, no. 3 (2006), 287–313.

——— *The Invention of the Eyewitness: Witnessing and Testimony in Early Modern France*, North Carolina Studies in the Romance Languages and Literature, 279. Chapel Hill, NC: University of North Carolina Press, 2004.

Gaggero, Christopher, 'Pleasure Unreconciled to Virtue: George Gascoigne and Didactic Drama'. In *Tudor Drama before Shakespeare, 1485–1590*, ed. Lloyd Edward Kermode, Jason Scott-Warren, and Martine van Elk, 168–93. London: Palgrave Macmillan, 2004.

Gardiner, Harold C., SJ, *Mysteries' End: An Investigation of the Last Days of the Medieval Religious Stage*. New Haven: Yale University Press, 1946; repr. Hamden, CT: Archon Books, 1967.

Gash, Anthony, 'Carnival and the Poetics of Reversal'. In *New Directions in Theatre*, ed. Julian Hilton, 87–119. New York: St Martin's Press, 1993.

Gaskill, Malcolm, *Crimes and Mentalities in Early Modern England*. Cambridge: Cambridge University Press, 2000.

Gieskes, Edward, *Representing the Professions: Administration, Law and Theater in Early Modern England*. Newark, NJ: University of Delaware Press, 2006.

Ginzburg, Carlo, *Myths, Emblems, Clues*, trans. John and Anne Tedeschi. London: Hutchinson Radius, 1990.

Girouard, Mark, 'The Architecture of the Halls of the Inns of Court'. Unpublished lecture, delivered at The Intellectual and Cultural World of the Early Modern Inns of Court, Courtauld Institute, London, 14–16 Sept. 2006.

Giuliani, Alessandro, 'The Influence of Rhetoric on the Law of Evidence and Pleading', *Juridical Review*, 62 (1969), 216–51.

Gleason, J. H., *The Justices of the Peace in England 1558 to 1640: A Later Eirenarcha.* Oxford: Clarendon Press, 1969.

Goodrich, Peter, *Law in the Courts of Love and Other Minor Jurisprudences.* London and New York: Routledge, 1996.

Gowing, Laura, *Domestic Dangers: Women, Words and Sex in Early Modern London.* Oxford: Oxford University Press, 1996.

——— 'Language, Power and the Law: Women's Slander Litigation in Early Modern London'. In *Feminism and Renaissance Studies*, ed. Lorna Hutson, 428–49. Oxford: Oxford University Press, 1999.

Goy-Blanquet, Dominique, *Shakespeare's Early History Plays: From Chronicle to Stage.* Oxford: Oxford University Press, 2003.

Gras, Hendrick, 'Twelfth Night, *Every Man out of his Humour* and the Middle Temple Revels of 1597–98', *Modern Language Review*, 84, no. 3 (1989), 545–64.

Graves, Michael A. R., *Thomas Norton: The Parliament Man.* Oxford: Blackwell, 1994.

Greaves, Richard L., 'Bernard, Richard (bap. 1568–1641)'. In *Oxford Dictionary of National Biography*, ed. H. C. G. Matthew and Brian Harrison. Oxford: Oxford University Press, 2004.

Green, Richard Firth, *A Crisis of Truth: Literature and Law in Ricardian England.* Philadelphia: University of Pennsylvania Press, 2002.

Green, Thomas Andrew, *Verdict According to Conscience: Perspectives on the English Criminal Jury, 1200–1800.* Chicago and London: University of Chicago Press, 1985.

Greenblatt, Stephen, *Hamlet in Purgatory.* Princeton: Princeton University Press, 2001.

——— 'Remnants of the Sacred in Early Modern England'. In *Subject and Object in Renaissance Culture*, ed. Margreta de Grazia, Maureen Quilligan, and Peter Stallybrass, 337–45. Cambridge: Cambridge University Press, 1996.

——— *Shakespearean Negotiations: The Circulation of Social Energy in Renaissance England.* Oxford: Clarendon Press, 1988.

Greg, W. W., 'Hamlet's Hallucination', *Modern Language Review*, 12, no. 3 (1917), 393–421.

Groot, Roger D., 'The Early Thirteenth Century Criminal Jury'. In *Twelve Good Men and True: The Criminal Jury Trial in England, 1200–1800*, ed. J. S. Cockburn and Thomas A. Green, 3–35. Princeton: Princeton University Press, 1988.

Gurr, Andrew, *The Shakespeare Company, 1594–1602.* Cambridge: Cambridge University Press, 2004.

——— 'Who is Lovewit? What is He?' In *Ben Jonson and Theatre: Performance, Practice and Theory*, ed. Richard Cave, Elizabeth Schafer, and Brian Woolland, 5–19. London: Routledge, 1999.

Guy, J. A., *The Cardinal's Court: The Impact of Thomas Wolsey in Star Chamber.* Tutowa, NJ: Rowman and Littlefield, 1977.

____ *Christopher St German on Chancery and Statute*. London: Selden Society, 1985.

____ 'The Development of Equitable Jurisdictions, 1450–1550'. *In Law, Litigants and the Legal Profession*, 80–6. London: Royal Historical Society, 1983.

____ 'Law, Equity and Conscience in Henrician Jurist Thought'. In *Reassessing the Henrician Age*, ed. J. Guy and A. Fox, 178–98. Oxford: Basil Blackwell, 1986.

____ 'Law, Lawyers and the English Reformation', *History Today*, Nov. 1985, 16–22.

Hacking, Ian, *The Emergence of Probability: A Philosophical Study of Early Ideas about Probability, Induction and Statistical Inference*. Cambridge: Cambridge University Press, 1975.

Haigh, Christopher, *English Reformations: Religion, Politics, and Society under the Tudors*. Oxford: Clarendon Press, 1993.

Halliwell, Stephen, *The Aesthetics of Mimesis: Ancient Texts, Modern Problems*. Princeton: Princeton University Press, 2002.

____ *The Poetics of Aristotle: Translation and Commentary*. London: Duckworth, 1987.

Halpin, N. J., *The Dramatic Unities in Shakespeare: A Letter Addressed to the Editor of Blackwood's Magazine*. Dublin: Hodges & Smith, 1849.

Hamilton, Donna B., 'The State of Law in *Richard II*', *Shakespeare Quarterly*, 34, no. 1 (Spring 1983), 5–17.

Hanson, Elizabeth, *Discovering the Subject in Renaissance England*. Cambridge: Cambridge University Press, 1998.

____ 'Torture and Truth in Renaissance England', *Representations*, 34 (Spring 1991), 53–84.

Harbage, Alfred, 'Intrigue in Elizabethan Tragedy'. In *Essays on Shakespeare and Elizabethan Drama in Honour of Hardin Craig*, ed. Richard Hosely, 37–44. London: Routledge & Kegan Paul Ltd., 1963.

Hasler, P. W., *The House of Commons 1558–1603*. London: HMSO, 1981.

Hassell Smith, A., *County and Court: Government and Politics in Norfolk, 1558–1603*. Oxford: Clarendon Press, 1974.

Havard, J. D. J., *The Detection of Secret Homicide: A Study of the Medico-legal System of Investigation of Sudden and Unexplained Deaths*. London: Macmillan, 1960.

Haynes, Jonathan, *The Social Relations of Jonson's Theater*. Cambridge: Cambridge University Press, 1992.

Heath, Macolm, 'Invention'. In *Handbook of Classical Rhetoric in the Hellenistic Period 330 B.C.–A.D. 400*, ed. Stanley E. Porter, 89–119. Leiden: Brill, 1997.

Helgerson, Richard, *The Elizabethan Prodigals*. Berkeley: University of California Press, 1976.

Helmholz, R. H., 'Assumpsit and *Fidei Laesio*', *Law Quarterly Review*, 91 (1975), 406–32.

Helmholz, R. H., 'Canon Law and the English Common Law'. Selden Society Lectures. London: Selden Society, 1983.

____ *Canon Law and the Law of England*. London: Hambledon, 1987.

____ *et. al.* (eds.), *The Privilege against Self-Incrimination: Its Origins and Development*. Chicago: University of Chicago Press, 1997.

Herrick, Marvin T., *Comic Theory in the Sixteenth Century*. Urbana, IL: University of Illinois Press, 1950.

Herrup, Cynthia B., *The Common Peace: Participation and the Criminal Law in Seventeenth Century England*. Cambridge: Cambridge University Press, 1987.

Hindle, Steve, 'County Government in Early Modern England'. In *A Companion to Tudor Britain*, ed. Robert Tittler and Norman Jones, 98–115. Oxford: Blackwell, 2004.

——— *The State and Social Change in Early Modern England, c.1550–1640*. Basingstoke: Macmillan, 2000.

Hirsch, Marianne, 'Past Lives: Postmemories in Exile', *Poetics Today*, 17, no. 4 (1996), 659–86.

Holland, Peter, 'Ian Judge's Stratford production, 1990'. In *The Comedy of Errors: Critical Essays*, ed. Robert S. Miola, 563–7. New York: Routledge, 1997.

Houlbrooke, Ralph, 'The Decline of Ecclesiastical Jurisdiction under the Tudors'. In *Continuity and Change: Personnel and Administration of the Church of England 1500–1642*, ed. R. O'Day and F. Heal, 239–57. Leicester: Leicester University Press, 1976.

Howard-Hill, T., 'The Evolution of the Form of Plays in English during the Renaissance', *Renaissance Quarterly*, 43, no. 1 (1990), 112–45.

Hudson, John, *The Formation of the English Common Law: Law and Society in England from the Norman Conquest to Magna Carta*. New York: Longman, 1996.

Hughes, Felicity, 'Gascoigne's Poses', *Studies in English Literature*, 37 (1997), 1–19.

Humphreys, Sally C., 'The Evolution of Legal Process in Ancient Attica'. In *Tria Corda: Scritti in onore di Arnaldo Momigliano*, ed. Emilio Gabba, 229–51. Como: Edizioni New Press, 1983.

Hunniset, R. F., *The Medieval Coroner*. Cambridge: Cambridge University Press, 1961.

Hurnard, Naomi D., 'The Jury of Presentment and the Assize of Clarendon', *English Historical Review*, 56, no. 223 (1941), 374–410.

——— *The King's Pardon for Homicide before A.D. 1307*. Oxford: Clarendon Press, 1969.

Hutson, Lorna, 'Civility and Virility in Ben Jonson', *Representations*, 78 (2002), 1–27.

——— 'The "Double Voice" of Renaissance Equity and the Literary Voices of Women'. In *'This Double Voice': Gendered Writing in Early Modern England*, ed. Danielle Clarke and Elizabeth Clarke, 142–63. London: Macmillan, 2000.

——— 'An Earlier Perspective' (Review of Alistair Fowler, *Renaissance Realism: Narrative Images in Literature and Art*, Oxford University Press, 2003), *Times Literary Supplement*, 30 May 2003.

——— 'Forensic Aspects of Renaissance Mimesis', *Representations*, 94 (2006), 80–109.

——— 'Fortunate Travelers: Reading for the Plot in Sixteenth Century England', *Representations*, 41 (Winter 1993), 83–103.

——— 'Liking Men: Ben Jonson's Closet Opened', *English Literary History*, 71 (2004), 1065–96.

____ 'Not the King's Two Bodies: Reading the "Body Politic" in Shakespeare's *Henry IV*, Parts 1 and 2'. In *Rhetoric and Law in Early Modern Europe*, ed. Victoria Kahn and Lorna Hutson, 166–98. New Haven: Yale University Press, 2001.

____ 'On Not Being Deceived: Rhetoric and the Body in *Twelfth Night*', *Texas Studies in Literature and Language*, 38, no. 2 (1996), 140–76.

____ 'Rethinking the "Spectacle of the Scaffold": Juridical Epistemologies and English Revenge Tragedy', *Representations*, 89 (2005), 30–58.

____ *The Usurer's Daughter: Male Friendship and Fictions of Women in Sixteenth Century England*. London: Routledge, 1994.

Ingram, Martin, *Church Courts, Sex and Marriage in England, 1570–1640*. Cambridge: Cambridge University Press, 1987.

Jakobson, Roman, 'Two Aspects of Language and Two Types of Aphasic Disturbances'. In *Fundamentals of Language*, ed. Roman Jakobson and Morris Halle, 69–96. The Hague: Mouton, 1956.

James, Heather, 'Cultural Disintegration in *Titus Andronicus*: Mutilating Titus, Virgil, Rome'. In *Violence in Drama*, 123–40. Cambridge: Cambridge University Press, 1991.

Janaway, Christopher, *Images of Excellence: Plato's Critique of the* Arts. Oxford: Clarendon Press, 1995.

Jennings, Margaret, 'Tutivillus: The Literary Career of the Recording Demon', *Studies in Philology*, 40, no. 5 (1977), 1–95.

Johnston, Alexandra F., 'The Plays of the Religious Guilds of York: The Creed Play and the Pater Noster Play', *Speculum*, 50, no. 1 (Jan. 1975), 55–90.

Jones, Emrys, *The Origins of Shakespeare*. Oxford: Clarendon Press, 1977.

____ *Scenic Form in Shakespeare*. Oxford: Clarendon Press, 1971; repr. 1985.

Jones, Norman, 'An Elizabethan Bill for the Reformation of Ecclesiastical Law', *Parliamentary History*, 4 (1985), 171–87.

Jones, W. L., *The Elizabethan Court of Chancery*. Oxford: Clarendon Press, 1967.

Jones, W. R. D., *The Tudor Commonwealth 1529–1559*. London: Althlone, 1970.

Jordan, Constance, and Cunningham, Karen, *The Law in Shakespeare*. Basingstoke: Palgrave Macmillan, 2007.

Kahn, Victoria, *Rhetoric, Prudence and Skepticism in the Renaissance*. Ithaca, NY: Cornell University Press, 1985.

____ *Wayward Contracts: The Crisis of Political Obligation in England, 1640–1674*. Princeton: Princeton University Press, 2004.

Kantorowicz, Ernst, *The King's Two Bodies: A Study in Medieval Political Theology*. Princeton: Princeton University Press, 1957.

Kehler, Dorothea, 'The First Quarto of Hamlet: Reforming Widow Gertred', *Shakespeare Quarterly*, 46, no. 4 (1995), 398–413.

____ 'Jaquenetta's Baby's Father: Recovering Paternity in *Love's Labour's Lost*', *Renaissance Papers*, 1990, 45–54.

Kelly, H. A., 'Inquisitorial Due Process and Secret Crimes'. In *Proceedings of the Eighth International Congress of Medieval Canon Law (UCSD 1988)*, ed. Stanley Chodorow, 407–27. Vatican City: Biblioteca Apostolica Vaticana, 1992.

—— 'The Right to Remain Silent: Before and After Joan of Arc'. *Speculum*, 68 (1993), 992–1026.

Kelly, J. M. *Roman Litigation*. Oxford: Clarendon Press, 1966.

Kennedy, George A., trans., *Progymnasmata: Greek Textbooks of Prose Composition and Rhetoric*. Leiden and Boston: Brill Academic Publishers, 2003.

—— 'The Rhetoric of Advocacy in Greece and Rome', *American Journal of Philology*, 89 (1968), 419–36.

Kent, Joan, 'Attitudes of Members of the House of Commons to the Regulation of "Personal Conduct" in Late Elizabethan and Early Stuart England', *Bulletin of the Institute of Historical Research*, 46 (1973), 41–71.

—— *The English Village Constable 1580–1642: A Social and Administrative Study*. Oxford: Clarendon Press, 1986.

Kerr, Heather, 'Aaron's Letter and Acts of Reading: The Text as Evidence in *Titus Andronicus*', *AUMLA: Journal of the Australasian Universities Language and Literature Association*, 77 (1992), 1–19.

Kerrigan, John, *Revenge Tragedy: Aeschylus to Armageddon*. Oxford: Clarendon Press, 1996.

—— 'Revenge Tragedy Revisited: Politics, Providence and Drama, 1649–1683', *The Seventeenth Century*, 12, no. 2 (1997), 207–29.

—— 'Shakespeare at Work: The Katherine–Rosaline Tangle in *Love's Labour's Lost*', *Review of English Studies*, 33, no. 130 (1982), 129–36.

Kiernan, Pauline, *Shakespeare's Theory of Drama*. Cambridge: Cambridge University Press, 1996.

King, Pamela M., 'Contemporary Cultural Models for the Trial Plays in the York Cycle'. In *Drama and Community: People and Plays in Early Medieval Europe*, ed. Alan Hindley, 200–16. Turnhout: Brepols, 1999.

Knafla, Louis A. 'John at Love Killed Her': The Assizes and Criminal Law in Early Modern England', *University of Toronto Law Journal*, 35, no. 3 (1985), 305–20.

—— *Law and Politics in Jacobean England: The Tracts of Lord Chancellor Ellesmere*. Cambridge: Cambridge University Press, 1977.

Kreps, Barbara, 'Contract and Property Law in *The Devil Is an Ass*', *Ben Jonson Journal*, 8 (2001), 85–122.

Langbein, John H., *The Origins of Adversary Criminal Trial*. Oxford: Oxford University Press, 2003.

—— *Prosecuting Crime in the Renaissance: England, Germany, France*. Cambridge, MA: Harvard University Press, 1974.

—— *Torture and the Law of Proof: Europe and England in the* ancien régime. Chicago: University of Chicago Press, 1977.

Lea, Henry Charles, *A History of Auricular Confession and Indulgences in the Latin Church* [1896], 3 vols. New York: Greenwood Press, 1968.

Le Goff, Jacques, *The Birth of Purgatory*, trans. Arthur Goldhammer. Aldershot: Scolar Press, 1990.

——— *Your Money or Your Life: Economy and Religion in the Middle Ages*, trans. Patricia Ranum. New York: Zone Books, 1988.

Lehmberg, Stanford E., *The Reformation Parliament 1529–1536*. Cambridge: Cambridge University Press, 1970.

Lehner, Ernst and Johanna, *Devils, Demons, Death and Damnation*. New York: Dover Publications Inc., 1971.

Levack, Brian P., *The Civil Lawyers in England: 1603–1641*. Oxford: Clarendon Press, 1973.

Le van Baumer, Franklin, 'Christopher St. German: The Political Philosophy of a Tudor Lawyer', *American Historical Review*, 42, no. 4 (1937), 631–51.

Levin, Harry, 'Two Comedies of Errors' (1966). In *The Comedy of Errors: Critical Essays*, ed. Robert S. Miola, 113–33. New York: Routledge, 1997.

Lewis, Ewart, 'King Above Law? "Quod Principi Placuit" in Bracton', *Speculum*, 39, no. 2 (Apr. 1964), 240–69.

Logan, F. Donald, *Excommunication and the Secular Arm in Medieval England*. Toronto: Pontifical Institute of Medieval Studies, 1968.

Lyons, John D., and Stephen G. Nichols, Jr., *Mimesis: From Mirror to Method, Augustine to Descartes*. Hanover, NH: University Press of New England, 1982.

McCoy, Richard, 'Gascoigne's "Poëmata Castrata": The Wages of Courtly Success', *Criticism*, 27 (1985), 29–55.

McCutchan, J. Wilson, 'Justice and Equity in the English Morality Play', *Journal of the History of Ideas*, 19 (1958), 405–10.

McEvoy, Sean, 'Hieronimo's Old Cloak: Theatricality and Representation in Ben Jonson's Middle Comedies', *Ben Jonson Journal*, 11 (2004), 67–87.

McLeod, Randall [Random Cloud], ' "The very names of the Persons": Editing and the Invention of Dramatick Character'. In *Staging the Renaissance: Reinterpretations of Elizabethan and Jacobean Drama*, ed. David Scott Kastan and Peter Stallybrass, 88–96. New York: Routledge, 1991.

McMillin, Scott, 'Casting for Pembroke's Men: The *Henry VI* Quartos and The *Taming of A Shrew*', *Shakespeare Quarterly*, 23 (1972), 141–59.

——— and Sally-Beth Maclean, *The Queen's Men and their Plays*. Cambridge: Cambridge University Press, 1998.

Mack, Peter, *Elizabethan Rhetoric: Theory and Practice*. Cambridge: Cambridge University Press, 2002.

——— *Renaissance Argument: Valla and Agricola in the Traditions of Rhetoric and Dialectic*. Leiden: E. J. Brill, 1993.

Macnair, Michael R. T., *The Law of Proof in Early Modern Equity*. Berlin: Duncker & Humblot, 1999.

Maguire, Laurie E., *Shakespeare's Suspect Texts*. Cambridge: Cambridge University Press, 1996.

369

Maguire, Mary Hume, 'The Attack of the Common Lawyers on the Oath *Ex Officio* as Administered in the Ecclesiastical Courts in England'. In *Essays in History and Political Theory in Honour of Charles Howard McIlwain*, ed. Carl Wittke, 200–9. Cambridge, MA: Harvard University Press, 1936.

Marchant, Ronald A, *The Church under the Law: Justice, Administration and Discipline in the Diocese of York, 1560–1640*. Cambridge: Cambridge University Press, 1969.

Marcus, Laura, 'Detection and Literary Fiction'. In *The Cambridge Companion to Crime Fiction*, ed. Martin Priestman, 245–67. Cambridge: Cambridge University Press, 2003.

Marcus, Leah S., *Unediting the Renaissance: Shakespeare, Marlowe, Milton*. New York: Routledge, 1996.

Marshall, Peter, *Beliefs and the Dead in Reformation England*. Oxford: Oxford University Press, 2002.

____ 'Fear, Purgatory and Polemic in Reformation England'. In *Fear in Early Modern Society*, ed. William G. Naphy and Penny Roberts, 150–66. Manchester: Manchester University Press, 1997.

Maus, Katherine Eisaman, 'Horns of Dilemma: Jealousy, Gender and Spectatorship in English Renaissance Drama', *English Literary History*, 54 (1987) 561–83.

____ *Inwardness and Theater in the English Renaissance*. Chicago: University of Chicago Press, 1995.

____ 'Transfer of Title in *Love's Labor's Lost:* Language, Individualism, Gender'. In *Shakespeare Left and Right*, ed. Ivo Kamps, 205–23. New York: Routledge, 1991.

Messac, Régis, *Le 'Detective Novel' et l'influence scientifique*. Paris: H. Champion, 1929.

Meyler, Bernadette, 'Substitute Chancellors: The Role of the Jury in the Contest between Common Law and Equity' (10 Feb. 2006). Cornell Legal Studies Research Paper No. 06-007. Available at ssrn.com/abstract=882829.

Michaels, Walter Benn, 'The Victims of New Historicism', *Modern Language Quarterly*, 54, no. 1 (1993), 111–20.

Miller, David, *The Novel and the Police*. Berkeley: University of California Press, 1988.

Milsom, S. F. C., *Historical Foundations of the English Common Law*, 2nd edn. Toronto: Butterworths, 1981.

____ 'Richard Hunne's *Praemunire*', *English History Review*, 76 (1961), 80–2.

Miola, Robert S., ed., *The Comedy of Errors: Critical Essays*. New York: Routledge, 1997.

____ *Shakespeare and Classical Comedy: The Influence of Plautus and Terence*. Oxford: Clarendon Press, 1994.

Mitnick, J. M., 'From Neighbor-Witness to Judge of Proofs: The Transformation of the English Civil Juror', *American Journal of Legal History*, 32 (1988), 201–35.

Montrose, Louis, *The Purpose of Playing: Shakespeare and the Cultural Poetics of the Elizabethan Theatre*. Chicago and London: University of Chicago Press, 1996.

Morgan, Teresa, ' "A good man skilled in politics": Quintilian's Political Theory'. In *Pedagogy and Power*, ed. Yun Lee Too and Niall Livingstone, 245–62 Cambridge: Cambridge University Press, 1998.

Moss, Ann, *Printed Commonplace Books and the Structuring of Renaissance Thought*. Oxford: Clarendon Press, 1996.

Mukherji, Subha, *Law and Representation in Early Modern Drama*. Cambridge: Cambridge University Press, 2006.

Mullaney, Steven, *The Place of the Stage: License, Play and Power in Renaissance England*. Chicago: University of Chicago Press, 1988.

Murphy, Andrew, ed., *The Renaissance Text: Theory, Editing, Textuality*. Manchester: Manchester University Press, 2000.

Musson, Anthony, *Medieval Law in Context: The Growth of Legal Consciousness from the Magna Carta to the Peasants' Revolt*. Manchester: Manchester University Press, 2001.

Nehamas, Alexander, *Virtues of Authenticity: Essays on Plato and Socrates*. Princeton: Princeton University Press, 1999.

Nelson, Alan H., *Early Cambridge Theatres: College, University, and Town States, 1464–1720*. Cambridge: Cambridge University Press, 1994.

Nuttall, A. D., *A New Mimesis: Shakespeare and the Representation of Reality*. London: Methuen, 1983.

Oakley, Thomas P., 'The Cooperation of Penance and Secular Law', *Speculum*, 7, no. 4 (Oct. 1932), 515–32.

O'Day, Rosemary, *The English Clergy: The Emergence and Consolidation of a Profession 1558–1642*. Leicester: Leicester University Press, 1979.

O'Donovan, Joan Lockwood, *Theology of Law and Authority in the English Reformation*. Atlanta: Scholar's Press, 1991.

O'Hara, Diana, *Courtship and Constraint: Rethinking the Making of Marriage in Tudor England*. Manchester: Manchester University Press, 2000.

Orgel, Stephen, 'The Authentic Shakespeare', *Representations*, 21 (1988), 1–25.

Parker, Patricia, *Shakespeare from the Margins: Language, Culture, Context*. Chicago: University of Chicago Press, 1996.

Parker, Robert W., 'Terentian Structure and Sidney's Original *Arcadia*'. In *Sidney in Retrospect*, ed. Arthur F. Kinney and the editors of *ELR*, 151–68. Amherst, MA: University of Massachusetts Press, 1988.

Patey, Douglas, *Probability and Literary Form: Philosophic Theory and Practice in the Augustan Age*. Cambridge: Cambridge University Press, 1984.

Patterson, Annabel, *Reading Holinshed's Chronicles*. Chicago: University of Chicago Press, 1994.

Phillips, James Emerson, *Images of a Queen: Mary Stuart in Sixteenth Century Literature*. Berkeley: University of California Press, 1964.

Pigman, G. W., 'Editing Revised Texts: Gascoigne's *A Hundreth Sundrie Flowres* and *The Posies*'. In *New Ways of Looking at Old Texts*, ed. W. Speed Hill, 1–9. Tempe, AZ: Renaissance Text Society, 1998.

Post, J. B., 'Equitable Resorts before 1450'. In *Law, Litigants and the Medieval Profession*, ed. E. W. Ives and A. H. Manchester, 68–79. London: Royal Historical Society, 1983.

Potter, Robert, *The English Morality Play: Origins, History and Influence of a Dramatic Tradition*. London: Routledge & Kegan Paul, 1975.

Powell, Edward, 'Jury Trial at Gaol Delivery in the Late Middle Ages: The Midland Circuit, 1400–1429'. In *Twelve Good Men and True: The Criminal Jury in England, 1200–1800*, ed. J. S. Cockburn and Thomas A. Green, 78–116. Princeton: Princeton University Press, 1988.

——*Kingship, Law and Society: Criminal Justice in the Reign of Henry V*. Oxford: Clarendon Press, 1989.

Prendergast, Christopher, *The Order of Mimesis: Balzac, Stendhal, Nerval, Flaubert*, Cambridge Studies in French, gen. ed. Malcolm Bowie. Cambridge: Cambridge University Press, 1986.

Preston, Jean F., '*The Pricke of Conscience* (Parts I–III) and its First Appearance in Print', *The Library*, 6th ser., 7, no. 4 (1985), 303–14.

Price, F. D., 'The Abuses of Excommunication and the Decline of Ecclesiastical Discipline under Queen Elizabeth', *English Historical Review*, 57 (1942), 106–15.

Prosser, Eleanor, *Hamlet and Revenge*, 2nd edn. Stanford, CA: Stanford University Press, 1971.

Prouty, Charles T., *George Gascoigne: Elizabethan Courtier, Soldier and Poet*. New York: Columbia University Press, 1942.

Putnam, B. H., *Early Treatises on the Practice of the Justices of the Peace in the Fifteenth and the Sixteenth Centuries*. Vol. vii of *Oxford Studies in Social and Legal History*, ed. Sir Paul Vinogradoff. Oxford: Clarendon Press, 1924.

Quintrell, B. W., 'The Making of Charles I's *Book of Orders*', *English Historical Review*, 95 (1980), 553–72.

Raffield, Paul, *Images and Cultures of Law in Early Modern England: Justice and Political Power, 1558–1660*. Cambridge: Cambridge University Press, 2004.

Rhodes, Neil, *Elizabethan Grotesque*. London and Boston: Routledge & Kegan Paul, 1980.

——*Shakespeare and the Origins of English*. Oxford: Oxford University Press, 2004.

Ricoeur, Paul, *Time and Narrative*, trans. Kathleen McLaughlin and David Pellauer, i. Chicago and London: University of Chicago Press, 1984.

Robertson, J. C., 'Reckoning with London: Interpreting the *Bills of Mortality* before John Graunt', *Urban History*, 23, no. 3 (1996), 325–50.

Romotsky, Sally Robertson, 'Henry of Monmouth and the Gown-of-Needles', *Intertexts*, 8, no. 2 (2004), 155–72.

Rueger, Zofia, 'Gerson's Concept of Equity and Christopher St. German', *History of Political Thought*, 3 (1982), 1–30.

Rummel, Erika, ed., *Erasmus on Women*. Toronto: University of Toronto Press, 1996.

Sachs, Leslie Raymond, *Thomas Cranmer's 'Reformatio Legum Ecclesiasticarum' of 1553 in the Context of English Church Law from the Later Middle Ages to the Canons of 1603*. Washington: Catholic University of America Press, 1982.

Sacks, David Harris, 'The Promise and the Contract in Early Modern England: *Slade's Case* (1602) in Perspective'. In *Rhetoric and Law in Early Modern Europe*, ed. Victoria Kahn and Lorna Hutson, 28–53. New Haven and London: Yale University Press, 2001.

Salamon, Linda Bradley, 'A Face in *The Glasse*: Gascoigne's *Glasse of Government* Re-examined', *Studies in Philology*, 71 (1974), 47–71.

Salingar, Leo, *Shakespeare and the Traditions of Comedy*. Cambridge: Cambridge University Press, 1974.

Sanders, Norman, Richard Southern, T. W. Craik, and Lois Potter, eds., *The Revels History of Drama in English*, ii: *1500–1576*. London and New York: Methuen, 1980.

Saunders, Claire, ' "Dead in his Bed": Shakespeare's Staging of the Death of the Duke of Gloucester in *2 Henry VI*', *Review of English Studies*, n.s. 35 (1984), 19–34.

Scafuro, Adele C., *The Forensic Stage: Settling Disputes in Graeco-Roman New Comedy*. Cambridge: Cambridge University Press, 1997.

Schoeck, Richard, 'The Strategies of Rhetoric in St German's *Doctor and Student*'. In *The Political Context of Law: Proceedings of the Seventh British Legal History Conference, Canterbury 1985*, ed. Richard Eales and David Sullivan, 77–86. London: Hambledon, 1987.

Schott, Holger, 'The Trials of Orality in Early Modern England' (Ph.D. dissertation, Harvard, 2004).

Senior, Matthew, *In the Grip of Minos: Confessional Discourse in Dante, Corneille, and Racine*. Columbus, OH: Ohio State University Press, 1994.

Shagan, Ethan H., *Popular Politics and the English Reformation*. Cambridge: Cambridge University Press, 2003.

Shapiro, Barbara, *'Beyond Reasonable Doubt' and 'Probable Cause': Historical Perspectives on the Anglo-American Law of Evidence*. Berkeley: University of California Press, 1991.

——'Classical Rhetoric and the English Law of Evidence'. In *Rhetoric and Law in Early Modern Europe*, ed. Victoria Kahn and Lorna Hutson, 54–72. New Haven: Yale University Press, 2001.

——*A Culture of Fact: England, 1550–1720*. Ithaca, NY, and London: Cornell University Press, 2000.

——*Probability and Certainty in Seventeenth-Century England: A Study of the Relationships between Natural Science, Religion, History, Law, and Literature*. Princeton: Princeton University Press, 1983.

Shapiro, James, ' "Tragedies naturally performed": Kyd's Representation of Violence'. In *Staging the Renaissance: Representations of Elizabethan and Jacobean Drama*, ed. Davis Scott Kastan and Peter Stallybrass, 99–113. New York and London: Routledge, 1991.

Sheen, Erica, and Hutson, Lorna, eds., *Literature, Politics and Law in Renaissance England*. Basingstoke: Palgrave Macmillan, 2005.

Sherman, William, 'Anatomizing the Commonwealth: Language, Politics and the Elizabethan Social Order'. In *The Project of Prose in Early Modern Europe and the New World*, ed. Elizabeth Fowler and Roland Greene, 104–21. Cambridge: Cambridge University Press, 1997.

Silverman, Lisa, *Tortured Subjects: Pain, Truth and the Body in Early Modern France*. Chicago: University of Chicago Press, 2001.

Simpson, A. W., *A History of the Common Law of Contract*. Oxford: Oxford University Press, 1975.

Sinfield, Alan, *Faultlines: Cultural Materialism and the Politics of Dissident Reading*. Oxford: Oxford University Press, 1992.

Skinner, Quentin, *The Foundations of Modern Political Thought: The Age of Reformation*, ii. Cambridge: Cambridge University Press, 1978.

Smallwood, R. L., '"Here, in the Friars": Immediacy and Theatricality in *The Alchemist*', *Review of English Studies*, n.s. 32, no. 126 (1981), 142–60.

Smart, Stefan J., 'John Foxe and "The Story of Richard Hun, Martyr"', *Journal of Ecclesiatical History*, 37, no. 1 (Jan. 1986), 1–14.

Smart, Walter K, 'Mankind and the Mumming Plays', *Modern Language Notes*, 32, no. 1 (1917), 21–5.

——— 'Some Notes on *Mankind*', *Modern Philology*, 14 (1916), 45–8.

Sokol, B. J., and Mary Sokol, *Shakespeare's Legal Language: A Dictionary*. London: Continuum, 2000.

Spencer, T. J. B., 'Shakespeare and the Elizabethan Romans', *Shakespeare Survey*, 10 (1957), 27–38.

Tentler, Thomas N., *Sin and Confession on the Eve of the Reformation*. Princeton: Princeton University Press, 1977.

——— 'The Summa for Confessors as an Instrument of Social Control'. In *The Pursuit of Holiness in Late Medieval and Renaissance Religion*, ed. Charles Trinkaus and Heiko A. Oberman, 102–19. Leiden: E. J. Brill, 1974.

Thatcher, David, 'Cover-up: The Murder of Gloucester in *2 Henry VI*', *The Shakespeare Newsletter*, 50, no. 4 (2000–1), 105–18.

Thayer, Anne T., 'Judge and Doctor: Images of the Confessor in Printed Model Sermon Collections, 1450–1520'. In *Penitence in the Age of Reformations*, ed. Katharine Jackson Lualdi and Anne T. Thayer, 10–29. Aldershot: Ashgate, 2000.

Thayer, James Bradley, *A Preliminary Treatise on Evidence at Common Law*. Boston: Little, Brown and Company, 1898.

Thomas, K., *Religion and the Decline of Magic: Studies in Popular Beliefs in Sixteenth- and Seventeenth-Century England*. New York and Oxford: Oxford University Press, 1971.

Thomas, Ronald R., *Detective Fiction and the Rise of Forensic Science*. Cambridge: Cambridge University Press, 1999.

Thomson, John A. F., *The Later Lollards 1414–1520*. Oxford: Oxford University Press, 1965.

Thorndike, A. H., 'The Relation of *Hamlet* to the Contemporary Revenge Play', *PMLA*, 17 (1902), 125–220.

Todd, Margo, *The Culture of Protestantism in Early Modern Scotland*. New Haven and London: Yale University Press, 2002.

Twining, William, *Theories of Evidence: Bentham and Wigmore*. Stanford, CA: Stanford University Press, 1985.

Urkowitz, Stephen, ' "If I Mistake in Those Foundations Which I Build Upon": Peter Alexander's Textual Analysis of *Henry VI parts 2 and 3*', *English Literary Renaissance*, 18 (1988), 230–55.

Usher, Roland G., *The Reconstruction of the English Church*, 2 vols. London and New York: Appleton, 1910.

———*The Rise and Fall of the High Commission*. Oxford: Clarendon Press, 1913.

Vodola, Elisabeth, *Excommunication in the Middle Ages*. Berkeley: University of California Press, 1986.

Walker, Greg, *The Politics of Performance in Early Renaissance Drama*. Cambridge: Cambridge University Press, 1998.

Wall, Alison D., *Riot, Bastardy and Other Social Problems: The Role of Constables and J. P.s in 1580–1625*, Wiltshire Monographs, 1. Trowbridge: Wiltshire Library and Museum Service, 1980.

Ward, Jenny, 'Brugis, Thomas (*b*. in or before 1620, *d*. in or after 1651)'. In *Oxford Dictionary of National Biography*. Oxford: Oxford University Press, 2004.

Ward, John O. 'From Antiquity to Renaissance: Glosses and Commentaries on Cicero's *Rhetorica*'. In *Medieval Eloquence*, ed. James J. Murphy, 25–67. Berkeley: University of California Press, 1978.

———'Renaissance Commentaries on Ciceronian Rhetoric'. In *Renaissance Eloquence*, ed. James J. Murphy, 126–73. Berkeley: University of California Press, 1983.

Warren, Roger, 'The Quarto and Folio Texts of *2 Henry VI*: A Reconsideration', *Review of English Studies*, n.s. 51 (2000), 194–207.

Waugh, W. T., 'The Great Statute of Praemunire', *English Historical Review*, 37 (1922), 173–205.

Weimann, Robert, *Shakespeare and the Popular Tradition in the Theater*. Baltimore: Johns Hopkins University Press, 1978.

Welsh, Alexander, *Strong Representations: Narrative and Circumstantial Evidence in England*. Baltimore and London: Johns Hopkins University Press, 1992.

White, Paul Whitefield, *Theatre and Reformation: Protestantism, Patronage and Playing in Tudor England*. Cambridge: Cambridge University Press, 1993.

White, R. S., *Natural Law in English Renaissance Literature*. Cambridge: Cambridge University Press, 1996.

Wigmore, John Henry, 'The Privilege against Self-Crimination: Its History', *Harvard Law Review*, 15 (1902), 610–23.

Williams, W. H., 'The Date and Authorship of *Jacke Jugeler*', *Modern Language Review*, 7 (1912), 289–95.

Wilson, John ['Christopher North'], 'Dies Boreales, no. 6, "Christopher under Canvass"', *Blackwood's Edinburgh Magazine*, 67 (Apr. 1850), 481–512.

Wilson, John Dover, *What Happens in Hamlet*. Cambridge: Cambridge University Press, 1935.

Wilson, Luke, *Theaters of Intention: Drama and Law in Early Modern England*. Stanford, CA: Stanford University Press, 2000.

Winston, Jessica, 'Expanding the Political Nation: *Gorboduc* at the Inns of Court and Succession Revisited', *Early Theatre*, 8, no. 1 (2005), 11–34.

____ 'Seneca in Early Elizabethan England', *Renaissance Quarterly*, 59, no. 1 (2006), 29–58.

Womack, Peter, *Rereading Literature: Ben Jonson*. Oxford: Basil Blackwell, 1986.

Woodcock, Brian L., *Medieval Ecclesiastical Courts in the Diocese of Canterbury*. Oxford: Oxford University Press, 1952.

Worden, Blair, *The Sound of Virtue: Sidney's* Arcadia *and Elizabethan Politics*. New Haven: Yale University Press, 1996.

Wrightson, Keith, 'Two Concepts of Order: Justices, Constables and Jurymen in Seventeenth Century England'. In *An Ungovernable People: The English and their Law in the Seventeenth and Eighteenth Centuries*, ed. J. Brewer and J. Styles, 21–46. London: Hutchinson, 1979.

Wunderli, Richard M., *London Church Courts and Society on the Eve of the Reformation*. Cambridge, MA: Medieval Academy of America, 1981.

____ 'Pre-Reformation London Summoners and the Murder of Richard Hunne', *Journal of Ecclesiastical History*, 33, no. 2 (Apr. 1982), 209–24.

Youngs, Frederic A. Jr., 'Towards Petty Sessions: Tudor JPs and the Divisions of Counties'. In *Tudor Rule and Revolution: Essays for G. R. Elton from his American Friends*, ed. DeLloyd J. Guth and J. W. McKenna, 201–16. Cambridge: Cambridge University Press, 1982,

Index

Altman, Joel, 18, 70, 92, 106, 157, 179,
 318–20, 328
Aphthonius, *Progymnasmata* 122, 124, 319
Apius and Virginia 237
Aquinas, St Thomas 55n
Arden of Faversham 259–60, 262
Ariosto, Ludovico
 I Suppositi 128–9, 190–4, 196, 199–201,
  209, 288, 292
Aristotle: *Nicomachean Ethics* 54
 Poetics 114–5, 122, 171–2, 316
 Rhetoric 106, 333
Assizes 7, 73n, 82–4, 89, 101, 162, 232, 273,
 276
Assize judges 162
Auerbach, Eric 217, 223–5, 233, 309–10
Augustine, St 74n

Babington, Zachary
 Advice to Grand Jurors 83–4
Bacon, Sir Nicholas 161–2, 188
bail 2, 44–5, 74, 211, 303
 in drama 97, 211–2
Bail and Committal Statutes 2, 74–5, 80,
 211–2
bailiff, bailiffs 34, 74
 in drama 166, 180–2, 184, 296
Beckwith, Sarah 19–20, 30–1, 39–40, 47, 51
Belleforest, Francois de
 Histoires Tragiques 111, 218
Bentham, Jeremy 90
Bernard, Richard
 A Guide to Grand Jury Men 147n
 The Isle of Man 43–6
 Terence in English 46–7, 140, 159, 168–70,
  172
Blount, Thomas, *Nomo-Lexicon* 76n
Boccaccio, Giovanni
 Decameron 173–4, 175, 176
Bowyer, Robert
 Parliamentary Diary of 81, 89, 90
Bradley, Andrew Cecil 116–28, 224
Brugis, Thomas

Vade Mecum 251
Buchanan, George
 Ane Detectioun 122, 216
The Bugbeares 288

Cambises, King of Persia 17, 18, 218, 237
Carletti, Angelico
 Summa Angelica 21
Castle of Perseverance 41, 266–7
Cave, Terence 157n, 171–2, 175, 223n,
 327
character
 'flat' v. 'round' 110–111
 Jonsonian 307, 311, 315, 317, 338
 mimesis of 111–2, 137, 223–4
 product of soliloquy 112
 relation to forensic rhetoric 75, 124, 219,
  235, 311
 subordination to plot 68, 114–5
 suppression of 106
 -witnesses (jurors as) 32, 45
character criticism 7, 223–4, 309
 and circumstantial narrative 116–120,
  128, 137–145, 154–5
 argued to be anachronistic 2, 109–112
characters
 illusion of individual mind, history 7, 4,
  152, 218, 292, 310
 in Plautus and Terence 123, 166–7, 182,
  188, 191, 292
 conjecturing, inferring 105–6, 146,
  149–50, 152, 205–7, 208–10, 216,
  223, 286, 290–1, 311, 314
 variety of in English drama 4
characterological effects (or character
  realism) 8, 10–11, 18, 107, 111,
  116–120, 155, 220, 312
Cicero 7, 92, 106, 132
 De inventione 1–2, 78–80, 121–3, 140,
  213–4, 251–3
 Pro Milone 122, 124–5, 127, 135, 137, 214,
  319
 Pro Roscio Amerino 127, 176, 214